THE EVOLUTION OF INTERNATIONAL SOCIETY

D1051404

This uniquely comprehensive historical study analyses and explains how international societies function. After examining the ancient states systems, the author looks in more detail at the European society of states and at our worldwide contemporary society, which grew out of it.

The book demonstrates that relations between states are not normally anarchies, but organized international or supernational societies regulated by elaborate rules and practices, which derive substantially from experience. Our present international society, for all its individuality, is the latest in the series.

The Evolution of International Society is a major contribution to international theory, and to our understanding of how relations between states operate. Current interest in international order and the hegemonial authority, and the renewed concern with history in political science, make this a timely book.

> 'A stunning success. Watson's book is a masterful piece of theoretical and historical analysis.'
>
> John A. Vasquez, *Rutgers University*

Adam Watson has been a British Ambassador and Assistant Under-Secretary of State, Chairman of the British Committee for the Theory of International Politics and, since 1978, Professor of International Relations at the University of Virginia.

THE EVOLUTION OF INTERNATIONAL SOCIETY

A comparative historical analysis

Adam Watson

London and New York

First published in 1992 by
Routledge
2 Park Square, Milton Park, Abingdon, Oxon, OX14 4RN

Simultaneously published in the USA and Canada
by Routledge
270 Madison Ave, New York NY 10016

Reprinted 1993 and 1999

Transferred to Digital Printing 2005

© 1992 Adam Watson

Phototypeset in 10/12pt Palatino by
Intype, London

British Library Cataloguing-in-Publication Data
Watson, Adam
The evolution of international society
I. Title
303.482

Library of Congress Cataloging-in-Publication Data
Watson, Adam
The evolution of international society: a comparative
historical analysis / Adam Watson.
p. cm.
Includes bibliographical references and index.
1. International relations–History. 2. State, The–History.
I. Title.
JX1305.W38 1992
327'.09–dc20 91–28666

ISBN 0 415 06998 X
0 415 06999 8 paperback edition

To the members of the British Committee
on the Theory of International Politics
and particularly in memory
of its three other chairmen
Herbert Butterfield
Martin Wight
Hedley Bull

CONTENTS

CONTENTS

INTRODUCTION

This enquiry is designed as a contribution to our understanding of how systems of states function. An understanding of how the contemporary society of states came to be what it is, and how it may develop in the future, requires a sense of how other societies operated and developed in the past. But we will not gain much understanding if we merely trace our present arrangements back in time. We need to examine the different patterns of relations between states in their own individuality and on their own merits; and then compare them.

This book accordingly sets out to ask, first, what were the institutions, and also the assumptions and codes of conduct, by which past groups of political entities tried to order and regulate the systems that bound them together. Past systems were differently organized, with different priorities. Secondly, what is the relevance for us today of the achievements of past societies and their trials and errors, even where our present society of states has not derived anything consciously from them? What light can past experience, and especially the hereditary elements in our society so to speak, shed on contemporary practice? How did our present global system and the society which manages it, unlike many others, come to be based on nominally sovereign and juridically equal states, linked by elaborate and changing rules and institutions to promote the advantage of individual members and to regulate the system itself? In our search for answers to these questions, as Gilpin says, 'believing that the past is not merely prologue and that the present does not have a monopoly on the truth, we have drawn on historical experience'.[1]

A clearer understanding seems badly needed. Our present international society is puzzling if looked at in isolation. Is there anything absolute or final about the political division of the world into some 180 nominally independent states? We gather that our present international practices, rules and institutions are recent, and changing, and that they have developed from very different arrangements in the past; but most of us are vague about what those former arrangements were.

1

We are also aware that what actually happens on the international scene does not correspond very closely with what is supposed to happen: why is there this discrepancy between the reality and the theory?

An adequate understanding of the past and the present is also necessary to see what may happen in the future and how we can hope to influence it. Many of us are unrealistic about the future. Sometimes we endow our current assumptions and beliefs, for instance about states being independent, with a permanence that the record in no way justifies. At other times we are apt to think that our present international practice has no inherent nature or characteristics, and that therefore almost any changes can be made to work. This is too mechanistic an approach to any society, too contrary to human nature. Even engineers do not usually design machines *in vacuo*; they draw on experience with previous models, and speak of a 'new generation' of computers or aircraft engines. How much more must we recognize that, without overworking the biological metaphor, our ways of managing the relations between diverse groups and communities of people have evolved from previous experience, and that future arrangements will evolve from ours.

THE BRITISH COMMITTEE ON THE THEORY OF INTERNATIONAL POLITICS*

The discussions and papers

In studying these questions I have greatly profited from the discussions and papers of the **British Committee for the Theory of International Politics**, a group of scholars and practitioners which for some twenty-five years (1959–84) met under the chairmanship first of Herbert Butterfield, then of Martin Wight, then of myself and lastly of Hedley Bull. Much of the work of that committee was concerned with the nature of states systems. I am indebted in particular to two valuable and original studies which emerged from it: Wight's *Systems of States* (a collection of papers which he wrote for the committee about the functioning of states systems, published after his death by Bull) and Bull's own *The Anarchical Society*.

The most important of **Wight's** essays is the general analysis which he called 'De systematibus civitatum', from the title of the essay by Pufendorf in 1675 that defined the concept and gave it its name.

---

* The title 'British Committee' was chosen to distinguish it from the American committee, also financed at first by the Rockefeller Foundation. It was a private and interdisciplinary group, which from the beginning included Irish and soon also Australian members.

2

Wight's paper followed several discussions by the committee and a number of essays, notably his 'Why is there no International Theory?' (published in *Diplomatic Investigations*, a set of papers written for the committee), and others by Herbert Butterfield, Desmond Williams and myself. The purpose of 'De systematibus' was to 'clarify the idea of a states system and to formulate some of the questions or propositions which a comparative study of states systems would examine'.[2] It provided a point of departure for the present book. The continuity between Wight's work and mine is best illustrated by Butterfield's statement in his first Martin Wight Memorial Lecture: 'When we decided to make a prolonged study of states systems in various parts of the globe throughout the ages, [Wight] took a leading part in the discussions; and we hope that the stimulus of these will secure that Adam Watson will complete his own book on systems of states.'

The European states system, leading to the present worldwide one, is not unique. There have been several others. The committee set out to compare the historical evidence, and see what the systems in various parts of the globe throughout the ages have in common and how they differ. We discussed the opinion of some scholars, that no other system is comparable to the European one, and that historical study of past practices can contribute little to our understanding of the predicaments and possibilities which we face today, because their circumstances were too different, and in particular because they were not 'really' systems of states. That opinion (where it is genuine and not merely special pleading for preserving the demarcation between academic disciplines) deserves consideration; but it seemed to us to be based on too parochial a concept of what constitutes a system, and what constitutes a state.

By states we conventionally mean sovereign states: independent political authorities (unitary or confederal) which recognize no superior. For states to form a system each must, as 'De systematibus' formulated the accepted view, 'recognize the same claim to independence by all the others' – not all other states, of course, but all members of the system. The sovereigns of the European system did so, as did the Greek city states and Hellenistic kingdoms. But Wight did not want us to be limited by the conventional view. 'De systematibus' cites the ancient Chinese system, the Roman system and the British raj in India as examples of groups of states in permanent relations with one another, 'but one among them asserts unique claims which the others formally or tacitly accept'. Since the claim in such systems was to suzerainty, Wight suggested that 'we might distinguish them from international states systems by calling them suzerain states systems'. But he described even the European international society as 'a succession of hegemonies, in which one great power after another

3

tries to transform the states system, or even to abolish it'. He wanted to look at the similarities as well as the differences between systems, and was unwilling to dismiss all but independent systems as out of date. As he put it in 'Why is there no International Theory?': 'the intellectual and moral poverty of international theory are due first to the intellectual prejudice imposed by the sovereign state, and secondly to the belief in progress'.[3]

I agreed with Wight and Butterfield about the need to study both kinds of system, and compare them. To understand even societies of more or less independent states requires a wider purview, which sees independence as only one end of the whole range of human experience in managing the coexistence of large and diverse communities of men. Indeed, in my subsequent examination of past and present systems, it has become increasingly clear to me that while systems of independent states certainly differ from suzerain or imperial systems, a simple dichotomy between them is inadequate to describe the actual realities. A system of absolutely independent states, and a heterogeneous empire wholly and directly administered from one centre, are theoretical extreme cases. In practice all known ways of organizing diverse but interconnected communities have operated somewhere between these two extremes. Nor does the management of a given group of communities occupy a static position along the spectrum that stretches between the two extremes: as it changes and evolves, it will become tighter or looser, and so move along the scale in one direction or the other.

The origins and development of this book also owe a great debt to **Hedley Bull**. He read an early draft and made several basic suggestions which I have adopted. The stimulus of his thought continued during our collaboration in editing *The Expansion of International Society*, which was originally his concept. Much of the material in my Chapter 19 and the section on the global international society derive from research and discussion with him for *The Expansion*. Most important for the clarification of my thought was his book *The Anarchical Society*, which also grew out of the papers he submitted to the British Committee. In it he makes the seminal distinction, which I have adopted in this book, between the impersonal network of pressures and interests that bind states together closely enough 'to make the behaviour of each a necessary element in the calculations of the others', which he calls a system, and the set of common rules, institutions, codes of conduct and values which some or all of such states agree to be bound by, which he calls a society. Bull wisely decided to limit his book to societies of independent states: partly to keep the book to a manageable size, and also because what interested him was our contemporary worldwide international society, as the title of the book indicates. 'In

4

terms of the approach being developed here,' Bull says, 'only what Wight calls an international states system is a system at all.'[4] However, Wight, Bull and I were agreed that a wider study was also needed. This book is an attempt to achieve it. At one point Bull wrote to me: 'The most important theme is what you say about hegemony and alternatives to it – or at least, that is what some 21st century historian of international thought is likely to single out.'

Herbert Butterfield had perhaps the most influence on the committee, and the most long-standing influence on me. This book reflects many of his ideas, particularly those in his *Whig Interpretation of History*. He was particularly concerned 'to clarify the principles of prudence and moral obligation which have held together the international society of states throughout its history, and still hold it together.'[5] The most relevant paper he wrote for the committee was 'The historic states-systems' of January 1965, in which as chairman he summed up and deepened its discussions on the nature of such systems and why they have functioned as they have.

> The salient fact about the international systems so far studied is that basically they do not seem to have been produced by the process of bringing together units which have hitherto been quite separate. The effective forces making for some sort of combination may be the elements of an antecedent common culture, but . . . the startling fact is the importance of an earlier stage of political hegemony – a political hegemony which may even have been responsible for the spread of the common culture. Granted that a states system is already in existence, it may not be difficult to add to it new units which were once outside it – even units that are of a quite alien culture. . . . It looks as though (in the conditions of the past at least) a states system can only be achieved by a tremendous conscious effort of reassembly after a political hegemony has broken down.[6]

Butterfield had in mind the Hellenistic or Macedonian society after the confusion following the death of Alexander the Great (see my Chapter 6), which Heeren said was the closest analogy to the European example, and the Westphalian achievement after the collapse of Habsburg hegemony (see my Chapter 17). He was using the term states system to mean what Bull calls an international society.

The shape of this book

Starting from the discussions of the British Committee, I have tried in this book to examine the wide range of experience offered by the principal independent and suzerain systems of the past, noting the development of each, and its relevance to relations between communities as a whole and to the problems of our own time. A general enquiry on these lines does not exist, so far as I am aware. Indeed, there is no convenient and generally accepted term to describe the subject. As Wight emphasized, 'international relations' is altogether too restrictive.

The emphasis of the enquiry is on practice. In this field theories have not normally preceded and guided operational practice, as has so often been the case with domestic government and constitutions, but have followed and interpreted the expedients evolved by experience. Moreover, the opposing rationales of independence and empire usually portray both as more absolute than they are, and ignore the compromises and limitations that move the reality away from the rhetoric. How far is it true that all systems of states, whatever they claim, are sisters under the skin?

The book is divided into three principal sections: the main states systems of the ancient world; the European international society; and our contemporary worldwide one. The committee felt that we, and especially the professional historians among us, were familiar enough with the general character of European civilization and the history of the European states system, and also of the present global system, and therefore did not need to spell them out to ourselves or other students of international relations. I have since wondered how widely this assumption was justified. Justified or not, in the second and third sections of this book I have taken some knowledge of the narrative history of Europe and of our own century for granted, and focused my examination on the evolution and workings of the European society of states and the system that stretched beyond them. On the other hand, the general cultural context within which other states systems originated is not so familiar, and therefore an account of how such systems functioned needs some exposition of the general context. Moreover, most of us are obliged to rely on secondary sources, that is on specialists who seem to us to be reliable authorities. The committee wanted to produce single papers on various past states systems. Since it is impracticable for such a single paper or chapter to include a description of a whole civilization and its general historical development, those papers confined themselves to what seemed necessary to make the relations between the political entities concerned intelligible. Following that practice, I have limited myself to what I consider is needed to explain the evolution and functioning of the systems themselves, and the resemblances and differences between them. I have not attempted chronological accounts of the relations between groups of civilized communities. Nor have I tried to describe or assess the general nature and achievements of past civilizations and their contributions to our

6

own heritage, which names like Athens, Jerusalem and Confucius invoke. And I have left more primitive pre-literate societies aside altogether.

SOME OTHER RELEVANT STUDIES

The extensive corpus of state and so-called diplomatic history has made use of diplomatic documents from the Tell el Amarna tablets to the latest releases by foreign ministries, from which the relations between states, independent and dependent, can be discerned. It has also brought in evidence from memoirs, public debates and other relevant sources to provide, at any rate in the European case, a continuous narrative and detailed analysis in which the views of scholars are collated and balanced against each other. Even so, many histories of international events concentrate on the narrative and on the policies and motives of individual states and personalities, from which it is difficult to disentangle the operation of the system as a whole. Moreover, such historical studies do not set out clearly the range and nature, especially outside Europe, of past experience in managing systems of states, and the relevance of that experience to our own time. Much writing about contemporary international problems by academic non-historians as well as journalists is marred by a haziness about the past, and by a tendency to dismiss all previous practice, the relevance and the variety of which such writers very inadequately understand.

These limitations do not, of course, apply to all writing on the subject. I have listed in the Bibliography at the end of this book those works, both specialized and more general, which I have found most useful, with brief comments that I hope will be helpful to the reader who wishes to pursue certain issues in more detail. I want here to point out at rather greater length the relationship to this study of a few books which I have found particularly relevant.

Butterfield emphasized to us the relevance to our study of states systems of the Göttingen school of historians; and particularly **Heeren**, that loyal Hanoverian who wrote his *Handbuch der Geschichte des Europaeischen Staatensystems und seiner Kolonien* under the Napoleonic occupation (the English translation introduced the term states systems into our language). Bull and I were much impressed by Heeren, especially the preface and introduction to the *Staatensystem*, from which there are extensive quotations in my Chapter 18. Eighteenth-century statesmen and scholars saw Europe not as an anarchy but as a family or commonwealth of states largely ruled by related princes. For instance, Voltaire in the brilliant summary that forms the second chapter of his *Histoire du Règne de Louis XIV* called it 'une espèce de grande république' (see my Chapter 18), and Gibbon in his general observations after Chapter 38 of the *Decline and Fall* claimed that 'a philosopher may be permitted to consider Europe as one great republic'. Eighteenth-century Europeans also recognized that the multitude of sovereigns which made up their republic were held in some sort of order by treaties and the balance of power, rather like the planets in Newton's solar system. Heeren set out to write the history not of the individual sovereigns but of the system itself. Bull and I planned to 'bring Heeren up to date' by an account of what has happened since 1809, as a complementary volume to our *Expansion of International Society*; but Bull's tragic death left our project unimplemented.

Power, not only between states, is a matter of great interest to academics. Much of their writing about states systems has focused on power, and the struggle for power between states in a system, rather than on the workings of international societies.[7] Scholars writing in English have addressed themselves especially to the problems of taming and controlling power, and of preventing war and aggression; and they have given less attention to the problems of authority in international societies, to 'prudence and moral obligation'[8] and to techniques of ensuring obedience and acquiescence. On the other hand, most practitioners, especially statesmen and professional diplomats from western democracies, are less interested in general analysis, and more keenly aware of the great limitations to which power in a society of states is now subject, and of the opposition of their publics (which they usually share) to the use of force or even inducement by the threat of it. Western practitioners have therefore concerned themselves more with expediency, prudence and compromise.

One of the most valuable studies of power in the international field is Sir Harry Hinsley's *Power and the Pursuit of Peace: Theory and Practice in the History of Relations between States* which, since its publication in 1963, has deservedly become a standard text. Hinsley traces the development of internationalist theories, and particularly plans for perpetual peace, in Europe from the seventeenth century. He sees Europe, and the world, as more of an anarchy and less of a society than Bull or myself. His observations are always to the point; and many of his insights into the workings of international society are echoed in my book. Most relevant is his Part II, entitled, 'A History of the Modern States' System to 1900', though it deals mainly with the comments of statesmen and theorists and with the search for peace. Indeed, Hinsley is principally concerned throughout with the history of prescriptions, particularly for ways to avoid war. He devotes less attention to descriptions of how the European society of states actually functioned (for instance, he does not mention Heeren).

A similar influential academic work concerned with power is Hans

Morgenthau's *Politics among Nations: The Struggle for Power and Peace*, first published immediately after the Second World War. Morgenthau, a political realist, saw international politics as determined by the interest of independent states defined in terms of power. He regarded his world of Nazism and the cold war as in essence even more anarchical than Hinsley: a world where powers might act according to *raison d'état* but not *raison de système*. *Politics among Nations* is political theory, and really interested in the functioning of an international society only in so far as its institutions impose some limitations on national power. Within this framework the book contains much shrewd and salutary observation. Especially relevant are Parts 4, 5 and 6 on specific limitations on the actions of states, and Chapter 27 on the concert of Europe and the idea of government by the great powers. In our sporadic discussions Morgenthau and I also agreed about the relevance of past experience to the understanding of current international affairs, and the inadequacies of behaviourist and games theory interpretations taken by themselves.

Another well-known and valuable recent study concerned with power in the international system is Paul Kennedy's *The Rise and Fall of the Great Powers: Economic Change and Military Conflict from 1500 to 2000*. It describes 'the interaction between economics and strategy as each of the leading states in the international system strove to enhance its wealth and power' in what he, like Morgenthau, sees as a nearly anarchical system.[9] But though Kennedy comments on the nature of the bipolar system from which we have just emerged, he only touches on the functioning of the European and contemporary societies of states, and does not discuss the role of the great powers in their co-operative development and management; wisely, it seems to me, because these themes are marginal to his closely reasoned work which musters a considerable wealth of statistical and other evidence. *The Rise and Fall of the Great Powers* thus runs almost parallel to the second and third parts of my book, touching but not overlapping them.

Since I started assembling material for this book some twenty years ago, a number of recent **sociological studies** of the ancient civilizations discussed in the first part of this book, though they are mainly concerned with power and other issues, have thrown valuable incidental sidelights on the nature of states systems and the relations between communities in the ancient world. This is particularly the case with hegemonial and imperial systems. The sociological approach to relations between political entities goes back to the Arab historian ibn Khaldun, of whom his biographer Schmidt says: 'To him, history was sociology.'[10] Historically minded sociologists are more likely than students of contemporary international relations to be aware of the substantial similarities between all societies of states, whether imperially regulated or substantially independent. They have mustered much of the evidence for which Wight and I were looking.

The most useful sociological study of power for the purposes of this book is the first volume of Michael Mann's *The Sources of Social Power*. I read this impressive work with increasing satisfaction, particularly the chapters on Sumer, the early empires of dominion and Persia, because Mann arrives at conclusions, coming at the subject-matter from another angle, which closely accord with those which I had tentatively reached. For like myself he is clearly interested not only in the generation of power but in how it operated, its radial nature, its limitations and the shifts and compromises which it made, and therefore in the characteristics and functioning of systems of states, some more imperially organized than others. This is in fact the sociology of societies of states or political entities. To read Mann on the ancient systems will confirm and illustrate much of what I have to say.

Two other books in the same category which I have also found useful are *Empires* by Michael Doyle, which discusses the nature of imperial control over other political entities, but not over a whole society of states, in Greece and Rome and by the Europeans overseas; and *Power and Propaganda*, a pertinent collection of sociological essays on the ancient empires edited by M. T. Larsen, which especially distinguishes the reality from the rhetoric. I discuss some of the ideas put forward by Doyle and Larsen in my Chapter 12. Robert Gilpin's *War and Change in World Politics* is not concerned with the ancient systems, but he also emphasizes the study of whole social systems, which primarily determine the behaviour of their members; and he has much of interest to say about hegemony, change and the relevance of the past. But like several other scholars mentioned here, and contrary to the conclusions reached in this book, he holds that relations between political entities were and are 'a struggle for power in a condition of global anarchy'.[11]

OTHER ACKNOWLEDGEMENTS

Many other scholars and practitioners have generously given me help and advice. I have perhaps learnt most over the last half-century, especially about constructive statesmanship, from a kindred spirit, George Kennan, who seems to me to be the profoundest scholar–diplomat writing in English in our time. I must also express my special thanks to Sir Michael Howard, whose lucid writings and personal encouragement over several decades have greatly fortified me; and John Vincent, who twice read the manuscript and suggested many detailed improvements, and whose recent early death I keenly feel. Both were members of the British Committee. At the working level I am indebted to Harry Temple and Peter Gellner, with whom I taught at the University of Virginia, and who helped me to shape and order the manuscript. My son Alaric did much detailed work on the chapters on Greece, Macedon and Rome. My wife has supported me with inexhaustible patience and editorial judgement during the abnormally long gestation of the book. I hope the many others who have helped me in a variety of ways will forgive me for not listing all by name.

I also wish to record my thanks to the Earhart Foundation of Michigan, and the Ford Foundation of New York, for personal grants to help defray the research and production costs of this book. The generosity of American foundations to foreign scholarship, both institutional and individual, is well known but none the less impressive. For instance, the British Committee was partly financed by the Rockefeller Foundation.

Polybius, born into the world of public affairs and engaged in a lifetime of statecraft, and also a gifted historian and interpreter to his fellow Greeks of the international scene, said that it is important for the historian to have had practical experience in shaping the course of events, as it is important for the statesman to have an adequate knowledge of history. His dictum has remained with me during the years of intermittent work on this book. I have also kept in mind Polybius' memorable injunction about the need to derive one's judgements from practice itself – *ex auton ton pragmaton* – and ibn Khaldun's similar requirement that theories should be in conformity with reality – *kanun al mutabaka*.

Nobody can be a specialist on every age. As Elie Kedourie says of Toynbee, it is difficult for a comparative historian to have the necessary knowledge to allow him to discriminate between the merits of alternative specialized accounts.[12] I hope that in the case of this book my concentration on states systems, rather than attempting to survey civilizations generally, has enabled me to exercise some discrimination. While apologizing to the reader for the errors there still doubtless are, I would ask him or her to bear in mind Montesquieu's plea in the *Esprit des Lois* (also quoted by Morgenthau in the preface to the second edition of *Politics among Nations*):

> I beg one favour of my readers, which I fear will not be granted me. This is, that they will not judge by a few hours' reading the labour of twenty years; that they will approve or condemn the book as a whole, and not a few particular phrases.

NOTES

1 R. Gilpin, *War and Change in World Politics*, Cambridge, Cambridge University Press, 1981, p. 11.
2 M. Wight, 'De Systematibus Civitatum', in M. Wight (with introduction by H. Bull), *Systems of States*, Leicester, Leicester University Press, 1977, pp. 21–46.
3 M. Wight, 'Why is there no International Theory?', in H. Butterfield and M. Wight (eds), *Diplomatic Investigations*, London, Allen & Unwin, 1966, pp. 17–24.
4 H. Bull, *The Anarchical Society*, London, Macmillan, and New York, Columbia University Press, 1977, p. 11.
5 Butterfield and Wight, op. cit., p. 13.
6 Text available in the Library of the Royal Institute for International Affairs, London.
7 In the Romance languages 'the being able' (*le pouvoir, el poder*, etc.) has softer and more neutral implications than the English term 'power', which has inescapable overtones of something alien and undesirable, or the Russian word *vlast* meaning lordship. This may be one reason why among classic twentieth-century writing on the subject Jouvenel's *Du Pouvoir* is a markedly better book than Bertrand Russell's *Power*.
8 Butterfield and Wight, op. cit., p. 13.
9 P. Kennedy, *The Rise and Fall of the Great Powers*, New York, Random House, 1987, p. xiv.
10 N. Schmidt, *Ibn Khaldun*, New York, Columbia University Press, 1930, p. 27. See also my Chapter 11.
11 Gilpin, op. cit., p. 230.
12 E. Kedourie, Review in the *New Criterion* (March) on Toynbee, 1990.

1

SCOPE AND DEFINITIONS

The purpose of the first part of the book, 'The ancient states systems', is to see what we can discern about the organization of relations between different peoples in other civilizations. In the light of our findings we will be able in the second part to examine 'The European international society', which derived much from previous experience. The third part examines 'The global international society'. The contemporary international system grew out of the European one, and many of the rules and institutions of the European society have simply been applied globally; but it also incorporates ideas and practices from earlier systems.

The other civilizations which we want to examine, and the relations between their communities, were of course highly individual and changed continually. What general terms can we use to describe and classify the great variety of these relations? Words like 'state', 'empire' and 'system' are useful so long as we remember that they are no more than broad categorizations which cover a considerable range of distinct individual phenomena, and that different users of these terms mean slightly different things by them. The simple distinction between free and subject peoples, or between sovereign and vassal rulers, is hopelessly overcharged with rhetoric, and obscures many of the issues we need to examine. We need more dispassionate terms.

I have become increasingly doubtful about sharp distinctions between systems of independent states, suzerain systems and empires. I now prefer to define the wider subject by saying that, when a number of diverse communities of people, or political entities, are sufficiently involved with one another for us to describe them as forming a **system** of some kind (whether independent, suzerain, imperial or whatever), the organization of the system will fall somewhere along a notional **spectrum** between absolute independence and absolute empire. The two marginal positions are theoretical absolutes, that do not occur in practice. It is convenient for purposes of comparison to divide the spectrum into four broad categories of relationship: independence, hegemony, dominion and empire.

There is in states systems an inevitable tension between the desire for order and the desire for independence. Order promotes peace and prosperity, which are great boons. But there is a price. All order constrains the freedom of action of communities and in particular their rulers. The desire for order makes constraints and voluntary commitments acceptable, for the reasons set out by Hobbes and others. But in so far as the order is imposed by the actual or potential force of a hegemonial authority, it can be felt as oppressive. This is especially the case with imperial and other authorities which intervene in the domestic policies of members. The desire for autonomy, and then for independence, is the desire of states to loosen the constraints and commitments imposed upon them. But independence also has its price, in economic and military insecurity.

The term **independent states** in a system indicates political entities that retain the ultimate ability to take external decisions as well as domestic ones. But in practice freedom in external decisions is limited by the constraints which involvement in any system imposes, and also by the voluntary commitments that states assume in order to manage their external relations more effectively. The greater the constraints and commitments, the tighter the system will be, and the further along the spectrum.

At the multiple independences end of the spectrum, the more closely sovereign states are involved with each other, the less they feel able to operate alone. The impersonal net of strategic and economic pressures that holds them together in a system induces them to make alliances. Alliances bring a form of order to what would be an inchoate system by co-ordinating, and thus modifying, the behaviour of their members. That is an aspect of what the European system called *raison d'état*. Order is further promoted by general agreements and rules that restrain and benefit all members of the system, and make it into a society. That is an aspect of *raison de système*, the belief that it pays to make the system work. In so far as such agreements, including commitments to collective security, are voluntary, and are not imposed by a victor power or group of powers, they fall within the multiple independences area of the spectrum.

In practice the freedom of action of independent states is always limited by the pressures of interdependence in a system, and often also by voluntary choice. Usually it is also limited, more effectively, by hegemony. As we move along the spectrum to the point where one or more powers are able to exercise a hegemony, the other forms of co-ordination shade off into the benefits which derive from the hegemonial authority ordering the system in such a way that all its members see a balance of advantage in accepting the hegemony. So also imperial powers usually find it advantageous to respond to the interests and welfare of subordinate peoples.

By a **hegemony** I mean that some power or authority in a system is able to 'lay down the law' about the operation of the system, that is to determine to some extent the external relations between member states, while leaving them domestically independent. Some scholars like to reserve the term 'hegemony' for the exercise of this authority by a single power. The difficulty there is that in fact the authority can be exercised either by a powerful individual state, or as is often the case by a group of such states. An example of dual hegemony is the Athenian–Spartan diarchy after the Persian wars, discussed in Chapter 5. The five great European powers after 1815 exercised a diffused hegemony, discussed in Chapter 21. Indeed, the rules and institutions of the European international society were far from purely voluntary: they were to a considerable extent imposed by the principal victors at the great peace settlements like Westphalia, Vienna and Versailles, and were to that extent hegemonial. I therefore prefer to use the term 'hegemony' in this wider sense of any authority, consisting of one or a few powerful states, that is able to determine the relations between the members of an international society, rather than resort to ugly words like 'para-hegemonial'. Moreover, a hegemony is not a dictatorial fiat. The hegemonies which I have looked at, whether exercised by an individual power or a small group, involve continual dialogue between the hegemonial authority and the other states, and a sense on both sides of the balance of expediency.

Suzerainty is a vaguer concept. In international law it usually means that one state exercises political control over another. In many historical contexts it means a shadowy overlordship that amounts to very little in practice. Some scholars like Wight and Bull spoke of suzerain systems or societies to mean those in which the members accepted hegemony as legitimate. There is a difference between systems whose members are in general agreement that there ought to be a suzerain authority, even when it is in abeyance in practice, and those whose members accept suzerain authority only tacitly. Tacit acceptance is the same as acquiescence, and is necessary for any effective hegemony, whether *de jure* or *de facto*.

Further along the spectrum **dominion** covers situations where an imperial authority to some extent determines the internal government of other communities, but they nevertheless retain their identity as separate states and some control over their own affairs. Examples are recent Soviet relations with eastern Europe, where the states were formally independent, the relation of the emperor Augustus to Herod's

15

kingdom and the relation of the British raj to the Indian princes. Here the part played by the ability to coerce is more obvious.

Finally there is **empire**, no more absolute in practice than independence, meaning direct administration of different communities from an imperial centre. The freedom of action even of imperial governments is limited in practice by the constraints which involvement with other communities imposes.

When we look at historical examples, in the world today or in the systems of the past, we are of course aware that these categories are not watertight with an abrupt transition from one to another, but rather a continuum, like wavelengths of light in a rainbow which we find it convenient to divide into different colours. No actual system remains fixed at one point in this spectrum.

The relation of the various communities to each other shifts constantly along the spectrum over time. The ways in which a system tightens or loosens, and one hegemonial or imperial power supplants another, will be of special interest to us. There is also, at any one time, a variation in space. Communities involved in a system do not all stand in the same relationship to each other, or to an imperial power. There are many gradations, even between independent states; and when looked at closely every relationship between two communities has in practice a special nature of its own, conditioned by history, geography and other differentiating factors. One question we must examine is the extent to which empires usually have a hard core of direct administration, beyond which lie layers of dominion and hegemony until fully independent states are reached that lie outside imperial control or influence. Such 'layers' are, of course, gradations along our spectrum and therefore concentric circles on a diagram rather than a map.

In addition to these continuing variations of reality in time and space, the communities which we have treated as the components of systems are far from being constants. A political entity means in essence a community held together by a common government. Obviously the area under the control of a government will fluctuate. A **community** which is also bound together by other ties, such as custom, ethnic descent, religion or language, may grow or shrink in importance and size: it may absorb other elements, or break up, or become assimilated or otherwise disappear. We must use terms like community and state also in as neutral a sense as possible. For instance, it seems to me that it obscures our understanding of the nature of states to maintain dogmatically that to count as states they must be independent.

Since systems and the communities which compose them vary greatly from each other, with widely differing cultures, past experiences and degree of development, and since within a given system the degree of control which one, or two, or five powers can exercise over other communities also varies, can we make any valid generalizations about the pressures which induce such changes? Especially, can we see any indications of the way our own system may develop? Has there been any general tendency away from the pole of centralized authority, empire and world government towards multiple independence, as some people claim? Has there been a corresponding counter-tendency in known systems of independent states for the strongest power to move towards hegemony, trying to control the foreign relations of client states and lay down the rules of the system; and for hegemony to develop into dominion?

A useful metaphor for a theory of systems is the pendulum. Imagine our spectrum laid out in the form of an arc, with its midpoint at the bottom of the pendulum's swing, somewhere between hegemony and dominion. Was there in ancient systems any noticeable pendulum effect, any gravitational pull on systems away from the theoretical extremes and towards some central area of the spectrum, even though the momentum of change and other factors may carry the system past that area? Or does the pattern vary too much from one system to another for us to make any valid general inferences?

Another important issue is how far the arrangements between communities in a system are accepted as legitimate. **Legitimacy** is the acceptance of authority, the right of a rule or a ruler to be obeyed, as distinguished from the power to coerce. It is determined by the attitudes of those who obey an authority. How does legitimate authority, as opposed to power exercised by compulsion or the threat of it, operate between communities in a system, and acquire international significance? The more closely involved independent states are with each other, the less they try to operate alone. They see that they can further some of their interests and their principles, especially the preservation of their independence, by co-operation with allies; which involves taking the views and desires of their allies into account and modifying their own behaviour accordingly. Other interests can be promoted by general agreements and rules that restrain and benefit all members of the system. This awareness of the advantages of co-operation between independent partners corresponds to the ways in which hegemonial and imperial powers find it advantageous to respond to the interests and welfare of subordinate peoples. To what extent do such policies depend for their success on a wide measure of acceptance? The rules and institutions and the accepted practices of a society of substantially independent states need legitimate authority to ensure habitual compliance. Is legitimate authority as necessary for the successful exercise of hegemony or dominion?

If we want to understand how the civilizations of the past organized the relations between their different communities, we cannot simply leave such evidence as historians and archaeologists have been able to uncover as a mass of uncorrelated data. It can be very useful to impose a diagram or a grid of categories on the multiple variety of actual relations, for possible classification and comparative analysis. There is nothing unusual about this. We have to group different individuals and communities together into categories for juridical purposes: for instance, when we say that all the very different nominally independent states in our present international system are equal in international law. And it was regularly done in ancient times, as it is today, in order to further a political goal. But while the division of reality into categories can assist our understanding of what actually happens, there is the inherent danger that our categories may come between us and reality. We may slip into the assumption that phenomena lumped together in a category are more alike than they really are, or that because some things are true about all of them, other things are true also. We have noted the danger of category words with emotional overtones like 'independence' and 'empire'. Equally misleading are the categories used by past civilizations to classify their communities, and especially those which rulers and political leaders proclaimed for their own purposes. It will therefore pay us to look a little more closely at the changing patterns of relationship of various systems in all their individuality, and then compare them.

THE ANCIENT STATES
SYSTEMS

PREFACE

In this section I want to examine a number of systems of states in the ancient world: that is, the world before the rise of European civilization.

It will not be possible, or necessary for our purpose, to examine every known system that binds together distinct political entities. We need to look at the more important and well-documented ones, and to cover a representative range of developed systems across our spectrum, from the most imperially integrated to the most fragmented clusters of multiple independences, in the same way that a general comparative study of states needs to extend from centralized and homogeneous examples to loosely federated and diverse ones.

We begin in the ancient near east with Sumer. This is the earliest point at which the archaeological written record enables us to discern, with some difficulty, how a states system operated; and what we find is a society of independent city states with hegemonial institutions, about halfway along the spectrum between anarchical freedom of action and rigid empire. The Assyrian system inherited much from Sumer but was more imperially organized; and its Persian successor larger and looser. We then turn to the much more familiar system of classical city-state Greece, where jealously defended independences were tempered by a succession of less institutionalized hegemonies and by continual involvement with Persia. The Greek and Persian systems merged after Alexander's conquest to form the diverse Macedonian system, which adapted practices derived from many predecessors. Its successor, the Roman imperial system, was the ultimate classical synthesis; which in turn developed into the Byzantine and Arab systems, and into the highly original society of medieval Europe discussed at the beginning of the next section of the book. This succession of systems will enable us to examine the problem of continuity: how a system can inherit and adapt from its predecessors institutions and practices, specific ways of organizing the relations between political entities, and also assumptions about what those relations were and ought to be.

Alongside this linked succession, we also examine two more distinct Asian systems: the ancient Indian, and the Chinese system of the warring states before the establishment of the Han Empire. The Indian society of states is interesting because of its elaborate indigenous development and because of the impact on it of Persian and Macedonian practices. The impressive practices and theories of the Chinese system developed in virtual isolation. These two systems will provide a useful basis of comparison with the near eastern succession.

When examining these ancient systems, we shall need to bear in mind two sets of fundamental questions that are also relevant to the European system and are of topical concern today. The first set concerns **cultural unity**. How far is a degree of cultural unity, or at least a dominant cultural matrix, necessary if the interests and pressures that bind political entities into a system are to find expression in the conscious rules and institutions of a society? How far are such rules and institutions determined by the culture in which they develop, and how far are they mechanically determined, as similar responses to similar interests and pressures? What regulatory machinery is required for the operation, the orderliness, of a system that is not dominated by a single culture?

The second set of questions concerns **hegemonial and imperial authority**. What can we learn from the ancient systems about the nature and degree of authority (as opposed to compulsion) exercised by the rules and institutions of the society itself, and also by its most powerful entity or entities? How far were these forms of order in practice combined? Does the evidence of the ancient systems support the generalization that all such authority curbs independent freedom of action but is in turn limited by anti-imperial and anti-hegemonial strivings for greater autonomy? In this context we shall need to remember how limited a degree of imperial coercion was practicable in ancient times.

We shall also assess the evidence for a **pendulum** effect, holding ancient societies towards the centre of the spectrum as they tightened and loosened over time. To what extent was there a propensity to hegemony in systems of comparatively independent states, and a propensity to autonomy in more imperial ones? Also, in so far as there were dominant or hegemonial powers in the ancient systems, how far were they political entities at the centre of the civilization and the system, and how far were they less civilized but more vigorous **marcher** communities?

Our examination of the evidence will also throw light on other concepts formulated in Chapter 1. We will be concerned with **legitimacy** in ancient societies of states. The authority which the conventions and institutions of a society, both formal and informal, were able to command, the degree of continuity of a society with its predecessors, and the degree of cultural affinity of its members, all helped to determine its legitimacy. What was the relation between the comparatively stable legitimacy of a changing and developing society of states, and the more rapidly evolving practice, concerned with expediency and the balance of material advantage? How did the legitimacies of individual member communities of the society, as opposed to those of the society as a whole, affect the society's stability?

In Chapter 12 we will consider what answers can be given to these questions, and what their implications are for a theoretical understanding of states systems.

2

SUMER

The original states system

Our study of the evolution of international relations takes us back to the earliest written records. Of course there were cities and kingdoms before that, and of course they had relations with one another. We can see from the archaeological record that there was trade, and war, and other exchanges. But until men developed the art of writing, and began to keep records of transactions between different communities, we cannot now, at this distance, any longer see what these were.

The first records of how communities, which were developed enough to write such things down, conducted relations with each other would be interesting in any case. The earliest records which have survived and which we can decipher are particularly interesting because they come from Sumer. Sumer was one of the earliest and most innovative civilizations, and particularly creative in its ways of managing public affairs. Fortunately for our enquiry, it was not a single empire, as Egypt for instance quickly became, but a cluster of separate communities within the framework of a common culture, each with its own distinct personality and corporate life. When the records of their dealings with each other begin, the Sumerian city-temple states had achieved a high level of civilization, with well-developed agriculture, seafaring, trade and accounting, held together by an impressive system of religion and government.

The Sumerian cities, Ur of the Chaldees and others like it, were grouped round the head of what we now call the Persian Gulf, where the Tigris and the Euphrates flow into the sea. They stood at the eastern end of the fertile crescent, which was more fertile then than it is now, and which sweeps north through Mesopotamia and Syria and then turns south again through Palestine towards Egypt. They were merchant cities, trading far up the Euphrates, which they called the copper river, and by sea down the gulf. The economic and cultural stimulation which they offered, particularly the diffusion of literacy and numeracy, spread into a periphery of independent communities far larger than the area of their political society of states.

24

What can we discern, at this distance, about the relations between the Sumerian cities, and the nature of their states system? They had an intensive agriculture based on irrigation, and depended on their crops to maintain their high standards of city life for a growing population and to export in return for what they imported from the lands around them. Consequently there were continual disputes between one city and another about water rights and the boundaries of fields. So far as we can see, the basic issue which dominated the relations between the Sumerian cities was how to regulate the commerce and the competition between them, and more specifically how to resolve the inevitable disputes over land, water and trade, so that they could prosper in their close involvement with each other but with each city preserving its independence. So by a stroke of luck we see poised for us at the beginning of our enquiry the central question facing an international society – how can a group of dynamic and closely involved communities preserve their independences and yet control their exchanges and competition to the point where they do not inflict unacceptable damage on each other?

The Sumerians conceived the world as dominated by gods, who created men to serve them. Each city belonged to a particular god or goddess. The people of that city were the people of that god's hand: the god provided them with water and grain and pasture, and their ships were under his protection. The affairs of each city were ordered by a king who was the representative of its god, the vicar of that god on earth. (This very old concept survives today in the Pope's title of Vicar of Christ.) A Sumerian king was a bailiff or manager of the god or goddess who owned the city and delegated divine authority to him. The Sumerian official religion was eminently practical, almost businesslike. In addition to keeping records, calculating the calendar and the appropriate times for various activities, the temple network was available as an inter-city diplomatic service. The Sumerians, with their keen sense of hierarchy and order, attributed to the gods the regular succession of the seasons and crops and of the stars in a divinely ordered cosmos. They attributed the irregularities of the harvest due to drought or flood, and the especial chanciness of trade and of war, to conflicts between the gods who controlled the forces of nature and the fortunes of men. But they saw that while the chanciness of human affairs might raise up or destroy individuals or whole cities, it had not since the legendary great flood destroyed Sumer altogether. This moderation they believed was due to the restraining hand of one god who was overlord over the others, 'a great king above all gods'. He did not interfere with the other gods and goddesses, each of whom had his or her own functions and cities; but he was the supreme arbiter between them.

25

The situation on earth was in Sumerian eyes a reflection of that in heaven. At any given stage of Sumerian history one city would have a similar authority over the others. The ruler of that city would be the great king over the other kings, and would act as moderator between them. He did not have the right to trespass on the domain of another god or, as we should say, to interfere in the internal affairs of another city: that would be contrary to the divine order. His legitimate function as great king was to moderate conflicts between cities, and to pronounce and where necessary enforce verdicts.

The Sumerian records show that in practice the decisions which the great king took in the name of the great god did need to be enforced. A clay cylinder from the city of Lagash in the Yale collection gives a picture of how the Sumerians saw the maintenance of order in the name of the god Enlil. The inscription begins as follows:

Enlil, the king of all the lands and the father of all the gods, marked out a boundary for the god of Lagash and the god of Umma [i.e. between the territories of the cities belonging to those gods] by his decree. The king of Kish measured it out in accordance with the word of the god of legal settlements, and erected a stone boundary marker there. [Later] a king of Umma violated the decree of Enlil and the word of the king of Kish, and ripped out the marker and entered the territory of Lagash. Then the god of Lagash, who was Enlil's foremost champion, fought against the men of Umma to maintain Enlil's clear decree. . . . He heaped up their bodies on the plain. The uncle of the king of Lagash marked out the boundary with the king of Umma, and dug a ditch and put boundary markers along it, and restored the king of Kish's boundary marker to its place. But he did not invade the territory of Umma. The men of Umma were allowed to eat the barley of the gods of Lagash to the amount of one measure each, and the king of Lagash levied a tax on them [presumably for the barley]. But because the barley remained unpaid [i.e. undelivered by Lagash?] the king of Umma again ripped out the boundary markers . . .

and so on until a new great king imposed another compromise which was apparently more favourable to Umma, a city that was seriously short of food to support its population. The great king was confronted with a dilemma which continues to vex modern statesmen: whether to maintain order by upholding the legitimate status quo and condemning the 'aggressor', or by making adjustments not on the basis of legal right, but of greater power and more pressing need.

A king's principal function was to carry out the will of the god of his own city, including the judicious administration of the city's god-given laws. Consequently, a great king, confronted with disputes between cities, understood from his domestic judicial experience the need for wise and balanced verdicts, which would maintain the order desired by the gods and especially by his god who was king and father of other gods. But at the same time the great king was the ruler of the most powerful city in Sumer; and no doubt, where the interests of his own city were directly involved, he tended to decide matters in his city's favour, at least so far as it was prudent to do so. That was the price of kingship, and the Sumerians seem to have accepted it. The system in Sumer, one realizes as one looks at the records, was summed up by their formula that 'the kingship must reside somewhere'. The kingship was legitimate in their eyes because it reflected the situation in heaven, because it was authorized by the holy city of Nippur and because it was necessary for the settlement of disputes. For several reigns the kingship would reside in one city. When the power and authority of that city weakened to the point where it was no longer strong enough to arbitrate, or perhaps its king abused his authority, then a number of other cities would band together and overthrow that kingship, usually by force. Another city would then become the kingly city and its king would become the moderator of the Sumerian society of city states. When this happened the Sumerians would add to the history of the gods. The victors would proclaim, and the defeated would admit, that the god of the former kingly city had obviously weakened and that the god of some other city like Uruk or Lagash had come to power in heaven.

In other words, the Sumerian state religion legitimated the administrative regulation of each city-temple state by its king-vicar, and the corresponding regulation of the relations between the cities of the Sumerian confederal society by the holder of the overall kingship. The sociologist Michael Mann has described Sumer as

> a singular civilization, fuzzy at the edges, that contained multi-power actors within a geopolitical diplomatically regulated power organization. . . . The numinous was immanent in [the] social structure. It was not opposed to, and did not transcend, the practical; it made sense of given power realities, the best sense available.[1]

Thus the Sumerian system of international relations was not a single empire like ancient Egypt, nor was it based on absolute independence such as prevailed between the Sumerians and their non-Sumerian neighbours. It was a **hegemony**, that is a system in which one city, through its ruler, was accorded legitimate authority to arbitrate between other cities and to keep competition and the use of force within acceptable limits, but not the right to interfere in their internal affairs. The Sumerian hegemony, and its limitations, were acceptable because they were legitimized by the religion of the culture itself. The verdicts of the great king did not depend only on his power to coerce those who resisted them, but also on his legitimate authority. His power and authority were effectively counterbalanced by the independent power, and the legitimacy, of the other city states. There seem to have been no specifically anti-hegemonial coalitions, in the sense of alliances directed against restraints on independence as such, rather than against a particular king who no longer had the power and authority to maintain acceptable order. In the Sumerian king-lists and inscriptions, the formula is regularly repeated: 'Then such-and-such a king was stricken by force of arms and the kingship was moved to another city.' But nobody demanded that there should be no kingship at all. The authority to keep the Sumerian system together had to reside somewhere, but its place of residence was not permanent. Rule over a particular city was normally hereditary, but the great kingship over all the cities depended on the power and the capacity to keep the whole society of states in order. It was a shifting hegemony.

It has been argued that the authority exercised by the ruler of one Sumerian city over the relations between his domestically independent fellow rulers was limited to a hegemony only because the ruler who exercised the kingship was unable to establish the degree of central control that would have welded all Sumer into a single state. This is a particular instance of the general view that dismisses all suzerain systems as irrelevant, and brackets the Sumerian hegemony with the empires of antiquity that we shall be considering in the next chapters, treating them as 'pre-state forms of domestic rule' or expanding governments that thought only in terms of overlordship over client communities that they were not strong enough to administer directly. In the case of Sumer this *a priori* assumption runs counter to the evidence. The Sumerian cities were internally independent states, able collectively to shift the hegemonial authority, which they considered necessary to regulate their inter-state relations, from one city to another. Both the practice and the legitimacy, so far as we can discern them, were hegemonial not imperial. Martin Wight pointed out that the city states of classical Hellas and the states of the European system were managed by 'a succession of hegemonies'; but Hellas and Europe were international societies of states rather than pre-state forms of empire, and the same is broadly true of Sumer.

Gradually the network of trade ties and military power involved the Sumerian city states more closely with the (doubtless genetically mixed) peoples of Semitic culture who lived further up the two rivers. The Semitic peoples are the most important group of communities in the ancient near east. The Semitic empires of Babylon and Assyria based on the two great rivers, and the smaller states of the Hebrews and the Phoenicians on the Mediterranean, are of special interest for our enquiry.

About 2300 BC a Semitic ruler made himself great king of Sumeria, and by means of superior military techniques spread a loose overlordship far to the north and west, to cover apparently the whole of the fertile crescent (already influenced by Sumerian trade and culture) including a large stretch of the Mediterranean coast. Given the difficulties of transport and communication in most of the area at that time, we must not suppose that in the remoter regions this overlordship amounted to more than a military incursion and the establishment of local rulers who were willing to acknowledge the great king's distant authority and permit an easier flow of trade. But the title 'Lord of the Four Quarters of the World' was a significant new claim to a universal imperial authority. Soon that authority weakened, and the Sumerians were able to assert their own more limited society of city states for a time. But by about 1700 BC the great Semitic city of Babylon ('the gate of god') had reasserted effective imperial control over the lands of the two rivers.

The Semitic empires which took over the Mesopotamian world forcibly imposed a more thoroughgoing and permanent dominion over the rulers of many diverse communities than the Sumerian hegemony of one independent city over the others. They did so partly in order to control the water rights of the whole Tigris–Euphrates watershed, which extended over a far larger area than the territories of the little Sumerian cities, and partly in order to control and facilitate trade. The kingship was firmly fixed in Babylon, which grew to be a metropolis of many races and tongues, as the word 'babel' reminds us. But except for a central core the Babylonian overlordship was a domination over client rulers, not a direct administration of territory.

The Semitic kingdoms upstream did not have a highly developed civilization of their own. They took over the advanced culture of Sumer almost entire, with the art of writing, the religious structure and the Sumerian tradition of statecraft which remained active for many centuries. We find Sumerian rules and records translated into the Semitic and used unchanged in the great empires further north. This was strikingly the case in the relations between what they perceived as the territories belonging to different gods. The god of Babylon was Marduk, 'the light of light'. In the inscriptions of Babylonia, written in a Semitic language recognizably like Hebrew and Arabic, we read how Marduk overthrew the other gods and established his kingship over them. It was therefore right and legitimate that his representative, the vicar of Marduk on earth, should rule over the many lands that made up the empire. Of course the other gods continued to exist, and local kings continued to rule their lands, though now as vassals approved or appointed by the great king of Babylon. In other words the new imperial legitimacy was sanctioned by religion, as the Sumerian hegemony had been, but without the Sumerian restraint.

Some of the local kings, temple priests and prophets, and their god-fearing peoples, resented the new and firmer dominion, and did not wholly accept its legitimacy. Babylon seemed to them the rich and powerful but corrupt city described in the Bible, the whore that sold itself for power and wealth:

> Her robes are purple and scarlet
> And kings have bent their knees
> To the gemmed and jewelled harlot.[2]

But the merchants welcomed the ban on warfare, the personal security and the opportunities which Babylonian rule provided over a wide area, as merchants trading over long distances are always ready to do. Under imperial rule they were doubtless also able to emancipate themselves to some extent from control by local kings and priests, and the commandments of local gods. The activities of the merchants over a great area in turn helped to make Babylon rich, and so helped to keep the system well towards the imperial end of the spectrum.

During the period of fluctuating dominion over the lands of the two rivers, there were other great imperial states in the near east. The two most important were Egypt and the Hittites.

The long-established and highly developed civilization of Egypt was unified by the valley of the Nile, which was exceptionally regular in its flood time and harvest, and largely insulated by desert and sea from the pressure of neighbours. Unlike Mesopotamia it was forged at an early stage into a single and unusually centralized empire. The Egypt of the Pharaohs produced what may fairly be called the most attractive as well as the most enduring of the ancient near eastern civilizations. Though it was almost self-sufficient, there was seaborne trade round the eastern Mediterranean and by land through the fertile crescent. For this commerce the Egyptians used the commercial lingua franca of the near east, the language of the Semitic trading cities of Aram (Syria), which conducted most of the trade. Periodically in Egypt's long history, a powerful and expansionist Pharaoh would establish a loose dominion over Palestine and up into Aram. The little kingdoms and cities of those areas temporarily lost their independence. But they were not Egyptianized: they remained autonomous, and in times of weakness Egypt lost control of them again.

Economic and military expansion beyond the geographically protected and centrally administered Nile valley brought the Pharaohs and their governments into contact not only with small vassal states, but also with other imperial structures that were completely independent. Where another state was too strong to be coerced and too near to be ignored, we can see from the surviving Egyptian and other records how Egypt was drawn into what we today call a diplomatic dialogue. Particularly interesting is the dialogue between Egypt and the looser and more practically minded empire of the Hittites, based in what is now Turkey. It was, as a matter of expediency, conducted in Aramaic, which all parties concerned understood, and Egyptian diplomatic records survive written in Aramaic with the Sumerian cuneiform characters.[3] The dialogue was concerned with regulating trade, averting or ending wars, determining where boundaries lay; and sometimes with the negotiation of elaborate bargains involving alliances against common enemies and the precise terms on which the troops of both parties might be stationed in border areas. The subject-matter of the Egyptian–Hittite exchanges was much the same as the dialogue between Sumerian cities. And though the style is very different, the subjects are strikingly like those which concern Egyptian diplomacy today.

Diplomatic dialogues between independent states grew out of the inviolability of messengers from one ruler to another. The immunity of heralds is an immemorially old convention, which has developed between different communities of men all over the world. Before a battle, for instance, a herald might come to a commander from the other side, carrying a white flag or an olive branch or whatever the local custom was, and he would be allowed to deliver his message and take back the commander's answer. It was obviously to the advantage of both sides to know whether one side wanted to surrender or make a truce on terms. This immunity became extended to more general exchanges. When the Pharaoh sent a trusted man to tell the king of the Hittites what was on his mind, the Hittite ruler would listen, and then let the envoy return to tell the Pharaoh how matters were seen at the Hittite court; and the reports of envoys were supplemented by direct correspondence in Aramaic.

The Egyptian and Hittite empires were not just in casual and random contact. They were the great imperial powers in a system of communities, involved with one another and with other neighbouring communities in a network of strategic and economic relations. Thus involved, the two very different civilizations developed fairly elaborate conventions and procedures for dealing with each other, which we can call rules and institutions to regulate their relations. To that extent they formed an international society. There were specific written treaties and agreements; but the general institutions were no more than a loose set of regulatory procedures, growing out of practices that had shown themselves to be useful, and probably not codified into a written contract. Such arrangements of convenience, even when they are quite elaborate, are very different from the rules and institutions of the Sumerian and Mesopotamian society, which developed within the matrix of a common culture and a common set of religious beliefs, and formed an integral part of a shared civilization. This difference appears again between the relations that the European states of Latin Christendom maintained among themselves, and those with the Ottoman Turkish empire, with which they were inescapably involved but which belonged to what both sides considered a different civilization.[4]

It is impressive that the oldest records of a states system that we possess show us an integrated society of city states, organized not as a directly administered empire or as multiple independences, but as an elaborate hegemony about halfway along the spectrum between the two extremes. The Babylonian supremacy was nearer to the imperial end of the scale, as were the loose dominions which Egypt and the Hittites were able to establish over neighbouring communities from time to time. But the relations between the great empires belonging to different civilizations were loose and regulatory, without any hegemonial legitimacy or practice.

NOTES

1 M. Mann, *The Sources of Social Power*, Cambridge, Cambridge University Press, 1986, Vol. I, p. 92.
2 See the Book of Revelation 17.
3 The most important of these are some 400 tablets found at Tell el Amarna in Egypt, and now mainly in the Berlin and British Museums. See J. D. S. Pendlebury, *Tell el Amarna*, 1935.
4 See pp. 216–18.

3

ASSYRIA

The first near eastern empire

During the period when the near east was dominated by the Hittites, Egypt and Babylon, another Semitic people was gradually struggling to importance, namely the people of the god Asshur whom we call the Assyrians. Their achievement is significant for our enquiry.

The Assyrians occupied an area round the upper reaches of the Tigris, at the centre of the fertile crescent. Their land was agriculturally rich, and also an economic crossroads for the trade routes of the whole region. But it had one serious drawback: it had no natural frontiers and was subject to enormous pressures from the organized and technically advanced Babylonians and Hittites, and also from wilder immigrant peoples who were pressing down on the fertile crescent from the north. The Assyrians were conquered several times, and subjected for a long period to the overlordship of Babylon, from which they learnt much. But each time they managed to reassert their independence. This they did by means of a determined emphasis on military prowess and political discipline combined with an exceptionally astute and realistic statecraft. The Assyrians learnt in a hard school, and they were a hard people. Because of their exposed position their army was the indispensable bastion of the state. Alongside well-trained infantry they were the first settled people in the area to make effective use of horses in war, and also the first to adopt iron weapons and armour on a large scale. The iron was made from local ore, but originally by smiths from further north whose superior product the innovative Assyrians were quick to appreciate.

Surrounded by enemies and potential allies who were very different from one another, the Assyrians learnt that success and even survival depended on finding out as much as possible about their dangerous neighbours. They made it their business not just to obtain advance information about the movements of other armies, but to know what mattered to the different rulers, and also to other groups like merchants or subject peoples, so as to be able to offer the most effective inducements and deterrents. They built up a remarkable stock of what

33

we should call military and political intelligence, much of which they apparently obtained from Assyrian and other friendly traders in foreign countries. Because their resources were limited, they were used to the most economical means to achieve their end. They seem to have relied on promises and threats where possible, and if it came to fighting they tried to induce others to do their fighting for them. Only when other options failed did they use their own army. They were more keenly aware than others of the chanciness of war, and of the danger of casualties to their own soldiers who were the ultimate bulwark of the nation.

The imperial system which this hard and calculating people established was the first real attempt to organize politically the whole ancient world. They could not govern it all directly, of course. They evolved a system of vassals, native governments with Assyrian garrisons. Cities were normally accorded municipal autonomy under generous charters. The contributions levied from conquered and vassal territories were used for the upkeep of the army, to defray the costs of imperial power and to protect long-distance trade. In contrast to many ancient rulers who were indifferent to what their subjects and their enemies thought, they took pains to extol the advantages of living under the overlordship of Asshur, and they deliberately encouraged stories of their ferocity in battle and the terrible punishments they meted out afterwards, especially to defeated rulers. It was usually easy to depose a rebellious ruler; but where a whole people showed itself prone to rebellion, the Assyrians deported the population to another part of their dominions and settled others in their place. The Assyrians considered that nationalism and a tendency to rebel were rooted in the soil of the homeland, and if people were moved away from their native land and their native gods, there would be more peace and more productivity in the empire.

The Assyrians first became a significant power in the fertile crescent about 1400 BC, and a great imperial state from about 1100 to about 600 BC. (This is about the same time span as the Roman Empire in the west, or from Columbus to the present.) In the first imperial centuries their main problem was what to do about Babylon, the great metropolis from which they had derived much of their culture and which was still the commercial focus of Mesopotamia. When the attention of the great king of Assyria was engaged elsewhere, tribal leaders from Aram (Syria) would seize control of the city or at least disrupt the Assyrian administration. The Babylonians on the whole preferred Assyria because the Assyrians granted them exemption from forced labour and imposed much lighter taxes than the Aramaeans. The merchants benefited from an imperial power which could assure security over a large area and which was interested in fostering trade. The great king, Sennacherib, decided that peaceful control of Babylon was impossible, so he moved the population (or most of it) further north into the Assyrian heartland. But some ten years later the Assyrians sent the Babylonians back, restored their property and provided resources for rebuilding the city. It became clear that the real answer was to conquer and police all of Aram. This policy brought the Assyrians into contact with the powerful empire of the Egyptian Pharaohs, who also thought it necessary to have a say in Aram, especially in the kingdoms of Judah and Israel in the south. The slow and experimental extension of Assyrian authority into these two kingdoms is described in the Bible and the Assyrian records, as well as to some extent in Egyptian inscriptions. It is worth looking at one incident in the Second Book of Kings, which illustrates clearly Assyrian techniques for managing their suzerain international system.

In the area south of Assyrian pacification King Ahaz of Judah found himself besieged in Jerusalem by the king of Israel and his allies. 'So Ahaz sent messengers to the king of Assyria saying "I am your servant and your son. Come up and rescue me from the hand of the king of Syria and from the king of Israel who are attacking me" '.[1] The Assyrians did so, killing the king of Syria and deporting some of his people, and making King Hoshea of Israel their vassal. 'But the king of Assyria found treachery in Hoshea; for he had sent messengers to the king of Egypt.' Therefore the great king decided to establish his authority in the area more effectively. The military campaign lasted three years – a measure of Assyrian caution in the use of their army – and after conquering the country the Assyrians moved most of the Israelites away to the north of their dominions and settled Israel with Assyrians and Babylonians. The prophet Isaiah warned Hezekiah the new king of Judah to recognize the power of Assyria which had shown itself friendly, and not to ally himself with Egypt. But the young king threw off his allegiance to Assyria and began military operations against his neighbours, trusting in the Lord and perhaps also the Pharaoh to protect him. After fourteen years of this defiance the great king, Sennacherib, decided to restore Assyrian authority by a demonstration of force. Hezekiah could not resist, and sent a message saying: 'I have done wrong: whatever penalty you impose on me I will bear.' Sennacherib let him off with a fine. When Hezekiah continued his independent operations, the great king sent a large army to Jerusalem with a Hebrew-speaking ambassador, the Rabshakeh. Chapter 18 of the Second Book of Kings describes how the Assyrians went about the assertion of their authority:

And the king of Assyria sent the Tartan, the Rabsaris and the Rabshakeh [senior envoys] with a great army from Lachish to

35

King Hezekiah at Jerusalem. When they arrived they came and stood by the conduit of the upper pool, which is on the highway to Fuller's Field. And when they called for the king, there came out to them Eliakim son of Hilkiah, the head of the household, and Shebnah the secretary, and Joah son of Asaph the recorder. And the Rabshakeh said to them: 'Say to Hezekiah "Thus says the Great King, the King of Assyria. On what do you rest this confidence of yours? Do you think that mere words are strategy and power for war? On whom do you now rely, that you have rebelled against me? Behold, you are relying now on Egypt, that broken reed of a staff that will pierce the hand of any man who leans on it. Such is Pharaoh king of Egypt to all who rely on him." But [the Rabshakeh continued] if you say to me "We rely on the Lord our God", is it not he whose high places and altars Hezekiah has removed, saying to Judah and to Jerusalem "You shall worship before this altar in Jerusalem"? Come now, make a wager with my master the king of Assyria: I will give you two thousand horses, if you are able on your part to set riders upon them. How then can you repulse a single captain among the least of my master's servants, when you rely on Egypt for chariots and for horsemen? Moreover, is it without the Lord that I have come up against this place to destroy it? The Lord said to me "Go up against this land and destroy it".'

Then Eliakim and Shebnah and Joah said to the Rabshakeh 'Pray speak to your servants in the Aramaic language, for we understand it; do not speak to us in the language of Judah within the hearing of the people who are on the wall'. But the Rabshakeh said to them, 'Has my master sent me to speak these words to your master and to you, and not to the men sitting on the wall, who are doomed with you to eat their own dung and to drink their own urine?' Then the Rabshakeh stood and called out in a loud voice in the language of Judah 'Hear the word of the Great King, the king of Assyria. Thus says the King. "Do not let Hezekiah deceive you, for he will not be able to deliver you out of my hand. Do not let Hezekiah make you rely on the Lord by saying the Lord will surely deliver us and this city will not be given into the hand of the king of Assyria. Do not listen to Hezekiah, for thus says the king of Assyria. Make your peace with me and come out to me; then every one of you will eat of his own vine, and every one of his own fig tree, and every one of you will drink the water of his own cistern, until I come to take you away to a land like your own land, a land of grain and wine, a land of bread and vineyards, a land of olive trees and honey, that you may live and not die. And do not listen to

Hezekiah when he misleads you by saying the Lord will deliver us. Has any of the gods of the nations ever delivered his land out of the hand of the king of Assyria? Where are the gods of Hamath and Arpad? Where are the gods of Sepharvaim, Hena and Ivvah? Have they delivered Samaria out of my hand?'

What a scene this was, with the wall of Jerusalem looking much as it is today, and the terrible Assyrian army drawn up outside. The people of Judah lean over the wall to listen while the Rabshakeh shouts out his offers to them, and the representatives of Hezekiah ask him not to speak in Hebrew in front of the people. But of course this was precisely the Assyrian purpose: this was why they had chosen as their ambassador someone who could speak the local language, probably a Hebrew in Assyrian service. So the Rabshakeh stood and called out in a loud voice: 'Hear the word of the great king of Assyria. Thus says the king!' It is like a modern broadcast, the Voice of Assyria.

This was the beginning of the imperial diplomatic technique of reaching out to influence the people, as opposed to merely talking to the rulers. We see the great king bothering to influence the people of Judah against their king, Hezekiah, hoping to avoid using his army, but having it there as a grim alternative, to be used as a last resort. It illustrates an important development in international relations.

The principal benefit of Assyrian suzerainty or hegemony was that it put an end to the destruction of the wealth and lives of the combatants by incessant local warfare. The siege of Jerusalem by the king of Israel and his allies, which led Ahaz to appeal to Assyria, was part of an intermittent destructive pattern which Ahaz hoped to end by putting Judah under imperial protection; and the imperial tribute or taxation which was the economic price of that protection was less than the additional wealth created by the king's peace. The *pax assyrica* brought other important benefits too. The development of long-range trade benefited the merchants who conducted it and who therefore supported imperial authority and also brought new goods and economic opportunities to communities that had been more isolated. Technology and ideas were also more effectively diffused. Such advantages need to be seen against the brutalities of conquest, and the deportations and ostentatious cruelties which the Assyrians used to suppress revolt. Several books of the Bible as well as other surviving sources describe the general relief and joy which the fall of the Assyrian Empire brought, though the joy was as usual in such cases short lived.

The Assyrian empire is a good example of the general rule that imperial authorities do not in practice administer the entire area which they dominate or influence. The inner core of direct administration is surrounded by a ring of dominion with a degree of local autonomy, and then a ring of hegemony where the imperial power controls external relations and exacts a financial contribution to the imperial structure. The Assyrians had a core area of direct administration round Nineveh and the city of Asshur, and dominion over Babylon and Sumeria. Beyond that, they wanted states like Judah to be client autonomous kingdoms, making a contribution towards the costs of the imperial structure and having no dealings with its enemies. If a client state like Judah did not comply, they would warn and cajole it, and perhaps subsidize it, but in the last resort they would coerce it, sometimes with ostentatious brutality. When the Assyrians invaded Egypt they did not try to administer that huge kingdom, but set up client Egyptian Pharaohs with a garrison under Assyrian command and an imperial governor, who would perhaps be better described as a commissioner or delegate. This early form of indirect rule left Egypt a separate state, no longer independent but with the imperial power in a position amounting to little more than hegemony. Beyond the reach of Assyrian power were independent states and political entities, some of them much less civilized than the peoples of the fertile crescent. They were involved with the empire through trade, and also sporadic warfare and diplomatic communication. The economic and cultural influence of the empire extended well beyond the area of its hegemonic authority – as had been the case with the Sumerian city states and Babylon.

The Assyrians certainly imposed a tighter system on the diverse communities of the fertile crescent and the Nile valley, and made them more interdependent than before. They increased the surplus of wealth; which, after paying for the court and imperial administration, the army and the subsidies to client rulers, also made possible a higher standard of living for a larger population. In particular trade benefited by protection from robbery and by the removal of local boundaries and other obstacles. Indeed, it was as traders that the Assyrians first emerged on to the stage of history. But the Assyrian organization of that great area was much looser, and further from the extreme end of our spectrum, than the overtones of our word 'empire' suggest. Historical atlases which paint empires of the ancient world one uniform colour are misleading. The ancient empires had no clearly delimited boundaries. Their activities and their authority were radial rather than territorial, and spread along lines of penetration. Trade especially, and more generally wealth, civilization, military power and diplomatic communications, were diffused along specific routes, which the Assyrians and the Persians after them took great pains to improve. The extent to which subject communities in the Assyrian Empire retained native administrations under its hegemonic overlordship is well illustrated by its downfall. After several centuries of suzerain imperial power, the rulers of subordinate states like Babylon and Egypt were still autonomous enough in practice, that is they still had enough freedom of action, to renounce their allegiance and negotiate an anti-hegemonial coalition with external enemies of the empire like the Medes. But the Assyrian achievement, and the advantages which it had brought, had acquired a certain legitimacy, and remained in the minds of men.

NOTES

1 2 Kings 16: 7.

4

PERSIA
Imperial moderation

The Persian Empire has an especial interest for the study of states systems. It was the climax of the methods evolved in the pre-Roman ancient world to manage many different communities in an imperial system. It exercised a radial rather than a territorially delimited authority; and at or beyond the fringes of that authority it also played a major part with the Greek city states in the Greco-Persian system and profoundly influenced the Indian system.

The Medes and Persians were Aryan peoples, originally nomadic horsemen from the steppes north of the Black and Caspian seas. By about 1000 BC the southward trickle of Aryan-speaking peoples had become a flood. These still half-barbarous communities, probably not of genetically pure stock but all with much the same language, religion and way of life, were pushing down and settling in the whole great area to the south of them, from India and Iran to Greece and most of Europe. The Medes and Persians settled in the area east of Mesopotamia, between Sumer and India, where their descendants still live today. They became typical marcher communities, independent of the fertile crescent but trading with it and absorbing much of its technology. Just as the Assyrians owed their great success in part to the use of iron for weapons, so the Persian success was partly due to their more effective use of the horse. Though the Assyrians used horses they were not born and bred to the saddle; and increasingly they found to the east of them horsemen from the steppe who could ride more swiftly and fire arrows from horseback with extraordinary accuracy.

Once the anti-imperial coalition had overthrown the Assyrians, the area which the empire had integrated was partitioned for a while between the victors. The fertile crescent remained in an imperial structure managed rather than governed from the great commercial metropolis of Babylon. Assyrian methods continued: Nebuchadnezzar deported to the capital many of the unruly people of Judah, now his frontier with Egypt. But half a century after the fall of Assyria, the more vigorous Persians and Medes moved the whole Assyrian area without much difficulty back towards the imperial end of the spectrum, and re-established a single nominal authority over the Assyrian empire and far beyond it. The ease with which Cyrus conquered the Median overlordship and Darius the Great extended and organized an enormous and heterogeneous area of Persian suzerainty suggests that imperial legitimacy was well established in most of its communities, and that powerful elements were eager for a restoration.

Like the Assyrians, the Persians assimilated Mesopotamian civilization, including the cuneiform writing and other inventions that derived originally from Sumer; and they fostered and diffused Egyptian skills in administration, science and medicine. They also took over the Assyrian governmental structure. In particular, because distances presented a major problem in a system twice the size of the Assyrian, they greatly extended the Assyrian network of roads and relays of messages. In large areas they conducted their dealings with local authorities in Aramaic, the Semitic *lingua franca*, because it was more convenient. Herodotus, who knew them well, says that 'no nation so readily adopts foreign customs as the Persians',[1] and they also absorbed much non-Persian stock, especially through political intermarriage. But they were more exclusive than their imperial predecessors, more aware of the differences between themselves and the many other communities under their suzerainty. They treasured the nomadic virtues that they had brought with them: to shoot straight and to speak the truth. They also held to their own religion, which had been reformed by their prophet Zarathustra into a belief in a cosmic god of light and truth, opposed by the powers of darkness. Their god was not, like the Assyrian Asshur and the Babylonian Marduk, elevated to be a great king above all the other gods in the same Mesopotamian pantheon, but remained entirely separate from the cults and divinities of Mesopotamia, Judaea, Greece, Egypt and India, which continued without interference.

The size and diversity of the 'empire' which the Persians established were so enormous that their suzerainty in all but a core area was looser, more decentralized and more prone to fission than its predecessors. The outlying areas were quasi-autonomous client states rather than directly administered provinces. Force was necessary to establish Persian overlordship, but they were too few to maintain it by military power. To deploy an imperial army at a remote point was a logistically formidable undertaking, though it had to remain a credible one, and the imperial forces were normally kept in reserve, as the Assyrian ones had been. The Persians recognized that they must operate through local authorities whom it was difficult to coerce, and they consequently relied on persuasion and consent – what we would call hegemonial diplomacy. The more effectively a suzerain system provides advantages to those who support it, the wider it spreads its radial authority. Recent sociological studies have described the Persian Empire as an imperially regulated confederacy, and a federated empire of native elites, in contrast to previous western historians who tended to make the Persian achievement implausible by giving too little weight to the Persian ability to manage a society of client states, and placing too much stress on tribute and coercion.[2]

How far the Persian rulers saw positive merits in tolerance and devolution, beyond expediency and their own exclusiveness, is hard for us to say. (Opinions differ about this aspect even of the much more recent British raj in India, some of whose leading figures had the Persian parallel consciously in mind.) Perhaps it does not much matter. What is clear from the surviving evidence is that, though Persian rule was extended and periodically reasserted by violence, like other empires before and since, once it was established an exceptional moderation came over all that part of the world. The cruelty and ruthlessness of the Assyrians and Babylonians gave way to a relative blandness, a proclaimed ideal of just rule and a desire to maintain authority by conciliating and winning the loyalty of at least the ruling groups in subordinate communities. But of course opposition to Persian overlordship and a desire for total freedom of action remained vigorous in many communities, notably Egypt and the Asian Greek cities. Atrocities were attributed to Cambyses, the predecessor of Darius the Great; and Darius apparently (allowing for hostile propaganda) put down the revolt of the Ionian cities with a severity unusual by Persian standards. There was thus a fund of anti-imperial resentment ready to be marshalled by opportunistic leaders.

The Persian system of administration is described in detail in Volume IV of the *Cambridge Ancient History* and other works listed in the Bibliography, and it is not necessary for the purpose of this book to set out the details here. The Persians adapted many features of Assyrian practice. They planted garrisons at strategic points, as the Assyrians had done, with Persian commanders. Greek and Phoenician mercenaries were conspicuous in many areas, including Egypt; but the Persians also relied on local levies of troops, each dressed and armed according to the fashion of their country. The civilian governors or commissioners, called satraps, were either Persians or, often, members of native royal and prominent families who acquired a new function or title and thus enjoyed local and imperial legitimacy. The satraps were aided by mixed councils of Persians and natives, and their jurisdiction was separate from that of the garrison commanders and of the imperial intelligence service. Below this thin top layer of imperial authority the local peoples retained and in some cases restored their

customs and their administrative systems. Some areas were administered by temple priesthoods, some by local kings or landowning aris-
tocracies, some cities by merchant families, and the Greek cities of the
Asian shore of the Aegean usually by what were known as tyrants
(Chapter 5). The local patterns of life were left as far as practicable
alone in their immense variety. The despotism of the great king,
proclaimed in Persian decrees and inscriptions, was constitutional and
rhetorical rather than real.

A striking example of the Persians' blandness and desire to work with
local populations which co-operated with their imperial authority is
shown by their policy towards the **Jews**. The Assyrians had deported
a substantial proportion of the population from the Kingdom of Israel
and the Babylonians from Judah. Many assimilated Jews, and also
several who avoided assimilation in exile, rose to prominence in the
Persian system. Esther who became queen of Persia and Mordecai
who became chief minister may be semi-legendary characters; but
Nehemiah was cup-bearer to King Artaxerxes, and other Jews occupied
prominent places at court and in the administration. Cyrus, the first
Persian king, and later Darius authorized the return to Judah of exiles
who wished to do so, and the re-establishment of a military stronghold
at Jerusalem. Artaxerxes appointed Nehemiah to be governor of the
area. Nehemiah records that other local rulers in the area protested to
the king about the refortification of Jerusalem, and also tried to prevent
it by armed force, which Nehemiah had to resist on his own without
aid from the Persian authorities. These accounts bear out other evidence that Persian imperial authority was superimposed on local political entities that were autonomous enough to have their own armed
forces and to use them not just to maintain domestic order within
their jurisdiction but on occasion against neighbours.

As imperial authority became consolidated, the Persians were able
to insist that the autonomous communities under their suzerainty
should not resort to force against each other, as for instance the Jews
and their neighbours in Palestine and rival Greek cities on the Aegean
coast were inclined to do, but should observe 'the king's peace'. War
for the Greeks and Phoenicians of that time was a summer occupation,
and was often an extension of the traditional practice of seaborne
traders capturing or sinking rival ships on the high seas. In a world
where a resort to armed force was considered a legitimate way of
advancing or protecting one's interests, many free spirits resented the
alien imposition of order, while others welcomed the security which
it provided.

During the reigns of Cyrus and Darius the Persians established a
loose authority over the **Greek and Phoenician cities** on the Asian

shores of the Mediterranean, which hardly affected the internal affairs of those cities but benefited their trading prospects. The Persians thought in terms of land rather than of trade. Their basic approach to taxation was to take for the imperial treasury one-tenth of whatever the tax on land was in any country which they brought into their empire, leaving nine-tenths to be used for local purposes. They did not tax profits from trade, though local governments could levy trade taxes. This suited the Greek and Phoenician city states, which had little land and lived mainly by seaborne trade. Moreover, Persian suzerainty assured easier access to a vast and orderly trading area in Asia equipped with the excellent Persian road system, as well as comparative peace between neighbours. A problem for the Persians was the involvement of the Asian Greek cities with peninsular Hellas. The Persian attempt to assert overlordship there also is discussed in the next chapter.

We have no record of how the empire, during the two centuries of its presence in the **Indus valley**, dealt in practice with the independent states of India beyond its borders, which had a highly developed international society and diplomatic tradition of their own, described in Chapter 7. But the surviving **Greek** evidence shows the Persians, after the failure of their early attempts to establish suzerainty over European Hellas, dealing with the independent city states there on a perceptive and realistic **anti-hegemonial basis**, supplying ships and money to a series of coalitions against the strongest Greek polis of the day, organizing congresses on the basis of mutually recognized independence and helping to define the legitimacies of the Hellenic inter-polis society. This defensive statecraft, discussed in the following chapter, stemmed from the Persians' awareness specifically of their military weakness in Hellas, including the Asian shore, and more generally of the limitations of their power and the need for tactical expediency. It was a political practice far removed from the arrogant rhetorical assertion of the great king's overlordship over the four corners of the earth, which was also part of the Persian political ritual, and is sometimes supposed to be the limit of their understanding of relations with other states. It is likely that corresponding techniques were used to protect the Persian position in India.

The nature of the system of communities which pivoted on the Persian suzerainty is also well illustrated by the position in the system of the rich and highly civilized but by then militarily weak land of **Egypt**. The Persian imperial authorities and the Phoenician and Greek trading cities had high stakes there. Egypt had helped to overthrow the Assyrian Empire, and briefly reasserted its independence by 650 BC. Connections with the Greek world developed actively, especially with the cities of the Asian shore which regarded Egypt as a major source of ideas and techniques as well as a natural trading partner. Egypt had made a valuable contribution to the Assyrian system, and the Persians wanted to recover it.

A century and a quarter after the reassertion of Egyptian independence the Persians invaded it; and soon afterwards Darius the Great re-established a loose imperial overlordship. Egypt, which according to modern estimates contained a fifth of the population of the entire Persian conglomerate, did not become a conventional satrapy; it remained a separate state with the Persian king as Pharaoh and an Egyptian administration which often resisted imperial demands, sometimes to the point of rebellion. The Persian connection stimulated Egypt's external trade. Under Darius a canal was cut from the Mediterranean to the Red Sea, which encouraged trade with India, part of which was also under Persian overlordship. That made Egypt even more attractive to the maritime Greek cities: both those under Persian suzerainty and above all Athens where many merchants from the Asian shore had settled. Elsewhere, in less developed lands, the Greek city states established independent daughter cities as colonies; but in Egypt merchants from many Greek cities had to trade from the joint city of Naucratis, which was perhaps something like an ancient Shanghai. The special rules and limits imposed by the Egyptian authorities on Greek activities in Egypt were something like those prescribed by the Ottoman Empire for European traders, described in Chapter 22. In the heyday of imperial Athens almost all Greek traders used Athenian money, which became widely accepted in Egypt.

The first period of Persian suzerainty over Egypt lasted some sixty years. In the moment of imperial confusion which followed the assassination of Xerxes, the anti-Persian faction in Egypt reasserted its external independence. The new Pharaoh found a willing ally in Pericles, who tried to help him ward off the Persians by the risky venture of sending an Athenian fleet, doubtless partly equipped by the 'Egypt lobby' in Athens. The Persians, whose forces included contingents of Greek men and ships, defeated the Athenian expedition in 455 BC, but the overlordship which they reasserted over Egypt appears to have been fairly nominal. The Pharaohs remained independent in practice, and in times of stress allied themselves informally with whatever corporation in peninsular Hellas was at war with the empire. In the era of the king's peace, when the Persians stood well with all the leading Greek cities, the Athenian connection seemed the most advantageous to the Egyptians, mainly for commercial reasons. The Athenian owl now appeared on the Egyptian coinage. The Spartans were also associated with Egypt, and a mercenary Spartan force operated there against the Persians. The links between Hellas and Egypt hindered the Persians from asserting even their mild degree of authority

45

in Egypt, and so helped to keep the whole east Mediterranean system nearer to the multiple independences end of the spectrum.[3]

In general, and taking into account the evidence in the next chapter, it can fairly be said that the Persians developed the concept and the practices of an imperial rule or influence so loose that the system approached a hegemonial society of states, and was therefore based on providing a balance of advantage to those willing to work with or at least acquiesce in Persian authority. The techniques of Persian statecraft were adapted by their Macedonian and Roman successors to different purposes. In dealing with states beyond the range of their military superiority, and (so far as the record survives) particularly in their involvement with the independent Greek cities, the Persians explored corresponding concepts of the rights and responsibilities of great powers in a society of states, which are still found in much transmuted forms down to our own day.

NOTES

1 Herodotus, Book 1: 135.
2 See Michael Mann, *The Sources of Social Power*, Cambridge, Cambridge University Press, 1986, Vol. I.
3 See the next chapter, and also J. Boardman, *The Greeks Overseas*, London, Thames & Hudson, 1980.

5

CLASSICAL GREECE
Independence and hegemony

Ancient Greece, during the four centuries from about 500 to about 100 BC, occupies a more central position in the evolution of modern international society than any other system in this part of our enquiry, and deserves our more detailed attention. It is important to us for two reasons. First, the city states and the Persians in the first half of the period, and the Hellenistic monarchies in the second, organized their external relations in very innovative and significant ways. Second, the Greco-Persian system exercised great influence on the European system, out of which the present system has developed; and for several centuries aspects of Greek practice served as models for the European society of states. There was a natural resemblance between the two societies. Both were in theory well towards the independences end of the spectrum; and the parallels were greatly reinforced by the classical education of European and American statesmen and thinkers who dominated international practice from the Renaissance to the early part of this century.

The history of the Greeks still awakens an extraordinary partisanship in many people. Few periods of the past have aroused anything like the same emotional commitment and bias in writers from Machiavelli down to our own day. In this century the main current of sympathy runs in favour of Athens and its incomparable cultural achievements, and in favour of European Greece and of the city-state period, and against Sparta, against Persia and the Asian side of Greece, and against the monarchical Hellenistic period. If we are to look objectively at the workings of the states system in classical times, our analysis must move away from partisanship and from an exciting story full of heroes and villains, towards a more balanced understanding of the predicament of all the actors. This attempt at objectivity will also help us to relate the Greek experience to that of other peoples.

It will be convenient to examine the inter-state pattern in Greece in three consecutive periods: first the fifth century and down to the end of the Peloponnesian War (500 to 404 BC); then the era of congresses (to 338); and finally, in a separate chapter, the Macedonian period (to about 80 BC). But first we must look at some general characteristics of the Hellenic world.

The Greeks called themselves Hellenes; and the area inhabited by them and their culture was called Hellas. Hellas, like Europe, was an area and a cultural tradition divided into a number of independent states. It was centred on the Aegean Sea, which is full of islands that acted as links between one side and the other. The cities of the Asian side were as prosperous and important as those in the rest of Hellas, but their external relations were subject to control by the imperial power of the day. The cities of what we may call central Hellas, namely the whole European peninsula south of Macedon and the Aegean islands (the southern half of modern Greece) were independent of any general overlordship, though many of them were dominated by a more powerful neighbour. Further to the west lay a third area of Hellas, the colonial settler cities of Greater Greece, mainly in southern Italy and Sicily. Pressure of population induced Hellenic cities to send out 'colonies' of their citizens to take advantage of greater economic opportunities elsewhere, especially in the west. A Greek colony was founded for much the same reasons as a European settler colony; but it was from the beginning an independent polis, in no way governed by the parent city, though usually in a special relationship with it.

The easiest form of communication in ancient Hellas was the sea. The land either consisted of islands or was so mountainous that land communication was not easy. This fact encouraged political fragmentation. The sea lanes south and west were fairly open to the ships of the rival Greek cities; but the economically vital northern route into the Black Sea ran through the straits of the Hellespont and the Bosporus, in earlier times held by Troy and in classical times by the city of Byzantium.

The early Greeks were not much interested in their own past. Unlike the other peoples of the near east, and especially the Egyptians and the Hebrews whose elaborate written records stretched back over millennia, the Greeks concentrated on the contemporary world; and even in the fourth century when they began to look to their own past, what they remembered about it was either very recent or largely mythological. As a result the classical Greeks were exceptionally uninhibited by their past experience in international relations as in most other fields, and felt substantially free to order matters as they wished. Whatever may have happened in the distant past when according to the legends there were kings like Agamemnon and his brother Menelaus who married Helen of Troy, by the time the mists of history clear away and we come to events which are recorded and not mythologized, we find a very large number of city states which treasured their independence. There were perhaps a thousand Greek cities, from large imperial states to the smallest townships.

The commitment of the Greeks to independence is legendary. They were passionately attached to the ideal that each city state, each polis, should manage its own affairs; and they resented any kind of overlordship or hegemony, by another polis or by a foreign power. The idea of uniting all Hellas into a single state did not often occur to them, and when it did, it was usually greeted with genuine abhorrence. In practice many Greek cities had to accept some degree of control by an overlord or a hegemonial ally, especially in their external relations; and it might seem the lesser of two evils. The Asian Greek cities were usually in this position, and so were many cities in the peninsula for long periods, but the western colonial cities less so. The Greek city states were thus, in their concept of legitimacy and to a large extent in practice, well towards the multiple independences end of our spectrum. The system was based on the independent polis, and attempts to pull it in practice towards hegemony and beyond had to find ways of accommodating the general presumption of independence. The Greeks were in this sense different from the other systems and communities we have discussed, which did not have such a strong dedication to freedom of external action. The Greek ideal of the city state was imported by the Renaissance into the European system, and the legitimacy of untrammelled independence remains a strong commitment of our international society today.

The Greek cities were on the western edge of the civilized world. In all the highly civilized communities to the east of them, from Persia and Egypt across to China, the normal form of government was a powerful king who took the decisions of state, and who derived his legitimacy from being the representative of a god. When the king prevailed, men accepted that his god prevailed in heaven; or in the Chinese system, if he was the real 'son of heaven' he would be able to prevail. The classical Greeks were not governed by kings in that way until Macedonian times, though certain kings held prescribed political or military offices in states of free citizens. Nor were Greek political leaders the representatives of gods, though tutelary deities were believed to protect their chosen cities. Each Greek polis was a limited **corporation of citizens** who were the hereditary armed proprietors of the corporation. A citizen had to be male, and to be descended from citizens, almost always on both sides; and he had notionally to own some property (though in Athens and several other cities many citizens came to own little or none) in addition to being a co-proprietor of the polis. It was extremely difficult to acquire the citizenship of most Greek cities. A citizen-proprietor had also to be able to bear arms, especially since the decisions which he and his fellow citizens made concerned not only the laws which governed the city but also peace and war. A Greek city state was small enough to allow the citizens who would do the fighting to assemble and decide for themselves whether to go to war. Common descent, common decisions, common military training and an acute awareness of a common destiny usually produced a high degree of solidarity among the citizens of a polis in the face of external enemies.

The Greeks distinguished between the city, its inhabitants and its citizen-proprietors. Our practice of talking about, for instance, the United States of America as an abstraction is derived from our greater sense of historical continuity and from the territorial rather than proprietory basis of our statehood. The Greeks did not say that Athens went to war with Sparta: they said that the Athenians, meaning the corporation of armed proprietors, went to war with the Spartans.

The city corporations felt little or no responsibility towards Hellas as a whole. War was always legitimate if the citizens saw advantage in it. The advantage was sometimes strategic, either directly or to support a valuable ally; but more often it was economic. War was always fairly probable; and encounters at sea between the ships of rival corporations, which fell below the level of formal war, were to be expected. The Greeks waged war very effectively. Both on land, with the citizens fighting as heavily armed infantry or hoplites, and at sea which was their element, the Greeks were, man for man, the pre-eminent military communities of the area. They easily outclassed the multinational levies of the Persian Empire at all times.

In practice the Greek city states did not live in a system of unremitting hostility, of all against all. They were bound together by a common language and culture, common religious observances which cut across city-state boundaries, common Olympic and other games in which all cities could take part and common theatre, architecture and other arts, which were of religious origin. There were active commercial and intellectual ties. In the more specific field of relations between states there were rules of war and peace, of mediation and of communication. Envoys came and went. Prominent citizens of a polis called *proxenoi* represented other corporations, spoke up for the corporation which they represented and gave it advice. These rules and institutions, based on a common culture, justify us in speaking of a Hellenic **international society** in Hedley Bull's sense.[1] But the Greeks themselves seem not to have thought in these terms. No Greek writer or philosopher described the inter-polis society as such. Aristotle has given us a detailed description of the internal government of a city state in his *Politics*, but there is no 'metapolitics' about the external rules and institutions that linked the city states, or about the wider international system in which the Persian Empire played a major part.

The Greek city corporations limited many of their inter-polis relations to other Hellenes, with whom they recognized a kinship that separated them from all other communities. Everybody else they called **barbaroi**. Such words change their meaning over time. Originally *barbaroi* did not mean uncivilized people, but those who could not speak Greek, and whose speech therefore sounded like 'bar-bar'. Herodotus recorded that some non-Greek speakers like the Egyptians and the Chaldeans were more advanced in the arts and the sciences than the Hellenes. Nevertheless the Greeks looked down on all non-Greeks, who, they alleged, did not have free, enquiring minds and thought it natural to acknowledge an overlord.

Three features of the Hellenic system, which were consciously in the minds of Greek and Persian political leaders in their dealings with each other, are of special interest to this enquiry. The first is **anti-hegemonialism**. There was a propensity to hegemony in the system. As the Athenians, the Spartans and the Thebans became in turn the most powerful corporation in Hellas, each desired to lay down the law and to establish a general hegemony. The Greek commitment to independence led other corporations to form one anti-hegemonial coalition after another. This was not inevitable. In the China of the warring states described in Chapter 8, for instance, the state of Zheng tended to move from one side to the other, always choosing the victor. Ancient Greece provides the first known examples of independent states that were anti-hegemonial on principle, and which held that to support the victor was dangerous for their independence. Anti-hegemonialism reflected the Greek sense of the legitimacy of multiple independences, and helped to anchor the Greek system towards the independences end of our spectrum.

Even more significant was a corollary of anti-hegemonialism, that it was unwise to destroy the defeated. A number of Greek corporations were in fact destroyed by their victorious rivals, who killed the male citizens and enslaved the women and children. The destruction of wealthy and perhaps monopolistic Sybaris by its commercial competitors in the toe of Italy sent a shiver through Hellas, and even in distant Miletus on the Asian side the citizens who did business with Sybaris shaved their heads in mourning. The same fate was proposed even for great corporations like the Thebans and Athenians. But more far-sighted statesmen saw that the independence and safety of their own corporation would be damaged in the long term by annihilating the enemy of the moment. The Spartans seem to have held this view because of their conservative tradition and respect for religious taboos. The Corinthians and some Athenians held it rather for reasons of expediency. The realization that the enemy of today might be the ally of tomorrow, that it was not in one's interest to destroy any of the essential elements of the system, later led European statecraft beyond anti-hegemonialism to the concept of the balance of power, which remains an important aspect of the present global system.[2] However, there is no evidence that Greek practice went beyond opposition to hegemony.

Stasis meant the use of armed force inside a city to alter the way it was governed. It involved revolution and counter-revolution, a resort to arms against one's fellow citizens. The bitterness engendered by stasis is always very high. It has been said that every citizen in Hellas hated some other polis more than he hated any non-Greek, and somebody in his own corporation more than he hated any other polis. In Hellas there were ancient traditions centred on aristocratic families and the land. The oligarchic families were a conservative force in a polis, upholding the old social system and performing the religious rituals. In most Greek corporations some citizens wanted to break down the old system, and some wanted government to serve the interests of the moneyed class rather than the oligarchy. The agitation of the reformers often led to the overthrow of the old constitutions and the establishment of a popular boss or dictator, called a tyrant, who was usually financed by the merchants and also supported by those people who wanted a more equitable distribution of purchasing and political power among the citizens. 'Tyrant' is another word that has changed its meaning over the centuries. It originally meant not a cruel despot but a sole ruler, and then someone who exercised power by non-traditional means. The authority of a single tyrant was in Greek eyes very different from democracy, the rule of those chosen by the majority of proprietors. However, tyranny generally led to democracy in the Greek sense, because the tyrants who wanted to stay in power acceded to the wishes of their followers, and because both tyranny and democracy were associated with financial enterprise and expansionist thinking. The early history of Athens was a long period of stasis, in which the forces that supported tyranny and then democracy gradually gained the upper hand; and many other corporations followed a similar course. The Athenian Thucydides summed up the trend in a memorable sentence: 'As the power of money grew in the cities of Hellas, tyrannies were established in nearly all of them, revenues increased, shipbuilding flourished, and ambition turned towards sea power.'[3] In the Assyrian imperial system the influence of merchants and manufacturers had been considerable. In Greek cities like Athens and Corinth their influence was more prominent, and intensified the rivalry between the corporations.

The importance of stasis for our enquiry, in classical Greece and

elsewhere including our own time, is that where states are closely
involved with each other and constrained to watchfulness by the pressures of their system, civil strife does not remain purely an internal
issue for the state concerned, whatever the formal legitimacy may say,
since the outcome affects other states. Consequently they **intervene**
and take a hand in the game. The Athenians, in the period of their
imperial expansion, knew that the cities where the oligarchic party
committed to the old ways remained in power would be likely to
oppose them and their plans; and that if they wanted a polis to be
friendly to them, or at least neutral, it would pay to help and subsidize
the populist and democratic faction there. Similarly, the Spartans knew
full well that their advantage lay in not having too many tyrannies
and democracies in Hellas. Both these great corporations understood
that, in the modern idiom, their own security was involved in the
internal affairs of other Greek states.

A perceptive passage in Thucydides on stasis deals with the con-
vulsion of Hellas during the Peloponnesian War as a result of the
opposition between the forces of change (tyrannic and democratic) and
the oligarchs:

> The former tried to bring in the Athenians and the latter the
> Spartans. In peacetime they would have had no pretext or desire
> to call in those states. But once war broke out, the faction that
> wanted to overthrow its own government found it easy to call
> in allies to upset its opponents and to promote its own cause.
> So revolution and counter-revolution brought calamities in many
> a polis.[4]

Thucydides goes on to say that the Athenians and Spartans did not
intervene out of altruism, to benefit another corporation, or out of
love for oligarchy or tyranny and democracy as such: they did it
because they saw advantage to themselves in doing so. In much the
same way the Soviet leaders considered it advantageous to them to
encourage and subsidize Marxist parties and stasis abroad, because
such parties usually looked to them. Similarly the British government
in its nineteenth-century heyday and the United States government
today have encouraged democracy in the different sense in which
we now understand it. Intervention in internal affairs, to the degree
necessary to ensure that the government of another community is
friendly to the intervening power, has the effect of integrating the
system, of shifting it in practice further towards the imperial end of
the spectrum.

The Greek concept of *dike* was a more sophisticated and less legal-
istic way of settling disputes than our present system has been able
to achieve. When *dike* refers to domestic issues inside a polis, it is

usually translated as justice, but that is a wholly unsatisfactory translation for external relations. *Dike* between one polis and another (for instance, between the Athenians under Kimon and the Spartans, discussed below), or with the Persian Empire (for instance, the king's peace, also discussed below), in the fourth century apparently meant what we should call a reasonable settlement, an adequate adjustment, consisting of three elements. The first element was what had traditionally been the legitimate and rightful position. The second was the actual position on the ground, the status quo. These were not usually the same. If the contesting parties could not settle the argument, the third element involved the good offices of some third person or state who was acceptable to both sides. *Dike* was not arbitration, in the way that the king arbitrated between two Sumerian cities, making a binding decision; much less was it like a judge within a state asserting the law. It involved patient shuttle diplomacy.

An early philosopher from the Asian side of Hellas, Anaximander, held that each force had its opposite. There was always a conflict between heat and cold, between the light and the heavy, between fire and water. Though fire could boil water away, water could extinguish fire. He pointed out that where one could find a middle position between these opposites, where the forces of nature and the forces of men could find some sort of balance, there conditions would exist where life, and the human spirit, could develop to their optimum. Anaximander's concept of the conflict of opposites, and his belief that when they were in equilibrium the good could flourish, was characteristically Greek; it was what we call scientific and objective. He seems to have considered equilibrium between extremes as a form of *dike*. Neither Anaximander nor others are recorded as applying this naturalistic way of thought to relations between cities; but for many Greeks it must have coloured the more specific senses of *dike* described in the previous paragraph. A man-made optimum or just compromise based on *dike* is very far removed from, for example, the Hebrew concept of international relations as part of almighty God's design and as a chastisement for transgression. This way of thinking also illustrates the difference between *dike* and justice. Justice is blindfold and uncompromising, and must give its verdict though the heavens may fall; *dike* was watchful and inclined to compromise, and its purpose was to keep the heavens up in their place.

Before Philip of Macedon established a dominion over central Hellas, four independent Greek city states there, the Athenians, the Spartans, the Corinthians and the Thebans, together with the Persians played the leading parts in the Hellenic system.

The Athenians were the most creative of the Greek city corporations.

They produced most of the classical Greek literature and thought which have come down to us. They were also, economically and at sea, the most powerful polis in Hellas. They earned their great wealth largely by manufacture and maritime trading, and as their economy and population grew they became increasingly dependent on imports, especially of food. Maritime trade was highly competitive and dangerous in Hellas. The Athenians considered it necessary to control the Aegean and the islands in it, which they did by means of a hegemonial alliance called the Delian League which became increasingly an Athenian dominion, and by a more equal link to remoter cities on the way to the Black Sea, like the geographically key polis of Byzantium.

In the great city, alongside the Athenian citizens who included many artisans and farmers, there gathered together a large trading community of foreign merchants and manufacturers, called metics, who were often very rich. They were not allowed to be citizens, but they made Athens a very cosmopolitan and wealthy city, and their money helped to line up the votes in the assembly of citizens for the expansionist and imperial policy that so alarmed other Greek states. The non-Athenians, and the women and slaves, together greatly exceeded the number of proprietors of the polis.

Sparta, the other great polis of peninsular Hellas, was in some ways the opposite of Athens. The Spartans were also, of course, a closed community of armed hereditary proprietors. They had a remarkably balanced constitution, with two kings who had special military functions, an assembly of the citizens and a panel of wise men called ephors. They had very different values from the trading cities: they were opposed to money playing a large part in the affairs of the state or the citizens, and they consciously championed the oligarchies and the traditional legitimacies. Spartan men lived together and shared frugal meals in conditions halfway between a monastery and a barracks, somewhat like the medieval military orders. They did not fortify their city, considering that they could defend it by force of arms. They maintained a rule by force over the large non-Spartan agricultural population of their state, called helots. The helots were not slaves and played an important part in Spartan armies; they cultivated Spartan land as sharecroppers, and produced most of the wealth that maintained the Spartan proprietors of the polis. The Spartans also controlled certain neighbouring cities by force, and were the leaders of a wider hegemonial alliance of cities, much as the Athenians were. The aim of Spartan policy was to make safe their area of dominion in the Peloponnese. They feared a helot revolt even more than the Athenians feared a revolt of their slaves.

The Corinthians are particularly interesting for a study of states systems. Corinth was one of the great trading cities of Hellas. Its position on the narrow land bridge that links the mainland to the Peloponnese gave it the big advantage of being able to trade easily into the western sea towards Italy as well as east through the Aegean. The Corinthians were a small and rich community, in many ways like their Athenian competitors, but with the crucial difference that they were never powerful enough to determine the way Hellas should be run. The main Corinthian interest, therefore, was that no other corporation should dominate Greece, or even lay down the law to the rest, and that the seas should be open for their trade. This is the policy that the Dutch adopted in seventeenth-century Europe, when they were in a similar position to the Corinthians. The interest to us of the Corinthians is that they were a systematically anti-hegemonial polis, the animators of one anti-hegemonial coalition after another. They sided regularly with the vanquished against the victors after wars, which required courage as well as foresight. They seem to have understood better than other Greeks the nature of the inter-polis system and how to use it in their interest.

Thebes was in some ways the most traditional of all the major Hellenic cities. It figured prominently in the ancient myths, and many half-legendary characters like Antigone and Oedipus were Thebans. In the centuries with which we are concerned the Thebans developed military skills which eventually won them hegemony over peninsular Hellas. Throughout the period they maintained a dominion over the cities in the country round them, called Boeotia, which they regarded as their vital zone of control, like the Spartan area in the Peloponnese and the Athenian islands in the Aegean. One independence-loving Boeotian polis, the Plataeans, were hostile to Theban dominion, and always on the opposite side to the Thebans in war. The Thebans were therefore anxious to suppress Plataea. Similarly in Renaissance Italy the Florentines continually tried to suppress the hostile neighbouring city of Pisa.

THE PERSIAN BID FOR HEGEMONY

The Persians became involved with the Greek world by taking over the Lydian imperial system in the west of what is now Turkey. They inherited from the Lydians a loose hegemony over several Greek trading cities, and gradually extended it to establish a degree of authority over all the Greek cities on the Asian side of the Aegean. The mild Persian overlordship hardly affected the internal affairs of the Greek corporations, and benefited their trading prospects. Nevertheless the independence-loving Greeks resented having Persian garrisons and governors who limited their freedom of action. The Persians soon discovered that Greeks on the European side of the Aegean continually aided the anti-Persian factions in the Greek cities in Asia. Athenians in particular were moved by the appeals of the malcontents and refugees from the Asian side, and became increasingly involved. Meanwhile the confused stasis in Athens between the traditionalist oligarchs and rival tyranny and democracy factions led the feuding parties to appeal for help to the Persians. These appeals seemed to the great king, Darius, an opportunity to intervene and impose a negative hegemony on central Greece, forbidding the cities there to help dissidents on the Asian side.

Athenian activities precipitated the close Persian involvement with central Hellas which continued until its conquest by Philip of Macedon. Darius' deterrent expeditions were a failure; but the Persians were still in a phase of expansion, and his successor Xerxes decided that he must establish some sort of hegemonial authority over the whole of central Hellas and Macedonia to the north of it. There is no evidence that the Persians wanted to include the Greek cities in Italy and Sicily. They gathered, rightly, that they would find some support from European Greeks, who were aware of the advantages which Persian enforcement of the peace conferred on the cities of Asian Hellas. A majority in many corporations of central Hellas saw advantages in having the Persians in, while in others the majority preferred absolute independence. The three corporations which led the independence camp were the Athenians, the Spartans and the Corinthians. The Thebans were conspicuous for favouring the Persians. When the Persians brought very large armed forces into Europe and sent ambassadors – Greek speakers rather like the Rabshakeh used by the Assyrians – the majority of the Greek city corporations opted to submit to the mild conditions of overlordship which the Persians offered to them, rather than to fight the empire which when in earnest had proved invincible.

However, the cities which did fight against Persia proved to be more than a match, on their home ground, for the mixed Persian levies that came from as far away as India. Generations of Europeans and Americans have been inspired by the accounts of how at Thermopylae the Spartans were defeated but with great honour, and the Athenians were able with outnumbered forces to defeat the Persians at the land battle of Marathon and the naval battle of Salamis. The decisive land battle was won under Spartan leadership at Plataea. That victory is one of the turning points of the Greco-Persian system. It established Spartan superiority in land warfare and made them the champions of the freedom of Hellas, that is of keeping the system well to the multiple independences end of the spectrum. The Corinthians played a characteristic part. They told the Athenians and Spartans at the beginning that if those two great corporations decided to resist, the

Corinthians would fight beside them; and they did so by land and sea from Thermopylae to Plataea.

The failure of Darius' expeditions and Xerxes' major attempt to establish suzerainty taught the Persians the important lesson that they could neither put into the field nor muster at sea a force able to stand against an alliance of Greek cities. Later they came to see that they were not a match for even one of the great cities of central Hellas. The Persian attempt to establish a hegemonial order in Hellas had failed. Henceforth they resigned themselves to limiting the threat from European Hellas by other methods than military force.

Why, in spite of the Greek love of independence, did the majority of cities in central Hellas accept the Persians, and many corporations actually fight alongside them? In addition to the reasons we have noted, there must have been real fear of the consequences of resistance. There was also mutual suspicion. The Thebans felt threatened by the Athenians. The citizens of Argos in the Peloponnese feared the Spartans. The maritime trading city of Megara lay between Athens and Corinth. These corporations decided (doubtless not unanimously) that the mild overlordship of the Persians was a lesser evil than the destructive harshness of their Greek enemies. Another important factor in the Hellenic system was the oracle at Delphi, whose political advice carried great weight. On this occasion the oracle advised against resisting the Persians. People have wondered whether the Persians, who were always ready to use money to further their aims, bribed the oracle. In any case the well-informed oracle was also probably genuinely impressed that the Asian side of Hellas was more tranquil and prosperous than the European side.

THE DIARCHY

When the defeated Persians recognized that European Hellas was too much for them, they also lost their authority over the Asian side. In the wake of their retreat, Hellas on both sides of the Aegean came to be dominated by a co-operative understanding between the Athenians and the Spartans. The defeated Greeks, called Medizers, now had little say. Many Athenians wanted to destroy the Theban corporation by killing the citizens. But the conservative Spartans and the wiser Athenians opposed the idea, considering that the Thebans ought not to be destroyed and had their role to play in Hellas. The Spartans' insistence on restraint earned them great respect in Hellas and later saved the Athenians too from destruction.

The second attempt at hegemony over Hellas succeeded where the Persian attempt had failed. For the first time we see hegemonial powers laying down the law in the system. It was not a single authority but a joint hegemony of the two great corporations, the Athenians and the Spartans, known as the **diarchy**. Athenian trade and wealth expanded rapidly, and the Athenians soon became stronger than the Persians or the Spartans. They drove the Persians out of Asian Hellas, bringing it under Athenian hegemony. Their imperial ambition before long extended beyond Hellas, along the maritime trade route to Egypt. Kimon, the architect of the Athenian imperial policy, saw clearly that if the Athenians were to expand eastwards and seawards, they must secure their rear by a firm arrangement with the Spartans. Most Athenians disliked the Spartans, who were very different from them; but Kimon argued that the two great corporations were 'yoke-fellows', like a pair of oxen, and that they must pull the plough together. Kimon made an agreement with the Spartans to settle their affairs never by war but by the methods of *dike*. This suited the Spartans, who did not look much beyond the Peloponnese, but who were committed to protect a number of corporations allied to them from Athenian encroachment. This is an early example of the idea that great powers which have wide-ranging commitments, and are bent on external undertakings, should also have a sense of responsibility towards each other.

Kimon's policies created favourable conditions for Athenian prosperity and maritime empire. But as the moneyed element became more influential, his conservative policies at home became increasingly unpopular. After seventeen years of power he was exiled and replaced by Pericles, who though an aristocrat was the leader of the money-and-democracy majority. Pericles believed in the expansion of trade and the power of money, and had the support of the rich metics; but he also believed in democracy and majority rule among Athenian citizens. He ended the diarchy: he had no use for the conservative and unpopular Spartans, thinking the Athenians were now so strong they no longer needed a yoke-fellow. Thucydides attributes to Pericles some splendid speeches about democracy, in the limited Athenian sense (he no more applied it to his slaves than did George Washington); and the power of that oratory still remains considerable. Some of the finest achievements of Greek culture and thought were achieved under Pericles, stimulated by the contact of many Athenians with strange lands and new opinions, and by the foreigners and the wealth that poured into the city.

THE ATHENIAN BID FOR HEGEMONY

The Athenian desire to dominate the system alone was the third bid for hegemony. But in making it, the great corporation outran its new-found strength. The Periclean faction became involved in quarrels with the Spartans at the same time as they were helping an Egyptian revolt against Persian overlordship. When the military operations in Egypt ended in disaster, it became politically necessary to recoup this setback nearer home. As more people thronged into Athens, and the need to import food and other necessities became more acute, a faction of Athenians wanted to suppress their commercial rivals, as a similar faction had wanted to destroy their Theban enemies two generations before. The Athenians first destroyed the corporation of Aegina, their nearest competitors, but only after a long siege which advertised Athenian aggressiveness throughout Hellas. Pericles then employed the Athenian navy to blockade the seaborne trade of other commercial rivals. On the isthmus leading to the Peloponnese between Athens and Corinth lay the smaller polis of Megara. The Megarians, who founded Byzantium, were particular rivals of the Athenians in the Black Sea trade for grain and slaves; and therefore the money faction and the majority wanted to suppress Megara. This issue precipitated the conflict known as the Peloponnesian War, between the Athenians and those who hated and feared them. The Corinthians in particular, though also commercial rivals of the Megarians, saw that if the Athenians succeeded it would be Corinth's turn next. So they appealed to their Spartan allies. The speech of the Corinthian envoys to the assembled Spartans, as given by Thucydides, illustrates well many of the issues which we are considering, and particularly the nature of anti-hegemonial coalitions:

Spartans! The confidence which you feel in your constitution and social order makes you inclined to doubt what we tell you about other cities. It is the source of your moderation, but also of your limited knowledge of foreign affairs. We have warned you time after time of the blows about to be dealt us by the Athenians, but instead of taking the trouble to find out about what we told you, you suspected us of being inspired by private interests. Now, instead of calling your allies together before the blow fell, you have waited till it struck us. Among your allies we have the greatest complaints to make, complaints of Athenian outrage and Spartan neglect. Long speeches are not needed where you can see slavery accomplished for some of us and meditated for others, our allies in particular, and prolonged preparations by the aggressor for the moment of war. . . . For all this you are responsible. It was you who first allowed them to fortify their city after the Persian war. You who, then and now, deprive of freedom not only those whom they have enslaved but those who are still your allies. For the true author of the subjugation of a polis is not so much the immediate agent as the power which permits it though it could prevent it; particularly if that power aspires to the glory of being the liberator of Hellas.

We are at last mobilized. It has not been easy to mobilize, and even now we have no defined plan. We ought not to be still enquiring into the facts, but into how to defend ourselves. The aggressors, with matured plans to oppose to our indecision, have ceased to threaten and begun to act. And we know the paths by which Athenian aggression travels, and how insidious its progress is. . . . You, Spartans, of all the Hellenes alone keep quiet. You defend yourselves not by doing anything but by looking as if you would do something. You alone wait until the power of any enemy is twice its original size, instead of crushing it in good time. And yet the world used to say that you were to be depended upon! . . . You fail to see that peace stays longest with those who use their own power in accordance with *dike* but equally show their determination not to suffer lack of *dike* by others. Your idea of *dike* is based on the principle that if you do not injure others you need not risk your fortunes to prevent others from committing injuries. You could scarcely have succeeded in such a policy even with a neighbour like yourselves.

Here at last let your procrastination end. . . . Do not sacrifice your allies and kindred to their bitterest enemies, and drive the rest of us in despair to seek some other alliance. The breach of a treaty cannot be laid to those who are deserted and forced to look for other support, but to the power that fails to assist its ally. But if you will only act, we will stand by you. It would be unnatural for us to change, and never could we find such a congenial ally.[5]

The Corinthians were the animators of the anti-hegemonial coalition, but the Spartans were the only polis that could lead it, and that was for the Spartans in arms to decide. The news that they were at last willing to do so evoked a tremendous wave of determination. Thucydides, who at an early stage of the war was an Athenian general, nevertheless describes how the Periclean policy met with universal opposition:

The sympathies of mankind were very much on the side of the Spartans, who proclaimed that their aim was the liberation of Hellas. Cities and individuals alike were enthusiastic to support them in every possible way, so bitter was the general feeling against the Athenians, whether from those who wished to escape from their rule or from those who feared that they would come under it.[6]

The Spartans had waited for a dangerously long time, and Athenian strength had become so great that the two sides were evenly matched and the war was long and damaging. The Spartans were only a land power. So long as the Athenians and their client allies controlled the seas they could withstand the anti-hegemonial coalition. The issue was finally decided by Persian financial aid to the coalition. At first the Persians were pleased to see the diarchy, which had enabled the Athenians to do them so much harm, split into two warring camps; and they hoped that Athenian power would be broken. But when it was not, the Persians provided the money for the coalition to build a fleet which finally destroyed the Athenian navy guarding the vital sea lane to the Black Sea, and so reduced the great city to starvation. The third attempt to organize Hellas on hegemonial lines had failed. Another Athenian historian, Xenophon, records that there was great rejoicing all over Greece at the downfall of his city, because people believed that the freedom of Hellas was no longer endangered.[7] But there must have been many who regretted the passing of the Athenian imperial system.

The Athenians were feared and hated not because they were barbarians or the enemies of Hellenic civilization. On the contrary, they were the acknowledged leaders in the arts, the most civilized as well as the richest of Greek states. They were feared because they were powerful, and did not hesitate to use their power to lay down the law; and hated especially because like the Assyrians they acted highhandedly and sometimes in a deliberately frightful way. We shall find this fear of hegemonial power again in Europe, directed against four highly civilized states: Venice in the Italian Renaissance, Habsburg Spain, the France of Louis XIV and of Napoleon, and nineteenth-century Germany.

Second, we must expect a power that is able to exercise hegemony in a states system, or even dominion, to do so. Some powers in this position may hesitate for a time, because of their traditions, post-war weariness or other reasons. But sooner or later the ability to move a system of independent states along the spectrum towards hegemony leads to action in that direction. This was to be the case with the Spartans and then the Thebans, as it had been with the diarchy and the Athenians.

CONGRESSES AND THE KING'S PEACE

The anti-hegemonial victory in the Peloponnesian War seemed to re-establish a looser system in European Hellas than the Athenians had tried to organize. But the belief that the freedom of the Greek city states was no longer endangered soon proved false. The Spartans found themselves in the position that the Athenians had held. They showed their traditional restraint by refusing to destroy the Athenians; but they soon began to assert their hegemonial authority over the whole of Hellas, and to interfere in the internal affairs of other cities in a way that they had not done before. They compelled their allies to accept their decisions, as the Athenians had done; and they adopted the Athenian policy of military operations against the Persians on the Asian side of the Aegean and even in Egypt (where their motives were more mercenary than hegemonial), in spite of the help they had received from the Persians in the war. This was the fourth attempt to establish a hegemony, and can be described as partially successful.

Though the conservative Spartans were somewhat more hesitant about their forward policy than the Athenians had been about theirs, other corporations which cherished their independence, and especially the democratic factions in them, found Spartan hegemony unacceptably oppressive. The Corinthians were again the anti-hegemonial animators; they offered the defeated Athenians their alliance and persuaded the Thebans and others to join a new struggle to end Spartan hegemony, which historians appropriately call the Corinthian War. The Persians also decided to protect their position in Asian Hellas by supporting the new anti-hegemonial grouping. A Persian fleet under Athenian command helped to get the Spartans out of Asia. But when Athenian power in the Aegean seemed to grow dangerously strong again, the Persians resumed their collaboration with the Spartans.

From the Peloponnesian War onwards, Corinthian and Persian policy ran largely on parallel lines. Both were anti-hegemonial in central Hellas, because neither was strong enough to support a hegemony of its own there. But the Corinthians, being Greeks, were more convinced of the need to reduce hegemonial power by military action, whereas the Persians inclined towards pacification.

Persian diplomacy, exercised largely through the Satrapy of Sardis, now took on a more active dimension. The Persians realized that they could neither conquer European Greece nor withdraw from contact with it. But with their hands full elsewhere, they wanted tranquillity on their western borders, and supporting anti-hegemonial coalitions in the European peninsula did not produce it. During the Spartan ascendancy they decided that the empire's interests would be best served by a general peace in the peninsula and the islands, similar to the one they tried to maintain on the Asian side, but on the basis of the independence of as many states outside their own domain as possible. None of the three major Greek states had this objective. The Spartans were the least opposed. When their attempt at hegemony met organized opposition they remembered their traditional support for the idea that every polis should be free; but they still wanted a position of recognized primacy and certain rights of intervention 'to preserve freedom'. The Athenians remained, and the Thebans became, ready for any hegemonial advantage which opportunity might offer.

Accordingly, when the Spartans sent envoys to the great king to renew their old alliance, he agreed, but the Satrap of Sardis enlarged the negotiations into a general peace congress by bringing in their enemies also. The Spartans agreed to a settlement based on the two principles of a universal peace and independence with appropriate exceptions, provided their primacy was respected. But the Thebans did not agree, and a second peace congress had to be convened. This time the Persians invited to Sardis not just the belligerents but every Greek polis. The Persian formula, known as 'the king's peace', now included peacekeeping arrangements:

> Artaxerxes the King thinks it in accordance with *dike* that the city states of Asia and certain islands should belong to him, and that all other Greek cities should be free except certain island cities which should belong to the Athenians as of old. If either of the two parties does not accept these terms, the King will make war on that party by land and sea, through the agency of those who do accept, supplying ships and money.[8]

Everybody knew that the king was in no position to enforce his proposals. They were balanced enough to command general acquiescence (the Asian Greek cities by now preferred Persian suzerainty to either Athenian or Spartan control) and a degree of active support. The reference to *dike* indicated that the empire, or more specifically the Satrap of Sardis, would use his good offices acceptably to all the major parties. Persian money, 'the archers of the king', was distributed impartially too. At the ratifying congress in Sparta the Spartan, Athenian and Theban leaders all accepted Persian subsidies as an element of the king's peace. This settlement has been compared to the Peace of Westphalia of 1648 which for the first time established a general peace in Europe based on independence and a general balance of power. But at Westphalia there was no power to play the Persian part of honest broker and to finance the settlement.

The king's peace was fragile. The leading Greek cities continued to oppose each other. The forward party in Sparta established a *de facto* hegemony over much of peninsular Greece that was just within the letter of the king's peace which the Spartans claimed to enforce. The Athenians expressly accepted the king's peace. They reorganized their maritime league on less hegemonial lines, with a congress of their allies meeting separately from them to ratify decisions; but they used other forms of pressure and many of their allies chafed under it or left the league. The Thebans developed a new military formation, the phalanx, which was able to defeat the hitherto invincible Spartans at Leuctra in 371 BC. Most cities in Greece hastened to applaud the victors, who had not hitherto shown hegemonial ambitions. But the Thebans quickly took the place of the Spartans as the corporation which enforced the law in central Hellas. The wary Corinthians renewed their alliance with the defeated Spartans, whose weight was needed to hold the Thebans in check.

Theban hegemony, the fifth in the series, was based on military superiority, and was as much resented as the others had been. But twenty years of the king's peace had changed the nature of inter-polis relations. The leading cities now acknowledged that they belonged to a politically organized system, which had rules and principles and which included the Persians. The general awareness of membership was strengthened by the convening of a number of further congresses, at which even the smallest Greek polis could have a voice. The basic principle was what most Greeks cared most about, independence; but the unwritten rules of the system allowed each of the three major Greek cities and Persia a back-yard of dominion, an area of predominant authority. The fact that the new international order was called the king's peace, and that the policy of *divide sed non impera* was Persian and maintained by Persian money, made it more acceptable to the three great corporations of Hellas. They accepted it, not because they trusted the Persians more than each other, but because they knew that the Persians were not strong enough to dominate the system as each of the three great powers of Hellas had shown itself to be.

The king's peace was in the Persian tradition of a unilateral pronouncement. But even the form was not that of a suzerain ruler. Everyone concerned, and not least the Persian negotiators in Sardis who took advice from Asian and other Greeks, knew that it was a negotiated formula for a new legitimacy – what was in accordance with *dike* – combined with an offer of naval and financial support to an anti-hegemonial alliance against a polis that tried to upset it. The new collective legitimacy was also ratified and made acceptable by the congresses, at which almost all the corporations of Hellas had some voice. The system established in Hellas by the king's peace and the congresses was further from the independences end of the spectrum than before; but in principle the law was laid down by an agreement between the major powers, rather than by one of them acting alone. Warfare continued in central Hellas, and the practice was more hegemonial than the legitimacy, but the legitimacy acted as a brake on the practice. The aim of the Persians, the Corinthians and the smaller independent corporations of Hellas was partly achieved.

The three regions into which Hellas of the classical city states was divided were involved with each other; but each occupied a different position along the spectrum. The eastern region was the most integrated. The city corporations of the Asian shore exercised internal autonomy, but externally they were accustomed to hegemony: Lydian, Persian, Athenian or Spartan. Their prosperity was due in large measure to their association with the Persian Empire, both for the market which it provided them and the peace which it usually managed to keep between them. In the early part of our period the eastern region was the most creative area of Hellas in art and thought.

At the other side of Hellas the western region consisted of newer colonial corporations in Sicily and Italy, which dealt with more primitive peoples, and remained in a very loose system of multiple independences. The region was wealthy, but looked east across the sea for the graces of civilization. Alliances shifted, trade rivalries provoked bitter conflicts in which cities were destroyed, and war was prevalent. The integrating force of Athenian expansion began the involvement of western Hellas in the more structured relationships of the central area; and later the king's peace partially extended to the western region as well.

Central Hellas, on the European mainland and the islands of the Aegean, lay between Asian and Italian Hellas, both geographically and in the organization of the inter-polis system. The middle region was the focus of the whole system, which included the Persians, and of the cultural society of Hellenic cities, which did not. It was there that what we value most in our classical Greek heritage was achieved. The city corporations of the region liked to think of themselves as free, in the sense of being able to decide their relations with other Greek cities and the outside world. Many corporations, especially the larger ones, were indeed independent; but long-standing leagues and alliances held most cities in a prescribed pattern of relationships, and so provided a structural order. Two main blocs gave the system a degree of polarity. When the Spartans and Athenians collaborated against the Persian invaders, their alliances and military efforts remained largely separate. The polarity continued through the subsequent period of diarchy, and intensified to the point of open warfare in the Peloponnesian War and again in the struggle against Spartan hegemony, with only a few independent corporations able to change sides.

Dominance within an alliance that covers only part of a system of states is of course not the same as laying down the law for the whole system. In the Hellenic system a power exercising or aspiring to hegemony was able to convert its client allies into an area of effective dominion, especially in alliances where coercion was used on recalcitrant corporations. Such alliances, like other imperial systems, can be represented in a diagram as having concentric circles or degrees of dependence, which in practice varied partly though not solely with geographical distance. The careful Athenian relationship with the remote but indispensable Byzantines was very different from their deliberate brutality on the closer island of Melos. The Macedonians' dominion of peninsular Hellas was equally shaded: they destroyed the Thebans, accorded the Athenians exceptional privileges and agreed to let the Spartans stay out of their federal league. Such imperial alliances were, as the Asian Greeks discovered, not very different in practice from the Persian Empire, which outside its directly administered core positively encouraged local ethnic identity and self-government. The Greek and Macedonian hegemonists, like the Persians, required three things from the communities whose external relations they determined. The three requirements were: a contribution to the imperial treasury; a military or naval contingent, furnished on demand; and the presence of an imperial commissioner or satrap and a military commander. The rhetoric and the legitimacies were certainly different, and kept Greek and early Macedonian imperial alliances somewhat nearer to the multiple independences end of our spectrum. But we should not let the difference of form obscure the administrative realities and their integrating effect on the system.

An alliance of client states round a powerful state making a bid for hegemony is also different from an anti-hegemonial alliance. When the Athenians were organizing anti-hegemonial resistance against Persian expansion, they and the city states on several Aegean islands formed a voluntary alliance. In the subsequent campaigns to wrest Asian Hellas from Persian hegemony, the Athenians organized the Delian League which convened on the island of Delos and took collective decisions, including contributions to joint naval defence. In their imperialist phase, and especially under Pericles, the league was converted into an Athenian dominion. Membership became compulsory, the treasury was moved to Athens, and some of the contributions for the navy were diverted to rebuilding the Parthenon. At that time the Spartan alliance was anti-hegemonial and voluntary, and the problem of the allies was to get the Spartans to act. The allies met first without the Spartans, who then heard their allies' views but took their own decision – so that there had to be negotiation and agreement to arrive at a joint policy. When the Spartans became dominant they reorganized their alliance as the Athenians had done.

A comparable situation existed in the organization of the two principal alliances in the cold war. The Soviets exercised what amounted to dominion over the internal affairs of the client members of their alliance, and openly said that they could not allow Czechoslovakia, Poland or any other member to secede. The European members of the NATO alliance were much more independent, and bound to America by fear of Soviet hegemony in Europe: they and the Americans often preferred different policies, so that a compromise had to be reached by negotiation. It is not a question of how 'democratic' a hegemonial power may be in its domestic affairs. The Athenian corporation was more democratic in its imperialist phase than before. The extent to which the Spartans were willing and able to assert themselves in the rest of Greece, not their domestic constitution, determined the structure of their alliance.

In spite of the commitment of the Greek cities to independence, the idea of hegemony over the whole of Hellas was always in the air. There were regular attempts to establish a hegemony over the central region, from the Persian invasions to the Macedonian conquest. The king's peace was designed to preserve the independences of central Hellas by an early form of covenant or guarantee, and so to provide collective restraints against any individual bid for hegemony.[9] Hellas became for a time an international society with elaborate rules, institutions and congresses, underpinned by Persian diplomacy and money. But the non-hegemonial structure of the king's peace was unstable. King Philip of Macedon established an overlordship over the central region which definitively moved it to about the same position along the spectrum as had been the practice for the corporations under Persian overlordship on the Asian shore.

NOTES

1 H. Bull, *The Anarchical Society*, London, Macmillan, and New York, Columbia University Press, 1977, p. 13.
2 See Chapter 18.
3 Thucydides, *Peloponnesian War*, Book I, § 13.
4 ibid., Book III, § 5.
5 ibid., Book I, § 6.
6 Thucydides, Book I, Chapter 3.
7 Xenophon, *Hellenica*, Book II, Chapter 2/23.
8 ibid., Book V, Chapter 1/30.
9 Peter Calvocoressi (*International Relations* volume XI, p. 286) has a useful formula. The Greeks and Persians 'cut down particular hegemonies in the interests of the hegemonial system when the particular hegemonies looked like destroying the system by moving too far along the spectrum towards its imperial end. They instilled a sense of the value of the system itself.' See also my comments on *raison de système* on p. 240.

6

THE MACEDONIAN SYSTEM
Hellenization of the Persian system

The Macedonian period is interesting to us for a number of reasons. It saw dramatic swings of the pendulum along the spectrum. Philip II established a hegemony which was close to dominion over central Hellas. Alexander brought the central area, and Asian Hellas which had largely reverted to multiple independences, with the Persian Empire into a single imperial structure. But his death led to its fragmentation into a group of independent imperial kingdoms and smaller states. The Hellenistic kingdoms dominated a new states system that was in many ways remarkably like the European one.

The original Kingdom of Macedon was a characteristic marcher state on the northern border of peninsular Hellas. For most of the period discussed in the last chapter it was a fringe member of the Greco-Persian system. Its royal and governing families became progressively Hellenized. Persian influence was also present: the king of Macedon was one of the envoys sent by Darius to persuade the peninsular Greek cities to accept Persian suzerainty, and after the Persian retreat Macedon expanded into areas conquered by the Persians. Philip II (king from 359 to 336 BC) was a determined expansionist. While a hostage in Thebes he learnt the new techniques of the Theban phalanx, and came to see the weakness of both the Hellenic city states and the Persian Empire. Back in Macedon he developed a standing army which combined an improved phalanx with well-drilled cavalry recruited from the wilder peoples of the north. Knowing how effective Greek hoplites were against Persian levies, he decided to make himself master of Hellas, and then, with the aid of as many Greeks as he could muster, to take over the Persian Empire.

Opinion in central Hellas was divided, with opposition to Philip especially strong among the dominant Thebans and the Athenians, while the Spartans inclined to neutrality. When Philip occupied the strategic straits into the Black Sea, the Thebans and Athenians went to war and were resoundingly defeated. Philip then used a shrewd mixture of force and diplomacy to form most of the Greek states, former allies and enemies alike, into what was nominally a league of cities under his military leadership but was in practice a highly hegemonial structure under Macedonian control. He wanted to avoid alienating the Greek cities, because he would need them to seize control of the Persian Empire. He legitimized and facilitated his control by preserving the forms of the polis and the alliance wherever these did not hamper him. The hereditary corporations of the cities continued to run their internal affairs. In practice Philip did not need to move the system of central Hellas so far along the spectrum as it might seem. The reality of multiple external independences had for some time been curbed there by the king's peace and by Spartan and Theban enforcement of their interpretations of it. The king of Macedon's peace extended the curbs and brought external freedom of action virtually to an end.

Philip thereupon began operations against Persia, but was assassinated in Asian Hellas. His enterprise was continued by his gifted son Alexander. Philip had trained his heir in the arts of war and statecraft, and ensured his Hellenization by summoning Aristotle (a Thracian who may have been a subject of Philip) to be the prince's tutor. Alexander was more confident of power than his wily father. He rigorously put down dissidence among his client allies in Greece. When the Thebans revolted he destroyed the corporation and the city itself, leaving only the house of the poet Pindar standing as a half-derisive gesture of respect for the ancient city's achievements.

From the point where Philip of Macedon effectively mobilized most of the central Greek cities under his command, the Persian policy there of *divide sed non impera*, of *dike* and subsidies, had visibly failed. The way lay open for the king of Macedon, with superior armed force, to take over the weak and acquiescent empire. Had Philip not been assassinated he would doubtless have achieved this goal. Alexander did so with comparative ease.

In one sense Alexander's war against Darius was to determine who should be king of kings. Persian aspirants to the throne had repeatedly put the issue to the test by similar military campaigns, usually with some Greek troops; one of these contests has been vividly described for us by Xenophon. To many and perhaps most politically conscious people in the non-Persian communities of the empire, the king of Macedon's bid must have seemed just another in the series. Indeed, Alexander took over the empire with its administrative structure more or less intact. In 330 BC he proclaimed himself the legal successor of the Persian kings and adopted Persian dress. His visits to remote communities like India and Egypt were affirmations of his personal succession. But there was a real difference. Authority in the empire was no longer to be purely Persian, but a blend of Macedonian and Persian; with two ruling races whom he encouraged to intermarry and to dominate the empire together.

The upper levels of Macedonian society were noticeably Hellenized; and they, assisted by large numbers of Greeks, provided the military basis on which Alexander's rule rested. That subtle blend of Greek and Persian ideas and techniques of government that we call **Hellenistic** had already begun to spread over the empire from the Greco-Persian area of interaction on the Asian side of the Aegean. Now it quickly displaced the purely Persian structure that had hitherto controlled the management of the near eastern congeries of peoples. The Hellenistic concept of authority accepted very varied forms of traditional local government under the overall rule of a semi-divine king. The Greeks, unlike the monotheistic Persians, regarded their mythical and historical heroes as semi-divine children of a god or goddess. Alexander's claim to be the son of the Greek supreme god Zeus (as well as the legitimate heir of King Philip) was widely accepted, and enhanced his right to rule the empire. Polybius records the widespread conviction nearly two centuries later that Alexander was a universal emissary sent from God to harmonize and save the whole world, bringing peace and concord to all men. However, Alexander was more attracted than his generals were by Persian ways, which had been shaped by long imperial practice; and had he lived the Hellenistic synthesis might have been more outwardly Persian in some of its forms. But he died of fever in 323 BC after only seven years on the Persian throne.

Each of the Macedonian generals who fought and intrigued for Alexander's inheritance would have liked to take the empire over more or less intact if he could; but failing that each aimed to secure as much as he could hold with Macedonian and Greek troops against his rivals. In order to hold the territories he conquered, a general needed to settle his fighting men and their families in garrison cities at strategic points. Since unlike Alexander he did not have the legitimacy of hereditary kingship, a general had to hold the loyalty of his European soldiers by paying them generously, and also by remaining sturdily Macedonian and substituting Greek manners and language for Persian.

Before long it became clear to the two outstanding men among them, Seleucus and Ptolemy, that since neither of them was strong enough to inherit the sceptre of Alexander and Darius, it would suit them better that nobody should do so, but that the spoil should be divided up according to what each general could hold. When after some years of desultory warfare and bargaining Antigonus One-eye made his bid for the whole empire, Seleucus became the animator of an explicitly anti-hegemonial compact of the kind familiar to the

Greeks, along with Ptolemy who had installed himself in the very rich and defensible province of Egypt, and others. They proclaimed the unified empire at an end and recognized each other as king or *basileus* (the Greek title for a hereditary sovereign ruler) in 305 BC. Each of the new kingdoms which was thus arbitrarily carved out of the empire remained administratively much as it had been. Each was a smaller replica of the Persian structure, with the general-king as *basileus* and successor of Alexander in the area he was able to hold. Seleucus in the east, threatened by Antigonus, realized that he did not also have the resources to hold the Indian territories against the Indian reassertion of authority that had found an outstanding leader in Chandragupta Maurya. He therefore struck a bargain with Chandragupta, recognizing him also as independent (with the consequences which we shall examine in the next chapter) in exchange for a large fighting force of war elephants. With these Seleucus and his allies defeated Antigonus at the battle of Ipsus in 301. Ipsus marked the triumph of a multiple anti-hegemonial system throughout the near east, which had for many centuries taken a single suzerain system or universal empire for granted. But the Hellenistic monarchies were themselves imperial conglomerates of diverse and largely self-governing communities.

Seleucus, who had at Alexander's instigation married a Persian wife, retained control of the ethnically Persian and Median heartland. He soon made over that part of his dominions to his half-Persian son Antiochus. The government of the core area of the former Persian Empire remained largely in Persian hands, and became gradually more detached from the Hellenistic system. The western half of Seleucus' domain, from the Tigris to the Aegean, became a separate kingdom, continually involved in conflicts with other generals and their heirs. In order to defend and govern it more effectively, Seleucid kings actively encouraged settlers from all over Hellas to form new Greek city corporations, which provided a privileged military and administrative class for the kingdom, replacing the Persian one. The Seleucid kings retained much of the former machinery for governing the non-Hellenic population, but left them less autonomy and taxed them with a heavier hand than the Persians had done.

The other major power of the new system, the Ptolemaic kingdom, was organized on the same general lines. In Egypt the Persian pattern of authority, which had never amounted to more than a hegemonial overlordship, disappeared; and a controlling layer of Greeks was superimposed on the age-old and still effective native Egyptian administration. The Ptolemies wrung as much wealth as possible from the subject Egyptian population. They spent it on the maritime extension of their kingdom, which stretched up into the Aegean, and on Alexandria, the greatest Hellenistic city of all, which became the centre of the Ptolemaic kingdom and the leading economic and cultural capital of the whole Hellenistic world.

The two secondary Hellenistic kingdoms, Macedon on the European side of the Aegean and Pergamon on the Asian, were more markedly Greek. But not all of the western half of the Persian Empire remained in the hands of Macedonian dynasties. In the course of time quasi-Hellenized local rulers, especially in the Seleucid area, were able to push their autonomy to the point of external independence.

The authority of the Macedonian general-kings depended on their military and political abilities. The area they were able to control was not a pre-defined territorial or ethnic entity. (We shall meet this phenomenon again in the Arab caliphates described in Chapter 11.) To help legitimize their succession to Alexander, they proclaimed themselves divine figures like him. In Egypt the Ptolemies took over the age-old and still generally accepted Pharaonic cult and iconography, which the monotheistic Persians had also done and Augustus was later to continue. Egyptian and near eastern cults blended with Greek ideas about demigods and heroes of divine parentage to produce a Hellenistic concept of divine kingship, which endowed the Macedonian kings with a religious legitimacy. It was supposed until recently that worship of the divine ruler was imposed by Hellenistic kings on their subjects; but modern scholarship emphasizes the extent to which the cult developed from below, especially among the Greeks who justified their obedience to royal authority by treating it as divine. Legitimation of authority makes things easier for those who submit to it as well as for those who wield it.

Since the armies and the administrations of all the Hellenistic kingdoms depended on the immigration of individual Greek mercenaries, it was important for each kingdom to maintain a position with various Greek cities and leagues, and to ensure that no rival kingdom was able to exclude it from Hellas. This competition benefited the Greek corporations, which were courted and subsidized. The Ptolemies in particular poured much wealth extracted from Egypt to buy, or rather to hire, the loyalty of Greek cities and individuals. But many cities in Hellas were occupied by garrisons and over time drained of their ablest men.

The struggles between the Hellenistic kings were for strategic territories, for influence over virtually autonomous local rulers and city states in Hellas and in Phoenicia like Tyre and Sidon, and for what Ptolemy called honour or prestige. The campaigns were conducted largely with Greek mercenary troops; and the interest of the men themselves and their employers was to keep casualties low. Each king also wanted to do as little damage as possible to the territory in dispute, so as not to alienate those who might incline his way and so as not to lessen the value of the prize. In addition, the Hellenistic dynasties intermarried in order to cement alliances and treaties and for other reasons. The Seleucid and Ptolemaic dynasties became one royal family and the disputes between them took on the flavour of family quarrels, with the women playing an active role. For all these reasons war, which had been a ruthless affair for the Assyrians, and waged by citizen armies intent on victory among the Greek city states, now became a means of adjustment, waged without passionate conviction by hired men, with a premium on keeping casualties and damage low.

The Macedonian system, from the mutual recognition of multiple kingship in 305 to the Roman conquest of the Seleucid kingdom (it became a Roman province in 65 BC), was a complex mixture of states that varied greatly in character and size and in the degree of their external freedom of action. The two great powers of the system were the Macedonian imperial kingdoms of the Ptolemies and the Seleucids, followed by the similiar kingdoms of Macedon and Pergamon. Alongside and between them were a large variety of smaller kingdoms, governments and cities, each usually composed of a single community. The smaller states enjoyed varying degrees of domestic autonomy under the hegemonial restraint of a great power. Some smaller states enjoyed periods of real independence in their external relations, with rival powers competing for influence. For instance, independent kingdoms came to control much of Asia Minor. Further south, the Phoenician merchant cities, situated between the two great powers, inclined to the Ptolemies or the Seleucids as prudence dictated; and the Jewish Maccabee state made itself independent of the Seleucids in 143 BC and maintained relations with the Parthian kingdom in Persia and with the Romans and the Spartans. In central Greece the Athenians and Spartans preserved a dignified though circumscribed independence, and leagues or confederacies of smaller Greek cities enjoyed the same status. The Rhodians, a rich merchant corporation who were in a sense the spiritual successors of the Corinthians, preserved effective independence by a discreetly anti-hegemonial policy, and made notable contributions to what we should call international maritime and commercial law.

Outside the Macedonian system were independent communities, connected to it by trade and cultural links and by strategic pressures. Among the highly civilized states in this category were the western Greek cities, Rome and Carthage, and the Maurya and Persian-Parthian empires to the east. The Macedonian system and expanding Rome were also subject to the pressures of the less civilized but warlike Celtic peoples of the north, who invaded and settled in northern

74

Greece and Asia Minor as well as in northern Italy, which the Romans called cisalpine Gaul.

This complex picture becomes clearer if we imagine it as a diagram. The system was dominated by the two similar great powers, the Seleucids and Ptolemies. But it was not a diarchy or shared hegemony like Kimon's. It was bipolar, turning on the axis of great-power rivalry. Neither was strong enough to establish a hegemony over the whole system, and indeed the two states derived their origin from the awareness of their founders that it was no longer possible for one power to dominate the whole Hellenistic world. But both of them were imperial states on the familiar near eastern model, with a core area of direct administration, a circle of dominion and beyond that a wider circle of hegemonial authority. In the third circle hegemony shaded off into fairly stable alliances based on mutual interest. One of the two secondary Hellenistic kingdoms, Macedon, suffered from Ptolemaic hostility to its position in Hellas and was therefore allied to the Seleucids; while Pergamon, which cut the Seleucids off from much of Hellas, relied on Ptolemaic support. In this way the rivalry of the two great powers brought the heterogeneous congeries of communities into an interconnected structure, and gave the Macedonian system a degree of order and predictability. The areas of hegemony inevitably fluctuated in extent, and the authority of each great power was necessarily loose at the fringes, because of the counter-pressure of the other. Bipolar systems provide opportunities for smaller powers to change sides or to avoid alignment.

This basically bipolar system flourished without a dominant power for some two centuries. But then, in the same way as the half-Hellenized Macedonian kingdom on the edge of Hellas had made itself master of the Greek city-state system, so the geographically marginal but militarily effective power of Rome extended its authority over most of the Hellenistic world, as described in Chapter 9. Rome restored to the western half of Alexander's empire a political unity that it had not enjoyed since his death.

The principal legacy of the Macedonian system was the creation of a great superficially Hellenistic area, centred on the eastern Mediterranean and stretching from the Adriatic to the Tigris and the Nile, which enabled the very diverse communities there to share a common culture and language in addition to their diverse ethnic inheritances. The Hellenistic expansion corresponds to the expansion of European civilization over the whole globe in the nineteenth century. Hellenistic civilization was attractive in itself, and an amalgam that facilitated the exchange of techniques and ideas. It spread downwards to the middle and lower levels of the local communities, and brought them closer together without destroying their individuality. It therefore proved impressively durable. The Romans took it over virtually intact. After the collapse of the Roman Empire in the west, it survived in Christianized form for another thousand years as the Byzantine civilization.

7

INDIA

Multiple independences and the Mauryan Empire

No system of diverse states and peoples developed a greater sophistication in ancient times than that of India. Largely isolated between the Himalayas and the sea, the Indian states constituted a world of their own. The great subcontinent was, and still is, inhabited by an enormous diversity of peoples speaking a great variety of languages. When the Aryans gradually flooded over the near east and Europe, they also crossed the Himalayas, and in the course of time imposed on all but the southern peninsula of India an Aryan dominion and a common Aryan language, Sanskrit. Aryan religion and ways of life blended into earlier Indian ones to form Hindu civilization. Hinduism in its many variants is one of the major civilizations of mankind, a complex culture affecting every aspect of religious, social and economic life and thought. We can examine only the nature of its political states system.

Hinduism conferred a greater similarity on the hitherto very different Indian communities. One of the interesting features of the Hindu tradition was that, as in classical Hellas or Europe since the Renaissance but in contrast to the near east, a strong sense of a common civilization distinguished Hindu Indians from other peoples. But it was taken for granted that the area of this civilization would be politically divided into a large number of independent units. India before the Maurya Empire was a patchwork quilt of independent and dependent communities, well towards the multiple independences end of our spectrum. Some independent states were more powerful than others, but all were aware that the welfare and expansion, and indeed the survival, of a state depended on its relations with its neighbours. In this inescapable net, rules and institutions developed, shaped by the Hindu cultural tradition. Most communities were governed by a king, though there were a few city republics and some elected rulers. Many states were matrilinear: the queen inherited from her mother, and her husband governed. Hindu kings belonged to the Kshatrya or second caste, whose function was to govern and to fight. They considered it legitimate and indeed praiseworthy to try to reduce a neighbouring king to vassalage: that enhanced their power and glory. But it was not legitimate to disturb the complex social and economic life of the conquered community. Indian civilization had great respect for all the various forms which nature took – vegetation, animal life, human customs. The Hindu tradition, perhaps learnt by experience during the gradual Aryanization of India, was that a ruler should not disturb the customs and laws of a subject community.

The Persian conquest of the north-west – approximately the area of modern Pakistan – changed Indian concepts. New ideas of empire were introduced into Indian minds: a new awareness of a huge imperial system through which people and commerce could move, and a grasp of how it might be kept together by roads and satraps and the other Persian administrative techniques.[1] When after two centuries of Persian presence (520 to 327 BC) Alexander and his Greeks came down into India, a flood of new Greek ideas was also let loose there. At the same time Buddhism (founded by Gautama the Buddha, 563–483 BC) and Jainism began to transform the religious and social values of Hindu life. Indian thought in all fields was greatly stimulated and became much more vigorous.

This new world gave Chandragupta Maurya his opportunity to found an empire based on Indian practice but Persian in scope and concept. It also produced a man of great learning and perceptiveness named Kautilya. He has been compared to Machiavelli, a man of the Italian Renaissance when a lot of new ideas, including Greek ones, were also bubbling up. Just as Machiavelli wrote a treatise called the The Prince as a guide to a man who might be able to conquer and unite Italy, so Kautilya wrote a manual called the *Arthashastra* or *Book of the State*. In it he described in detail the nature of the Indian states system and the relations between one ruler and another, and explained how a prince, whom he called the conqueror, might exploit the pattern in order to bring all India into a Persian type of empire. Kautilya also found a man capable of doing this, which Machiavelli did not. Kautilya's conqueror, Chandragupta, established the first historical empire to unite not the whole but most of India.[2] Since Kautilya compiled the core of the *Arthashastra*, additional passages have crept into it, smatters of ancient Indian wisdom and statecraft, other people's suggestions and ideas, rules about being respectful to brahmins and much else. It is as though Napoleon had inserted some passages, Jefferson others, into *The Prince*. The *Arthashastra* must therefore be read with some circumspection.

The *Arthashastra* deals with how to conquer and govern an empire, how to move the whole system far towards the imperial end of the spectrum. It has additional significance for us in that it sets out a

major theoretical analysis of international relations as an integral part
of the problems of statecraft. Kautilya's analysis is not complete.
Because he aims to establish an imperial system in place of the warring
independent kingdoms, he is not interested in alternative ways of
managing the system. He does not discuss anti-hegemonial coalitions
or co-operation between independent states to promote the general
welfare. But when we remember that the Greeks, who produced such
outstanding analyses of the domestic government of a state, wrote
nothing comparable about a state's foreign relations or about the workings of their international system, we realize the importance of this
pioneering Indian achievement.

Kautilya's diagram of a states system, what he calls circles of states,
consists of seventy-two variable components. Each state or kingdom
(most though not all Indian states were kingdoms) consists of six
elements:

(a) the king;
(b) the government or the ministers;
(c) the country and its population;
(d) the fortifications of the country;
(e) the treasury, or financial resources available to the king;
(f) the armed forces.

All these will vary in each state. The diagram consists of twelve states,
divided into four primary 'circles' or potential alliances. The most
important passages for our purpose run as follows:

> The king who is possessed of good character and whose [other
> five] elements of sovereignty are at their best, and who is in
> control of his state's policy, is here called the conqueror.
>
> The king who is situated anywhere on the circumference of
> the conqueror's territory is called the enemy.
>
> The king who is situated equally close to the enemy, and
> separated from the conqueror only by the enemy, is called the
> friend [of the conqueror].
>
> Any neighbour of considerable power must be considered an
> enemy. When he is involved in difficulties or has taken to evil
> ways, he becomes assailable. When he has little or no help, he
> becomes destructible; otherwise he should be harassed or his
> power reduced. Such are the aspects of an enemy.
>
> In front of the conqueror and close to his enemy there will
> happen to be situated kings like the conqueror's friend, next to
> him the enemy's friend, and beyond him the conqueror's friend's
> friend and finally the enemy's friend's friend.
>
> In the rear of the conqueror [if he has decided to attack an

enemy in one direction] there may be situated a rearward enemy, a rearward friend, an ally of the rearward enemy and an ally of the rearward friend.

That enemy who is equally of high birth [i.e. is an equally legitimate ruler] and rules a territory next to that of the conqueror is a natural enemy; while he who is merely antagonistic and makes other enemies for the conqueror is a factitious enemy.

The king whose friendship is derived from father and grandfather, and who is situated next to the territory of the immediate enemy of the conqueror, is a natural friend; while he whose friendship is courted in order to maintain the conqueror's position can be called an acquired friend.

The king who occupies a territory close to both the conqueror and his immediate enemy in front, and who is capable of helping or resisting either of the kings individually, is called a *madhyama* [mediatory or balance-holding] king.

He who is situated beyond the territories of any of these kings, and who is very powerful and capable of helping the enemy, the conqueror or the *madhyama* king, together or individually, or of resisting any of them individually, is called an *udasina* or neutral king.

These are the [twelve] primary kings in the diagram.

The conqueror, his friend and his friend's friend constitute a primary **circle of states**. As each of these three kings possesses the five elements of sovereignty, namely his ministers, his country, his fortifications, his treasury and his army, a circle of states consists of eighteen elements. Obviously the circles of states which have the enemy, the *madhyama* king and the neutral king at their centre are in addition to the conqueror's circle. Thus there are four primary circles of states, twelve kings, and sixty elements of sovereignty, making seventy-two variables in all.

All twelve types of king have their sovereignty, power and ultimate purpose. **Strength is power, and happiness is the end or ultimate purpose of power** [my emphasis] . . .

A king shall always try to augment the power and elevate the happiness of his state.[3]

The pressures of the Indian international system described by Kautilya were such that no independent state, and certainly not a state that wished to expand into an empire, could operate alone; but each must look for allies to help it take the strain. Kautilya wanted to reduce the complexity of the system to a formula. Relations with other states followed a pattern which in diagram form resembled a chessboard. He says to Chandragupta, in effect: 'Any state that touches yours must be considered an enemy, because that is where you want to expand and because he may want to expand against you. Any state beyond the enemy, who touches him but not you, can be considered your friend.' This is the important maxim that as you look out across your enemy there is doubtless some other state that has a quarrel with him, and that state should be your friend. The rule that my enemy's enemy is my friend was a guiding principle of French policy in Europe for centuries. China and the United States were not drawn to each other in recent years by any ideology or political sympathy: the Chinese leaders saw in America and western Europe states 'on the other side of' the Soviet Union that like them opposed Soviet imperialism.

Kautilya next takes the diagram further by pointing out the chain effect of alliances. Beyond the conqueror's friend and the enemy's friend are the conqueror's friend's friend, who helps to take the strain and so with the conqueror and his friend makes up the diagram alliance or circle of three states; just as the enemy with his friend and his friend's friend make a second circle. And this pattern, which the conqueror faces in the direction of his expansion, is repeated in his rear. Kautilya saw the difference between an actual enemy in front and a potential or rearward enemy who must be kept quiet for the time being; just as he saw the difference between a natural and what he calls an acquired friend. He then proceeds, in a still more sophisticated way, to describe two other categories of king, each with a similar circle. A king who is involved with both circles but uncommitted to either and strong enough to tip the balance between success and failure Kautilya calls a *madhyama* or mediatory king. The *Arthashastra* contains elaborate instructions on how to deal with *madhyama* kings in various circumstances, particularly in order to prevent a *madhyama* giving anti-hegemonial support to the conqueror's enemy. Fourth, there is a neutral king, 'beyond the territory of all these kings, a great and powerful ruler'. This may be the first instance in a text of the concept of neutrality, and of the steps which a conqueror or someone resisting conquest should adopt towards a neutral state. No such distinctions between a mediatory and a neutral power are to be found in the writings of the near east or Greece; and the European system rarely got beyond allies, enemies and neutrals.

Kautilya's idea was that the conqueror should limit himself, if possible, to one enemy at a time. But each diagram had seventy-two variables to reckon with, and there might well be more than one actual state in some of the categories in the diagram, such as friend or friend's friend. Moreover, the whole Indian scene was several diagrams big. The odds that the conqueror had to calculate were therefore very complicated, and required a great deal of information and preparation. The conqueror must work to bring all the variables to their optimum point. Especially the six elements in his friend's country should be good, and those in his enemy's country bad. Then would be the moment to strike. Kautilya regarded any means of affecting the variables, any clandestine or what we should call dirty trick in an enemy's country, as permissible, in the same way as Machiavelli. This is particularly clear when he describes the functions of what we would call an ambassador. In the Indian society of states ambassadors were usually brahmins, of the highest, priestly, literate caste, and they were not residents but envoys who came and went. Their functions, listed by Kautilya, included the delivery of messages and bringing or sending back replies, the maintenance of treaties and in particular the need to insist that the king whom the ambassador is visiting should observe the treaties with his own king. Another important task was to win friends among the subjects of the king being visited. These respectable functions have been considered legitimate in all systems of independent states. Kautilya adds intrigue, causing the break-up of hostile alliances, organizing secret armies and weapons, the use of spies and the suborning and bribing of enemy officials. Modern books about covert operations make no allegations beyond the Indian practices that Kautilya described in detail as desirable.

Financial support by the conqueror for his friends, bribery and subversion of his enemy's population might make war more successful; but they could also reduce its scope or even make it unnecessary. The *Arthashastra* stresses that peace should be preferred to war, and peace should even be preferred to armed and watchful neutrality in wars between other kings, because of the cost in men and money of waging war or even maintaining armed neutrality, and the chanciness of war. If by the use of bribery or in any other way a king can attain his goal while avoiding the actual use of force, then that king is reaching his goal on the cheap, because no expenditure on bribery or subversion will cost as much, in the lives of his own people or his treasure, as open warfare. Kautilya does not question the goal of empire, of course; but he stresses the advantage of keeping the cost of attaining that goal as low as possible. Warfare was not something to be avoided: on the contrary, it was something to prepare for by every means, and to be able to wage; and this ability to wage war if necessary might make it possible to achieve one's objective without actually having to do so. We can recognize this and many other precepts of the *Arthashastra* as derived from Persian and ultimately from Assyrian experience – what one might call the accumulated wisdom of statecraft of the near east distilled through Persia and formulated by Kautilya to Chandragupta Maurya.

There was in India of that time no central source of legitimate authority over the whole system, and no valid memory of a previous empire to appeal to. Kautilya does not say that the emperorship must reside somewhere. Neither the conqueror nor any other king had a right to be emperor. The Indian system was in this respect like that of Greece, and very different from the near east, where imperial authority was familiar and legitimate. Kautilya therefore listed prudent rules for treating conquered countries, that some commentators think he learnt from the Persians, though they often also correspond to Indian beliefs. There was no place for a defeated king, but otherwise states brought under the conqueror's control should continue to be governed as before. The wise conduct for the conqueror as he rides his horse into the conquered country is to show virtue, to observe all royal duties, to reward all his supporters, to remit taxes among the defeated (also a Venetian practice, but in contrast to the usual practice in other systems of exacting tribute), to bestow gifts and honours on those who want to serve him and above all to respect the way of life, the dress, language, customs and beliefs of the area, and encourage learned men (like Kautilya, one supposes). Kautilya's advice aimed at dominion with very substantial local autonomy, leaving the local legitimacies as far as practicable intact. He attached great importance, like the Persians, to winning over conquered communities to the empire.

Finally Kautilya asked what was the ultimate purpose of establishing an empire. For him the end of power was not the service of the gods, or an ideology, but the happiness of the state. He believed, like the Persians but unlike the Greeks and unlike the conventional legitimacy of today, that a multitude of independences was not the most desirable state of affairs, and that on the contrary greater happiness could be attained by establishing a benevolent imperial rule. It is curious that from the *Arthashastra* to the American Declaration of Independence (which opposes imperial rule) no other text puts the pursuit of happiness quite so high.

Chandragupta was an outstanding organizer and general, and he and Kautilya calculated their chances well and took opportunities as they came. Following the death of Alexander they established the Mauryan Empire over most of northern India. The forms and practices of the empire were Indian, with some Persian elements of style and organization such as a network of good roads, a central bureaucracy and a land tax. The Mauryans were strong enough to defeat Seleucus' attempt to reconquer Persian India in 305 BC, but came to a friendly understanding cemented by a marriage alliance between the two adventurer kings, who had the same unsentimental approach to statecraft. Chandragupta's empire assured security over an exceptionally large area, and trade flourished by land and sea (the *Arthashastra* contains detailed rules for shipping). But his rule was more oppressive than the bland Persian Empire, in spite of Kautilya's moderate advice; and, aware of the enemies he had made and the risks he ran, he became wary and isolated himself from the world by a large bodyguard of armed women.

The empire-building process continued under his son and then his famous grandson Asoka (272–231 BC). Asoka at first expanded the Mauryan Empire by ruthless methods: there is a record of 100,000 people killed and 150,000 deported in one campaign. But he later became a devout Buddhist, increasingly concerned for the welfare of all his subjects, which was in accordance with Buddhist teaching and was also Kautilya's justification for the establishment of the empire. The extent of his rule and the standards of ethical benevolence which he observed and enjoined on others make the later Asoka one of the greatest and most saintly of all known imperial rulers. He combined loftiness of purpose with a direct and standardized pattern of administration wherever possible, so that an unusually large proportion of his empire was included in the core area; but inevitably the fringes were under a looser dominion shading into hegemony over domestically independent states. However, even the benefits of such a benevolent empire, and a duration of nearly a century, were not sufficient to legitimize it and hold it together. On Asoka's death local traditions and the submerged desire for independence reasserted themselves. The empire was fragmented, and India quickly reverted to the patchwork quilt of independent and warring states described in the *Arthashastra*.

NOTES

1 These included the use of iron and coined money.
2 For the controversies surrounding Chandragupta's origins and relations with Kautilya, see R. C. Majumdar, H. C. Raychandhuri and K. Datta (eds), *An Advanced History of India*, London, Macmillan, 1984.
3 Kautilya, *The Arthashastra*.

8

CHINA

Hegemony, warring states and empire

The Chinese system of independent states is of great interest for our enquiry. Like Chinese civilization generally, the structure of authority and relations with non-Chinese neighbours developed separately from the experience of western Asia which influenced even the Indian system. The Chinese patterns evolved in virtual isolation. The Chinese classified all their non-Chinese neighbours as 'barbarians', and regarded them as culturally inferior. So did the Egyptians and the classical Greeks. But educated Egyptians and Greeks knew that they had to deal with other peoples that were as advanced and sophisticated as they, and in some respects more so; whereas the communities surrounding China were still at a more primitive stage of development, sometimes vigorous and militarily formidable, but pre-literate. Though some other civilizations, for instance that of Mexico, also developed independently of western Asia and the Mediterranean, only the Chinese reached a level of sophistication in managing the relations between different communities held together in a system, and left written records of their achievement, which we can usefully compare with those discussed in previous chapters.

The monumental Chinese achievement in the field of statecraft is usually held to be the more or less effective imperial unity that has assured domestic peace and order for most of Chinese history. But for five and a half crucial and creative centuries China consisted of a number of genuinely independent states. The second half of this period is known as the 'warring states', because warfare later appeared to be a salient characteristic. The system of independent Chinese states, with its antecedents, and the establishment of effective empire form the subject of this chapter.

The Chinese system of multiple independences operated from 770 to 221 BC. The contending states of that period developed from fiefs of the kingdom of Zhou (formerly transliterated as Chou). Zhou previously held some sort of suzerain authority over the Chinese cultural area, which was then confined to the basin of the Yellow River. The

Zhou kingdom had a cult of 'heaven' (*tian*) as a supreme deity, which conferred upon the royal family a mandate to rule (*tian ming*). An individual ruler could forfeit the mandate by impious or sacrilegious behaviour. The Zhou kings had a small core territory under their direct administration, and the rest of China was parcelled out into fiefs, which according to tradition were originally 70 but later grew to 1,770. The fief-holders were members of the royal family or commanders of garrisons sent from Zhou, or else local chiefs prudently recognized. The title of king was reserved for the Zhou suzerain alone.

In 770 BC, the Zhou capital was sacked. The Zhou king survived to rule a much smaller area, but his suzerain authority could not be restored, and the fief-holders became independent of central control. They continued to recognize the nominal primacy of the king, but they ignored his wishes and contended among themselves for *de facto* supremacy. So independent were these princes that some modern scholars regard the concept of effective royal authority over all China before 770 as largely mythical. They suggest that Confucius and others who lived in the period of independent states postulated an age of order and obedience to ceremonial rules as an idealized alternative to the wars and lack of order that they saw around them. These scholars consider that administratively and politically there never was much of a Zhou kingdom to break to pieces. But the ceremonial deference for many centuries after 770 is hard to explain if it was not a survival from a more effective authority. Perhaps the Zhou king with his divine mandate at the apex of a feudal pyramid was something like the Holy Roman Emperor in the European Middle Ages (Chapter 13).

At all events, the collapse of effective Zhou authority pushed the Chinese system far towards the multiple independences end of the spectrum. The former fiefdoms which were now independent jealously guarded their freedom of action and their status as sovereigns. Internal autonomy was not enough: the attributes of independent statehood were the ability to preserve one's territory, to wage war, to change allies and to make treaties. The states which maintained their independence in these ways treated each other as formal equals; and surviving treaties show that in matters of war and alliance 'barbarian' powers that had the same capacities were treated in the same way. Those states which could not effectively assert their independence were relegated to a position of inferiority. At a conference in 546 which brought together the representatives of most states, the representative of Lu asked: 'Zhu (Chu) and Teng (T'eng) are like private possessions of other states that we treat as equals. Why should we be ranked with them?'

The states formed two geographical groups. The relatively small central states occupied most of the old Chinese cultural area. They continued to observe the traditional usages of the Zhou kingdom, including the ceremonial primacy of the Zhou king, and the ultimate derivation of their legitimacy from the old Zhou fiefs. They agreed that war should be regulated by customary rules that reduced bloodshed and favoured skirmishing rather than pitched battles; and that war might lead to the loss of a ruler's independence but not the destruction of states as entities or the dispossession of legitimate ruling families. The central states prided themselves on conserving Chinese civilization, and looked down on the peripheral states as semi-barbarous, ignorant of the traditions and mixed with non-Chinese peoples.

The peripheral or marcher states spread out into non-Chinese territory in all directions, and so became larger and stronger. The states on the southern fringe along the Yangtse were particularly concerned with extending their power, and contemptuous of the old order. They observed the old rules only when they found it expedient to do so. From 500 BC the peripheral states introduced important innovations into the art of war, which made it more intense and its results more decisive. They equipped large numbers of foot soldiers with iron spears; new methods of drill produced disciplined infantry formations; they learnt from the nomads how to use cavalry; and they developed an efficient crossbow. At the same time the rulers of the new states organized more effective control over their populations. All these innovations gave the peripheral states an advantage over the more civilized rulers and communities in the old Chinese area. The most important new states for our purposes are the efficient and aggressive southern state of Chu, which was the first to establish effective hegemony over the system; the colony state of Yuch, which was founded by Chinese adventurers south of the Yangtse and had never belonged even in part to the old Zhou kingdom; and the innovative western state of Qin (Ch'in), which extended its sway over nomadic horse-breeding peoples, and in due course conquered all of China.

The Chinese system after 770 was too disintegrated to be stable. The more powerful states aspired to hegemony. Before long the ruler of Chu assumed the title of king, thus declaring himself separate from and equal to the whole central system where that title was reserved for the Zhou monarch. Other peripheral rulers quickly followed suit. The growing power of the efficient Chu state led to an anti-hegemonial league of the central states with other peripheral enemies of Chu. A significant conference of the league in 679 BC, which included the ceremonial Zhou king, recognized the need for a single effective leader, to be called the *ba*, to conduct war and diplomacy on the league's behalf. In practice the ruler of the strongest state opposed to the hegemony of the day was elected *ba*; and when another state became stronger, its ruler was elected instead. The central states regarded the *ba* as a vice-regent on behalf of the Zhou monarchy, but in fact the league and its *ba* were an important innovation. They integrated the new Yangtse states with the old Zhou system, and moved the whole loose relationship between the communities of the expanded Chinese world an appreciable way back along the spectrum towards a more hegemonial pattern.

The league managed for some time to restrain Chu and its client allies. But in the long run it was not strong or well organized enough. After some seventy years a ruler of Chu defeated the league and cynically had himself elected *ba*. So an institution intended to curb Chu was transformed into a means of legitimizing Chu hegemony. Then, about two hundred years after the original institution of the *ba*, Chu was overthrown, not by the rest of the league which it now dominated, but by another half-Chinese state in the Yangtse valley; and after nine years of struggle a new dominance was established by Yuch, the least Chinese of all the states.

Below the great powers of the day were middle states, able to insist on a degree of external independence. They enjoyed a much greater freedom of action in the league than in the subordinate alliance controlled by Chu. The secondary powers on the fringes of the Chu alliance therefore tried to switch their allegiance to the anti-hegemonial league when they thought it safe to do so. The most interesting of the middle powers for our enquiry was Zheng (Cheng). Zheng was an important commercial state situated between the two alliances, with a watchful government and considerable armed forces. The adherence of Zheng was regarded as indicating the superiority of one side or the other. In 140 years Zheng is recorded as changing the general bias of its alignment fourteen times, without losing its freedom of action. Its shifts of alliance were usually in response to superior pressure; but were sometimes deliberate and anticipatory, when it perceived that the group with which it was aligned was growing weaker and that the other side was on the way up. Zheng showed mobility in its alignments and put calculations of state interest before its commitments. It regularly joined the stronger side.

The whole system, which now covered twice the area of the old Zhou kingdom, thus became steadily more integrated. The military and political process of integration was carried out by the new states. But for all their innovative practices and contempt for the old traditions, their authority in the system continued to derive in some measure from the old concept of a single Zhou kingdom. The *ba* claimed to be acting on behalf of the ceremonial Zhou king and his nominal vassals, whether he was genuinely elected by them or imposed himself on them.

It is instructive to compare this stage of the Chinese system with the corresponding and nearly contemporary stage of the Greco-Persian system (Chapter 5). There were two main alliances in each case. The league corresponded to the anti-hegemonial period of the Spartan alliance; and the Chu alliance designed to support its hegemonial aspirations corresponded to the Athenian. The *ba* or anti-hegemonial protector had a role similar to that of the Spartans down to the end of the Peloponnesian War. How like the reluctant Spartans criticized by the Corinthians are the words of a *ba*'s envoy to an apprehensive ally about Chu:

> If we are careful of our conduct, maintaining our good faith and observing the rules, correct in our first acts and thinking at the same time of our last . . . if our service is performed according to the ancient laws and our duty discharged according to the ancient kings and regulated by due consideration of what our states need, however extravagant the ruler of Chu may be, what can he do to us?

There was even a treaty between Chu and the *ba* in which the two rival groups agreed not to go to war and to have common friends and enemies, though there was no equivalent of *dike* and Chu broke the treaty in three years. The later dominance of Yuch is analogous to that of Macedon. The most striking contrast is between the anti-hegemonial instincts of the Hellenic corporations and the opportunism of the smaller Chinese states. Zheng and the Corinthians were equally elastic in their alliances; but while the Corinthians systematically supported the weaker side, Zheng regularly supported the stronger. No outside power comparable to the Persian Empire played a major constructive part in the Chinese system: but the hegemonial Chinese states, like Macedon, drew strength from beyond the confines of Chinese civilization.

The period of the warring states also saw the greatest creative and intellectual activity in Chinese history. Under the imperial dynasties Chinese civilization, in philosophy, literature and the arts, was very largely a continuation and refinement of what had been achieved in the centuries of multiple independence, when different communities offered a competitive range of opportunities, and men could move from one community to another.

Many of the controversies of that creative time turned on the legitimacy of power, the goals of statecraft and remedies for the increasingly violent wars. There were four main currents of political thought, stretching from the anarchic pacifism of the **Dao** (Tao) through the Confucians and the Mohists to the champions of despotic authority and unification through conquest. The first group, the followers of the

Dao, believed in a natural order, which could best be achieved through non-violence, and held that all active government was interference in the natural order. A second and more important school, the **Confucians**, accepted the state as a necessity. Society was an aggregate of families under a paternal ruling family. Confucius emphasized the ethical duties of paternal rulers, whose example and persuasion would lead the people in the path of virtue. Similarly all states should be under one kingly family which had the mandate of heaven to rule the world; and the restoration of virtue and imperial unity would end strife among the warring states. The traditional aristocratic order implicit in Confucian teaching was modified by the provision that rulers should choose their ministers according to merit not lineage. The Confucians believed that the ablest scholars and merchants, and the simple peasants, would flock from everywhere to live under a just ruler. To some extent this in fact happened. The Confucian doctrine of a society of states reflected the aspirations of the central states that acknowledged the titular supremacy of Zhou.

Mo-zi (Mo-tsu), the prophet of the third school, also reflected the ideas of the old Chinese culture. But he was less idealist and more pessimistic than Confucius. He was concerned with the conduct of individual men and individual states rather than with the ordering of societies. Mo-zi agreed with Confucius that in the existing condition of China a state bent on supremacy could prevail over others by combining the attractiveness of good government with offensive military strength. To prevent that policy succeeding, Mo-zi developed a doctrine of defensive war as the key to peace among states. The Mohists held that a state which renounced offensive war could make itself so proficient in defensive techniques that no other state would attack it. If this plan were generally followed, all states would become invulnerable to attack, and would have to live in amity with each other. The Mohist programme of armed neutrality was genuinely anti-hegemonial: the only theoretically formulated Chinese concept of international relations that was. But Mohists did not think in terms of a structured relationship between the Chinese states, as the Confucians did, and their concept of peace and amity amounted to little more than coexistence between multiple independences that hardly constituted a system. In practice defensive strategy, especially without alliances, proved inadequate to protect its civilized practitioners from the vigorous states of the periphery.

The fourth school of politics was that of the so-called **legalists**. The conventional use of this word to translate the Chinese *fa-chaio* gives it misleading overtones, suggesting a rule of law to which kings and executive governments are subject. The law of the Chinese legalists was the will of an autocratic ruler, formulated in precise legal decrees, to which all his subjects including his officials must conform without question. A word like 'authoritarian' conveys the views of this school better. The legalists were anti-democratic, allowing the ruler's subjects no say in political affairs, and anti-aristocratic, for they insisted on extinguishing the private jurisdictions and hereditary privileges of the feudal nobility which were endorsed by Confucius and existed in all Chinese states. All land, according to the legalists, should pay taxes directly to a central royal treasury. All administrative authority should be vested in officials chosen and dismissed by the ruler, who would ensure their loyalty and competence not by a Confucian education in virtue but by a pragmatic system of rewards and punishments.

In external relations the legalists repudiated both the moral restraints and respect for tradition inculcated by Confucius and the defensive war of the Mohists. The legalists claimed that their domestic political order would make a state stronger externally. Its ruler would not have to rely on poorly disciplined feudal levies or mercenaries, but could train as many of his subjects as he needed to be disciplined soldiers, and would have greater financial resources. The legalist ruler should train his troops for attack, with the aim of decisively subjugating all hostile states. Such policies would lead realistically to peace, the legalists argued, because the more states were suppressed the wider the area of unity and order would become, until only one state existed and there would be no more war. One legalist expounded the doctrine in revolutionary and imperialist language which has modern echoes, in China and elsewhere:

> If the poor are encouraged by rewards they will become rich, and if penalties are applied to the rich they will become poor. If the ruler of a state succeeds in making the poor rich and the rich poor, his state will have great strength and will attain to supremacy over other states.

The legalist school developed in the new peripheral states, and appealed to rulers concerned with power rather than ethics. Legalist ideas on organizing the state for war and achieving peace through universal conquest reflect the policies actually pursued by those states. The legalists were innovative and pragmatic, impatient with the traditions and virtues that the central states and Confucius valued. They wanted to move the states system as far as possible towards the imperial end of our spectrum. In this they were utterly opposed to the Mohists; but they had some common ground with the Confucians, who also advocated imperial unity for all China under the mandate of heaven. That common ground was where the traditional legitimacy of the Chinese warring states system wishfully lay.

The state in which the legalists got the most favourable hearing was Qin, the most north-westerly and marginal state in the system. Qin was strong in cavalry, and wealthy from the increasing trade between China and central Asia, which it largely monopolized. **Li Si** (Li Ssu), a native of the former hegemonial **Chu**, adopted legalism, entered the service of the king of Qin and quickly became his chief minister. Under his direction Qin between 230 and 221 BC fought a series of wars in which all the other states of China were either decisively crushed in battle or annexed by Qin. Li Si fought these wars with an unprecedented ferocity, aiming in each campaign at the total destruction of the enemy state. Armies which surrendered after protracted resistance were massacred; those which scarcely opposed Qin were incorporated in the Qin forces. Rulers and their ministers were executed. Nobles whose lives were spared were deported to the Qin capital, where their administrative experience was used in minor employment. Governors and prefects were sent from Qin for the direct administration of the conquered states.

China was thus reunified. But the Qin Empire was on a far larger scale and with far more centralized control than that of the semi-mythical Zhou kings. The ruler of Qin, a man of no great ability who depended on Li Si, was now given the title of 'first emperor'. The word which we translate as emperor had hitherto applied only to gods; but Li Si considered that the title of king had been devalued by the rulers of many states using it at once. The new rulers were revolutionaries who relied on force. They hated variety, local custom and prescriptive right. They gave all China by decree a unified script, a standard system of weights and measures and a standard cart-axle so that the wheel ruts would be the same width all over their empire. But they found that the passive resistance of the peoples of China to their innovations was more formidable than the armies of the other states had been, and was encouraged by the scholars and intellectuals, most of whom were Confucians determined to preserve the traditions. Li Si and his colleagues resolved to obliterate the very memory of the old system, its institutions and its ideas, and especially Confucianism. The notorious 'burning of the books' decreed that all writings with a few specific exceptions were to be burnt, and scholars who refused to give up their libraries were put to death. Immense damage was done to Chinese history and literature. Though some records were safely hidden, most were irretrievably lost, and later restorations produced more forgeries than originals.

The legalists' belief in power and success and their rejection of moral standards enabled them to conquer the whole of China in nine years and to institute a cultural and technical revolution. But it did not ensure the loyalty of the new rulers to each other or protect them from popular resentment. Revolutions devour their children. Fifteen years after the proclamation of the 'first emperor', Li Si was assassinated; and the government, torn apart by treacherous struggles, was overthrown by a popular rebellion. Qin became for posterity, under the influence of Confucian moralists, an object lesson in the consequences of impious violence.

The unifying and standardizing work of Qin was nevertheless done too thoroughly to be undone. Traditional unitary legitimacy and real economic advantage combined to ensure that the rebellion did not lead to a restoration of the old states, whose rulers and feudal families no longer existed, but to the maintenance of the centralized bureaucratic empire. The new son of heaven, in fact the son of a peasant, founded the Han dynasty which endured with a brief interval for four centuries. The Chinese states system was now firmly anchored far to the imperial end of the spectrum. In a sense Qin imperial statecraft and the legalist programme were historically victorious. But the Han rulers formally repudiated legalist doctrines and the repressive harshness of Qin rule. They became the patrons of a revised Confucianism, which taught obedience to the son of heaven, and justified the Han by portraying the Zhou system as a direct bureaucratic administration of all China. The creative period of the warring states was depicted as merely a prolonged interregnum of chaos between ages of political unity, and the title of emperor was accorded retrospectively to the Zhou kings. The Han fusion of Confucian and legalist ideas became the intellectual orthodoxy of China for two millennia.

NOTES

This chapter owes much to the paper on the states system of ancient China written for the British Committee by Geoffrey Hudson, and the subsequent discussions. For the political philosophers or theorists, see especially Vitaly Rubin, *Individual and State in Ancient China*, New York, Columbia University Press, 1976; Rubin is a Soviet scholar who compares the legalists to Stalin.

9

ROME
The final classical imperial synthesis

With Rome we reach the climax of the long, gradual, irregular shift of the near eastern and Mediterranean world towards the imperial end of our spectrum, which began with Assyria and developed through that empire's successors in the east, the Persian and Macedonian systems.

Rome began as a city state in central Italy, on the western margin of the high civilizations of the east Mediterranean which became the Hellenistic world. Over several centuries the city expanded its authority and adapted its methods of government to bring first Italy, then the western Mediterranean and finally almost the whole of the Hellenistic world into an empire larger than any which had existed in that area before or has done since. The Roman imperial structure not only was accepted by the diverse communities which it encompassed, but came to be regarded by the citizens of the empire as the only acceptable and legitimate authority. This unique and astonishing achievement, and the cultural transformation which it brought about, laid the foundations of European civilization and influenced almost every aspect of its life and thought. The traditions of the church, the general use of Roman law and the classical education of the governing classes since the Renaissance transmitted Roman experience and ideas to Europe. Rome helped to shape European and contemporary practice and opinion about the state, about international law and especially about empire and the nature of imperial authority.

The Romans traced their origin mythically to a band of Trojans fleeing from the sack of Troy, and dated their calendar from the supposed founding of their city by Romulus in 753 BC. In any case the Roman city state was of Etruscan origin but based on a Latin population and language. It was for many centuries a turbulent and restless city, much given to stasis and to expansion by conquering its neighbours. The legendary murder by Romulus of his twin brother Remus is symbolic of the city's internal violence. At the same time the Romans developed a remarkable practical sagacity, a talent for

94

organization and engineering, a businesslike shrewdness and most significantly a respect for law. Law had played a great part in the civilizations of ancient Mesopotamia which Rome in some ways inherited; but the concept of the law as standing above every citizen, and the tendency to frame all disputes in legal terms, is essentially Roman. In republican Rome as in the Greek city states a boy would learn soldiering as a matter of course, since to bear arms was a distinguishing feature of citizenship; but whereas an educated Greek boy would learn poetry and philosophy, Roman upper-class education concentrated on the law.

After getting rid of its Etruscan kings the Roman republic was made up of two castes, the patricians and the plebeians, but with power in the hands of 'noble' families drawn from both castes. Executive authority was entrusted to two consuls, of whom at least one had to be a plebeian, both elected by all the citizens for a one-year term, exercising equal powers alternately. The plebeians also elected tribunes of the people who acted as watchdogs for their interest and corresponded to the leaders of the tyranny-democracy faction in a Greek city state. Spengler in the *Decline of the West* perceptively described the Roman tribunate as

> the happiest inspiration of the classical polis. It was the tyrant raised to the position of an integral part of the constitution, and set in parallel with the old oligarchical offices, all of which remained in being. So the social revolution was carried out in legal forms. The tribune with his immunity could carry out revolutionary acts that would have been inconceivable without street fighting in any other polis.[1]

The difficulty was that this division of power, designed to mitigate domestic social stresses and to prevent monarchy or the domination of a single ruler, reduced the continuity of the formal executive almost to nothing. Important decisions and the general lines of Roman policy were decided in the senate, a largely hereditary body representing the important 'noble' families, strengthened by co-opting able plebeians. Nevertheless the complex, elastic and balanced Roman government functioned remarkably well during the centuries of expansion. The power of the senate grew steadily. There was popular discontent and sometimes stasis, but the successful expansion of Roman rule and the wealth which it brought enabled the senate to strengthen its hold. Republican Rome was governed by an outstandingly able and acquisitive oligarchy.

The Roman conquest of the whole Italian peninsula was a remarkable feat. It is true that Italy was very fragmented, with individual Etruscan cities to the north of Rome and even more individual Greek cities to the south, as well as many other native and immigrant peoples. There was no united opposition, so that Roman acquisitions could proceed piecemeal. But the shrewd and practical senators, however eager they may have been for the spoils and profits of war, saw the advantages of reconciling the populations of the newly acquired areas. They tempered their initial economic gains, and other unpopular measures like the settlement of colonies of Romans in conquered areas and the ruthless suppression of all opposition, by introducing the advantages of Roman order, Roman law and the extension of various degrees of citizenship. Roman rule at this stage followed the familiar imperial pattern of direct government with voting rights for the area around the city and Roman settlements outside, then dominion over areas where the people enjoyed some privileges of citizenship, and beyond that a firm hegemony over client allies who managed their own internal affairs. Success made the earlier precautions seem less necessary. The stronger Rome grew and the further from the city its conquests extended, the greedier its exploitation seemed to become. The acquisition of southern Italy, which was then Greater Greece, greatly increased the civilizing influence of Greek culture on Rome. It also led Roman eyes across the sea to Sicily and beyond that into the heartland of Greece.

Involvement in Sicily brought the Roman republic up against an imperial city, an adversary equal in wealth and power but very different in tradition and outlook. This was the great Phoenician city of Carthage, also situated on the western fringe of the civilized world, in what is now Tunisia opposite Sicily. Like its parent Tyre and many Greek cities but unlike Rome, Carthage was a city governed by a merchant aristocracy dedicated to seaborne trade, and it had made itself maritime mistress of the western Mediterranean, and had colonized the Mediterranean areas of Spain and what is now Algeria. The struggle lasted for half a century (roughly from 250 to 200 BC). Carthaginian armies were largely made up of mercenaries, like those of other Phoenician cities and the Hellenistic kings, and commanded by a series of brilliant war leaders among whom was Hannibal, the most formidable enemy of republican Rome. The Romans, hitherto very much a land power with a citizen army, saw the need to build a fleet, which ultimately gave them victory. But Hannibal raised a land army in Carthaginian Spain which crossed the Alps with a train of elephants and ravaged Italy, defeating the Romans on their home ground. The ability of Rome to retain the loyalty of most of its Italian conquests in such circumstances is striking evidence of the success of the senate's policy in conquered territories.

The Punic Wars (the Romans called the Carthaginians Poeni because of their Phoenician origin) have been seen as the victory of Roman peasants over Carthaginian traders and an example of the importance of sea-power. They are also of interest to us because of the policy of Syracuse. This Sicilian daughter polis of the Corinthian corporation was, like its parent, inclined to support the weaker side, on several occasions switching its aid to the loser after a turn in the fortunes of war, in order to prevent either from establishing a dominion which would cost the Syracusans their independence. But in the end the Romans conquered and sacked Syracuse. An anti-hegemonial policy has limitations.

The Punic Wars gave the Romans control of the Carthaginian empire in the western Mediterranean. In the closing stages they also turned their attention eastwards to peninsular Greece and the Macedonian kingdoms, and so became major actors in the Macedonian system. The small communities of central Italy, which were similar to the Romans, had been effectively Romanized. But the senate did not have a conscious policy of conquering the much vaster Hellenistic world, let alone Romanizing it. Roman intervention in the east was usually a reprisal against an attack on some Roman interest or client, or else by invitation and in order to prevent the consolidation of a strong power in opposition to Rome. Nevertheless, Roman military superiority and the inability of the Greek and Macedonian states to form an anti-hegemonial coalition led fairly rapidly to Roman domination over the whole area. The anti-hegemonial corporation of Corinth was destroyed (by killing the men and enslaving the women) in the same year as Carthage. As the Romans became involved with the bipolar Macedonian system, they found it easier to co-operate with the Ptolemaic alliance structure. Consequently Macedon and the Seleucid kingdom were broken up; but the Ptolemies became client allies, and the last ruler of Pergamon left his state to Rome in his will.

The senate made the areas acquired by Rome outside Italy into provinces, with a Roman governor and taxes, which led to much ruthless exploitation. The inhabitants did not become citizens of an expanded city state, but subjects of an imperial power. But the conquerors left Hellenistic civilization more or less intact, with client kingdoms and local autonomy for cities within the provincial system; and most of the land remained in the hands of the previous owners. Under Roman protection commerce thrived. The large estates acquired by senators and others in middle distant areas like Sicily were profitably worked with slave labour. Hellenistic art, culture and ideas were imported wholesale into Rome, and the upper classes became steadily more Greek in outlook, while consciously retaining their own language, traditions and practical competence. But Hellenistic civilization was not just Greek: it was a synthesis of Greek, Persian, Jewish and other near eastern elements, all of which played their part in forming

Roman imperial civilization. The river that Juvenal complained was flowing into the Tiber was not a Greek one but the Syrian Orontes, the river of the Seleucid metropolis of Antioch.

Before long it became apparent that the senate, which had directed Roman affairs so effectively during the centuries of expansion, was able to manage neither the sprawling imperial acquisitions which stretched from Spain to Asia Minor nor the domestic discontents which followed the wars. The Roman Empire had become too large to be governed by a city state, especially one controlled by an oligarchy and with a pitifully weak and discontinuous executive. Into the executive lacuna stepped military leaders who made the armies they commanded personally loyal to them by grants of land and money and by victories in the field. More than a century of stasis periodically erupted into civil war. In the struggle between rival commanders ostensibly representing the oligarchy and tyranny-democracy factions, the senate was obliged to depend on the military commander most willing to support its interests.

The conservative military dictator, Sulla, restored the senate to power and then voluntarily retired; but within ten years another military hero, Pompey, undid much of Sulla's restoration. The senate, which was becoming increasingly rigid, refused to ratify Pompey's administrative arrangements in the eastern provinces or his payments to his veterans; whereupon Pompey made an arrangement with Caesar, the heir of the radical tradition. Pompey restored order in Rome where stasis had come near to anarchy, and stepped into Sulla's shoes as the protector of the senate. But Caesar built up an army by his conquest of Gaul and returned to defeat Pompey and his senatorial allies in campaigns that ranged all over the empire from Spain to Egypt. He was proclaimed *dictator perpetuus* and *imperator* or commander-in-chief. Under Caesar a more explicit imperial authority and administration began to take shape. He administered the eastern territories in Hellenistic fashion. Some Hellenistic cities accorded him the divine honours paid to Macedonian kings and to other Roman conquerors like Pompey. After his assassination by a group of senators, further civil wars devastated the Roman world. The final victory went to Caesar's adopted son Octavian.

Octavian was a man of quite remarkable statesmanship, whose long period of rule marks a turning point in Roman and indeed in world history. He won the civil war by exceptional ruthlessness and the military ability of his commanders. But he then showed an equally exceptional moderation and reorganized the war-weary Roman world by a constructive compromise. He concentrated executive control in his own hands, but legitimized his authority with his fellow Romans by restoring the forms of the senatorial republic. Like most of his contemporaries, he had come to see the real advantages of domestic peace after a long period of civil wars. He symbolized the introduction of the *pax romana* within the empire by building an altar to peace on the field of Mars where Roman armies had traditionally been mustered. *Pax* stood for the peace and order which are the principal advantages of the imperial administration: it did not mean the end of wars of conquest. However, Augustus, as he now styled himself, also suspended the expansion of the empire, partly because of the danger from other generals in command of victorious armies. His Roman titles of *princeps* (first among equals) and *imperator* sounded republican enough, but the monarchical reality gave Europe its titles of prince and emperor. For in practice Augustus was much more than a populist Greek tyrant; he was the Roman version of the Macedonian generals who became kings. He made Egypt, the richest prize of all, his personal possession, as Ptolemy had done. The communities of the Hellenistic east accorded him some of the titles of his Macedonian predecessors, and paid him the customary divine honours. After his death his imperial authority, known as the principate, remained for the next five reigns in his family.

Augustus' immediate successors lacked his reconciling touch. But they implemented his basic achievement, which was to transform the Roman governmental system from haphazard administration by senators or generals to co-ordinated executive government headed by an imperial monarch. They were personally a sorry lot, though not as bad as they were painted by Roman historians who hankered for the old senatorial republic and resented the increasing and arbitrary power of the emperors and their often low-born officials. Then, after a moment of renewed stasis with four emperors in one year had reminded the Romans how fragile their universal peace and order were, came the golden age of the emperors (AD 96–180). The concept of autocracy hereditary in a single family, with its bureaucracy and its obvious advantages, had now become so established that the legitimacy itself shifted from a nominal republicanism to a nominal hereditary monarchy. Whereas the successors of Augustus had been members of his family with republican titles, in the second century the emperor chose an able successor and conferred legitimacy on him by formally adopting him as son and heir.

Throughout the great area now controlled by Rome the power of the executive was much greater than it had been in Roman Italy in the early centuries of the republic. As the emperor's personal household proved increasingly inadequate to administer the empire, a central bureaucracy gradually developed. Government was more executive and less in the hands of a free oligarchy, but also less arbitrary and rapacious than it had been in the heyday of senatorial expansion. Centralized bureaucratic administration is characteristic of the imperial end of our spectrum; but in the Roman Empire it was slow to develop. Augustus did not set up an administration, but relied on his personal household and on individual delegation. This practice proved increasingly inadequate to administer the empire, and from the second century a central bureaucracy gradually developed. Augustus and most of his successors thought it prudent to use the minimum of autocratic power necessary to achieve their ends, and to disguise that power under conventional forms. Just as they saw the advantages of conserving the forms of the Roman republic, so they were inclined to enlist other legitimacies throughout their immense and varied dominions. The Roman emperors in the first two centuries, like their Persian and Macedonian predecessors, preferred indirect rule and the preservation of local authorities where these could be relied on. Augustus removed the Roman armies of occupation from tranquil provinces to station them on the frontiers. Local monarchies like the succession of Herods in Palestine ruled large areas under the emperor's supervision. Several Greek and other states retained the formal status of client allies. Cities in the former Hellenistic monarchies continued their local autonomy, including responsibility for law and order, and they rather than distant Rome remained the focus of their citizens' loyalty. They dealt with the Roman governor of the province, whose functions were not very different from those of a Persian satrap, but also negotiated by letters and embassies with the emperor and the developing central bureaucracy in Rome. New local legitimacies also developed. Germanic and other peoples were allowed to settle within the empire, at first as subjects but in time more often as client allies, retaining their national organization and co-operating with Roman armies to defend their new homes against later invaders. These were forms of dominion rather than direct administration, autonomies varying with local custom and the history of the acquisition or settlement. The empire remained a conglomerate rather than a uniform blueprint, and respect for local legitimacies made it easier to govern.

Consequently below the level of imperial control ethnic loyalties retained their hold, especially where peasants as opposed to imported slaves worked the land. Civic loyalties, the sense of belonging first and foremost to a hereditary group or people in a defined territory, such as the citizens of Nicaea or the tribe of the Aedui, remained strong. The Egyptian language and customs survived very cohesively beneath the layers of Hellenization and Roman government. The Semitic areas from Mesopotamia and Syria through Carthage to Spain retained some Semitic identity, which later resurfaced to facilitate the Arab conquest. In western Europe, Celtic and other languages and traditions flourished underfoot like the shamrock, while Gaul and the northern provinces became increasingly Germanic.

The advantages of empire were plain to see. Law, currency, weights and measures were standardized. Commerce and industry thrived under the *pax romana*, with goods moving largely by sea over a Mediterranean now at last substantially free of pirates. Life, especially in the cities, reached standards of physical comfort, housing, cleanliness, food and personal security which were not achieved again until the eighteenth century. Education became more widespread, and learning, which had hitherto been a private affair in Greece and Rome, now became institutionalized. Gibbon, writing in the eighteenth century at the height of the classical revival, when the two centuries following Augustus were as familiar to his readers as their own history, summed them up as follows:

> If a man were called to fix the period in the history of the world during which the condition of the human race was most happy and prosperous, he would without hesitation, name that which elapsed from the death of Domitian to the accession of Commodus. The vast extent of the Roman empire was governed by absolute power, under the guidance of virtue and wisdom. The armies were restrained by the firm but gentle hand of four successive emperors whose characters and authority commanded involuntary respect. The forms of the civil administration were carefully preserved by Nerva, Trajan, Hadrian and the Antonines, who delighted in the image of liberty and were pleased with considering themselves as the accountable ministers of the laws.[2]

As time went on, and the standardizing effects of a central bureaucracy asserted themselves more firmly, men's horizons widened and the Roman imperium acquired a legitimacy of its own. In the civilized east the upper classes were already Hellenized, and public life and thought continued to be conducted in the Greek koine or universal language. In the previously more primitive west of the empire, Latin came to occupy a similar position. Long military service, and the settlement of many veterans in the west, facilitated absorption, as did the presence of a Latinized upper class of administrators, landowners and businessmen. A wider unity of trade and learning developed throughout the empire, fostered by the extent and safety of personal mobility. Educated people especially saw themselves as individuals in a universal imperium. Though Caracalla's decision to confer Roman citizenship on the whole free population of the empire in 212 had many motives and effects, it marked the formal culmination of this process. In addition to the old loyalties, increasing numbers of the mixed population of the empire joined voluntary associations that cut across ethnic lines, particularly religious fraternities that offered their members spiritual meaning and social solidarity. The most important for the future were the various Christian groups: not yet standardized into a single catholic or universal church, but already possessing a more impressive organization and code of conduct than their rivals. Ethnic and civic loyalties increasingly found their place within an imperial political and cultural horizon. The will and the capacity to assimilate subject peoples, and their eagerness to be assimilated, were greater in the Roman Empire than in any other imperial system of antiquity. In this respect the only empire comparable to Rome has been China.

In the third century AD the system of the principate virtually collapsed, and the empire itself, with the order and security which it provided, seemed close to disintegration. The serious challenge was a twofold threat from without. The civilized and politically highly organized empire of the Persian Sassanids invaded Roman territory from the east as far as the Mediterranean. The Persians were driven back; but the troops required to do this were drawn from the long European frontiers of the Rhine and the Danube, where, since Augustus, the great preponderance of Roman military strength had been stationed. In the west the distinction between Roman and 'barbarian' had become increasingly blurred. The more recent Germanic client allies within the empire were not yet Romanized or reliable; the similar but looser structure of client alliances that stretched beyond the frontiers taught the barbarians Roman techniques; and the legions themselves were increasingly recruited from barbarian stock. By the third century the tribes north of the European frontier had learnt Roman military and other skills, and their great confederations such as the Allemanni broke through the weakened frontier to conduct far-ranging raids into the settled lands of the empire. It became necessary to encompass Rome itself with defensive walls.

An emperor could not be everywhere at once, to defend the frontiers from the North Sea to Mesopotamia. In these circumstances regional priorities reasserted themselves for lack of cohesive power at the centre. A succession of generals took the title of emperor and gradually restored order by military might, sometimes only in a few provinces. A degree of cohesion was also provided by the frightened cities and provinces. Those most threatened by external invasion or internal brigandage and chaos wanted not just a remote emperor involved in a campaign in some far-off part of the empire, but an emperor on the spot; and they accepted, at least passively, any general capable of ensuring the advantages of empire to them. One hard-pressed emperor allowed a general who had defeated the Persians to set up a client kingdom in the east; this soon extended from Babylonia to Egypt and proclaimed itself independent of Rome. The brief resurgence of a Semitic imperial state in the third century echoed the Assyrian achievement and anticipated the Arab caliphate of the sixth. How far this or that general proclaimed emperor on the Rhine or elsewhere also thought in terms of a separate imperium, or whether he aspired to rule the whole Roman world – whether in the German terms he was a *Sonderkaiser* or a *Gegenkaiser* – is a matter of debate. But certainly pressures from without, and the corresponding demands from within for defence against those pressures, combined to push the pendulum back from the unified imperial principate of the early third century towards a looser and more fragmented pattern.

The restoration of imperial control and order and the parallel tendency to military autocracy were gradual processes. The republican attachment of the educated to the values of *romanitas*[3] and their scruples against kingship and autocracy lost practical significance. People's lives, and especially their economic relations, were increasingly regulated by heavy-handed decrees, administered by a more systematized central bureaucracy. These tendencies reached their climax under two outstanding generals, Diocletian and then Constantine. They reinforced their authority by focusing the loyalty of their subjects more directly on their own person as *dominus* and *princeps legitimus*, dispensing with the lip-service previously paid to the traditions of the Roman city state dear to the senatorial and upper class. The effort required to reassert imperial authority moved the Roman system further towards the imperial end of the spectrum than the earlier principate. The more nakedly authoritarian style of government (called the dominate by some modern scholars) was accepted because the successful generals were able to coerce by armed force both external enemies and rival aspirants to the purple, and it was welcome to the communities of the empire who had suffered badly from war and disorder. Its military harshness was tempered by Christianity, which under Constantine and his successors became the established religion.

Yet a succession of competent generals with strengthened authority were unable to hold the whole empire together in the changed circumstances. Over the century and a half following the death of Constantine in AD 337 the more fragile west of the empire became increasingly separate from the more solid east. Constantine decided to move away from Rome, where the emperors had not resided for some time, and to create a new capital of the empire at Byzantium, the crossroads of the Greek east, which he renamed Constantinople. That shift of focus came to symbolize the tendency of his successors to concentrate on the east, and reluctantly and temporarily to let the west, including even Rome itself, go.

The eastern Roman Empire in its more tightly knit Byzantine form, discussed in the next chapter, showed remarkable powers of resilience. In the Hellenized area of the Macedonian system and its imperial predecessors it continued for another thousand years. But the Roman Empire in the west came to a formal end in 476, and the Latin world round the western Mediterranean was partitioned into kingdoms dominated by vigorous, semi-civilized Germanic peoples.

There has been much argument about why events took the course they did, with all its momentous consequences. There are specific explanations. The Hellenized world of the east was richer, more effectively administered and more profoundly civilized. It was therefore more worth defending against Persia than the west was against the European barbarians, who tried to invade the east too but were bribed and forced westwards. The fact that the empire split along the cultural divide between the Latin west and the Greek east was also more than mere coincidence, and is regarded as a major determinant by those who consider distinct civilizations as the basic units of human development. The establishment of Germanic kingdoms in the west took a stage further the previous Germanization of that area, and was followed by the conquest of the basically Semitic areas of Asia and Egypt by the Islamized Arabs two centuries later. Both Germanic and Arab rule increased the differences between the areas once united by imperial Rome. More general explanations, such as decadence and the decline of material and moral standards, may help to explain why the whole empire could not be held together, but not why one half of it continued while the other half collapsed.

One factor which was certainly not a cause of the collapse of the empire in the west was any general desire on the part of its constituent communities to secede or regain political freedom. The disappearance of Roman authority was bitterly regretted by the local populations that had known Roman rule. For generations they looked back to a safer, more universal and more civilized *res publica* than the half-barbarian kingdom in which they found themselves. What were these kingdoms, educated men like St Augustine asked contemptuously, but great robber bands, if justice was absent?

In what had been the western empire the memory, the language and the traditions of Latin civilization were kept alive, largely by the Christian churches, whose bishops became the representatives and intercessors – one might say the tribunes – for their communities with the new Germanic rulers. Moreover, the immigrant Germanic peoples, and especially their kings, also had a great respect for Roman civilization. They took over as much of the administrative practice as they could understand and operate, and they became devout though not always Catholic Christians. Theodoric's kingdom in Italy after the dissolution of the empire in the west was conscientiously Roman, with a strong regard for law and even for the shadow of legitimacy represented by the senate. But the eastern emperor Justinian's wars of reconquest ruined Italy, and the first-hand experience of the *res publica* did not last in the west much beyond the year 550. The assimilation and fusion of the Latin and Germanic populations proceeded apace, though they were periodically set back by the irruption of new and less Latinized Germanic peoples. The Roman civilization to which men in the west looked back was their own Latin one, inherited or adopted: they did not, in the main, want to be governed by alien, Greek Constantinople, which would treat them as inferiors. It took rather more than three centuries for the Roman Empire to be proclaimed again in the west. And when the pope crowned the Frankish King Charles Holy Roman Emperor in Rome on Christmas Day of the year 800, they did not between them restore the Roman Empire, but inaugurated a new and unsubstantial realm based on Germanic and Latin practice and dependent on Frankish arms.

The later Roman Empire stood far along the imperial end of our spectrum. It was an autocratic and often harsh form of rule, based on a heterogeneous and rapacious professional army. What were its attractions that made the populations of the western half of the empire look back to Roman authority with such nostalgia and such a desire to restore it? Certainly what is familiar seems legitimate; and over the centuries the empire and the authority of the emperor had come to be taken for granted. Moreover, the Roman imperium was a markedly more civilized and orderly form of government than Germanic practice, so that those who had experienced Roman rule understandably wanted to maintain it. In this sense the desire for a restoration in the fifth century was much the same as in the third. The Latinized population continued to honour the memory of Rome and to look to the empire as their civilization, and they resented their later Germanic overlords as aliens and often as heretics. The Roman Empire was indeed a higher civilization. In principle, and for the most part in practice, it established the rule of a single familiar code of law. It seemed universal, covering the known world. As in other imperial systems, the advantages of security and safe travel, and thus the possibility of long-distance trade, appealed to merchants and the consumers of their wares, and to certain types of scholar. Scholarship after 500 became largely concentrated in the church, and helped to make it the conscious heir of the Roman tradition.

There are times and places where remote central authority is felt to be oppressive, and liberty and the pursuit of happiness seem to be more attainable by secession, at least for those who then become the governing elite. That view, set out for instance in the American

Declaration of Independence, is today almost an axiom of western 'international theory'. But the history of the Roman Empire from the time of Augustus, and especially the loyalty to its institutions during the difficulties of the third century and to its memory after its collapse in the west, is evidence that liberty and happiness are not necessarily increased by the absence of a universal authority or central control. We shall come to this point again when we look at the twentieth-century desire for an international authority or world government.

NOTES

1 Oswald Spengler, *The Decline of the West*, London, Allen & Unwin, 1934, p. 395.
2 Gibbon, *Decline and Fall of the Roman Empire*, Chapter III, p. 96 in the 1782 edition.
3 *Romanitas* meant the distinctive values and traditions of the Roman city-state republic. The most important, for our purpose, was the ideal of government by the 'senate and people' rather than by a god-like lord and master and a professional army.

10

THE BYZANTINE *OIKOUMENE*

The Roman Empire in the east, which we call Byzantine, was much longer lived than other empires in the near east or Europe, surviving for about a thousand years. During that exceptional span of existence, periods of military expansion, notably under Justinian in the sixth century and under the Macedonian dynasty (870 to 1070), alternated with periods of great difficulty and loss of power. During much of their history the Byzantines were militarily, and in other ways, on the defensive, and were confronted with an expanding Islam which was more powerful than they were. Their ability to maintain their brilliant civilization in such difficult circumstances for so long, and actually to spread it far and wide among more primitive peoples beyond the limits of their rule, must still excite our admiration. The means they used are very pertinent to our study.

The Byzantines might well have regarded themselves as one state among others, perhaps the most civilized but not the most powerful; and therefore inescapably subject to pressures from without, against which they must be ready to defend themselves at all times and to expand when opportunity presented itself. The more thoughtful Byzantine rulers and statesmen admitted that in a superficial sense this might be the case. But they saw themselves, and the nature and purpose of their empire, very differently. They had inherited consciously from the Romans and less consciously from the previous empires of the near east the belief that their imperium ought to cover the whole civilized world, the *oikoumene*, and ought to spread the true faith and the true civilization to all the still uncivilized peoples of the earth. It was God's purpose that the imperium should be a light to lighten the Gentiles and the glory of His own people, the Christian Romans. The emperor or *basileus* (the title that the classical Greeks had used for the Persian 'king of kings' and which the Macedonian kings had adopted) was the sole legitimate sovereign, the only viceroy of God on earth: other rulers had legitimate authority only by delegation from him. He was both lay autocrat of the *oikoumene* and head of the Orthodox Church. The world ought therefore to be organized politically with Constantinople the great city, both the new Rome and the new Jerusalem, at the centre; surrounded by the Orthodox, Hellenized, Roman empire of the elect; and beyond that an ordered hierarchy of outlying principalities obedient to the universal *basileus* at the centre of the *oikoumene*. This was God's design for the world, and in due course it would come to pass. It was the duty of the *basileus*, of the clergy and of the whole Byzantine people to further God's design as best they could, to spread the Orthodox faith and the authority of the empire. Byzantine society was dedicatedly imperialist and dedicatedly missionary, and absolutely convinced of the superiority of its own civilization.

The Byzantine concept of the world has obvious affinities with that of China, where also an emperor exercised the mandate of heaven by spreading a manifestly superior civilization to an ever-widening periphery of subordinate and grateful peoples. But the Chinese version corresponded more with realities than the Byzantine. Since God had not provided his viceroy in Constantinople with adequate military power, but for His own inscrutable reasons allowed usurpers and barbarians to resist and menace the empire, military strength must be supplemented by other means.

The Byzantine imperial system was organized like other empires. It consisted in practice of a heartland which was Greek-speaking, Orthodox Christian and permanently under direct though sometimes feudal administration from Constantinople, and a very fluctuating penumbra under gradually decreasing degrees of Byzantine control or influence. The second circle of our diagram, the area under imperial dominion, which under the Macedonian emperors of Byzantium stretched from Syria and the Caucasus to the Danube and southern Italy, was made up of peoples of many races and languages, united under the formula 'one master and one faith'. It was a political principle of the Byzantine Empire, born of inherent weakness and almost always observed, not to coerce conquered peoples, but to leave every ethnos in possession of its own customs and laws. What mattered was loyalty not conformity. This was the Persian principle, and that of the *Arthashastra*. Loyalty to the *basileus* conferred enjoyment of the advantages of membership of the *oikoumene*, made more tangible by prudent tax concessions. The second aim of Byzantine statecraft in the areas of its dominion was the establishment of a common faith, for which God had created the empire, and for which a vigorous and well-educated priesthood worked tirelessly. Being Byzantine virtually meant being Orthodox. The third aim was to win over the subject peoples gradually to the customs, language and civilization of the empire. Thus the Hellenizing policy of Alexander and his successors, which had continued discreetly in the east during the centuries of Roman dominion, now again received official support and encouragement.

Outside the areas under Byzantine dominion lay others, inhabited by equally or even more different peoples, whose allegiance or at least alliance the Byzantines were anxious to win and retain. There seems to have been one great exception to this policy: for most of its existence the Byzantine state, even in periods of military strength, was basically on the defensive against the great rival missionary imperial power of Islam in the south and east which continually menaced and eventually destroyed it. To the north, round the shores of the Black Sea in the Caucasus, the steppe and the Balkans were less civilized semi-nomadic peoples, particularly Slavs and Turks; and to the west the Germanic kingdoms and the heretical papacy that had usurped, as the Byzantines saw it, the western half of their Roman Empire. Here there was real hope of spreading the light and of bringing independent peoples once again, or for the first time, into the *oikoumene*. The basic techniques for dealing with the Latins and the northern barbarians were established as early as the sixth century by Justinian. Professor Obolensky says:

> It was above all Justinian who developed and bequeathed to his successors that conception of diplomacy as an intricate science and a fine art, in which military pressure, political intelligence, economic cajolery and religious propaganda were fused into an almost irresistible weapon of defensive imperialism.[1]

Like the Assyrians, the Byzantines understood that the first need was adequate information. They organized a remarkable intelligence agency and centre for relations with these less civilized peoples, in which we find recorded even the personal tastes and suitable gifts for every ruler, members of his family and his rivals. To supply this intelligence they manned remote observation posts in places like the Crimea; they impressed traders (who welcomed the spread of Byzantine order) and missionaries into supplying information; and they maintained in Constantinople large numbers of pretenders and exiled leaders who became the emperor's men and gave him advice in the hope that with his help they might one day be restored to power among their own people.

In this area of hegemony the chief means of persuasion, as in the Persian case, was money. The Byzantines believed that every man, and certainly every 'barbarian', had his price; and even the large sums used to manage the situation in the penumbra of Byzantine influence seemed to them cheaper and less chancy than military operations. In the main their policy was the Persian one of *divide sed non impera*, and they were well pleased when dangerous neighbours took Byzantine gold and advice and turned their destructive energies against each other. 'In many cases', says Professor Obolensky,

> this money was undoubtedly tribute, exacted by the barbarians [from the Empire] at the point of the sword. But the Byzantines themselves, characteristically enough, regarded these contributions, especially when they were periodic, as payments of the beneficent emperor for services the recipients had rendered, or would render, to the empire. Thus tribute itself became a means of associating the barbarians with the Oikoumene.[2]

The recipients of Byzantine money usually signed some sort of agreement, and were then described as fighting together, as allied, as bound by treaty or as clients of the *basileus*. They undertook to put a certain number of armed men at the emperor's disposal, and were an important source of troops. Further, they formed a semi-reliable buffer or line of defence almost the whole length of the northern frontier against the wilder and more dangerous enemies beyond. The treaties included advantageous trade arrangements and economic privileges for the client ruler's merchant subjects throughout the empire. The allied rulers received Byzantine titles and insignia such as crowns, which flattered them and helped to establish a formal relation of dependence on the *basileus* and membership of the imperial system.

The treaty rulers, and even the remotest barbarians, were also brought into a dependent relationship with the empire by intensive missionary activity and cultural attraction. The most powerful instrument of Byzantine influence was the Orthodox faith, which won them over by its splendour and its spiritual values and also bound them to the *basileus* as head of the church. The converted rulers became the emperor's godsons. In accordance with the Byzantine policy of respect for other cultures, Orthodox missionaries translated the liturgy and scriptures into local languages. The Slavs who came to populate most of eastern Europe and the Balkans thus received their Christianity as well as their alphabet and other foundations of their culture from Byzantium without fear of losing their national autonomy. Byzantium achieved for the Slav and east European peoples what Rome at an earlier stage had done for the Celtic and Germanic peoples of the west. If these peoples could not be fully Hellenized, they could acquire a smattering of and a taste for the dazzling Roman–Greek–Christian civilization of the *oikoumene*. An important part of this civilizing process was effected by the women of good families, including in special cases the imperial family of the day, who were married to barbarian rulers and to other leading figures of the periphery including military chiefs and wealthier merchants.

Byzantium's relations with its Latin and barbarian neighbours were never easy. Many western rulers, from the Holy Roman Emperors to the popes and the Venetians, were alienated by Byzantine arrogance and duplicity. Byzantine diplomacy was adept at stirring up stasis by encouraging and subsidizing dissidents and rebels against Latin rulers, but it paid a heavy price in the hostility of those in power. It also gradually alienated the Slavs whom it had done so much to convert and civilize. Once they had learnt from Byzantium how to organize a competent administration, they wanted to establish realms that were independent of the empire and sometimes even to seize control of it. Nevertheless, in the main, Byzantine diplomacy was remarkably successful, both in the more mundane task of saving the empire many times from invasion and destruction, and in the missionary and imperial purpose of attracting so many less civilized peoples into the orbit of Greco-Roman civilization. Many features of Byzantine civilization, including notably Orthodox Christianity and an imperial missionary purpose, were inherited by Russia and carried by the tsars to the shores of the Pacific, and still in some ways colour the outlook of the Russians on the world. It is sometimes stated that Byzantine policy combined to an outstanding degree an uncompromising belief in the truth of its own values with an elastic ability to negotiate with its opponents. In fact, Byzantium did not just negotiate with opponents, in the modern sense of bargaining with juridical equals. It tried to manage the whole area round it, by a combination of military force, trickery, financial subsidy and religious and cultural proselytizing. It did so in the conviction that its God-given mission was to bring the whole world in due course under its sway, combined with the realistic awareness that meanwhile it was not as strong as its neighbours.

NOTES

1 D. Obolensky, 'Principles and methods of Byzantine diplomacy', in *Actes du Deuxième Congrès International d'Etudes Byzantines de 1961*, Belgrade, 1964.
2 ibid.

11

THE ISLAMIC SYSTEM
Adaptation of many traditions

In the early Middle Ages before the revival of Europe, another Semitic people, the Arabs, spread out over the southern and eastern half of the Roman Empire. The first great wave of Arab expansion covered the other Semitic lands of Syria and Mesopotamia; and the second soon afterwards brought in Persia, north Africa, Spain and the islands of the Mediterranean. In France the Arabs nearly reached the Loire, but were thrown back to the Pyrenees. With the Mediterranean effectively lost, Latin Christendom was confined to western Europe.

This astonishing expansion of the Arabs, without parallel in history, was made possible by their new religion of Islam. The Islamic era is normally dated from 16 July 622, when Muhammad and his band of faithful followers were driven out of Mecca and organized themselves into a military and religious movement. The Muslims – those who surrender to Islam – achieved their conquests with remarkable speed. There were many reasons for this accomplishment, of which we need to note two in particular. First, Muhammad was a religious leader of the first magnitude and also a statesman. He was inspired by Judaism and by Christianity, to which he added a clear and distinctive moral code, and also elaborated a system of law and a practice of government. Most important for international relations, Islam was from the beginning a universal missionary religion, without ethnic or geographic limitations and directed towards the conversion of all mankind. It quickly became clear that the principal features of Islam had a great attraction for many people all over the middle east. The Arab conquest was also a religious and political conversion. Second, Semitic languages were still generally spoken in much of the near east and along the African coast of the Mediterranean round as far as Spain. Once the Arabs had driven out or deposed the Greek- and Latin-speaking administrations that survived from the Roman Empire, they found it easy to establish a relationship with the Semitic-speaking population. Many of these people were also deeply committed to a more rigorous monotheism than the Orthodox Christianity of Byzantium and the Catholicism of the Latin West, which in addition to theoretical concepts like the Trinity and the Mother of God had allowed many local cult practices to survive transmuted into the veneration of saints. Those who held that 'Thou shalt have no other gods but me' welcomed the principal Muslim article of faith: 'There is no god but God.'

The areas which the Arabs overran and into which they were invited were at that time among the most civilized in the world; and the Muslims rapidly adopted much of this civilization. The Arabs had come out of the desert largely unfamiliar with higher civilization or culture, or – what especially concerns us – the techniques of managing empires made up of many diverse communities. Like other nomadic conquerors before them, they quickly and willingly adopted these skills from Islamized Syrians, Mesopotamians, Egyptians and Persians, and also from the Byzantines whom they displaced. The result was an eclectic and mixed culture and system of government which spread over much of the world. The Muslim synthesis was very successful in practice for about a thousand years. Some of the reasons for that success are relevant to international society today.

Like many other imperial systems, the Muslim empire found a measure of toleration expedient, and perhaps inevitable. Because so few Arabs had expanded over such an enormous area they needed converts to help them govern their new empire, and they actively encouraged conversion. But to force everyone to become a Muslim would have meant killing or driving out too large a number of their new subjects whom they needed to populate the countries which they had taken over, as well as provoking dangerously fierce resistance. Moreover, it is a tenet of Islam that conversion by the sword is no conversion at all. So the Muslims quickly evolved a formula of autonomy, rather like the Persian one in former times. They treated Christians and Jews as subordinate and inferior peoples, who were liable for extra taxes but remained organized in autonomous communities with their own religion and many of their laws. This toleration contrasted with the Christian insistence on conformity. It made possible, for instance, a medieval Spain of three religions and three cultural traditions which continually influenced each other.

The Muslims thought of the world as divided into the *dar al Islam*, the area of acceptance (of the will of God) or the area of peace, and the *dar al harb*, the area of war, where conflict with non-Muslim powers was to be expected and where war to expand the *dar al Islam* (but not, in theory, to make forcible conversions of individuals) was not only legitimate but positively virtuous. The *dar al Islam* was, or ought to be, one seamless cloth, with no regard to ethnic differences and no independent domains. It was an empire governed by a single 'commander of the faithful', who was a lay *imperator* rather than a religious leader, the successor (*khalifa* or caliph) to Muhammad in his secular not his prophetic capacity. The area over which the caliph was assumed to rule was in Islamic theory one of peace and harmony, which would in God's good time encompass the whole earth. The Muslim concept of the *dar al Islam*, and of the divine purpose regarding it, corresponds to the Byzantine view of their empire, and was doubtless substantially derived from it. It also corresponds to the communist concept of the socialist countries as the area of classless social harmony, and the rest of the world as the area of class war.

The early caliphs in fact exercised effective authority. But the Arab Empire, unlike its Byzantine predecessor, soon became too big, and the land communications which held it together too long and tenuous, for a single authority to maintain itself. The great schism between Sunni and Shia' had its origins in an early rivalry between claimants to the caliphate. Soon after the schism a new dynasty of caliphs supplanted the old at the centre, but the former dynasty continued in Spain, claiming that they were the only rightful successors of the Prophet. Areas loyal to the new dynasty but distant from the capital, Baghdad, also came to be quite separately administered. There were, inevitably, disputes between rival claimants to these distant governorships, and about the territorial limits of their power. How could the theory and the practice be reconciled? Muslim political thought continued to regard the *dar al Islam* as a single political structure, and did not evolve the concepts of states or rulers within Islam who were legitimately independent of each other politically. A ruler who was independent in practice therefore had to acknowledge nominal allegiance to some suitably remote caliph or claim the supreme position for himself. This was the issue of 'mosque and mint' – in whose name prayers were said and coins minted.

Outside the *dar al Islam*, on the other hand, in the area of war, it was permissible to make temporary agreements, truces and alliances with infidel rulers as a matter of expediency. But such arrangements must not become permanent, or confer immunity on infidel powers, since that would hinder their incorporation into the *dar al Islam;* agreements with non-Muslims should have a fixed time limit, such as ten years. The Muslims further divided infidels into the Jews and Christians who followed the two traditions recognized by Muhammad as divinely inspired forerunners of his teaching, and the kaffirs or heathen. This distinction had some effect on Muslim practice. Christians and Jews in conquered territories were more easily tolerated than kaffirs, and more easily than Muslims were tolerated in areas reconquered by Christians.

From about the year 1200 the Muslim conquest of India brought

114

Islam into direct dealings with the great and highly developed yet apparently idolatrous and kaffir civilization of Hinduism. The early Muslim Indian sultanates and then the Mogul Empire soon evolved the familiar pattern – concentric areas of direct administration, dominion, loose hegemonial control of domestically autonomous realms and agreements with wholly independent powers beyond the reach of imperial authority. Hindus occupied important positions throughout the structure, which usually prospered better the more their advice was heeded. It was difficult, as some pious Muslims complained, to say where the *dar al Islam* ended and the *dar al harb* began. But in spite of these compromises with Hinduism, and the other usual advantages of a suzerian empire which the Muslim sultanates had in common with their predecessors like the Mauryas, Muslim rule remained very distasteful to most caste Hindus.[1]

Iberia also provides an instructive example of this process, especially so for us because of the major roles which Spain and Portugal were to play in the European states system and in European colonization overseas. The Arabs under Tariq landed in AD 711 at Gibraltar (Gibr al Tariq = mount of Tariq), and spread very quickly all over the peninsula, almost without a military conquest. Recent scholarship in Spain has shown how willingly whole areas seem to have accepted the new Islamic rulers. The Muslims represented a higher level of material civilization, and the Catholic population was at odds with its Visigothic rulers who, though Christian, were aliens and heretics. There was also a large Jewish population in Spain which found Muslim rule less onerous than Christian. Before long the Arab conquerors established an independent caliphate in Cordoba, based on the old dynasty which had been overthrown in Baghdad. It had a core area of direct administration, with a substantial Muslim population, in al Andalus (the modern Andalucia), and a looser dominion elsewhere shading off into nominal suzerainty in the north. After two golden centuries the caliphate broke up into a number of principalities under Christian or Muslim rulers and mixed populations. In the struggles for power between these successor states of the caliphate we almost always find one coalition of Christian and Muslim rulers against another alliance of similar composition.

The greatest Christian knight and military commander of medieval Spain was the Cid, a liegeman of the King of Castile but with a title derived from the Moorish *sidi* (= my lord). He was a military contractor, like the Italian *condottieri;* and often fought for Muslims against Christians until finally he conquered himself a territory round Valencia which his wife ruled after his death. But at the same time he was a Christian champion whose legend became part of the folklore of the Christian reconquest. What began as a struggle for local power and territory gradually became more polarized as the Christians invoked the aid of the rest of Christendom and the Muslims brought in military-religious brotherhoods from north Africa, who between them turned the local conflicts into a crusade and holy war. In the end the Christians won, because the bulk of the population was Christian and because the knights and soldiers who came down from the rest of Europe proved the better soldiers. But it took them a long time. The emirate of Granada survived as an outpost of cultivated but enfeebled Islamic civilization in Spain until 1492.

When the strength of the Arab caliphate in Baghdad began to falter, Islam was mightily reinforced in the east by the influx of the Turks. These nomadic peoples came from the Eurasian steppe, with much the same primitive vigour as the Arabs who had created the *dar al Islam*. They easily adopted a religion which had arisen in social conditions similar to theirs, and it gave them a new unity and strength of purpose. They also displayed a gift for organization comparable to that of the Normans. In the eleventh century, when the Normans were establishing new and more effective governments in England and Sicily, the Seljuk Turks reorganized the government and the educational system of Persia and fostered a revival of a more native and less Arabized Persian culture. Later, the rule of the Turkish Mameluks in Egypt (*circa* 1250 to 1500) made their realm, including the holy places of Mecca and Jerusalem, the most prosperous and civilized in the Islamic world, and the intellectual focus of the *dar al Islam*. The Mogul Empire in India was founded by the military and organizing genius of the Turkish leader Babar. Most remarkable of all for its impact on the European system and on the evolution of international society was the Ottoman Turkish Empire that survived into the twentieth century. We shall need to look at the Ottomans more closely in later chapters.

Islam is the clearest example we have of a messianic religion permeating and shaping a whole culture. It was concerned from the beginning with government and administration as well as personal conduct and salvation. The code of conduct for a ruler was different from that which governed private behaviour but, as in the Byzantine Empire, equally strict. Not all rulers obeyed it, of course, and those who did were singled out in popular memory, like the great Caliph of Baghdad, Harun al Rashid (Aaron the Just), who was a contemporary of Charlemagne and the nominal hero of many of the tales in the *Arabian Nights*. Similarly Islam in its great days had a code of conduct in war which applied to all wars and campaigns, including those in the *dar al harb*. The Muslim warrior must not kill a woman or a child or those who surrendered. This was not because a Muslim owed anything to infidels, but because God required such conduct of those faithful to him.

116

Thus the conduct expected of the noble Arab corresponded to that expected of the noble Christian knight. These chivalrous codes were not concerned with such modern concepts as crimes against humanity or human rights, but with personal honour and obedience to God's commands. It was dishonourable to kill a woman in the same way as to lie or to break one's pledged word.

The most original Muslim thinker about the formation of empires and hegemonies, and the management of different communities of men, was **ibn Khaldun**, who wrote in the second half of the fourteenth century. At that time Islam was much fragmented politically, but educated men moved fairly freely over the whole great area. Ibn Khaldun came from a Yemeni family that had settled in Muslim Spain but were driven out to Tunis, where he was born; and he finished his life as a judge in Egypt, then the most prosperous and civilized part of Islam. He worked out a general philosophy of history or science of culture. He was especially concerned with the rise and fall of what we might call states but he saw as centres of authority, within the *dar al Islam* and generally.

We are so used today to thinking of authority and dominion spreading out from more developed centres to more backward ones, and of the European empires expanding into the primitive continents of the Americas, Africa and Siberia, that we are apt to lose sight of the fact that in previous ages the opposite has more generally been true. Thus the Assyrians were less civilized than the Babylonians and Sumerians when they established their empire, and the Persians again more primitive than the areas they subdued, as were the Germanic conquerors of the Roman Empire in the west and the primitive imperial conquerors of the Indian and Chinese civilizations. To ibn Khaldun this seemed the normal pattern of history. He had of course particularly in mind the *dar al Islam*, from the first conquests of the primitive Arabs to the coming of the Turks in the east and the Franks and Berbers in the west. The basic distinction he makes in his study of the rise and fall of authority is between primitive or bedouin culture and civilized culture. Primitive peoples, he said, may be settled or nomadic; their significant characteristic is that they lead a simple existence which makes them tough and used to hardship, closely knit by tribal loyalty and uncorrupted by the enervating vices of civilized cities. But their political and economic institutions fall far short of what is required to realize man's full capacities. One primitive group may come to dominate others; but in order to conquer an empire or dominate more civilized peoples, primitive tribes need the unifying force of an inspiring religion. This they may either evolve for themselves like the Hebrews or the Arabs, or adopt like the Turks (and he might have added the Germanic peoples who were converted to Latin Christianity and became its champions). Ibn Khaldun saw religion as a social force shaping law and custom. The historical record showed that the conquered civilized peoples often adopted the religion, language and other customs of their new masters, as was most strikingly true of the Arab conquests and the establishment of the *dar al Islam*. But the more primitive conquerors tended to learn from the conquered the advantages of civilization. Among these advantages ibn Khaldun included cities, which he considered indispensable for the development of civilized life; the ordering of an advanced economy which generated the wealth required for civilization; and the flowering of the arts and the sciences. A civilized order of this kind, often including many different peoples, was a fragile affair, subject to constant threat from within and without; and it therefore needed to be held together and defended by a firm framework of authority. This had been particularly the experience of Islam. The difficulty was that the unified force of a primitive people weakened when they acquired imperial authority. They spread out to govern and defend their new realm; they became enervated by civilization; and the rulers were transformed from leaders among equals to masters served by functionaries and slaves. In this way, he said, the duration and limits of any realm are set.

Ibn Khaldun concluded that an area of civilization is not ethnically determined but follows the establishment of a powerful imperial authority, is limited in extent to the area controlled by that authority, and disappears or is transformed when that authority declines or is conquered. This is an important general proposition, which runs counter to some modern assumptions. The examples that came to his mind are those which he and his family experienced in the shrinking of civilized Muslim Spain, the confusion of north Africa and the prosperous order of Egypt. The word *daula* which he used for 'authority' can also be translated as 'state'; and indeed, his areas of authority were territorial states, independent in practice within the nominal unity and single sovereignty of the caliphate. But because of the Muslim concept of the *dar al Islam*, neither ibn Khaldun nor his contemporaries saw their *duala*-states as jointly operating a system, and for all his interest in economics and trade he was not primarily concerned with the relations between his areas of authority.

The interest of this objective and thoughtful statesman scholar for us lies in his pioneering attempt to understand the general laws and forces that govern the establishment and decay of imperial authority, a subject which had hardly been attempted before him in the civilizations round the Mediterranean. By imperial authority I mean one which is not ethnically or geographically limited, but is capable of indefinite expansion. Such were the areas of authority within Islam,

118

and the Macedonian kingdoms. The unifying force that held together such states was Hellenistic or Islamic civilization. Islam especially was a way of life open to all; and within Islamic society individuals were exceptionally mobile, changing their geographical location and how they earned their living more easily than in most others. Islam aimed at homogenization of all Muslims, and the ultimate conversion of all non-Muslims. Ethnic origins, which elsewhere have often played and still play so large a part in ensuring loyalty to authority, were at a discount. In some respects, therefore, the impact of Islamic beliefs and ideology in the centuries of their expansion can be compared to the impact of the French Revolution, and of modern communism, which has been called the Islam of the twentieth century. We shall come back to these analogies. Moreover, both in concept and in practice Islamic authority was well towards the imperial end of our spectrum, far removed from the small corporations of hereditary armed proprietors who made up the Greek city states. The limited context of our contemporary concept, of an international society of independent member states, is well illustrated by the fact that neither of the great systematic analysts of politics, the Arab ibn Khaldun, who saw authority as potentially universal, and the Greek Aristotle, who saw it as limited to the city, seriously considered anything of the kind.

NOTES

1 For a detailed account of relations between Muslim and Hindu states and communities, see A. Watson, *The War of the Goldsmith's Daughter*, London, Chatto & Windus, 1964.

12

THE ANCIENT STATES SYSTEMS
Some theoretical implications

We may now be able to answer, or at least formulate more precisely, some of the questions raised in Chapter 1 and in the preface to the present section. What provisional theoretical deductions can we draw from this cursory survey of the relations between different communities in the ancient world, before we proceed to a more detailed look at the European experience?

RULES AND CULTURE

The ancient world knew of many ways of managing the relations between different communities that were involved with each other sufficiently to constitute a system. But some arrangements always existed. Whenever a number of states or authorities were held together by a web of economic and strategic interests and pressures, they evolved some set of rules and conventions to regulate their intercourse.

The sense in a community or group of communities of belonging to a distinctive culture is clearly discernible from the earliest civilizations to our own day. It was perhaps particularly acute among peoples who belonged to the same culture but were divided politically into a number of independent states, like the city-state Greeks, the Indians and the warring Chinese. There are many theoretical definitions of what constitutes a culture or civilization, and many theoretical conclusions have been based on the importance of cultural differences. We are not concerned with those wider issues, but with the question: what was the relevance of a **common culture** or civilization, or at least a dominant cultural matrix, to the integration of the ancient systems?

We saw that in the ancient world a strategic and economic system could reach sophisticated levels of organization even when the leading communities belonged to very different cultures. Where the leading states, as well as organizing relations between themselves on a basis of *de facto* independence and equality (whatever their ostensible claims), also exercised a hegemonial control over a more tightly knit group of client communities or dependent states, the wider arrangements are sometimes called secondary systems. The relations between Egypt and the Hittites in the second millennium BC provide an example. Neither could dominate the other, or establish a hegemonial control of the whole system; and they were bound to each other and to the smaller powers in the system by trade and strategic rivalry. Trade and strategy both have complementary as well as competitive aspects. Negotiation and bargaining, which are necessary both for trade and also for the political adjustments induced by war, were co-ordinating factors of even the most culturally diverse systems of independent states in the ancient world. The machinery of communication which we saw reflected in the Tell el Amarna tablets was designed to regulate economic and strategic relations: it included codes of conduct and specific agreements based on expediency and mutual convenience. But not every system is a society in Bull's sense (Chapter 1). The secondary systems did not go beyond the merely regulatory; they did not develop a set of rules and institutions consciously based on shared assumptions and theories, which would justify our calling them inter-state societies. The arrangements of the secondary systems have greater relevance to the relations between the European international society and the Ottoman Empire, which will be discussed in Chapter 19.

Ancient systems were notably more integrated when the communities enmeshed by the pressures of trade and strategy were also bound together by a culture, which provided a set of common assumptions about their relations with each other and shaped the rules and institutions of their system. The corporations of citizens that controlled the Greek city states were conscious of being Hellenes, with a common culture, language and religion that distinguished them from non-Greeks. Within this shared framework they were able to develop their complex and distinctive system of inter-polis relations: which most of the time included a number of powerful corporations each with a penumbra of dominion around it, and a shifting general hegemony of the strongest polis or diarchy of the two strongest. The Indian system described in the *Arthashastra* was an equally elaborate and institutionalized international society, bound together even more than the Greek by a very distinctive common culture based on the horizontal caste organization of society that cut across the individual, politically independent states. Hindu cultural values moulded every aspect of public and private life, including the rules and institutions governing the relations of Indian states with each other. The sense of cultural unity among the Chinese of the warring states was as strong as the Greek or Indian, and their inter-state society as distinctively Chinese.

Thus the differing cultures of these three ancient civilizations went far towards determining the distinctive forms and institutions by which

121

communities within the culture conducted their relations. The dominant culture in a society of states shaped the conscious response of its members, the methods which they used to cope with the network of interests and pressures that held them together. More especially the cultural framework helped to prescribe the position along our spectrum which seemed legitimate and proper to the communities concerned, and to which the society tended to gravitate. This was the case from the Greek commitment to the independence of the polis, through Indian ambivalence, to the Chinese belief in the system-wide mandate of the son of heaven. The rules and conventions of such unicultural systems were not merely regulatory: they incorporated shared values and aspirations. We also saw that where a culturally alien power was involved with a group of states that had evolved a society within a common culture, it was usually prepared to adopt much of the regulatory machinery and even the assumptions formed within the matrix of that culture. For instance, the Persians adopted Greek forms and recognized Greek assumptions about independence when dealing with the Greeks.[1]

POSITIONS OF SYSTEMS ALONG THE SPECTRUM

The evidence is that it was difficult for ancient systems to stay anchored near either extreme of the spectrum postulated in Chapter 1. The further the pendulum swung up the arc, either towards independent states or towards empire, the greater was the gravitational pull towards the centre, between hegemony and dominion. Sometimes the momentum of the pendulum carried it across the midpoint towards the other end of the spectrum. The Maurya Empire is a good example. The gravitational pull is a metaphor for what in sociological terms are the constraints exercised by the impersonal net of interests and pressures that hold the system together: constraints which become greater as a system moves towards the extremes of independences or empire. But the pendulum metaphor must be used with caution; there was no regularity in time or rhythm of the swing.

At the independences end of the spectrum, where there was no overarching authority, communities tried to increase their security by forming what Nozick pertinently calls protective associations, which in this context means leagues or **alliances**.[2] Such alliances were either between equals or, more often, composed of a stronger power protecting and dominating weaker ones. Then, as now, alliances provided some structure for what would otherwise be a very anarchic group of communities. The structure of the system extended when competing associations made agreements, to settle a dispute or to register the results of war. Such agreements established precedents, which became conventions. Similarly there were conventions governing trade, and sometimes other understandings, for instance regulating religious observances. Together the alliances and the conventions maintained a varying but usually considerable degree of order. They formed the rudiments of the conscious integration into a society of the system held together by a web of interests and pressures. Even the most heterogeneous systems, which fell short of a conscious society like that which involved Egypt and the Hittites, were a long way from anarchy.

However, such minimal systems were exceptions. There usually was some overarching authority, incorporated in a powerful state. A central fact about systems with a large number of substantially independent states in the **propensity to hegemony**.

Hegemonial authority sometimes extended over the whole system. Where the system became a society within the compass of a common or dominant culture, this was normally the case. A good example, especially impressive because it occurred so early, is the sophisticated Sumerian system, where the hegemonial authority was established and transferred by force of arms, but legitimized by religion and by the assumption that the kingship must reside somewhere. Or there might be two or more centres of hegemonial authority, polarizing and balancing the system. The Macedonian kingdoms and the Chinese warring states are examples, and so is Kautilya's theoretical diagram of allies, enemies and neutral powers. The Greek cities also provide graphic illustrations of the propensity to hegemony among independent states. Hegemonial authority seems to have grown out of, or resulted from, unequal alliances. It was a more developed, more induced form of international order, tolerated and indeed sometimes welcomed for that reason. The greater the degree of hegemonial authority in a system at a given time, the more integrated the system then was, and the further down the arc of the spectrum towards the borderline with dominion we must place it.

The distinction between hegemony, where a powerful state controls the external relations of its client allies, and dominion, where it also intervenes in their domestic affairs, is clear in theory; but it was smudged in practice. We saw that a hegemonial power, struggling against a rival alliance or trying to assert control over an entire system, found itself driven by the pressures of the situation to ensure that strategically or economically important lesser states conformed to its policies by maintaining in those states governments amenable to its wishes. Typical examples are the relations of Judah and Egypt with expanding Assyrian dominion, and the interventions of hegemonial Greek city states in support of the factions in weaker cities that favoured them, as also the Persian and Ptolemaic practice of extensive subsidies. It is difficult for hegemonial authority, whether of a single state or a diarchy, to order the external conduct of lesser states without some degree of intervention in their internal politics. While in Sumer there were apparently religious and conventional taboos on such intervention, most hegemonial authorities had no compelling reason to refrain from it.

The establishment of what we may call an area of dominion, involving a degree of control over the domestic affairs of subordinate states (which some modern scholars include in their use of the term 'empire'), does not necessarily involve formal suzerainty or the loss of the nominal independence of the weaker community. But in practice in the ancient world, as our metaphorical pendulum moved past the central point of its arc and up the imperial side of the spectrum towards increasingly direct rule, formal imperial overlordship became more likely. The claim to empire naturally came sooner in areas where imperial rule or suzerainty was traditional, and met with less resistance because those communities regarded a degree of imperial control as the natural order of things. Where it allowed them a substantial autonomy it was widely welcomed for the peace and security which it brought. But **autonomy** is an important proviso. The more imperial rule suppressed cherished local autonomies and customs, the more irksome it seemed to the subject communities. The further our metaphorical pendulum swung up the arc of the spectrum, the greater was the gravitational pull on it towards the low central point in the arc.

The frankly imperial powers of the ancient world – the Assyrians, the Persians, the Mauryas, the Macedonian kingdoms, Rome – understood this very well, as a matter of practical statecraft if not as a theory. Whatever they proclaimed, they were willing to leave local legitimacies substantially intact so long as they could obtain what mattered to them. Their principal requirements were compliance with the king's peace, political alignment in international relations, a financial contribution to the imperial treasury and sometimes a quota of troops on demand. The local communities were prepared to concede these things, if need be, and to acknowledge imperial suzerainty, which after all made them more secure and more prosperous. What really mattered to them was to keep their community out of the core area of direct administration and retain the political and religious autonomy of their society. The need for the 'conqueror' to respect local forms and traditions is emphasized with particular clarity in the *Arthashastra*. The acceptance of autonomy can bring benefits to both rulers and ruled, whereas the enforcement of direct administration may require more effort, money and even blood than it is worth. In the imperial half of the spectrum there is a **propensity to autonomy**, which corresponds to some extent to the more marked propensity to hegemony in the independences half of the spectrum.

The evidence is that in practice the independences half of our spectrum is not a reverse replica of the imperial half, and the corresponding pull on the metaphorical pendulum is not quite the same. The communities to which men are loyal change over time. But the members of whatever community exists at a given time and place want it to develop free from alien constraints. In the ancient world the commitment to independence was naturally strongest among those who exercised local authority: the rulers, religious leaders and those citizens who had some say in political decisions. It was less so among the sections of the population customarily excluded in practice from a political say. Among free men it seems to have been least strong in long-distance traders, especially where they did not control the government of their community.

The advantages of the imperial side of the spectrum are practical; but the pull towards independence is mainly a moral and emotional one, associated with cultural identity and a heroic ideal. In the imperial half of the arc, where alien dominion regulated to some degree the internal governance of dependent communities, the first and essential aim was the maintenance of a separate identity and then the enlargement of local autonomy. In more loosely controlled areas, where the pendulum was on the independences side of the arc, the desire for greater independence inspired struggles by states to weaken the regulation of their external relations by the hegemonial authority of the time. One anti-hegemonial aim was to lessen the ability of any outside authority to impose its solutions to disputes. Consequently the independences end of the spectrum left more disputes to be settled by the arbitrament of war. Warfare was not considered reprehensible in the ancient world. Indeed, the ability to decide when to go to war was the hallmark of independence, for a king or a city corporation.

STRUCTURE OF IMPERIAL SYSTEMS

In our preliminary definitions, we provisionally divided our spectrum into four categories: multiple independences (never absolute), hegemony, dominion and direct administration or empire (also never absolute). Our examination of the complex realities of the relations between states with varing degrees of dependence in the ancient world showed that imperial systems, or in Bull's terminology imperially organized societies of states, were not administratively homogeneous. We saw that imperially organized systems were conglomerates, radially managed rather than territorially administered. They were composed of: (a) a directly administered core; (b) a penumbra of dominion where subject communities have varying degrees of domestic autonomy; shading into (c) an area of hegemony where the centre does little more than control or influence external relations; and (d) outside the imperial structure, but included in the network of interests and pressures that make up the system, genuinely independent states and other imperial structures. On an analytical diagram (though not of course in geographical reality) these areas can be represented as concentric circles. We have described systems with a greater degree of imperial authority radiating from the core as tighter and more integrated, and those with less imperial authority as looser and less integrated.

Some historians argue, or assume, that imperial powers want to make their administration more direct; and that they practise the less absolute forms of control if they are not strong enough to enforce more direct rule. The argument is sometimes part of the doctrinaire general theory that all sources of power within a state tend to make themselves as absolute as they can, and that all members of an international society of independent states will expand whenever they can. The evidence seems to me on the contrary to show that almost all the established imperial powers which we have examined in this section of the book, whether they dominated a whole system or only part of it, showed considerable restraint in dealing with traditional legitimacies. This was conspicuously true of the Persian system and the Roman principate. The clearest theoretical formulation, if we may call it that, is the advice in the *Arthashastra* to leave local legitimacies alone.

Indeed, many imperial systems were established by aggressive expansion of the dominant power, but then became, and for a considerable proportion of their existence remained, largely on the **defensive**. During such periods an imperial authority might certainly decide, or try, to reduce the degree of autonomy in a given area and institute more direct administration; but the purpose of such actions was often to defend rather than to expand its overall control. Defensive imperialism has been discussed, for instance, by Garnsey and Whittaker in general, by Garelli in the case of Assyria, by Meiggs in the case of Athens and by Luttwak in the case of Rome. On China, Owen Lattimore writes in *Power and Propaganda*:

Chinese chroniclers began very early to disguise the nature of trade granted as a political concession by describing the barbarians [i.e. the non-Chinese periphery] as bringing 'tribute' and receiving 'gifts' in return. The real character of these transactions is quite clear, however: the Chinese 'gifts' always exceeded the 'tribute' in real value. . . . [W]e repeatedly find that in periods of Chinese weakness the barbarians demanded the right to send 'tribute missions' more frequently.[3]

Notice the categorical 'always'. This passage provides a significant comment on symbolic representations of imperial power, such as those at Persepolis of the various peoples of the Persian imperial system bringing tribute to the great king. The dependent states or 'provinces' in the area of dominion, and even more so the domestically self-governing states in the area of hegemony, often – perhaps more often than not – had more autonomy and thus more potential for independent action in practice than the imperial or suzerain power claimed or pretended. Ancient imperial authority had an element of prestige, in the French sense of something not wholly real but partly a conjuror's illusion.

We therefore need an adequately comprehensive and neutral definition of an imperial system. Definitions that refer to only one aspect of such complex structures, like 'a mechanism for collecting tribute' (Wallerstein) or a lust for conquest and domination are pitifully inadequate. Doyle has a usefully comprehensive formula:

> Empires are relationships of political control imposed by some political societies over the effective political sovereignty of other political societies. They include more than formally annexed territories, but they encompass less than the sum of all forms of international inequality.[4]

His definition extends the term 'empire' to include what we have called the area of dominion and even the area of hegemony. He speaks of 'opportunities and incentives for domination by the metropole as well as vulnerabilities to conquest and incentives for collaboration in the periphery': I would prefer 'radial influence' to 'domination', and would include in the incentives for collaboration of the periphery economic subsidies and protection against third parties.[4] The definition I favour is Larsen's suggestion 'that an empire be defined as a **supernational** [my emphasis] system of political control, and such a system may have either a city state or a territorial state as its center'.[5] This formulation recognizes the existence of separate dependent states with varying degrees of autonomy. It also suggests to us a corresponding formula for a system of multiple independences, as an **international** system of political control, and such a system may have either a city state or a territorial state as its hegemonial focus. In practice if not nominally, some degree of hegemony is apparently always present, and societies of states near the multiple independences end of the scale also have some core or focus of authority. The difference between one pattern and another is one of degree rather than of kind. There is no abrupt break between supernational and international societies. The position of any supernational or international system in our spectrum at any given time therefore refers to the general tightness or looseness of the rules and institutions of the society of states concerned, dependent and independent, and the degree of central or hegemonial control.

THE PERIPHERY AND THE CENTRE

The nature of imperial structures is determined not only by the impact of the centre on the periphery but also, as Lattimore's observation reminds us, of the impact of the periphery on the centre. This aspect of the problem raises the question of **marcher states**. The evidence of the role of marcher communities in ancient systems was indicative, but not decisive. The impulse towards the imperial end of the spectrum, tightening up a loosened system, and establishing or usually re-establishing a greater degree of central authority and stricter rules and institutions for a society of communities, usually came from vigorous peripheral communities hardened on the dangerous frontiers or 'marches' of a civilization whose centre had become softer and more refined. Marcher communities were obliged by their environment to develop stronger government and superior military techniques in order to survive; but they admired the civilization which they came to dominate: they made themselves its standard bearers, and inherited the hegemonial structures that already knitted the system together.

Assyria, the Medes and Persians, Macedon (with both the Greek cities and the Persian empire), the Mauryas, Rome and the Arab caliphate are all examples of marcher states. All of them recognized the value of the administrative experience of the centre, and while they established their dominance by force they were quick to adapt to their purposes the previously existing but now weakened patterns of imperial authority which they found to hand. There was a remarkable continuity of imperial administration from Assyrian Nineveh to Arab Baghdad. It was a family likeness that was sometimes a conscious inheritance: as with Alexander, who was both a Macedonian kinglet and a Persian imperial ruler; and Augustus, who acted not as a Tarquinian city state *rex* but as a Hellenistic *basileus* in all but official title. The quite separate unification of China by the Chin dynasty followed a significantly parallel pattern. All these imperial marcher states moved the organization of their system, or moved it back, a considerable distance towards the imperial end of our spectrum.

Even the wilder nomadic invaders were rarely wholly alien to the civilization they overran. They had usually lived for some time on its fringes, and their leading figures included nomad traders like Muhammad and former mercenary soldiers from civilized armies, who were well aware of its general nature. The barbarian Medes and Persians had assimilated a considerable degree of Mesopotamian civilization by the time they took over its imperial power. The same is true of the Germanic peoples who irrupted into the western half of the Roman Empire, the Arabs who swept into the south and east, the Slavs in the Byzantine Balkans and the Turks who reorganized the *dar al Islam*. They were extreme examples of the broad and continuing interaction between barbarian vigour and civilized decadence, which ibn Khaldun saw as a regular and recurring rhythm between communities in a system.

In so far as an enlarged imperial domain or conglomerate was able to ensure order and promote economic well-being, it was in many people's interest to take part in it; and the looser and more indirect (that is, the further from the empire end of the spectrum) it was, the less people minded who the overlords were. The more civilized and politically sophisticated areas, which made up the inner core of a marcher dominion or suzerainty, were able to influence the administrative practice of the wider imperium in proportion to their cultural achievements and their wealth. Familiar examples were the influence of Sumer on the concepts and practices of subsequent suzerain systems, and of Hellas and Persia on their Macedonian conquerors. So was the influence of the Hellenistic east (Juvenal's Orontes) on imperial Rome. The east of the empire had a social structure that knew how to use a nominally divine monarchy to its own advantage, by conducting a client–overlord dialogue with the ruler and his bureaucracy. The local authorities in the Asian provinces found the Roman senate less easy and more faceless; and because they were richer and more civilized, they were able to pull the Roman principate away from senatorial practices towards more Hellenistic forms of managing a hegemonial society of political entities.

But the ancient societies were not always ordered by marcher hegemonies or dominions. A highly civilized central power was sometimes able to achieve primacy or dominance. We noted the position of Babylon after the collapse of Assyrian authority; that of the culturally pre-eminent Athenians in classical Hellas; and above all that of the Hellenistic world from the time of Constantine, expressed in the form of the millennial Byzantine *oikoumene* whose cultural superiority reinforced its internal moral strength and its external legitimacy. We shall examine the position of peripheral and central powers more specifically in the European section of the book, when we look at the remarkable position of France, particularly under Napoleon, in the European society of states.

LEGITIMACY AND FLEXIBILITY

The practice of an ancient system rarely coincided with its legitimacies (any more than it does in our contemporary international society). When therefore we ask how integrated a system was at any given point in its history, we must consider both what the relations between its component entities actually were, and also what men claimed they were and what the rules and institutions stipulated. People are influenced by what they believe is or ought to be the position *de jure (das Sollen,* as Kant might say) as well as by what they perceive is happening *de facto (das Sein);* and they are inclined to favour what they believe ought to be, even when it is not in their material interest. Law and theory and the sense of what is proper and fitting are culturally conditioned and associated with tradition and precedent. They are therefore comparatively solid and resistant to change; and so is the legitimacy which they confer. Practice, on the other hand, is much more influenced by expediency and empirical advantage. It is fluid, and like water adjusts quickly to new levels as circumstances alter. But while legitimacy holds back changes in the rules, it shifts imperceptibly over time, to come closer to long-established realities. Time and familiarity legitimize practice.

In the ancient world the relations between members of a community, and the relations between communities, were determined partly by practical realities, but also to a considerable extent by what the relations were proclaimed and believed to be. The assumptions about these relations varied considerably in different cultures. For instance, the Chinese commitment to an imperial authority, in contrast to the legitimacy and vigour of the Indian tradition of a system of independent states, puts the two great Asian civilizations on either side of an important dividing line of legitimacy. Similarly the loose but effective Persian structure of authority over the domestically autonomous Greek cities of Asia was not very different in practice from the Delian League at the height of Athenian domination; but the Persian system was an imperial or suzerain one in which Greek city corporations were not formally independent (though their own legitimacy told them that they ought to be); whereas the Delian League, whatever the realities, was nominally an alliance of sovereign city states. In all these cases there was an element of make-believe in the claims of the imperial or hegemonial power, which were attempts to legitimize its authority by asserting that the society was tighter or looser than it really was.

Legitimacy pulled the management of a society of states or communities towards the point along the spectrum where the communities concerned felt most comfortable. In so far as it influenced the way a society was managed, it was usually a force for stability and continuity.

However, the nature of every ancient system was subject to changes, which were often abrupt. Our metaphorical pendulum was constantly swinging. In such circumstances legitimacy mattered as much as performance in obtaining the consent of the governed; and authority (as opposed to forceful compulsion) was respected and obeyed to the extent that it was believed to be right and proper. Even in the most innovative Greek cities there was a presumption in favour of legitimate authority. Legitimation was particularly important in the management of a system of different communities. For instance, government by a lawful ruler, especially a native one from the same community as the governed, was usually more acceptable than materially better government by an unlawful or alien one, even if the legitimate or semi-legitimate ruler was to some extent under the influence, or actually carrying out the instructions, of an imperial authority. Thus the forms of independence could be preserved by a shrewd hegemonial power, while the reality shifted a long way towards the imperial end of the scale; and the converse was also true, as Persian and Byzantine practice and the experience of the caliphate vividly illustrate. Retention of established forms (whatever they may happen to be) can lend a cloak of legitimacy to a reality that no longer corresponds to them, and gain greater acceptance for changes which are not at first clearly perceived, and which as they become more visible also in time become more legitimate. Provided the legitimacies seemed to remain fairly intact, the fluidity of practice enabled the systems of the ancient world to tighten or loosen – to move along our spectrum – more easily and further than was realized by the governed or even by most of their rulers and leaders. The more the management of a system was considered to be legitimate, the more smoothly it functioned. Legitimacy was often, in the ancient world, the oil that lubricated the operative machinery of a system.

We may therefore provisionally arrive at the following formula. Three factors play major parts in determining what point in our spectrum is the most stable and generally acceptable for a given system at a given time. The first is the *Sein*, the balance of material advantage, both for the rulers and the ruled. The second is the *Sollen*, the point of greatest legitimacy, also for all concerned. The importance of the dominant culture in ancient systems is that it largely prescribed the point of legitimacy. Third there is the gravitational pull of the pendulum away from the high points of the curve, from direct empire towards autonomy and from anarchical independence towards hegemony. **Thus the most stable point along the curve is not some invariable formula, but is the point of optimum mix of legitimacy and advantage, modified by the pull on our pendulum away from the extremes.** This optimum mix was different in each of the ancient systems we have looked at, and shifted in each system over time.[6]

NOTES

1 In this context I would refer the reader back to the extract from H. Butterfield's paper, 'The historic states-systems', written for the British Committee on the Theory of International Politics in 1965 and quoted in my Introduction.

2 R. Nozick, 'The state of nature', in *Anarchy, State and Utopia*, New York, Basic Books, 1974, pp. 10–25.

3 O. Lattimore, in M. T. Larsen (ed.), *Power and Propaganda: A Symposium on Ancient Empires*, Copenhagen, Copenhagen University Press, 1979. See also p. 110 of this book.

4 M. Doyle, *Empires*, Ithaca, Cornell University Press, 1986, pp. 19, 20.

5 Larsen, op. cit., p. 91.

6 Professor Fulvio Attinà of the University of Catania, Sicily, has suggested the following valuable alternative formula in a letter to me about the importance of legitimacy in international societies. 'I see the organization of an international system located in a space defined by two dimensions: that of high/low hierarchy [among states, i.e. hegemonial structure] and that of high/low legitimacy (or acceptance by states) of the rules and institutions on which the high or low hierarchical organization is based.'

THE EUROPEAN
INTERNATIONAL
SOCIETY

PREFACE

We can now turn to a more detailed examination of the European society of states. We need to look at it in its individuality, its unique and individual nature, because only in that way can a historian understand it and perceive its original features. We also need to compare and contrast it with the other societies of states discussed in the first section of the book. In doing so we shall consider the questions we asked about the ancient systems, formulated in the preface to that section and in Chapter 12.

The historical chapters, 13 to 21, examine the nature and unfolding of the European society of states. They are not a telescoped survey of the history of Europe, and refer to individual states and to political, military, economic and social developments only in the context of that society, and of the wider and expanding system – the network of interests and pressures – which involved the European society beyond its geographical borders.

The European example throws valuable light on the question of **continuity** between one society and another. Looking back to its predecessors, we shall note how the European society was the heir not only of its medieval past but also of the Greek, the Macedonian and the Roman societies: both historically, and by conscious European adaptation of classical models. Looking forward, in this section and the next, we shall see how the European society also transmitted many of its institutions and practices to our present worldwide society.

The European society of states provides us with instructive evidence on the question of **cultural unity**. It did not include the whole system of interests and pressures whose members felt obliged to take close economic and strategic account of each other. That distinction raises two questions. First, what did determine the geographic scope of the European society? Why was it not system-wide? How far were its rules and institutions formed within the highly original cultural matrix of Latin Christendom? Second, what were the relations of the society itself, and of its individual members, to polities beyond its bounds?

We shall look particularly at European relations with the Ottoman Empire, which for most of the period controlled up to a quarter of geographical Europe and bulked large in the strategic and economic calculations of the Europeans. We must also examine European relations with other eastern polities. How did the arrangement which regulated those relations before the nineteenth century differ from the rules and institutions of the European society? In the period of European domination of the world, which roughly coincided with the nineteenth century, how did European arrangements with the outside world change? What ideas and practices of international society did the Europeans transmit to political entities outside their society?

This section will also examine the way in which the European society of states evolved. What were its **basic principles** and its **organizational institutions and practices?** Its characteristic feature is sometimes said to be independent statehood. We shall examine the claim of states and their rulers to sovereignty, meaning internal and external freedom of action: from the Renaissance *stato*, through the princes' club, to the nation states that destroyed the European society in two twentieth-century world wars. We shall look at the legitimation of claims to sovereignty at the Westphalian and subsequent settlements.

We must also examine the opposing propensity to hegemony and the nature of hegemonial practice in the European society. So entrenched was the concept of sovereign independence that the powers that exercised hegemony were periodically overthrown by anti-hegemonial coalitions that proved to be economically and militarily stronger. How does the European society compare in this respect with classical city-state Hellas and other ancient societies from Sumer onwards? How much **hegemonial authority** was there in fact in the European society? Is Martin Wight's description of it as a 'succession of hegemonies' justified?[1] How necessary was hegemony for the maintenance of order in the society? In what condition was the hegemony exercised by one power, or diarchic, or else shared by a group of great powers?

In the ancient states systems we noted the importance of **legitimacy**. How were the legitimacies of the European society established? How much did they diverge, at different stages, from the practice? In particular, how legitimate, that is how consciously acknowledged, was hegemonial authority? What were the origins and the role in the society of international law, and the concept of juridically equal independence for all member states?

In the context of hegemony we will also look at the evidence for a **pendulum effect** in the European society. How far did the pendulum swing, at its furthest point under Napoleon, towards an imperial order for the whole society? How far did the society in its anti-hegemonial periods approach genuine freedom of action for all its members? To what extent were the powers that exercised hegemony those at the centre of the civilization and the system, and how far were they more vigorous marcher communities, and states that derived their power from areas outside the society?

NOTES

1 M. Wight, *Systems of States*, Leicester, Leicester University Press, 1977, p. 42.

13

MEDIEVAL EUROPE
The originality of Latin Christendom

The society of medieval western Europe was exceptionally creative and original in almost every field. We must limit our attention to those aspects which concern the relationship between different communities, and which have contributed to our present principles and practices.

THE NATURE OF MEDIEVAL SOCIETY

The society of medieval Europe, in which the later European states system and international society have their roots, was very different from the classical civilization that preceded it. If a Roman in the great days of the empire had been asked to imagine what could come after, he might have foreseen the developments which led to the Byzantine system, but his wildest speculations would not have conceived of anything like the Middle Ages in western Europe. The medieval world has been much maligned, and the very word 'medieval' has acquired a pejorative sense; but it was one of the most remarkable and creative periods in all world history. Perhaps only in the city states of ancient Greece and in the warring states of China can we find parallels to medieval creativity. Of course the concepts and institutions that were evolved in western Europe in the Middle Ages were not perfectly implemented. But it does not detract from the idea of parliamentary democracy, for instance, which evolved in the Middle Ages, to say that neither did it then nor does it today function perfectly, any more than it detracts from the idea of chivalry to recognize that many noblemen in medieval Europe behaved like beasts.

From the fall of the Roman Empire in the west in AD 476 down through Charlemagne's short-lived empire in the ninth century to about the year 1000, western Europe went through a period of great difficulty. Barbarian peoples from across the Rhine formed a number of kingdoms out of the prostrate empire. Communication became more difficult, and literacy and trade shrank. Towards the end of the period, Muslim Saracens and Moors occupied the Mediterranean islands and

Spain, and raided France and Italy; the Norsemen raided and settled from the north; and the Huns and other peoples from the steppes hammered Europe from the east. Many of the barbarian invaders were influenced by Roman civilization before they settled in the empire, and all of them quickly learnt from the communities over which they ruled. But the Muslims saw themselves as standard bearers of a more developed civilization, which had already absorbed much Roman practice; so that they learnt little from the Latins whose territories they occupied, and in the latter part of the Middle Ages taught them much.

In those centuries of disorder and of dramatic decline in material and other standards, the Latin population of western Europe managed to preserve some of its Roman civilization. First there was the memory of the Roman Empire, more civilized and universal than the circumscribed and dangerous conditions of the day. The Holy Roman Empire was 'restored', or more objectively was founded, by the Frankish king Charlemagne with the active aid of the church, and included most of Latin Christendom. On his death the western third, which had been colonized by the Germanic Franks, gradually acquired the name of France. The eastern two-thirds, comprising Italy and central Europe, retained the other name of Charlemagne's great realm, and continued to be called the Holy Roman Empire. Second, Italy, Spain and Gaul, though not Britain, retained their varieties of the Latin language, which became the Romance languages of today. The incorporation of the Germanic peoples, including the English and the Scandinavians, transformed Christendom from a Latin-speaking and Mediterranean-oriented survival of the imperial past to a society as much Germanic as Latin, and also larger, more vigorous and forward-looking. Third and most important, the population remained or became Christian and Catholic, and were organized and represented by the administrative machinery of the Catholic Church, which negotiated on their behalf with the Germanic rulers of the new kingdoms. The universal Latin-speaking church, directed from Rome, was the most specific survival of the lost imperium, and transmitted a sense of universality and common membership to all Latin Christendom.

The Latin Christians of west and central Europe continued throughout the Middle Ages to think of themselves as members of **Christendom**. The term in practice included only Latin Christians, and left out the Greek-speaking Byzantine Empire. The later sense that all Europe was a great commonwealth derived from the medieval sense that Christendom was one, and ultimately from the universality of the Roman Empire. Medieval Christendom was a single society, for all its diversity. It was not divided vertically into large and small independent states, each sovereign within its own borders, as the world nominally is today. It was horizontally stratified into four broad classes:

the nobility, from kings to simple knights; the clergy; the townspeople, artisans and merchants; and the mass of the people who were mainly concerned with agriculture. A man or woman's position in medieval society tended to be hereditary; but in practice the divisions were fairly fluid.

The function of the **nobility** was to bear arms and to govern. As military service was the obligation of the hereditary proprietors of the Greek city corporations, so in the Middle Ages those who governed bore arms. At the head of the nobility were kings and autonomous princes. A medieval king had very little authority or wealth outside his own family possessions. He depended on his feudal vassals, the dukes and counts and barons, who had as much right to their positions and functions as he to his, and had corresponding administrative and military responsibilities. A lord owed his king certain feudal obligations, just as those under him owed obligations to him. In practice many great lords were powerful enough to withhold their obligations; and some had different obligations for separate fiefs.

The analogy with later centuries in Europe, when many kings and sovereign princes ruled despotically, can lead to our projecting absolute power back to medieval kings; but that was not the case. Governmental power and military capacity were still very diffused, and it was difficult for any medieval ruler to concentrate much of either in his hands, or to raise revenues other than those assigned to him by custom or derived from his own possessions. So fragmented and localized was the authority of the medieval nobility that an entity or realm like the Holy Roman Empire or the Kingdom of France was not a single political unit. Medieval Europe was not a system of states. Our next chapter is concerned with how the determination of kings and princes to increase their real power led in the Renaissance to the reorganization of Christendom vertically, into what we can recognize as states.

The nobility shared the government of medieval Christendom with the **church**. As early as AD 494 Pope Gelasius spoke of 'the two powers by which this world is chiefly ruled, the sacred authority of the clergy and the imperial power'. The dual authority of the Middle Ages grew out of the coexistence of the Roman Church and the barbarian kingdoms; and the two powers shared authority, so that all men owed allegiance to both. The church was responsible for almost everything that we call social services. Medicine and hospitals, literacy and education (as opposed to apprenticeship for nobles and townspeople) and charity, such as they were, came into the church's domain. The church was also concerned with religion, which played a much greater part in people's lives in the ages of faith than today, and with the ethical issues of what was right and wrong.

Unlike the nobility who were largely tied down to the local rights and functions that went with their inherited or newly won fiefs, the church remained truly universal. The clergy were recruited from all classes and all over Christendom; and since they were celibate and had no heirs, they were recruited anew in each generation. They preached and fostered among laymen an awareness of membership of all Christendom, as well as of a particular locality. Originally a bishop was a local man, but the medieval clergy from the popes downward might come from anywhere in Christendom, and the greatest clerics moved about.[1]

The civil government was responsible for the administration of law for the layman; but the clergy came under a separate legal system known as the canon law, and were thus emancipated in practice and in theory from the control of lay rulers. The universal and separate church influenced the conduct of lay government in two ways. First, rulers recognized it as the custodian of the ethical principles which they were expected to follow. Second, kings and other rulers used the clergy, who were much more literate and familiar with written records than they, to do much of their administrative work; so that the clergy penetrated the governmental functions of lay rulers. The term 'clerical work' originally meant work performed by the clergy.

The third horizontal stratum of medieval society was made up of townspeople, artisans and merchants: the **burghers**. Many towns and cities had survived from Roman times, and preserved an individual identity. They were independent of both the nobility and the church in varying degrees. Many cities governed themselves, and their elected mayors or burgomasters could be powerful figures. Some like Cologne were governed by a prince-bishop. Others, especially in England, were substantially under royal control. The chief functions of the towns were manufacturing and trade. Medieval cities provided channels of contact between one part of Christendom and another, parallel but separate from those of the church; and also contacts beyond the Latin world, which brought in new goods, techniques and ideas. The concepts and practices of law, especially maritime law, of long-distance trade and of banking were preserved and developed in the cities, particularly those of Italy and Germany. In all these activities the Jewish communities played a notable part.

The peasantry, who made up the bulk of the population, were usually serfs attached to the soil. The Middle Ages did not inherit the classical institution of slavery; but the peasants were obliged to remain on the land and to work it, partly for themselves but partly for their lord or the church. They may be compared to the **helots** and **coloni** of antiquity. But there was more upward mobility. Most important was the continuous recruitment of bright peasant children into the clergy; some even became popes. The population of the towns and cities was also augmented by enterprising serfs who had run away from their lords and who could find employment there, substantially free from the danger of being handed back. Many good warriors, who served a great lord well, were knighted, and so recruited into the lower ranks of the nobility.

The age of faith and chivalry was an age of enormous dynamism. From about the year 1000 Christendom, further reinforced by Norse and Slav vigour, began to find itself a match for the Moors and Saracens in the south and the heathen in the east. Europeans became richer and stronger. The population greatly increased. The lands which had gone out of use or reverted to forest after the collapse of the Roman Empire were brought back into cultivation, their fertility increased by the long period of regeneration. New techniques of farming and building, suitable for the north of Europe, were developed, along with metalworking, seamanship and the other arts of war and peace. Many innovations were developed and diffused by the church. The prodigious developments of civilization, government, social services and ideas achieved by the governing strata of the church and the nobility were supported by the wealth produced by the two strata of medieval society principally concerned with its production: the peasantry and the townspeople and traders. The prosperity of Christendom increased so much that the burghers and the peasantry steadily improved their own material conditions as well.

THE ORIGINS OF NATIONALITY AND STATEHOOD

Though Christendom was all one, government and authority functioned differently in its two geographic halves. The difference affected the development of the European society of states.

In the later centuries of the Middle Ages the western half of Christendom was dominated by the civilization associated with the French language, Gothic architecture and the reform of the church. That civilization grew up in the north of France, was also dominant in England and played a large part in the reconquest and settlement of Spain and Portugal. The kings of France, who in the twelfth century were still weak and overshadowed by their great vassals, gradually turned their nominal overlordship into an increasingly effective royal authority. So powerful did the French monarchy become that in the fourteenth and fifteenth centuries it was able to remove the popes from Rome and set them up in Avignon. In England the Norman and Plantagenet kings were able to make royal authority effective earlier than elsewhere. The three main Iberian kingdoms and the duchy of Burgundy were also gradually forged into coherent entities by a suc-

142

cession of firm rulers and foreign wars. The machinery of government and the legal justification of territorially defined realms made it increasingly easy for kings in the west of Europe to defy a particular pope (or in some areas emperor), though without formally repudiating the universal authority of these offices.

However, the new embryo states in the west, if we may call them such, were still royal domains: administrative areas rather than linguistic or cultural units. Loyalty was focused on the crown and whoever was legitimately entitled to wear it. Educated and wealthy townspeople, and increasing numbers of humbler folk, looked to the king and his justice for protection against the demands of the local nobility and even the church. Joan of Arc symbolizes a stage in this process. She stood for the Kingdom of France, loyalty to its crown and the crown's rightful heir (whose rights were in fact in dispute), against the English, the Burgundians whose loyalty was to their duke, and those with traditional Plantagenet allegiance.

On the other hand, in the eastern half of Christendom, in the Holy Roman Empire which consisted mainly of Germany and Italy, the Catholic Church, headed by the pope with those cardinals, bishops and monasteries that supported him, waged a continuous struggle to assert itself against the temporal power of the emperor. A pope had to be elected by the cardinals from all Christendom, and an emperor by the electoral princes of the empire, who included three cardinals. Both, therefore, had to make political concessions to attain their high office. On the whole the pope and the church were stronger than the emperor, in contrast to the 'Avignon captivity' of the popes by the kings of France. But many people did not want the church to dominate the lay side. They held that it should determine what was right and wrong and lay down the law as a modern legislature does, but that the lay rulers – what we would call the executive and judiciary – should be independent. Our ideas about the separation of church and state, and of the legislature from the executive and judiciary, go back in part to this struggle.

The contest was not on national lines, with the Italians for the papacy because Rome was in Italy and the Germans for the empire because the emperor was usually a German. On the contrary, in Germany there were always great dukes and princes who opposed the elected emperor of the day; and Italy was a land of semi-independent cities, in each of which there was a faction that wanted the peace and order of the empire and opposed the local tyranny of the church or of the anti-imperial faction. The greatest medieval poet, the Florentine Dante, was a strong supporter of the empire, and his *De Monarchia* argued that peace in Italy as elsewhere in Christendom could only be maintained by a strong single universal authority separate from the church.

The great royal families had no sense of being limited to a particular 'nation' or territory.[2] Great families reigning in many realms, like the Plantagenets in the west and the Hohenstaufen in Germany and Italy, foreshadow later dynasties like the Habsburgs and Bourbons who could aspire to organize all Europe on a hegemonial basis; but that was beyond the power of any medieval ruler.

The very great families were exceptions; the function and livelihood of the lesser nobility usually bound them to their fiefs almost as securely as the peasants and serfs who worked their land. For many centuries attachment to the land, the sense of belonging to a locality, did not mean a sense of nationality as we understand it today. Feelings of solidarity were very local, hardly extending beyond a city or a well-defined region. One dialect shaded almost imperceptibly into the next, the Romance languages from the Low Countries to Portugal and Sicily and the Germanic from Holland to Vienna. But the concept of quasi-ethnic German, French and other 'nations' already existed. In the west from the twelfth century a sense of belonging to a royal realm developed in addition to men's more local ties and their sense of membership of all Christendom. In the eastern part of Christendom princes and – to a much greater extent than in the west – autonomous cities gradually also established territorially defined realms. But the structure of the 'Holy Roman Empire of the German Nation' and the intense local patriotism of Italian and other cities hindered the development of what later came to be called nation states, and loyalties remained diffused and uncertain. Germans and Italians were to become aware of linguistic and cultural nationhood long before there was a single administrative state to focus their loyalty. This difference between western and central Europe complicated the subsequent development of the European society of states, and remained unresolved until late in the nineteenth century.

MEDIEVAL ATTITUDES TO WAR AND JUSTICE

Medieval Christendom was an age of diffused and local violence, to which the fractured nature of authority certainly contributed. Though random violence and pillage occurred frequently enough, they were generally condemned by responsible men, in the nobility as well as the clergy. Such men were therefore concerned to establish when the particular and organized resort to arms called war was legitimate and right in the eyes of God. Before about the year 1000, when the Arabs, Vikings, Huns and Magyars were ravaging Christendom, fighting to defend it was clearly a necessity, and also fitted in well with the ideals of the Germanic peoples who had imposed their kingdoms on Europe. But as Christendom became more settled and more civilized, the

144

church took a great interest in the question of whether any war
between Christians was permissible and, if so, what kind of war was
just and how it should be waged. There was no significant doubt in
ancient Greece that war was a permissible way of settling disputes
between one polis and another, though there were arguments about
individual acts of war and high-handedness, such as the Corinthian
accusation that the Athenians were establishing a tyranny over all
Hellas. The idea that a war could be unjust, contrary not merely to
the will of a particular deity which protected a city but to the will of
all heaven, was not a Greek one. It can be detected in Chinese philosophy: the defensive concept of the Mohists can be regarded as incorporating this idea. But as a seminal and conscious issue in modern
civilization, it derives from the concern of the medieval church and
the more enlightened nobility.

The basic position of the medieval church was that all acts of warfare
against other Christians were essentially wrong. For instance, the pope
pronounced that William the Conqueror had just cause to invade
England to claim his rights against Harold in 1066; but the church
required every man, on the winning side as well as the losing one,
who had taken a life in battle to do penance for it. What then was a
just war between Christians?

St Thomas Aquinas, the greatest of the medieval church philosophers, devised a series of categories to determine which resorts to
force between Christians were just. 'For a war to be just', he wrote,

> three things are necessary. First, the authority of the sovereign
> by whose command the war is to be waged. For it is not the
> business of the private individual to declare war. . . . It is the
> business of those in authority to have recourse to the sword of
> war in defending the common weal against external enemies. . . .
> Secondly, a just cause is required, namely that those who are
> attacked should be attacked because they deserve it on account
> of some fault. Thirdly, it is necessary that those who wage war
> should have a rightful intention, so that they intend the advance-
> ment of good. . . . For it may happen that a war is declared by
> a legitimate authority, and for a just cause, and yet be made
> unlawful through a wicked intention.[3]

Aquinas quoted with approval St Augustine's list of wicked intentions,
including the cruel thirst for vengeance, an unpacific and relentless
spirit, the fever of revolt and the lust for power, and also endorsed
Augustine's dictum that we go to war that we may have peace.

The ideals of the church and those of the nobility blended in medieval civilization. Michael Howard describes the process as follows:

To bear arms, to have a crest on one's helmet and symbols on one's shield instantly recognizable in the heat of battle, became in European society for a thousand years a symbol of nobility. In the Middle Ages it was a symbol of *function* and available to all who performed that function. The nobility was not yet a close hereditary caste; war was still a career open to the talents. But having achieved nobility through military prowess, the man-at-arms was expected to comport himself according to a certain code of conduct. . . . The concept of 'chivalry' itself, which was in essence simply the behaviour of chevaliers or knights . . . hymned the virtues not only of courage, but of honour, gentleness, courtesy and, by and large, chastity. The chevalier had to be not only sans peur but sans reproche. Knighthood was a way of life, sanctioned and civilized by the ceremonies of the Church until it was almost indistinguishable from the ecclesiastical orders of the monasteries. Indeed, in the twelfth century military orders – the Templars, the Knights of St John, the Teutonic Knights – were established in conscious imitation of the monastic foundations. The sword-belt and spurs set the knight apart as distinctively as the tonsure did the monk and the priest; and in the mythical figures of Parsifal and Galahad priest and knight became indistinguishable, equally dedicated, equally holy, the ideal to which medieval Christendom aspired. This remarkable blend of Germanic warrior and Latin sacerdos lay at the root of all medieval culture.[4]

A holy war, against infidels outside the bounds of Christendom, was a different matter from quarrels between Christians. The church especially still remembered vividly the long struggle of Christendom to defend itself from the attacks of the non-Christian Saracens, Vikings and peoples of the steppe. It held that when Goliath and his Philistines went up from the plains against Jerusalem, it was just of David to kill him in order to defend what was rightfully the Lord's. So, by extension, wars against the Muslims and the heathen to rescue (Latin) Christians in occupied territories like Spain, or to redeem the Holy Land, were holy wars or crusades. A crusade was an enterprise of all Christendom and had to be proclaimed by the pope, preached and organized by the clergy as well as by lay rulers and open to all Christians. It was not a matter for unilateral decision by a lay ruler for his own advantage. The Muslims had much the same ideas about the distinction between holy wars against unbelievers and wars between Muslim rulers.

Of course princes and other men went to war for all sorts of reasons. But in the Middle Ages they could not, in practice, admit that they were resorting to war for reasons of expediency or to assert their power, as became possible later. War against other Christians needed careful justification. The argument was usually a legal one, concerned with who was the rightful ruler of a territory or whether he had forfeited that right. Medieval Christendom, like the Arab world, inherited from the Roman Empire a great concern with law and justice; and the judicial function was the particular domestic responsibility of the king or prince. Therefore justice and legal argument were very present in the minds of medieval rulers in their quarrels with each other. Justice in the Middle Ages was not an abstract ethical concept, nor was it based on equality: each person had certain rights particular to his station in life and to him as an individual, and justice meant assuring to each what was rightly and legitimately his or hers. In French the word *droit* still means both right and law.

This association between war and the concepts of legitimacy and justice continues to colour our thinking on the subject, and makes the arguments of Aquinas seem surprisingly contemporary. At a more mundane level the aim of the medieval church, and responsible lay rulers also, was to enlist the use of **force in the service of order**. Aquinas's rules for just war between Christians were designed to enhance the security of legitimate possession. The duty of the knight was to champion just causes against wrongful oppressors. The church's proclamation of crusades derived from the need for collective action to make all Christendom more secure. Augustine's dictum that we go to war that we may have peace shows an awareness of the need to maintain order similar to the modern concept of a peacekeeping force. In an age when lay authority was exceedingly fragmented and the authority of the church had no force under its command, all these aspirations reflected the desire to achieve the benefits of peace, order and security which in ancient systems were associated with the imperial half of our spectrum. It is not surprising that the church, which preserved the memory of the Roman universal empire and its advantages, was especially interested in order. But neither the church, which regarded its independence from lay authority as indispensable, nor most responsible lay rulers challenged the legitimacy of fragmented feudal power. Only burghers opposed to the church and the immediate supporters of powerful rulers looked towards an *imperator* of all Christendom who would possess real and universal power: the ideal described in Dante's *De Monarchia*.

There were in the Middle Ages two main ways of settling disputes about rights, when the authority of a king or the church was not strong enough to ensure compliance with a verdict. Both are relevant to our present international society, where there is also no overarching authority. One was trial and verdict by a man's peers: not any twelve people, but those in a similar station in life to the disputants. Today judgements on the action of a state, or on disputes between states, are pronounced by other states: for instance, in the Security Council of the United Nations or by judges who in practice follow the policies of their states in the International Court of Justice. Such judgements, like the jury system in domestic law, have roots in medieval practice.

The other way of settling disputes, especially between nobles, was the duel. Many medieval 'wars' were extended duels between two lords and their retainers disputing a legal claim. The concept of war as a duel is a very old one, which still plays a part in international relations. In the Middle Ages it was generally believed that the man with the just cause, he whose heart was pure (on the issue), would have the strength of ten, and that in battle God would uphold the right. The belief that the just cause tended to win may have had some foundation in fact.[5] It certainly represented an attempt to give even the duel a bias towards order and legitimate possession.

THE EXPANSION OF EUROPE

No aspect of medieval society is more important for this study than the beginnings of the long process of expansion. The expansion of Europe carried European civilization over all the rest of the world, and actual European rule over most of it. European power and influence reached their climax in the nineteenth century, and still continued to spread in certain areas in the first half of the twentieth. The consequences of that worldwide expansion, and its decline in our time, constitute one of the most important aspects of contemporary international society. We must therefore observe its beginnings, and note its progress at each stage of the development of the European system.

By the year 1000 Scandinavia, Poland and Hungary had been brought into the fold of Latin Christian civilization. Medieval Europe was then strong and dynamic enough to expand in three directions. The most lasting was south and south-west, to push the Saracens and Moors out of Italy and Spain, and to reconquer lands which were still predominantly Latin and Catholic in population but ruled and extensively settled by Arabs and Moors. As the great area of the Iberian peninsula was reconquered, the Islamic population was gradually driven out and its place taken by immigrants of all classes from France and other parts of Christendom. The native Catholic population had learnt much from the more developed Islamic civilization, from agricultural techniques to the ideas of Aristotle; and the Christian monarchies which replaced the Arab emirates continued to learn from the *sabio Moro*, the wise Moor, and from the large and civilized Jewish communities whose origins went back to the Carthaginian settlements.

The corresponding reconquest of southern Italy and Sicily was carried out by Norman adventurers from the north of France. The techniques learnt from the Muslims which were relevant to conditions further north quickly spread through Christendom. Among the most valuable was the reintroduction into Christendom of Greek philosophy, which illuminated and transformed the Latin Church in the fields of religion and science, so that Aristotle acquired an authority alongside that of the Hebrew prophets and the fathers of the church.

The second direction of European expansion was south-east, across the Mediterranean to recover for Christendom the Holy Land of Palestine, and to establish Latin Christian kingdoms and lordships in wider areas of the Levant. These crusading incursions into the heartland of Islam met with a partial success. 'Outremer' – as the Frankish, that is west European, colonies in the eastern Mediterranean were called – maintained themselves perilously for some centuries. They were established largely by the martial vigour of the French and Normans, and were finally evicted by the recruitment to Islam of the equally martial Turks. At the same time trade between Christendom and the Levant flourished and expanded. It was organized by the Europeans and transported in European ships; and it greatly enriched the Italian trading cities, particularly Venice which was geographically well placed to deliver eastern produce into central Europe and to provide a channel for European goods to the markets of the Muslim world. In these various ways there developed a strategic and economic involvement of the Latin west with Turkish-dominated Islam, and rules and institutions to regulate that involvement, which also played a major part in the evolution of the European states system.

The third direction of European expansion was eastwards into the pagan or heathen lands round the Baltic between western Christendom and the fragmented, Byzantinized world of Russia. The eastern crusades were partly a Christianizing mission, a continuation of the Carolingian conquest of Germany. The Poles, Germans and Scandinavians pushed forward the frontier of Christendom to the western fringes of Russian settlement, converting the local peoples to the Latin Church (to whose Protestant and Catholic traditions they still belong) and bringing into the area western nobility, clergy and especially townspeople and artisans. The consequences of this eastward expansion for Russia, for the European states system and for the expansion of Europe were to prove equally momentous.

All three thrusts of medieval expansion were primarily religious in inspiration, and it was the Cross which conferred legitimacy and approval on them in medieval eyes. But there was also land hunger, and the desire of restless nobles for glory and lordship, and of artisans and traders for new markets. All the elements which in varying proportions have made up the amalgam of motives for European expansion were present. But in the Middle Ages religion – not fanaticism but the acceptance of an obligation – seems to have played a larger part than since. It is an anachronism to attribute to the Middle Ages the more important roles which the other motives came to play in subsequent centuries.

The Middle Ages provided the Europeans who followed them with a dynamic, developing and expanding civilization. The period also left them a very distinctive heritage, not least in the field of our concern, the management of closely involved communities. Authority and administration were divided and diffused, while ethical standards and assumptions developed new insights. The long relative continuity of the imperial tradition of the ancient world, from Assyria to the caliphate, was sharply broken, in spite of the organization of the church and the memory of the Roman Empire.

The subsequent development of the European international society of states was conditioned by its medieval origins. Abstract reasoning and expedient ways of dealing with new problems played their part, as did the revival of the classical tradition. But the distinctive medieval inheritance was equally important. The patterns which evolved later in Europe were shaped by the continuing interaction of reason and experience with men's attempts to defend or alter the ideas and institutions of the Middle Ages. The worldwide expansion of the European international system was itself a continuation of the expansion of medieval Christendom, and spread the rules, institutions and values elaborated in Europe over the whole world. Our present global society of states, which is derived from the European system, contains much that is comprehensible only in the light of the medieval heritage and the reaction against it.[6]

NOTES

1 For instance, St Anselm was born in the Alps and became a leading bishop in Normandy and then Archbishop of Canterbury; St Thomas Aquinas from Naples spent much time teaching in Paris; St Boniface was born in England and spent much of his life in Germany.

2 Perhaps the best example of a royal line whose eminence lifted it beyond any one realm is the Plantagenets. Henry II of England, who did more than anyone to establish the English common law, came from the Loire as Count Henri d'Anjou. His mother had been Holy Roman Empress. His wife Eleanor of Aquitaine, perhaps the most remarkable woman of the twelfth century, was the effective ruler of about a quarter of France in her own right, and had been married to the King of France before marrying the King of England. She and Henry saw themselves as the first family of Christendom; many of their sons became kings and their daughters queens. One

daughter, Eleanor, Queen of Castile, is notable for being the only woman in European history who was the grandmother of two saints, both crusaders, one a king of France and the other a king of Castile.

3 St Thomas Aquinas, *Summa Theologica*, 2–2, question 40. See also A. Holmes (ed.), *St Thomas Aquinas: War and Christian Ethics*,

4 Michael Howard, *War in European History*, Oxford, Oxford University Press, 1976, pp. 4–5.

5 Ornithologists report that this is the case in territorial disputes between birds.

6 I should have liked to include this brilliantly creative period, the foundation of European civilization, in our list of systems and indeed societies of states. Medieval authorities – the elected pope and his appointed bishops, the elected emperor in the eastern half of Christendom, the hereditary kings and other nobles, and the free cities – all had legitimacy in their elaborate and overlapping governance, and engaged in co-operation and conflict within the same cultural matrix, with recognized rules, institutions, codes of conduct and values. But the longer I considered the matter, the surer I became that medieval government was too diffused, and mostly too local, for us to consider it as divided into separate states. For instance neither the realm of France, nor the lands of the Plantagenets which included large parts of it, were what we mean by states. Nor did the communities of Christendom form a system in the sense defined in Chapter 1, even to the extent that this was true of the 'seamless cloth' of Islam; and the rules and institutions of Christendom were not devised to manage the pressures of a system, which is how we have described a society of states. Towards the end of the period central administration of territorially defined realms gradually began to crystallize out; but the vertical division of Europe marks the dissolution of the medieval pattern.

14

THE RENAISSANCE IN ITALY
The *stato*

The Renaissance is important both generally and culturally in the history of Europe and the world, and also in particular for the evolution of the concept of the state and of relations between states. The Renaissance was essentially an Italian phenomenon.

The seminal contribution of the Italian Renaissance to the states system was made during the century from 1420 to 1527. But of course its origins reach back into the Middle Ages and classical antiquity, and outside Italy it continued for a long time. In the year 1420 Pope Martin V, himself a Roman nobleman, rode into Rome and put an end to the schism of the papacy and the alternative popes in Avignon. In 1453 the Ottoman Turks captured Constantinople, causing a large number of Greek scholars to flee, mainly to Italy, and so to help the revival of classical Greek learning that was a major feature of the Renaissance. In 1492 Columbus, an Italian from Genoa in the service of Castile, 'sailed the ocean blue' and discovered the New World, and in 1498 the Portuguese Vasco da Gama found the ocean route to India, cutting out the Mediterranean. These discoveries had immense consequences for Europe and the relations between its communities. One result was to displace Italy from its position as the focus of Latin Christendom. But the Italian Renaissance was over before men realized this. The sack of Rome by the army of the Habsburg emperor in 1527 finally established the long domination of Italy by the Habsburgs and the French that lasted until well into the nineteenth century.

It so happened that for a century after 1420 the other powerful rulers of western Europe were absorbed in their own affairs. There was a hundred-year lull in the regular French and imperial interventions in Italy which had marked the preceding centuries and which resumed at the end of the period. During that century also the Ottoman Turks were building up their strength ominously in the east but were not yet strong enough to threaten Italy. The peninsula was largely left to itself.

The essence of the Renaissance was humanism. The word has changed its meaning over time, like so many others. In the Renaissance it meant no longer seeing God as the measure of all things, but concentrating attention on man and his potential achievements. Two aspects of Renaissance humanism concern us. One was direct access to the classical and especially Greek experience, which had been accessible to only a few west Europeans and only in Christian guise. The other was the diffusion of a liberal spirit of enquiry, and a feeling that men could and should think things out anew.

Suddenly in Italy in that century a great number of men and a few women used their imagination both in learning and in the arts. There was tremendous speculation about the real nature of the world and man's purpose in it, absolutely free from the teachings of Christianity which had hitherto inspired and confined such speculation. Similarly there was an uninhibited quest for beauty, for the new forms which had been recovered by digging up the remains of Roman and Greek civilization which were then plentiful all over Italy. Because man was now the measure of things, beauty and truth were especially associated with the proportions of the human body and the human mind, as they had been in classical Greece. Humanists did not care whether the shape of the body and the ideas of the mind which they saw and copied were unethical or indecent by Christian standards. In the Middle Ages the question had been whether something was right or wrong: now it was a question of whether it was true or untrue, beautiful or ugly, effective or futile. A new spirit of earthy realism and new scientific formulae were applied to painting and to politics, to war and to statecraft.

But the Renaissance humanists, in discarding medieval Christendom, fell in love with ancient Greece and Rome. Men do not always see with objective realism what they fall in love with. So the humanists, realistic in other matters, were unrealistic about the wisdom of the ancients. It seemed to them so new, so beautiful, so profound that some of them got drunk on it. Politically the Italian humanists were attracted to the individual city state of republican Rome rather than the memory of the universal authority and security of the empire which had been cherished in the Middle Ages. In Greece they loved the ideals and the teaching and the arts of the city-state period, because they themselves lived in city states. Italy during that century was in fact remarkably like ancient Hellas.

The buoyancy, the animation, the excitement of discovery of the Italian Renaissance were bought at a price. The sense of liberation, the quest for realism, for beauty, for the classical world, were the affair of a small educated elite. In the Middle Ages everyone, from princes to peasants, however different their way of life, shared a common set of beliefs. In a medieval cathedral like Chartres the blaze of colour, the sense of awe, the Bible stories told in pictures, impressed everybody alike and seemed a foretaste of paradise. The Renaissance created a new educated class with different values from the rest of the people. But it produced within this elite class a new unity of culture, of purposes and of techniques; and as it spread beyond the Alps to France and England, Germany and Spain, it carried this unity of the elite with it. The painter, the philosopher, the poet, the adventurer were not in rebellion against society, not left to starve or driven into exile, as they have tended to be in later times. The world of the Renaissance was a princely world, and many independent and semi-dependent rulers of Italy acted as patrons of artists and intellectuals, scientists and soldiers. They founded centres of learning to study, not Christian doctrine like the medieval universities sponsored by the church, but classical learning and humanist speculation. And, being princes, they were particularly interested in government and in relations with each other.

THE ITALIAN STATES

Italy was at that time a patchwork quilt of cities and principalities ranging from the substantial to the tiny. Its five main powers were the Kingdom of Naples in the south; Rome and the territories controlled by the popes in the middle; the trading city of Florence to the north of Rome; the great city of Milan in north Italy; and the island city of Venice at the head of the Adriatic. Interspersed between these powers were a multitude of smaller territories, some independent but most of them subject in one way or another to a more powerful neighbour while enjoying extensive local autonomy.

The focus of the Renaissance in Italy was the city of **Florence**, and the Florentines were its intellectual and artistic leaders, as the Athenians had been in the classical Greek culture. Florence came to be dominated – not constitutionally, but in practice, which is what counted in Renaissance Italy – by the Medici family. The Medici were bankers on a European scale; and their power was in large part the power of money intelligently used. The most famous member of the family was Lorenzo the Magnificent, a splendid and wealthy patron of all the arts, a great beautifyer of Florence. The model for Botticelli's *Venus*, the nude pagan goddess which is a symbol of the Renaissance, was generally recognized as a mistress of Lorenzo. But he was also the shrewdest of the leading Italian statesmen: concerned to control not only the difficult and factious city of Florence, but also the whole Italian political scene in order to ward off the dangers that threatened Florence and the Medici bank from the outside.

Politically the most important city in Italy was once again **Rome**. The extensive area under papal government was geographically central, and Rome was pre-eminent in its possession of acknowledged authority. A series of Renaissance popes stopped thinking of themselves primarily as the spiritual heads of the church throughout Christendom, and became instead local Italian princes, great patrons of pagan classical learning and the arts. Their real aim was to carve out an area in central Italy which they and their family could dominate. The most remarkable was Alexander Borgia, a Catalan bishop who became a worldly Italian prince and shocked pious Christians by his secular and cynical approach to the papacy. (His exploitation of the papacy for dynastic ends is well illustrated by his practice of leaving his daughter Lucretia in charge of the papacy during his absences from Rome.) His son Cesare Borgia was something of a military and political genius, utterly unprincipled and remarkably effective. He was the hero of Machiavelli's *The Prince*, and might have succeeded in uniting most of Italy under Borgia control if luck had been more with him. Most Renaissance popes pursued, with variations, the policy of the Borgias.

The third great power of Italy, in many ways the most impressive of all, was **Venice**. The spectacular trading city, built on islands at the head of the Adriatic, was originally a Byzantine settlement, and provided the principal commercial link between the Levant and Christendom north of the Alps. Like the Corinthians, and like the Dutch later in the European system, the Venetians were a community which lived by trade and shipping. Until the end of the Middle Ages they imported most of their food, but then they began to acquire territory on the mainland of Italy in the fertile Po valley, as well as holding a string of islands and fortified bases down the Adriatic and in the eastern Mediterranean. The Venetians elected their doge or prince, and the city was controlled by a directorate or committee of the merchant aristocracy, called the *signoria*. They were also known for the high place which they gave to their law, which was perhaps an echo of classical Rome. Whatever upredictable decrees and verdicts other Italian rulers might hand down, in Venetian territory everyone knew where he stood. The Venetians developed, rather later than Florence, the most luxurious and perhaps the most beautiful of all the European traditions of painting, music and civilized living.

The fertile plain of the Po was the richest land in Italy, and its focus had since Roman times been the great city of **Milan**. Landward expansion brought the Venetians into conflict with Milan, where in 1450 an able professional general, Francesco Sforza, had established himself as duke with effective control but without legitimate authority. The fifth major power in Italy was **Naples** in the south, an old-fashioned feudal kingdom but with disputed legitimacy. Its crown was claimed by the royal families of both Aragon and France, and its *de facto* ruler, Ferrante of Aragon, was himself illegitimate.

THE *STATO*

The Italian Renaissance produced a great concentration of power in the hands of princes. They were often new men, whose position depended on their own skill and wits rather than on legitimate authority. Some aspects of the power of all five major Italian governments were illegitimate. Not only the Sforzas and the Medici, but also the popes who misused their power for territorial conquest, the land-hungry Venetians and the cynical rulers of Naples, all wanted to turn the real but naked power they had acquired *de facto* into something more legitimate, an authority which they exercised by right, *de jure*, and which would normally be obeyed without compulsion. Power – *il potere, le pouvoir,* the being able to – has always been the central issue of politics in a political society, as opposed to one so ordered by tradition and custom that all exercise of authority is fixed. The Renaissance Italian contribution was to develop new techniques of acquiring and consolidating real power, within a territorial area and extending beyond it. The naked power which an Italian ruler wielded was called a **stato**. The word then meant a state or situation, in the sense in which we use the term 'status quo'. After several transformations it became our word 'state' in the sense of a governmental authority or the political form of a nation. The central political problem of the Italian Renaissance rulers who had established the naked power of a *stato* was how to give the authority of legitimacy to it.

Machiavelli's description of Cesare Borgia paints a vivid picture of the authoritarian Renaissance *stato*, consolidating its power internally and expanding where possible at the expense of its neighbours. Machiavelli hoped for a strong man to unify Italy and keep out the foreigners. He was sent by Florence to report on Cesare's conquests which were coming very close to Florentine territory, and was much impressed:

> I will give two examples which have occurred within our memory, those of Francesco Sforza and Cesare Borgia. Francesco, by appropriate means and through great abilities, rose from a citizen to become Duke of Milan, and what he attained after a thousand difficulties he maintained with little trouble. On the other hand Cesare Borgia acquired his position by his father's influence, and lost it when that influence failed, although he adopted every measure and did everything that a prudent and

capable man could do to establish himself firmly in those positions that the arms and favours of others had given him. I know of no better precepts for a new prince to follow than may be found in his actions; and if his measures were not successful, it was through no fault of his own but only by the most extraordinary malignity of fortune.

After describing various stratagems of the Borgias to gain control of various parts of central Italy, Machiavelli continues:

By suppressing the leaders and making their partisans his friends, the duke [Cesare] laid a very good foundation for his power, having all the Romagna with the Duchy of Urbino, and having gained the support of the inhabitants, who began to feel the benefits of his rule. And this part is worthy of note and of imitation by others. When he took the Romagna, it had previously been governed by weak rulers, who had despoiled their subjects rather than governed them and given them more cause for disunion than for union, so that the province was a prey to robbery, violence and every kind of disorder. He therefore judged it necessary to give them a good government in order to make them peaceful and obedient to his rule. For this purpose he appointed Remirro de Orco, a cruel and able man, to whom he gave the fullest authority. This man was highly successful in making the country orderly and united in a short time; whereupon the duke, thinking that such excessive authority was not expedient . . . decided to show that if any cruelty had taken place it was not by his orders but due to the harsh disposition of his agent. He had him cut in half and placed one morning in the public square at Cesena. The ferocity of this spectacle caused the people both satisfaction and amazement.

For the future, he [Cesare] had to reckon that a new head of the Church would not be friendly to him and would try to take away what Alexander had given him. He thought he could insure himself against this in four ways: first by killing all the relatives of those rulers whom he had despoiled; second by winning over all the Roman nobles, so as to hold a new pope in check through them; third by getting as much control over the college of cardinals as he could; and fourth by acquiring enough power [*imperio* is Machiavelli's interesting word] before the pope died to resist a first attack. At the death of Alexander he had managed three of these four things, and almost managed the fourth. . . . If at Alexander's death he had not been ill, everything would have been easy for him.

Looking back on the duke's actions, I cannot blame him. He

seems to me someone to hold up, as I have done, as an example to all who have risen to power by fortune and the arms of others. For with his great spirit and high intentions he could not have governed otherwise, and only the shortness of Alexander's life and his own illness worked against him. Any new ruler who thinks it necessary to protect himself against enemies, to win friends, to conquer by force or by fraud, to make himself loved and feared by the people and followed and respected by the hired troops, to destroy those who could or might harm him, to introduce new ways into old traditions, to be severe and kind, magnanimous and liberal, to suppress a disloyal militia and create a new one, and to keep the friendship of kings and princes so that they are glad to help him and hesitate to harm him, can find no more vivid example than the actions of this man.[1]

Allowing for all the differences between Renaissance Italy and Maurya India, *The Prince* reminds us of Kautilya's advice to Chandragupta. Machiavelli looked cold-bloodedly at politics, both domestic and external, and described statecraft as he saw it, explaining how a prince could seize power and conquer territory, and taking current and classical models to learn what was expedient. Machiavelli's *Prince* corresponds in politics to his fellow Florentine Botticelli's *Venus* in painting: a statement of what the human body or human behaviour is like naked, when stripped of Christian inhibitions and moral respectability.

HIRED ARMIES

Military operations were now a matter of realism not rights, as they had been in the Middle Ages. The motto of the Plantagenet kings was 'Dieu et mon droit' – God and my right: Renaissance Italians fought for neither *Dieu* nor *droit* but for material advantage. Kings had needed money to wage war before the Renaissance. Now it became evident that money was the sinew of war, that military power was a factor of economic power. The reasons which move rulers to go to war and men to fight, in different times and places, almost always include gain, even in wars of religion; in Renaissance Italy gain played a dominant part, in the minds both of rulers and of the troops they hired.

For some time the Italian cities had hired **mercenary armies** to fight for them. The Medicis and the Venetian *signoria* well understood that in the predatory and dangerous condition of Italy they needed armed force to defend themselves; and that if they had the armed force they could increase their security and their power by territorial expansion.

Whatever else the Medicis and the *signoria* were prepared to do for their city, they were not prepared or able to lead a military campaign like a medieval king. Instead they hired a professional military commander, and gave him a *condotta*, a contract to conduct a given campaign. A **condottiere** was more than a professional general; he was a military contractor, prepared to serve one employer and then another, hoping for the opportunity to acquire a realm or *stato* for himself. The men he commanded were also fighting for money, as a profession. They were not citizen warriors like the hereditary armed proprietors of the Greek city states and early Rome, but soldiers, a word derived from the Italian *soldi* meaning money or pay, and they were determined not to get themselves killed if they could help it.

The hiring of troops was nothing new. In the times of the Greek city states there were *condottieri* and paid soldiers, like Xenophon and his ten thousand who were hired by a Persian pretender and the Greek mercenaries employed by the merchant rulers of Carthage. In the special circumstances of medieval Spain the Cid was a *condottiere* who worked for Christian and Muslim princes and finally acquired a realm like the successful Italians. In the Macedonian system mercenary armies became the rule, and war was largely waged with them by rulers who had carved out *statos* and then legitimized them. The same was true of the Italian Renaissance. In such conditions military operations tend to become a display of power and resolve, calculating and unfanatical, conducted to cause the minimum damage compatible with the success of the contract.

RESIDENT DIPLOMACY

The Italian Renaissance princes also made a seminal contribution to the development of the diplomatic dialogue, one of the major integrating mechanisms of the European system. Since the Assyrians, successful rulers have understood the importance of being well informed about their neighbours. In the dangerous world of the Italian Renaissance a sustained flow of reliable intelligence about strategic and economic threats and opportunities was particularly necessary. In medieval Europe there was no regular system of news, and men lived on travellers' tales and rumour. But two powers in Italy had agents throughout Europe reporting accurately what was going on. The papacy had clerical envoys and nuncios in every Christian court and realm, who maintained close contacts with the local clergy, so that a great stream of information about the rest of Europe poured into Rome. Many of these records survive. Reports also came in from all over Europe and the Levant to the merchant princes of Venice. The Venetian *signoria* were the best-informed rulers in Europe; and the documents they received are still invaluable for the reconstruction of European history. In the Renaissance a third set of reports began to be important, those which the Medici received from the managers of foreign branches of the Medici company.

These reporters were not noblemen: they were usually humble people, skilled servants of their employers, who knew how to get reliable information and report it back shrewdly, cynically and of course secretly. The popes, the *signoria* and the Medici increasingly used them to talk to kings and princes and even the Ottoman sultan, because they understood the business which their employer had instructed them to handle. Kings and princes wanted to hear a message in confidence from the great Italian rulers and to send a confidential answer back. These humble agents who resided abroad were the origins of our network of embassies and our diplomatic dialogue of today.

This was the beginning of a new kind of diplomacy. No state discussed in the first section of this book sent out permanent representatives to other independent states, though the Persian satraps and their equivalents fulfilled some of these functions in the different context of overlordship over other communities. One of the most important technical inventions of the European system of managing relations between independent communities was the resident agent of a power, the envoy who stayed on the spot.

But there were also, in the rest of Europe and even in Italy, embassies of another more medieval kind. When for instance the King of France wished to communicate with the Holy Roman Emperor, he would send a great personage, perhaps a member of his family, on an embassy with the display and the military escort that worthily reflected the dignity of the realm; and if it was a question of a marriage the princess and her retinue would go too. The great cavalcade would order its affairs according to its own rules and customs, a detached bit of France in another realm. But because of family quarrels such embassies were not always effective instruments of a king. Today the fading ceremonial and glitter of embassies, and more importantly the concept of extraterritoriality and diplomatic immunity, come from those noble cavalcades and not from the useful but humble agents of Italian rulers.

THE BALANCE OF POWER

Many rulers of the new Italian *statos* were eager to expand their power outwards as well as strengthen it at home, and they all understood the need for vigilance against other rulers whose expansion threatened them. Much of the diplomatic dialogue between the mutually suspicious Italian rulers concerned such opportunities and threats, and projects for joint action to deal with them. This anti-hegemonial concern led to the development of a new concept unknown in the ancient world, the conscious aim of a **balance of power**.

Sforza, who had seized power in Milan with Lorenzo dei Medici's support, became worried about the expanding power of Venice across northern Italy towards his own domain. Venice might become so strong that it would overshadow the whole peninsula. Sforza therefore invited Lorenzo to join him in opposing the Venetians. He pointed out that the *signoria* could afford the best *condottieri*, and that when they conquered a territory they reduced the taxes and posted up the laws in the public squares to show that Venice meant the rule of law and not the decrees of one man. Sforza did not say that the Venetians were wicked: that was not a Renaissance idea. His complaint was that they were dangerous because they were too successful. If things continued in this way, said Sforza, then the Venetians would soon be the *signori di tutta Italia*. Sforza meant not a direct administration or dominion but a Venetian hegemony, the ability to lay down the law to other rulers.

Lorenzo was shrewder than Sforza. He agreed that it was indeed necessary to oppose Venetian ambitions. But if Milan and Florence destroyed Venetian power altogether they would find themselves threatened by the pope or the Holy Roman Emperor, whom Venice helped to keep in check. Lorenzo also thought that if Sforza came to control the whole Po valley he too would threaten Florence. It was therefore not a question of this or that particular enemy, but of prudently assuring that nobody, not even his closest ally, became too strong. So he answered Sforza with the seminal phrase that the affairs of Italy ought to be kept in some sort of balance. This banking concept was remarkably apt. A conscious balance was to become one of the key elements of the European system. The discerning Florentine bankers saw that the problem was not Venice but power itself, and that the way to manage power was not to destroy it but to balance it with other power.

To sum up, the most significant contribution of Renaissance Italy to the evolution of the European states system was the territorial concentration of independent power, *de facto* and partly or wholly illegitimate, which was called the *stato* of a ruler. Renaissance Italy was a dangerous place, and a ruler who wanted to preserve and extend his *stato*, and to deal with other similar *statos* around him, had to be guided not by standards of right and wrong but by cool calculation of what was expedient. This calculation was called **ragione di stato**, reason of state. The watchful Renaissance rulers developed a new way of conducting a continuous dialogue with each other by means of permanent resident agents, who could also report accurately on conditions in the countries in which they resided. Rulers learnt to regard force as a technique of the *stato*, and as something to be bought for money, especially in the form of a hired *condottiere*, so that economic power translated into military power. The most far-seeing of them also perceived that the way to deal with a powerful *stato* was not to destroy it, which would release the power of other *statos* held in check by it, but to bring all the powers of the system – in this case Italy – into a complex and constantly shifting balance. These major innovations developed from the practices of Renaissance princes under the pressures of establishing and holding a *stato*. The practice preceded the theory. Theoreticians like Machiavelli described the practice after the event, sometimes with much insight. The hard statesmen of the Renaissance looked to Greek and Roman history for practical examples, but they were rarely guided by theory in calculating *ragione di stato*; and when they were, the results were usually unsuccessful.

NOTES

1 Machiavelli, *The Prince*, Chapter IX.

15

THE RENAISSANCE IN EUROPE
The *stato* outside Italy

We now need to look at the effect which the spread of the Italian Renaissance had on the organization of the rest of Christendom. Late medieval Europe down to about 1460 was still organized horizontally, held together especially by the universal church. Throughout Europe what were to become the issues of international relations, that is the relations of territorial lay authorities with each other and the disputes between princes and between them and the church, were still regarded as coming under a universal system of customary law, based on individual and local inheritances, rights and charters.

The western half of Christendom was made up of the independent realms of its kings and one or two almost-kings like the dukes of Burgundy. Each king stood at the apex of his kingdom's pyramid of government, with symbolic authority, and with his actual power more consolidated than before but still severely circumscribed by custom, by the autonomy of his vassals and by the local rights of towns and other holders of feudal privilege that operated more or less as they saw fit. These western kingdoms, stretching in a great arc from Iberia through France and Britain to Scandinavia, were still confederal structures. They had weak central governments with almost all power devolved not merely to the provinces but to the local level, and a whole range of social and economic activities were controlled from outside the realm. However, a certain national sentiment was beginning to weld together the populations of each kingdom.

The eastern half of Christendom, from the North Sea and the Baltic down to Sicily, was still formally subject to the dual universalism of empire and papacy. Emperor and pope were elected rulers representing rival coalitions of power, the twin peaks of a complex hierarchy. During the century of the Italian Renaissance this dual authority was in practice crystallizing out into a number of territorial *statos*, especially in Italy but also in the Netherlands and Germany. Many of these *statos* had real local power but much less legitimate authority than the western kingdoms.

In the second half of the fifteenth century the wonderful new world of Renaissance Italy began to fascinate the rest of Europe. The arts and sciences, the revival of classical learning, the amoral and realistic attitude of mind of the Italians penetrated courts and universities and the more educated nobility and bourgeoisie on the other side of the Alps. From the Renaissance *stato* developed new relations between princes, and the concept of a Europe organized as a system of sovereign and independent states, closely involved with one another but all jealously guarding their sovereignty. When the techniques evolved in Italy spread to the rest of Christendom, it was practical rulers and their counsellors who introduced them.

Western kings, in particular, came to realize the significance of the *stato* and of the much greater power which Italian rulers were able to concentrate in their own hands within the territory which they controlled. True, the most conspicuous Italians, from the Medicis, the Sforzas and the Borgias down to dozens of smaller rulers, had power without legitimacy. The western kings had legitimacy without much effective power. Those rulers who understood best the political lessons to be learnt from Renaissance Italy set about turning the legitimate but shadowy medieval overlordship of their realms into a territorial *stato* on the grand scale, with themselves as the real and absolute masters within the boundaries of their kingdom. The whole medieval diffusion of authority, including the independent power of the vassal nobility and the church, the charters and *fueros* of the cities, the parliaments and assemblies representing the various estates of the realm, must be made to yield actual power as far as possible to royal absolutism, even though it might be expedient (that favourite Renaissance concept) to let the outward forms continue to a large extent.

These new ideas and aspirations spread over the rest of Europe quite suddenly and quickly. The rulers who controlled the political destinies of western Christendom began to think of it as divided vertically into territorial *statos*, each able to do what it liked subject to the pressures which other *statos* were able to exert. However great the continuity in Europe in many other fields, the rapid spread of Italian ideas to other rulers marks a significant watershed for the evolution of the European states system. The words of the introduction to *The Cambridge Modern History*, written nearly a century ago, retain their validity. The Renaissance was

> the period in which the problems that still occupy us came into conscious recognition, and were dealt with in ways that are intelligible to us as resembling our own. It is this sense of familiarity which leads us to draw a line and to mark out the beginnings

of modern history. . . . Anyone who works through the records of the fifteenth and sixteenth century becomes conscious of an extraordinary change of mental attitude, showing itself on all sides. . . . [In the Middle Ages] a definite conception had been promulgated of a European commonwealth, regulated by rigid principles; and this conception was cherished as an ideal, however much it might be disregarded in actual practice. . . . This system wore away gradually, and was replaced by the plain issue of a competition between nations, which is the starting point of modern history.[1]

The process was indeed gradual. At the beginning of the sixteenth century there was not yet a competition between nations, or even between states in the modern sense of that term, but rather between *statos* dominated by monarchs determined to assert their sovereignty both internally over their own subjects and externally against the commonwealth of Europe or Christendom.

The ruler who most effectively learnt Italian ways, living in Italy until he almost seemed an Italian, was the king of the largest and richest realm in the west, Louis XI of France. In the twenty years after he came to the throne in 1461 he systematically reduced the power of the great noble families, the church and the parliaments of his realm, by force and fraud on Machiavellian lines. He established an Italian *stato* in France which was welcomed by many of his subjects, especially the townspeople, in spite of his high-handed ways. To the south in Iberia, Ferdinand of Aragon and Isabella of Castile, whose marriage made the united Kingdom of Spain, did much the same from about 1480. Ferdinand supplied the craftiness and a new Italian style of foreign policy, and Isabella the piety and the moral values esteemed by Spaniards; but both were equally determined to forge their realms into a *stato*, governed by the personal will of the 'Catholic kings'. At the same time Henry Tudor put an end to the prolonged stasis of the Wars of the Roses in England and established a strong monarchy. But Burgundy and the Netherlands were not welded into an effective *stato*, partly because some of their duke's rather scattered possessions were in the Holy Roman Empire and others in France, with populations that had little sense of belonging together in spite of their loyalty to the same princely house.

In the empire and Italy there were no independent kings. The Kingdom of Naples was held by the royal family of Spain, though the royal family of France also claimed it; and by the end of the fifteenth century the kingdoms of Bohemia and Hungary belonged to the Habsburg monarchy. Though the empire's electoral college of princes and cardinals chose one of their number to be emperor and king of

Germany in the same way as the cardinals chose one of their number to be pope, the imperial crown had no direct domain or revenue attached to it, and the emperor did not govern the lands of other princes, only his own. His authority may be compared to the Sumerian kingship: it was a hegemony for life, and like the Sumerian it depended in part on the authority of the office, which might shift at the next election, and in part on his own power. Getting anything done in the empire consequently involved prolonged and multiple negotiation. However, the electoral princes were still autonomous feudal lords and not yet sovereign rulers; and the smaller lords were even less so.

Renaissance ideas spread north of the Alps at a time when imperial authority was weakening internally, and was also shrinking at the fringes, so that the area to be consolidated became more wholly German. With the examples of Italy and France before them, some German magnates wanted to consolidate a single authority in Germany, and turn the whole empire into a *stato*. The imperial machinery of government was woefully inadequate for this purpose. The three elector archbishops from the Rhineland had a more statesmanlike vision of how to reform it than the lay princes. Berthold of Mainz took the lead in trying to establish an efficient central German government, which would be capable of maintaining order and raising revenue and armed forces like Louis XI and the Tudors. But the princes and cities of the empire were already more autonomous than the English or French nobility, and Berthold and his princely backers wanted the power of the emperor limited by an effective *Reichsrat* or imperial council, with himself as chancellor. A Renaissance *stato* could only be forged by the unfettered will of a single ruler. No such ruler of all Germany existed. Consequently the empire became a number of *statos* instead of one, with major consequences for the European states system.

The most powerful ruler in the empire in the late fifteenth century was Maximilian of Habsburg, an attractive, ambitious, able Renaissance prince. For fifty years a succession of Habsburgs had been elected emperor; but it soon became clear to Maximilian that he could not forge the whole empire into an Italian-style *stato* under his direct rule, and that Berthold and the major princes wanted to leave him the shadow of a strengthened authority while they controlled its substance. Maximilian therefore concentrated his efforts and used his authority as emperor elect (he was never formally crowned) to develop and consolidate a great personal Habsburg *stato*, a *Hausmacht*, by means of dynastic marriages and Italian techniques of power. As crown prince he had married the heiress of Burgundy and the Netherlands; and soon he inherited this great prize in the west. In the east he expelled the Hungarians from Vienna and arranged his own succession as king of Hungary. He later married a daughter of Sforza, the Duke of Milan. Maximilian thus held a broad but intermittent belt of hereditary realms and alliances stretching across the middle of Europe from Antwerp to Budapest. But the Habsburgs were still far from aspiring to exercise the hegemonial power in Europe which they later attempted. Maximilian's policies tended not to unite Europe but rather to fragment the empire.

The rival great princely families of the empire were equally interested in turning their dominions into *statos*, and in checking the power of the emperor and each other. The domains of the Wittelsbachs based on Bavaria, of the Wettins based on Saxony and of the Hohenzollerns in the north-east were better governed, safer and more prosperous than the parts of the empire fragmented into many small and quarrelling lordships; and as they became welded into *statos* they moved steadily towards more real independence.

It is possible to regard the failure to unify and modernize the empire into a German national kingdom on the same lines as France and Spain as one of the tragedies of Europe. But many people were glad to see the powerful forces there checking and balancing one another; for if the whole Holy Roman Empire, or even the German lands, had been unified into a single *stato*, its strength would have put it in a hegemonial position in all Christendom. The fragmentation of Germany into a number of *statos* left France the strongest power in the new Europe. And it became the settled policy of France in particular to support any group or movement that would help to keep the empire divided.

The power of the French crown had been greatly strengthened by Louis XI; and when from 1494 the kings of France invaded Italy to assert their claims in the peninsula, they seemed to be irresistible. To prevent French domination of Italy, the pope, perhaps with Avignon in mind, organized an anti-hegemonial coalition, called the Holy League. The league was based on Spain and the Habsburgs, who both had interests in Italy and elsewhere to protect against France. The anti-hegemonial alliance was cemented by a dynastic marriage between the Spanish and Habsburg families. (Ironically and by the accidents of inheritance this marriage was to bring Spain under Habsburg rule and so create the greatest hegemonial dynasty of Europe.) The Holy League brought most of Latin Christendom into a single system of *statos* for the first time. At that stage the Catholic kings in Spain and Maximilian in eastern Christendom were each concerned to weld diverse realms together into a single *stato* and to expand their rule geographically as opportunity offered. Beyond the area of their own authority they asked no more than the Medici formula writ large, namely that power, not just in the Italian peninsula but in the whole of Christendom, should be broadly balanced. That meant in practice that other *statos* should co-operate to some extent to curb the most powerful single monarch in Europe, the King of France. It was an anti-hegemonial aim. Neither the Spanish kings nor the emperor, nor on the other side the kings of France, yet had any constructive or overarching plan for the management of the whole of Christendom.

Thus the effect of Renaissance ideas in Europe north of the Alps was to push the area from the loose unities of medieval Christendom towards a new European system fragmented into territorial *statos* that acknowledged no general authority. The system moved towards the multiple independences end of the spectrum. But the newly forming *statos* of Europe impinged too much on each other to dispense with co-ordination of their foreign relations. As a compensation for the loss of medieval restraints, those rulers who felt most threatened by the power of the strongest *stato* began to form an anti-hegemonial protective association which covered much of what was still called Christendom, and gave Europe a measure of strategic cohesion and structure.

NOTES

1 S. Leathes (ed.), *The Cambridge Modern History*, Cambridge, Cambridge University Press, 1903, pp. 1–2.

16

THE HABSBURG BID FOR HEGEMONY

The Renaissance and the Reformation dislocated the horizontal structure of medieval Christendom. Three aspects of the sixteenth-century struggles to replace it with a new organization of Europe are of special concern to us. The first is the impulse which the Reformation itself, and the resulting massive religious stasis, gave to the fragmentation and verticalization of Europe. Second, we must look at the ways those who wanted to consolidate independent *statos* tackled the stasis, and their consequences. The third aspect is the Habsburg bid to establish a hegemonial authority in Christendom and to move the emerging states system away from fragmentation and towards the imperial end of our spectrum.

THE EFFECT OF THE REFORMATION ON THE EUROPEAN STATES SYSTEM

The immense and passionate explosion of the European spirit that we call the Reformation, including the Protestant movements and the corresponding reforms in that part of Latin Christendom which continued to call itself Catholic, was religious in origin and purpose. We shall not discuss those religious differences, but confine ourselves to the impact of the Reformation on the evolution of European international society and on the management of diverse groups and entities within a system. The Reformation complicated and distorted into unexpected shapes the new practices of statecraft associated with the Renaissance. In particular the religious stasis encouraged the recasting of the horizontal society of medieval Christendom into territorial *statos*. It distorted the gradual growth of 'national' loyalties within the new territorial centres of power. It opposed the concept that the distribution of power between the new *statos* should be in some way balanced, regardless of religion, in order to prevent the strongest of them from dominating the whole system. Beyond the confines of Christendom, it changed the nature of the continuing dramatic outward thrust of

169

European society, and it provided opportunities for the Ottoman Empire to expand in Europe.

The religious Reformation divides broadly into two parts. The first, associated with the German Martin Luther who proclaimed his doctrines in 1517, favoured moderate reform of the church. The Lutherans accepted a breach with the 'unredeemable' papacy; but they relied on Protestant bishops and on kings and other lay rulers to maintain order and authority both in religious and in lay affairs, and to defend the reformed areas from Catholic attempts to bring them back to the fold by force. Lutheranism was a movement native to the eastern half of Latin Christendom, and took hold particularly among Germans and Scandinavians.

The second part of the Reformation, associated with the Frenchman Jean Calvin who began his effective career at Geneva in 1536, was more radical. It rejected not only the papacy and certain doctrines but the hierarchical structure and tradition of the universal church, preferring that each congregation should choose its own ministers. Many Calvinists extended this principle to republican forms of lay government, on the theory that political like religious authority inheres in the body of the people, who may therefore choose and control those who govern on its behalf. The *Vindiciae contra Tyrannos* of 1579 asserted the right of a community to resist an oppressive ruler and to call in outside help if the local authorities agreed: it was a recipe for stasis. When existing governments tried to suppress these politically revolutionary ideas, the Calvinists formed quasi-military organizations capable of taking over the government. Calvinism and other radical sects spread mainly in the western half of Christendom, particularly in French-speaking lands, the Low Countries and Great Britain.

As the humanists of the Renaissance idolized the Greek and Roman classical texts and found there the lessons they wanted, so the Protestants used the Bible as another huge quarry of precepts and examples, from which they selected lessons for every walk of life. In the domain of statecraft and the ordering of society the Calvinists were particularly impressed by the independent Jewish states of the judges and the prophets, the chosen people of God standing alone against the surrounding kingdoms and empires, rather than by the imperial Roman world of St Paul. To them the word 'Roman' meant their persecutors, the Catholic Church and the Habsburg Empire, and evoked fear and hatred. The Protestant and especially the Calvinist interpretation of the Bible confirmed their commitment to a disintegrated Europe of wholly independent states, in some of which at least they would be free to enforce their religion and institute their form of society.

The Catholic Counter-Reformation was unable to restore the medi-

170

eval unity of Christendom by military force. The breach was much too wide for that. But reforming movements like the Society of Jesus gave that part of the church which remained loyal to the pope and the old traditions a new power corresponding to the increased power of the Italian *stato*, and new doctrines to justify it. The Catholic wing of the fragmented Latin Church remained committed to the imperial vision which had sustained it during the Dark Ages. It attracted the loyalty of those who still held to the traditional doctrines and rituals of their faith, and also those who retained the political ideal of a united Christendom and saw the Habsburgs as its standard bearers.

The momentous religious and political issues raised by the Reformation invoked the conscience, or the judgement, of each individual. Where the conscience of a subject differed from that of his ruler, the political effect was to weaken if not destroy the subject's acceptance of that ruler's authority and his unquestioning solidarity with his fellow subjects. For both Protestants and Catholics agreed that adherence to the true faith transcended all other loyalties. The result was colossal and prolonged stasis. Religious and civil wars, which pit men against their neighbours rather than against an external foe, are usually the most bitter of conflicts. The religious persecutions and the wars of religion engendered by the Reformation and the Counter-Reformation were the most damaging ordeal experienced by European civilization.

RESPONSES OF EUROPEAN RULERS

The tide of stasis and conflict developed between the subjects of almost every ruler in Europe, just when he or she was trying to transform a medieval realm into a *stato*. This turbulence might be expected to have hindered and perhaps disrupted the formation of integrated states whose inhabitants would acknowledge a primary loyalty to each other and to their prince, and thus to have enabled what we should recognize as a states system to come into being. In fact the turbulence had the opposite effect. The breaking of the unity of Christendom, and especially of that most horizontal of all medieval institutions, the universal church, reinforced rather than diminished the concentration of power into the hands of the rulers of states. The Lutherans in particular, but not only they, openly looked to princes for protection, and enjoined obedience to those who provided it. Lutheran support encouraged the independence of German princes who were organizing their own *statos*, and speeded up the spread of the new statecraft of power politics from Italy to the German parts of the Holy Roman Empire. The alienation of many subjects from their rulers, and the threat or reality of destructive civil war, posed very serious problems for the emerging states. Moreover, passionate religious loyalties cut across the new boundaries which rulers were trying to impose, and helped to involve the states increasingly with each other. All Europe, including the Ottoman Empire, seemed to be forming into two camps, Should a prince align himself with the greatest power in Europe, the Habsburg family, which was committed to the Counter-Reformation, or with those who for different reasons opposed the Habsburgs? Four examples of how sixteenth-century rulers tried to deal with these problems are relevant to our enquiry.

In **Spain** the new 'national' state created by the Catholic kings was identified with the Catholic Church and cemented by the successful conclusion of the reconquest from the Muslims. When Charles of Habsburg became King of Spain in 1516, church and state suppressed political and religious opposition to the monarchy. Most Spaniards, accustomed to the expulsion of Muslims, apparently regarded enforced conformity as a lesser evil than the religious civil war which was ravaging other parts of Europe. The Spanish option of enforced conformity was also fairly generally accepted in Italy, most of which was under Spanish or papal domination. It succeeded in keeping the peace and avoiding material destruction. Many dissident members of those communities emigrated or fled, and were partially replaced by the influx of Catholics from the domains of Protestant princes. This policy enabled the Habsburgs to turn the energies of Spain and Italy and the wealth of the Indies outward to establish their hegemony in Europe.

In **England** the active classes, especially merchants and townspeople and the new nobility and gentry, became increasingly Protestant in the course of the sixteenth century; but they looked to the monarchy to transform England from a feudal realm torn by conflicts between noble families into a national state. All but one of the Tudor rulers were *politiques*, people who put expediency before principle. They were engaged throughout the century in establishing an effective royal *stato*. Henry VIII made himself independent of the papacy, without becoming a Protestant. Two of his heirs and many of their moderate subjects wanted to avoid the havoc of religious war by establishing a single religious denomination broadly based enough to include the majority. The Church of England was a *politique* compromise, which kept the domestic peace. But England could not escape the meshes of the European system. The extent to which it could be governed according to the wishes of the Protestant majority depended internally on who wore the crown, and externally on how far other states could keep Habsburg power on a leash and thus tilt the emerging European system towards the multiple independences end of the spectrum. Three foreign policy options were theoretically available; but one, a whole-hearted commitment to the Protestant cause, was too dangerous to attempt. The English *politiques* opted to avoid commitment to either the Habsburg or the anti-hegemonial camp, and to keep England as the 'tongue of the balance'; but they also felt obliged to support other Protestant powers. Henry's daughter Mary, a cousin of the Habsburg Charles V and married to his son Philip II, chose the third option of the Catholic Counter-Reformation and a Spanish alliance, which made England a part of the Habsburg hegemonial structure. Her successor Elizabeth restored a balance at home by active support of the Church of England, and resumed the balancing act between France and the Habsburgs abroad. Philip II of Spain, legitimist, anti-French and somewhat *politique* in foreign policy, was prepared to leave Protestant Elizabeth alone so long as her heir was his enemy Mary Queen of Scots, a Catholic but half French and a former queen of France. When Protestant public pressure obliged Elizabeth to execute Mary, Philip tried unsuccessfully to bring England back into the Habsburg camp by force.

The Spanish option and its English variant were not available in the **Holy Roman Empire**, which was not a single *stato*. But the empire in Germany and the Netherlands evolved the most significant expedient for the future of the European states system. The medieval Guelf tradition of princely particularism and opposition to imperial authority, and the new Italian techniques of government which were teaching princes to turn their realms into *statos*, now combined with Lutheranism to divide the German areas of the empire in practice into a number of autonomous principalities. The rulers of these new *statos* increasingly saw the need for loyal subjects in order to avoid destructive internal stasis. Moreover, by the middle of the sixteenth century, after thirty years of inconclusive religious contention, warfare and negotiation, the German princes on both sides were war-weary, and wanted a lasting peace. So in 1555 they accepted the Augsburg settlement on the basis of *cujus regio ejus religio*. The essence of the *politique* Augsburg compromise was to allow rulers large and small, and even some individual towns, the right to choose the religious denomination of their *stato*, and to allow dissatisfied subjects to 'vote with their feet'. An extensive transfer of populations within Germany followed. Most migrants were glad to move to a territory where they could practise their variety of religion, and princes were equally pleased to gain loyal subjects in place of dissident ones. The migrations also confirmed the 'Calvinist' claim that the authority of a prince over his subjects was not to be taken for granted, but depended to some extent on a congruence between the prince and his people. The awareness of the rulers that they had a common interest was also the effective beginning of the 'princes' club' which was later to play a major part in the management of the European society of states.

The effect of the Augsburg compromise was to consolidate the separate states and mini-states into which the empire was crystallizing. But it also had hegemonial aspects. The rulers gained increased autonomy, but were not yet recognized as independent in the same way as, for instance, France or Sweden. The imperial institutions continued to be recognized as the legitimate authority. The princes accepted that the settlement should be partly negotiated and ratified by the Diet of the empire, but that those issues on which they did not want to commit themselves formally would be decreed by the Habsburg emperor. The Augsburg compromise brought peace to the empire for nearly sixty years, a long lifetime in those days, and greatly increased the personal happiness of many Germans.

The Netherlands were with parts of Italy the richest and most advanced provinces of the empire, and of Christendom. The emperor Charles V was born there; but his absentee government was widely resented and half the population became Calvinist. Partition and considerable movements of people according to their individual loyalties proved to be the painful but most practical answer to religious strife in the Netherlands too. The division was more cleanly cut than the mosaic in Germany. The predominantly Calvinist northern provinces seceded from the Habsburgs and from the Holy Roman Empire, and proclaimed their formal independence in 1581 after a long struggle. The United Provinces became a new type of state, a republic based on popular will and immigration. Its particularist provinces had federal and republican hankerings; but the times required a strong executive and monarchical authority, and under the pressure of the struggle with Spain the military and other aspects of statehood were largely forged by the elected princely family of Orange. The southern Netherlands became homogeneously Catholic and loyal to the Habsburgs, and remained so until at length they became the modern kingdom of Belgium.

The two options in the emerging states system – collaboration with, or anti-hegemonial opposition to, the Habsburg hegemonial structure – are most clearly visible in the case of **France**. France too was rent by Calvinism and by the dissidence of powerful noble families. The crown and the majority remained Catholic, so the Calvinists, called Huguenots, turned for protection to independent-minded nobles, including notably Henry of Bourbon, king of Navarre. They built up armed forces of their own, fortified strong-points, administered large territories, especially in the south and west, and defied the authority of the crown without formally rejecting it. The Counter-Reformation faction, the Catholic League led by the Guise family, acted in the same way in the north and east and in Paris. They wanted a Catholic Europe; they accepted hegemony as its necessary means, and they looked to the Habsburg enemies of the French crown as the champions of their cause. But France, unlike the empire, had been forged into a *stato* by Louis XI, and the fissiparous forces had less legitimacy. Many *politiques* and others who favoured a strong central authority supported the crown, and the wind blowing in favour of kings helped to hold the state together against the fragmenting forces.

Francis I's foreign policy, based on opposition to Spain and alliance with the Ottomans, proved unsuccessful. As the stasis between Catholics and Huguenots increasingly disrupted the power of the state, his son Henry II saw the Habsburg hegemonial structure as less dangerous to him and to his kingdom than the disintegration of royal authority inside France. Henry therefore came to favour an alliance with the Habsburgs so that the two great rulers of Christendom could deal with Protestantism and maintain order in Europe. The agreements associated with the Treaty of Cateau-Cambrésis in 1559 – four years after Augsburg – envisaged a joint dominion which was reminiscent of the Athenian–Spartan diarchy and foreshadowed the Holy Alliance to establish a hegemonic order and to deal with revolutionary stasis after the fall of Napoleon. But the Spanish option was not to be tried in France. Henry II was killed before his agreements with the Habsburgs could take effect, and the dissidence inside France continued to grow. His Florentine widow Catherine de Medici, who became regent, cared nothing for quarrels over dogma, but was determined to re-establish a strong *stato*. At first she thought that toleration might open the way to increased royal power. But when she saw that this was impracticable she tried to achieve a Medici-like balance between the Catholic League and the Huguenots, and to weaken both factions by killing their leaders. Prolonged stasis and religious war divided France into pockets of territory controlled by the league and the Huguenots, so that it nearly became as divided as Germany, and the great weight which France normally carried externally was temporarily much reduced.

An expedient compromise was finally adopted, as in England and the empire. In due course the Huguenot leader Henry of Navarre came to the throne as Henry IV. But inheritance was no longer the only legitimacy: to gain the acceptance of the Catholic majority Henry became Catholic. His Edict of Nantes in 1598 re-established the authority of the French state, at the price of recognizing the Huguenots whom Henry had led for so long. Calvinist noble families consolidated their semi-independent fiefs, and Huguenots continued to nourish rebellious sentiments against the Catholic crown. The Edict of Nantes was an uneasy compromise to serve a temporary purpose; and as the power of the state strengthened in France the autonomous rights of the Huguenots were steadily whittled away. The emigration of French religious dissenters was only deferred. Externally Henry, now secure of the allegiance of most Catholics, rejected the league's links with the Habsburgs and continued the Huguenot foreign policy, which corresponded to the state interests of an independent France. In place of the diarchy with the Habsburgs which had been cultivated by Henry II, Henry IV organized an anti-hegemonial league against them with the Calvinist Netherlands and the Protestant princes in Germany, and with Ottoman support.

In all these examples **expediency prevailed**, fostered by a Renaissance appreciation of *ragione di stato*. In Spain, and in England during the sixteenth century, the crown and the forces that rallied round it were strong enough to maintain an effective state. In France this was barely possible. In the empire both expediency and *ragione di stato* operated against imperial coherence, and in favour of separate *statos*, of which the Habsburg dominions were the most important. Protestantism was not originally directed against hegemony in the states system. It became anti-hegemonial because of the commitment of the Habsburgs to the Catholic side. In practice it helped to make the states of Europe, and especially the emerging states inside the empire, more different from one another, and more emancipated from any central or collective lay authority. The pendulum moved fitfully but increasingly towards the multiple independences end of the spectrum.

The **migrations of religious dissenters** reinforced the vertical division of Europe. They increased the power of princes, and the loyalty to them of both their subjects who remained and the new ones who immigrated. But individual subjects were now determined and able to choose their allegiance, though often at great cost. The exercise of individual options made allegiance a more voluntary matter, involving the consent of the governed, and foreshadowed new concepts of what constituted a state. **Toleration** between states and princes, the basis of the Augsburg compromise, became the policy of the day in the anti-hegemonial camp. But Protestants and Catholics agreed that there ought to be only one religion in a realm, and even more so in a *stato*. Toleration within a state was therefore considered shameful, and people who advocated it were denounced as worldly and irreligious. Readiness to tolerate in one's own community what one condemned and thought wicked came through weariness and a desire to avoid further material destruction.

The contrast between the substantial nations which were forming in the west of Europe, and the fragments into which Germany and Italy were divided, accentuated the long-standing difference between the western and eastern halves of Europe. This contrast led to two different concepts of statehood and nationality in the European society of states, both of which have spread from Europe over the modern world.

THE ROLE OF THE OTTOMAN EMPIRE

The development of Latin Christendom into a system of states was complicated by the expansion in eastern Europe and the Mediterranean of a technologically advanced and militarily successful non-Christian great power, the Muslim Ottoman Empire. The Ottomans regarded the Habsburgs as the principal obstacle to their westward expansion. The army of Suleyman the Magnificent reached the gates of Vienna in 1529. Thereupon the French under Francis I took the initiative in organizing co-operation with the Ottomans against what they saw as the Habsburg aim of general and unassailable predominance in Europe. The Franco-Ottoman agreement of 1536 took the form not of an alliance between equals but of a unilateral regulation by the sultan of economic relations with France; however, it provided the basis for political and military collaboration, and was so understood throughout Europe.[1] Through French contacts with the Protestant princes opposed to the Habsburgs, the Ottomans developed a general policy of fostering disorder in Christian Europe and weakening their Habsburg enemies by offering political and military co-operation and economic inducements to anti-hegemonial states and rebellious movements there. For instance, in their detailed negotiations with Philip II in the 1570s, they took the lead in trying to co-ordinate William of Orange's moves with their own. By and large the Ottomans achieved their diplomatic objectives in Europe in the sixteenth century, and the development of the European states system suited them well. The effective union of Christian Europe under Habsburg leadership was averted, and the area moved increasingly towards multiple and feuding independences.

Thus the Ottoman Empire became, and for some centuries continued to be, an integral and major component of the European states system. Yet it regarded itself, and was regarded, as too different from the Christian family of states to become a member of their evolving international society. This distinction had major consequences, discussed in Chapter 19.

The imperial expansion of Ottoman power in the sixteenth century was not confined to Europe. It encountered two principal centres of opposition: the Habsburgs, usually supported by Venice and other allies, in the west and the Safavid Persians in the east. Both struggles had religious justification: the Safavids were Shia' heretics, and campaigns in Europe had the additional merit of expanding the *dar al Islam*. The more or less continuous involvement on two fronts imposed limits on the formidable military capacity of the Ottomans, both in terms of their overall resources and also in terms of time, since it took several months to move an army from Istanbul to Vienna or Tabriz. The Ottomans' need to take simultaneous account of the forces arrayed against them in both east and west led them to look for potential allies and to negotiate periods of respite with their enemies, and in particular to become actively involved diplomatically with the emerging Christian states. These are the impersonal constraints that we have associated with systems of states. However, the contacts between the Persians and the Europeans remained sporadic, and they only occasionally entered into military agreements with each other against the Turks. Their relations were not regular or systematic enough for us to regard them as members of the same system.

THE HABSBURG HEGEMONY

It was against this unpromising state of affairs that the Habsburg family made its prolonged and complex attempt to establish a hegemonial system in Christendom.

A number of factors operated in favour of a Habsburg hegemony. Most important, the Italian ideas of Renaissance statecraft, the Reformation and the growth of national consciousness combined to make European society more turbulent and its rulers more independent. Consequently the fear of anarchy, and also the fear of the Turks, became widespread. These fears, combined with the desire of sixteenth-century statesmen to establish peace and order within their states, made men realize through all the passions of the Reformation that **some wider order** between states was also required in the new Europe to replace the old collectivity and the increasingly disregarded rules of Christendom. It is important to note, alongside the desire of princes to control individual *statos*, that propensity to hegemony and order between states which we have observed in similar systems in the past, and which made the Habsburg bid plausible.

Second, Habsburg power was diffused over most of Christian Europe. Charles V presided over a disparate range of inherited and elected realms, principalities and offices, each with its own interests and its own constitutional limitations on its ruler. The Habsburg territories were too geographically separated and too diverse to forge into a single *stato*. (The principal elements of the Habsburg conglomerate were: Charles's immense Spanish inheritance that covered Spain itself, much of Italy and the Americas; his position as Holy Roman Emperor; the great concentration of Habsburg territories along the Danube, partly under his brother Ferdinand; the Burgundian inheritance which included the rich and virtually autonomous cities and provinces of

Charles's native Netherlands; and some small lordships elsewhere.)
The Habsburgs were therefore obliged to frame their policies in terms
of all Europe. Ironically their primacy in the emerging system was
born of the dynastic marriages designed to underpin the earlier anti-
hegemonial alliance against France, and they found themselves by
accident rather than by design powerful enough to try to lay down
the law. None the less they responded to the logic of their fortuitous
pre-eminence of power by a bid to establish a new order with an
accepted hegemonial structure.

The Habsburg vision of Charles V and Philip II thus had the merit
that it looked beyond their own territories to the welfare of the whole
of Latin Christendom, rather than merely to the welfare and independence of a single *stato*. Sir Stanley Leathes's verdict on Charles, that
'He and he alone of the Princes in Europe formed a just opinion of
the religious danger and did his best to meet it',[2] may be too favourable; but Charles's sense of responsibility and leadership is not in
doubt. No alternative constructive plan for a new general order
between princes was seriously advocated.

The Habsburg solution was essentially conservative. In many ways
the family looked back to the medieval past: they wanted to restore
the unity of Christendom and defend it against Islam outside and
heresy within. They upheld dynastic legitimacy, to which they owed
their own position; but the suppression of heresy involved interference
with that legitimacy and intervention in the internal affairs of other
states as well as their own. Charles did not want to acquire territories
which he did not consider legitimately his. He favoured a Europe
which would leave each realm and province with its own lands and
administrative traditions, and maintain all legitimate princes in their
places, so that his family's possessions would exist in their variety
alongside others. In such a Europe the great concentration of legitimate
power in his hands would ensure a Habsburg hegemony. He hoped
by means of it to prevent what he saw as the slide of Christendom
towards anarchy, and to unite its rulers behind him to suppress heresy
and oppose the Turks. He was eager to enlist the King of France, the
Catholic ruler of the most powerful single state in Christian Europe,
as a junior partner in these enterprises with a position in the hegemonial order second only to his own.

Charles's aims were moderate, and in victory he was careful to
show restraint. He was therefore able to exercise a *de facto* hegemonial
authority, in the sense that his primacy was recognized, even by his
opponents, and that he was largely able to control the functioning of
the developing states system. But his attempt to establish a legitimate
and accepted hegemony or suzerain system in Europe was unsuccessful. The chief liability of the Habsburg design for Europe was that its

acceptance of diversity did not genuinely extend to Protestantism: the Habsburg concessions to Protestants, such as the Augsburg compromise, were made only under military or political necessity. The great power and honourable intentions of the Habsburgs were not enough to deal at the same time with the Reformation, the military struggle against France and the Ottoman Empire and the opposition of many lesser rulers who wanted a free hand to turn their holdings into *statos*.

Charles finally concluded that his responsibilities were more than one man could discharge. He turned over the emperorship and the Habsburg positions in Germany to his brother Ferdinand, who was already King of Bohemia and Hungary, and his other possessions to his son Philip. The Habsburg collection of states now became more obviously what it had essentially been under Charles: a Europe-wide dynastic alliance. Philip II was the effective king of the powerful Spanish state, and inherited Portugal which made him the legitimate lord of all Europe ultramar. But the Habsburg fiefs in Italy and down the Rhine had no independent and resident rulers to forge them into *statos*, and the earnest and unimaginative Philip was only partially able to win their loyalty to his Spanish state across the barriers of custom and culture. In the German lands the exchanges of populations following the Augsburg settlement consolidated loyalties round the emerging states rather than the empire. Ferdinand welded those of his domains which were not under Ottoman control into the most powerful of these states; but parallel development elsewhere in Germany also made some non-Habsburg states independent enough in practice to form alliances, first with each other and then outside the empire.

Had the Habsburgs succeeded (which would have involved realistic acceptance of the Reformation), Europe might have become a suzerain system something like those existing in Asia at the time, rather than a patchwork quilt of independent and juridically equal states. The expansion of Europe would have continued as it began (see Chapter 19), within a single orderly framework and without the stimulus of competition, doubtless with the rich and innovative Netherlands playing a leading part. The brilliant creativity of Europe, which flourished in the diversity of its independent states, might have been seriously curtailed.

Confronted with the Habsburg aim to establish a hegemonial Catholic European order, France had two options: the policy advocated by the Catholic League and the Guises of collaboration with the Habsburgs, and the national policy advocated by the Huguenots of systematic opposition to their pretensions. A substantial body of French opinion supported the league policy, especially during the periods of exceptional weakness. But except for a few brief periods, most notably under Henry II, the French state, personified by the king, was not prepared to play second fiddle in a Habsburg order, and pursued a Huguenot policy. France became the animator and leader of the loose anti-hegemonial coalition. Protestant German princes and cities and the secessionist Dutch opposed the Habsburg design for religious reasons as well as the desire to establish independent *statos*. They became leagued with France and the Scandinavian powers, and thus by proxy also with the Ottoman Turks, in a loose anti-hegemonial collaboration against Habsburg and Catholic dominance. The Protestants who joined this coalition had no great fear of the Turks, from whom they were partly insulated by the coincidence that Habsburg power was concentrated in the south and east of the empire.

The anti-hegemonial resistance to the integrationist aim of the Habsburgs in the sixteenth century was particularist and local, and ostensibly committed to differentiation and multiple independences. The anti-Habsburg rulers were themselves integrated to some extent by strategic pressures and by a network of alliances which together covered the whole system including the Ottomans. However, while the alliances gave a degree of coherence to the policies of the anti-hegemonial camp, and were thus some substitute for hegemonial order, there was no co-ordinating grand design, and co-operation was a matter of temporary expediency. The general idea of a balance of power was present, especially in the minds of Venetian and English statesmen; but at this stage of the development of the European society the desire for a balance merely operated against the Habsburgs, and provided a justification for co-operation with the Ottomans.[3] Specific rules for managing a general balance, including the strongest power, had not yet developed. Even in France, those who aimed to destroy the power of Habsburgs hardly thought beyond replacing them at the top of the hierarchy. Not until the seventeenth century would Europeans try to elaborate something new in the history of states systems, the rules and institutions of a consciously anti-hegemonial international society.

NOTES

1 The nature of these relations is most clearly described in Thomas Naff, 'The Ottoman Empire and the European States System', in H. Bull and A. Watson (eds), *The Expansion of International Society*, Oxford, Oxford University Press, 1984.
2 S. Leathes (ed.), *The Cambridge Modern History*, Vol. II, Cambridge, Cambridge University Press, 1903, p. 79.
3 The concept of a balance was of course not limited to foreign policy, but was also a *politique* formula for managing rival factions within a state.

17

WESTPHALIA
An anti-hegemonial commonwealth of states

The seventeenth century saw the effective establishment of a Europe of legitimately independent states that recognized each other as such. They still felt themselves to be parts of the wider whole that had been Latin Christendom, and the interaction between them was now such that each state, and especially the more powerful ones, felt obliged to take account of the actions of the others. They recognized that, since the medieval restraints had disappeared or become irrelevant, new rules and procedures were needed to regulate their relations. In Hedley Bull's terms they needed to constitute a new international society.[1] The European society of states evolved out of the struggle between the forces tending towards a hegemonial order and those which succeeded in pushing the new Europe towards the independences end of our spectrum. The decisive feature of this process was the general settlement negotiated in Westphalia at the middle of the century after the exhausting Thirty Years War. The Westphalian settlement was the charter of a Europe permanently organized on an anti-hegemonial principle. It also affected the growth of national consciousness, which was in due course to transform the relations between the European states, and the role played in the ordering of Europe by states on its periphery. Europe's 'colonial' expansion landward and overseas, and the consequent expansion of the European system worldwide, requires a separate examination, and is discussed in Chapter 19.

RICHELIEU AND THE ANTI-HEGEMONIAL ALLIANCE

In the sixteenth century the grand design for Europe had been the hegemonial vision of the Habsburgs. Its opponents had been particularist, leagued together to oppose the Habsburgs but with no general picture of an alternative organization. In the first half of the seventeenth century the French state pursued a new grand design in opposition to the weary and weakening Habsburgs. The design was anti-hegemonial, and still essentially negative; it assigned to France the leadership of the anti-Habsburg coalition, corresponding in effect to that of the Spartans in the Peloponnesian War and to the Chinese *ba*. Men like Henri IV's minister, Sully, contributed to the concept; but its principal architect was King Louis XIII's chief minister, Cardinal Richelieu.

Inside France, Richelieu pursued a policy of consolidating royal authority after the prolonged stasis of the religious wars, reapplying the techniques of the Italian *stato* introduced by Louis XI. He held that to establish a state, meaning the effective government of a kingdom, it was necessary to combine the concentration of power of a *stato* with the acknowledged authority of a legitimate king; and that indeed the king must be the personification of the state. His aim was to unify France under an absolute monarch, and to destroy all effective opposition, especially the fortified castles of the nobles and the garrisons of Huguenot cities that were designed to resist the king. This was the policy known as **raison d'état**. In Italy *ragione di stato* amounted to a justification of any policy, including force and fraud, that consolidated a *stato*. Richelieu meant something more principled, a right and reason of state that recognized the obligations of a ruler to all those committed to his charge.

Richelieu's concept of *raison d'état* abroad was almost the counter-image of his domestic policy. He considered that the welfare of the kingdom of France and of the king's subjects, which he regarded as a sacred trust of King Louis, also required the removal of the external threat represented by the ability of the Habsburg family to lay down the law in Europe, though Habsburg power was legitimate and Catholic. Externally therefore this devout prince of the Catholic Church continued the Huguenot foreign policy of the previous century. While France was the largest and most populous kingdom in western Europe and occupied a geographically central position, it was still weaker than the Habsburg combination, so that expediency was needed. Richelieu encouraged in the Holy Roman Empire and in Spain those elements of stasis which he suppressed at home. For example, he described the Huguenot stronghold of La Rochelle as a wasps' nest, but maintained that the German Protestant princes (who were in a similar relationship to the empire) were legitimate allies.

Richelieu had to build an anti-hegemonial coalition or counter-network out of very diverse components, not on the basis of authority as the Habsburg system was able to do, but by patient negotiation and persuasion. He accepted the basic premiss of anti-hegemonial coalitions, that any ally was acceptable, especially if it would do the fighting. In his *Political Testament* he stressed the need for continuous foreign negotiations, which enabled him 'to transform completely the nature of affairs in Christendom', and the 'unbelievable' value of which he says he realized only from the experience of office.[2] To carry out the task of activating and co-ordinating his coalition he built up the best-informed and most effective diplomatic service in Europe. French policy also made effective use of money. It provided subsidies and support to anti-imperial German princes, most of whom were Protestant, to the Protestant kings of Denmark and Sweden and to the independent Calvinist Netherlands. It encouraged the Turkish enemies of Christendom to harass the Habsburgs. The French used their own troops, augmented by hired mercenaries, only as a last resort, after the death of the warrior king of Sweden threatened the Protestant cause in Germany with collapse. The policy of subsidizing allies to do the fighting was used in the Italian Renaissance, as earlier by Assyria and Persia and later by England. In other words, the cardinal was a *politique*, and like other *politiques* concerned less with heresy than with *raison d'état*. He wanted to lift the French state from the low ebb to which its fortunes had fallen, and to free it from both hegemonial pressure from above and the pressure of stasis from below.

The Huguenots were in a dilemma. They favoured the foreign policy of alliance with all Protestants against the Habsburg standard bearers of the Counter-Reformation; but their hard-won military and political power within France, which protected them from persecution, also weakened the state and the king's ability to wage war. The Dutch found the choice equally bitter. The French alliance was indispensable to save the independence of their new state; but the Huguenots were the heroes of the Calvinist struggle and needed the help from outside which the Dutch had found so precious at an earlier stage. *Raison d'état* prevailed over ideology in the Dutch case also, and they paid the price of the French alliance by agreeing not to aid or encourage the Huguenots. The Protestant princes were weaker than the Catholic ones, and therefore found it expedient to ally themselves with the cardinal and to welcome Ottoman victories, whatever their subjects thought.

Neither Richelieu's anti-hegemonial expediency nor the struggle of the dissident German princes against the authority of the empire yet amounted to a concept of a new European order. But the Franco-Protestant coalition and its ramifications co-ordinated and gave a structure to the forces opposing hegemony in the chaotic first half of the seventeenth century, before a new general order had been negotiated and brought into effect. The co-ordination necessarily accepted a wide diversity of interests and indeed (especially with regard to the Ottomans) also of principles and values. In a sense it was the extension to the whole system of the Augsburg formula of *cujus regio ejus religio*.

The Habsburgs had the advantage of singleness of purpose, but they showed themselves less flexible and more committed to principle. Whereas Richelieu was concerned with the interests of the French state, the policy of the Habsburgs was based on the maintenance of all the hereditary rights assigned to them by God, which taken together put them in a hegemonial position, and on the belief that what mattered was to save one's soul, so that one must have no truck with heresy. It was almost impossible for the Habsburgs to accept the independence of their Dutch territories. But the makings of a deal existed with the Protestant kings of Denmark and Sweden; and Wallenstein, the *politique* Habsburg general, explored arrangements with Protestant German princes that could have brought peace to the empire. Furthermore, since France was the main enemy, the Habsburgs could have aided the Huguenots in the same way that the French helped the Protestant dissidents in the empire and in the Netherlands. Olivares, the Spanish counterpart of Richelieu, saw these opportunities and the dangers of rigidity, but could not persuade his king. The Thirty Years War achieved an anti-hegemonial solution to the concentration in a single state of German power, but allowed a concentration of French power.

The Habsburg rejection of a Spanish *raison d'état* meant that the state interests of Spain were sacrificed to the aims and interests of the Habsburg family, including its hold on Italy and the Netherlands, and to the Catholic Church and the Habsburg sense of order in Europe as a whole. It is difficult to say how useful the reconquest of the northern Netherlands would have been to Spain, or how valuable were the southern Netherlands which the Spanish crown retained, measured against the Spanish blood and treasure expended in the struggle. Certainly Spain paid the price of a foreign policy based on general principles rather than national interests. Even more serious was the devastation of Germany. There Habsburg intransigence, the ambitions of the princes, the operations of the Swedish army and the French and Ottoman policy of encouraging independence and dissidence brought about those disasters from which the Habsburgs had saved Spain and Bourbon domestic policy rescued France.

The **north European states system** round the Baltic was still a separate network of pressures at the beginning of the seventeenth century. It was dominated by two rival marcher states tempered in the expansion of Latin Christendom, the kingdoms of Sweden and Poland–Lithuania, which were often in conflict with each other as well as with their eastern neighbours. Sweden had become a homogeneous national state, and it also controlled a number of subordinate non-Swedish territories around the Baltic. The kingdom of Poland had increased its power and influence by a dynastic union with Lithuania and expansion eastward, and had made itself the principal bulwark of Latin Christendom on the eastern marches. But the heterogeneous population, the dual governmental structure of Poland–Lithuania and the practice of elective monarchy prevented its consolidation into an effective *stato*.

The Thirty Years War involved the Scandinavian powers in central Europe, and French statesmen saw advantage in collaborating with both Sweden and Poland, which were geographically on the other side of the Habsburgs. The western and northern European systems merged. The Swedes understood more clearly than the western states that 'all the separate wars of Europe have become one universal war',[3] and Swedish arms and diplomacy played an active part in shaping seventeenth-century Europe. The main and ironic contribution of Poland–Lithuania was the Polonization and westernization of Russia, which was destined to conquer Poland and become a major European and world power (see Chapter 19).

THE NEW WESTPHALIAN ORDER

The long struggle was brought to an end by the complex parallel negotiations known collectively as the **Westphalian settlement** of 1648. Though it was a negotiated settlement rather than a dictate, by and large it registered the achievement of the victors. Dame Veronica Wedgwood's familiar verdict that 'the peace was totally ineffectual in settling the problems of Europe' refers to the rearrangement of the map and the claims of princes.[4] Nevertheless the negotiations in Westphalia amounted in practice to something new and significant: the first general congress of the effective powers of Europe. The electors and all the princes and imperial cities of the Holy Roman Empire who were capable of conducting an independent foreign policy were separately represented at the negotiations.

The Westphalian settlement legitimized a **commonwealth of sovereign states**. It marked the triumph of the *stato*, in control of its internal affairs and independent externally. This was the aspiration of princes in general – and especially of the German princes, both Protestant and Catholic, in relation to the empire. The Westphalian treaties stated many of the rules and political principles of the new society of states, and provided evidence of the general assent of princes to them. The settlement was held to provide a fundamental and comprehensive charter for all Europe. It also formulated some general ideas which have been echoed in subsequent settlements and at the permanent congresses of the League of Nations and the United Nations, such as the medieval condemnation of the evils of war and the need for a new and better order. But of course many things that later European statecraft held to be important were not yet achieved. A balance of power, which was necessary to maintain the conditions in which non-hegemonial rules and institutions could operate, and which was therefore central to the concept, was not effectively established. The indispensable role which the Austrian Habsburgs were to play over the next two centuries, in maintaining the balance which they had previously combatted, was not foreseen; and the smaller victors had not yet developed the maxim that the great enemy of yesterday would be the ally of tomorrow.

The medieval realms and Renaissance *statos* of Christendom had now become a **hierarchy of constituted states**, which we can divide into three classes. Some sovereigns, with the emperor and the kings of France and Spain at their head, were universally recognized as independent, both *de jure* and *de facto*. Their status was not affected by the Westphalian settlement. The second category were independent in practice, but not altogether in juridical theory. The most significant members of this category were the lay princes of the empire. The electors of powerful *statos* like Bavaria, Saxony and Brandenburg, who with three archbishops chose the emperor, were by the end of the war obviously independent in all but name. Over a hundred lesser princes and some fifty free imperial cities had also acquired considerable freedom of action. Under the settlement the German princes and city governments were still nominally not permitted to go to war without the consent of the empire. But they were formally authorized to make alliances with states outside it. They were thus recognized as independent components of the states system, and mobile participants in the institutions of the new international society of princes. Third were the states separately constituted, with their own laws and institutions, but dependent. Such were the Habsburg southern Netherlands and various states in Italy and round the Baltic, and also the European colonies in the New World. Some might aspire to achieve independence in due course, as the German states had done.

The independent states were obviously not equal in power, and were still thought of as ranked in a hierarchy, with issues like the precedence of their representatives hotly disputed. But though not juridically equal, the first two classes of states in practice recognized each other's independence and dealt with each other on an equal plane. That had been the practice among the members of the victorious anti-hegemonial alliance, and is characteristic of such alliances; and under the Westphalian settlement it became the customary rule in Europe. Moreover, the kings and princes of Europe, whose position depended on hereditary right and therefore on genealogy, were extensively related to each other by blood and marriage. European sovereigns might differ greatly in power and rank, but they were actually or potentially members of the same extended family.

The Westphalian order negotiated by the sovereign rulers thus legitimized a patchwork quilt of independences in Europe. The frontiers separating the states of these sovereigns were clearly drawn, with a thick line; and what happened inside that line was for the government of the state alone to determine. Sovereignty, especially as it applied to the principalities of the empire, legitimized the extension of the concept of *cujus regio ejus religio*; the break-up of the universal church was now reflected in the break-up of lay structure in Europe. In its emphasis on the separateness of the European states rather than on the unity of Christendom, and its rejection of any idea that a pope or emperor had some universal authority, or that a dominant state should lay down the law to the others, the Westphalian settlement was anti-hegemonial. On all these issues the settlement reflected the views of its architects, France, Sweden and Holland, which were Protestant powers or pursuing a so-called Protestant policy. The Westphalian order was imposed by the victors on the vanquished; and the aims of the victorious coalition became the public law of Europe. The Habsburgs were obliged to abandon their hegemonial aims. The pope understandably denounced the settlement as invalid and inane.

The Ottomans, whose arms had greatly helped to make the settlement possible, took no part in it. They wanted to weaken their Habsburg enemies, but they did not think in terms of an anti-hegemonial order for Christian Europe, and nothing in their policy corresponded to the Persian aim of establishing a 'king's peace'. Habsburg weakness seemed to them an opportunity. Some forty years after Westphalia the Ottomans were besieging Vienna.

The sovereigns of Europe were no longer bound by the universal laws which were deemed to regulate the conduct of lay rulers in medieval Christendom. Their relations were dangerously near the anarchic end of the spectrum. In order to function, they needed not merely the territorial and juridical settlement which established an anti-hegemonial society, but also **new rules and institutions** in place of the old ones. The rules and institutions in their developed eighteenth-century form are discussed in the next chapter.

One new institution needs to be mentioned here. The seventeenth century developed a new concept of **international law**, as a set of rules devised by and for sovereign princes to regulate their dealings with each other. The princely *statos* of Europe had already begun to develop such arrangements and practices, based on expediency. The task of formulating and codifying the existing practices into a body of international law was undertaken mainly by the Protestant states in the anti-hegemonial coalition, especially the Netherlands. Some Catholic thinkers considered international law a 'Protestant science'. The codification was, inevitably, the work of lawyer-diplomats, men who combined experience of international negotiation and practice with a legal training and turn of mind. The most eminent was Hugo Grotius, the Dutch author of the monumental *De Jure Belli ac Pacis*, the 'Laws of War and Peace', who after representing the Netherlands in negotiations with Richelieu served for eleven years as a Swedish diplomat, but who died before Westphalia. Grotius wanted order rather than Machiavellian anarchy in the relations between states, but an order that did not depend on a hegemonial power. His aim was to set out a body of rules largely derived from divine fiat or ancient tradition but now legitimized by explicit consent: rules acceptable to God and to princes, describing actual practice and suggesting how it might be made more rational and more conducive to order and peace. While Grotius combined the regulatory with the ethical, a more theoretical German, Samuel Pufendorf, also in the service of Sweden, was more concerned to base international law on universal natural rights. He wanted war to be lawful only to redress infractions of natural law. Seventeenth-century international law was in fact a substitute for universal law. Its corner-stone was the principle of independent hereditary sovereignty. It was essentially regulatory, and did not control the relations between sovereigns so much as facilitate them. The ethical content that it possessed reflected, as always in such cases, the common cultural tradition of Europe, derived from Latin Christendom and the classical and biblical heritage, as seen through the eyes of the victors in the last great struggle.

THE HEGEMONY OF LOUIS XIV

The Westphalian settlement marked the failure of the Habsburg concept of hegemony, and the final defeat of Spain by France eleven years later seemed to confirm that hegemonial order in Europe was a dream, or nightmare. There was one of those brief periods of general hope and rejoicing, because it seemed, as Xenophon said of the defeat of the hegemonial Athenians, that all Europe would be free. But the hegemonial vision and practice were no sooner abandoned by the Spanish and Austrian Habsburgs than they returned in the person of the greatest king of France, Louis XIV, who reigned effectively from 1661 to 1714. Personally Louis was a French Habsburg, and was much influenced by his Habsburg mother, Anne of Austria. He supported Catholic causes. The style of his court, though animated by French genius, reflected that of Habsburg Spain. The crumbling of Spanish and Austrian power enabled France, now again the strongest, the most populous and perhaps the best-administered kingdom in Europe, to assert itself once more. Louis found himself in a position to act hegemonially in the new order, as the Spartans did after the Peloponnesian War.

189

Louis's hegemonial plans combined Habsburg and traditional French aspirations. In the Habsburg pattern, at the beginning of his effective reign he married the daughter of the Habsburg king of Spain, and one of his main aims later was to establish his grandson on the throne of Spain, and so replace the Austro-Spanish axis of Habsburg hegemony with a similar Franco-Spanish axis. The Holy Roman Empire had been disintegrated by the Thirty Years War and the Westphalian settlement into a mosiac of principalities linked by dynastic or other alliances to a number of different powers. Louis took over the Habsburg policy of focusing on himself the allegiance of as many of the princes and cities of the empire as possible. In order to do so he set about acquiring another main source of Habsburg authority, the position of Holy Roman Emperor, for himself or, as the compromise he achieved, for a client German prince. In continuation of the French tradition he aimed to extend French direct rule (which involved a measure of local autonomy) up to the Rhine, including the Netherlands. Beyond an enlarged France and outside the area of his dominion Louis was able to exercise a hegemony over the whole of Christendom, largely by means of financial subsidies. The outer bastions of Louis's hegemonial structure were England and Scotland under his first cousins Charles II and James II, and France's old allies Sweden and Poland–Lithuania. His Ottoman associates were wholly independent and outside the grand design, but useful as a permanent restraint on the Austrian Habsburgs. However, Louis was also the heir of Westphalia. He worked to establish his hegemonial order where possible within its framework. He inherited Richelieu's diplomatic machine, and built up Europe's most formidable army and solid financial resources. With these instruments he and his able ministers worked to hold his elaborate and constructive grand design for Europe together, and induce the separate parts to function as he wished, by Richelieu's techniques of continuous negotiation, subsidy and bribery on the one hand but also by intimidation and war on the other.

This was a **French order for Europe**, more systematic and less oppressive than the Austro-Spanish one. French ideas and practices, and especially the French language, became the model for most of Europe; and had Louis's hegemonial order been more permanently established, other forms of standardization, as well as a *pax gallica*, would no doubt also have prevailed. But Louis's French order was contrary to the anti-hegemonial aims of Sully and Richelieu, and to the spirit of Westphalia. The sun king Louis incarnated the state and the nation, and his apotheosis represented him as a divinely appointed figure before whom every other ruler in Europe should bow. When the princess Sophia, the mother of the future George I of England, formally visited Versailles, Louis's queen offered Sophia the hem of her robe to kiss.

The commitment of Europe to multiple independences was so strong, and so legitimized and reinforced by the Westphalian settlement, that Louis's plans were inevitably opposed by another anti-hegemonial coalition. The Netherlands played in the European system the part of the Corinthians in classical Greece. The power of the Dutch was economic rather than military and they were anti-hegemonial on principle. In face of the new threat from their former ally they were therefore prompt to ally themselves with the defeated Habsburg enemy of yesterday as well as with any other members of Richelieu's coalition that they could persuade of the danger. In 1688 Louis's client King James II was driven out of Britain and replaced by his son-in-law William of Orange, the *de facto* ruler of the Netherlands, and by the anti-hegemonial Whig party. Thereafter the two Protestant maritime powers took the lead in organizing and financing the anti-hegemonial coalition, which came to include the papacy. The maritime powers also negotiated a peace between the empire and the Ottomans so that the Habsburg power could be more effectively used to contain France.

In the course of the century *raison d'état* replaced religion as the determining principle of alliances between European princes. The alliance structures became secularized. As the Habsburgs and their associates and the Franco-Protestant coalition had between them organized and canalized the pressures of power in Europe in the first half of the century, so Louis's network of client alliances and the anti-hegemonial coalition organized those pressures against each other in the second half.

Those who opposed Louis's pretensions in Europe did not claim that France was uncivilized or tryannical. They acknowledged French pre-eminence in civilization and the arts, among which many included the arts of war and government. Louis personally was held in great respect. The charge against him was the same as that made against the equally civilized Athenians, that they aimed at a tyranny over all Hellas; and against the Venetians in the Renaissance, that they were becoming the *signori di tutta Italia*.

Finally after a prolonged and fairly destructive struggle, Louis's power was cut down to the point where he could not exercise hegemony, though his grandson was installed as king of Spain. The Habsburgs, who were bitter about the Spanish succession, and also other states wanted to continue the war; but the newly constituted United Kingdom of Great Britain opposed it. The Tory and Stuart tradition of association with France was still strong, and thoughtful Englishmen did not want to destroy France. They also had a grand design for Europe. They wanted an order which was free of hegemony, but based on an equilibrium of power rather than a victorious coalition. They saw a reduced France as a necessary and major weight in the complex mobile balance, in a way that the victors at Westphalia had not seen a reduced Austria. The resulting Utrecht settlement, discussed in the next chapter, laid the basis for the eighteenth century.

While France was the strategic and cultural focus of Europe, England and Holland became the centres of scientific, technical, banking, industrial and maritime skills so innovative and so mutually reinforcing as to represent something quite new in the world. This extra dimension was the achievement not of the concentrated power of the monarchical state but of an educated independent middle class. The maritime powers now also took the lead in overseas expansion and colonization. During the Habsburg bid for hegemony Spain derived strength from the New World: silver from the Indies helped the hegemonial side. But Louis did not inherit the orderly division of European overseas expansion between the Iberian powers; nor did he evolve a French grand design for outremer. While the French had their own colonial ventures, the Dutch and English secured the bulk of Europe's trade with Asia. The Dutch formulated a new and disputed anti-hegemonial regime for trade, colonization and other activities outside Europe. They extended to the Indian Ocean the principles of no monopoly, the open door and freedom of the seas, which were Dutch ideas about how to manage relations between states in Europe. Those principles were in due course adopted by Great Britain and by the United States.

STATEHOOD AND NATIONHOOD

By the beginning of the seventeenth century most of western and northern Europe had been forged by its rulers into **states**. The ruler was sovereign, owing allegiance to nobody; all his subjects owed him a personal loyalty and obedience. The nobility, the clergy, certain towns and others still had internal rights and privileges that enabled them to participate in internal government according to their ranks or charters, and some states had parliaments or assemblies; but the sovereign ruler denied the right of any subject to deal separately with external powers, and his subjects in the main upheld that right. In this way the security of the state could be assured; and the security of the state meant the safety of its inhabitants. Many who were aghast at the suffering and destruction caused by religious strife felt that obedience even to a bad ruler offered better security than a resort to arms. The state was encompassed in what Hobbes called the hide of a leviathan, and internally each leviathan was politically independent of the others.

The concept of distinct **nations** or peoples within Christendom, based on common language and culture, existed in the Middle Ages. To be Spanish, French, English, German or Italian had an ethnic meaning which transcended political allegiance. Now the populations enclosed within the west and north European leviathans developed a primary loyalty to the state and to each other. Membership of the same body politic reinforced the old concept of the nation and gave it a new meaning. The vertical organization and national awareness of the populations of the western half of Latin Christendom, which had been slowly developing for centuries since the time of Joan of Arc, was for practical purposes complete. In no part of western Europe was a sense of nationhood stronger than in Spain, which thus stood in contrast to the other Habsburg dominions. The new state nationalities normally – with historical exceptions like the Catalans, the Huguenots and the Gaelic-speaking Irish – crystallized out round a dynasty and in the territories over which that dynasty was sovereign. But a state did not have to be monarchical, and certainly its population did not have to be loyal to an unacceptable individual ruler, for a sense of nationhood to strengthen. The Calvinist struggles against the Habsburgs in the Netherlands and against the Stuarts in Scotland and England had a republican flavour; but where they succeeded they reinforced the hide of the leviathan and the concept of nationhood in western and northern Europe.

In the eastern part of Christendom, which we may now call central Europe, the sense of nationality developed very differently. The spread of education, the development of printing, the increasing use of the vernacular in place of Latin, all tended to reinforce a linguistic national awareness. Nevertheless both in Italy and in Germany the development of the *stato* led to the formation of political units which usually had a local tradition but were too small to encompass a decisive part of the medieval nation. In Germany the institutions of the 'Holy Roman Empire of the German Nation' had seemed to Berthold of Mainz and others to be capable of development into a national German state. But the divisive effects of Protestantism and the multi-ethnic character of the domains ruled by the most powerful dynasties, the Habsburgs and later the Prussian Hohenzollerns, ensured that state and nation would remain until the nineteenth century two separate concepts competing for the loyalties of Germans and Italians.

The contrast between the substantial nations which were forming in the west, where the administrative and ethnic units broadly coincided, and the fragments into which Germany and Italy were divided, accentuated the long-standing difference between western and central Europe. This difference grew greater in the seventeenth century. The middle classes, who in the west were among the most loyal supporters of the national states, in central Europe became increasingly dissociated from their local prince and especially from his negotiations and wars with other princes.

THE MARCHES AND THE CENTRE

What characteristics and capacities enabled a state to bid for hegemony in the European system? In former systems, communities on the marches or periphery of an area of civilization, such as Assyria, Macedon, the Mauryas, Ch'in and Rome, were obliged by constant contact and struggle with alien neighbours to develop a greater military capacity and a firmer administrative structure than the more civilized, gracious and tradition-conscious communities in the relatively shielded heartland, as well as a greater readiness to innovate and to learn from experience. In all those cases a more vigorous and competent marcher state was able to establish a hegemony over the system and a dominion over much of it. In Europe the role of the peripheral states was also significant. The situation was more complex and the results were different, but not as different as is sometimes claimed.

The three directions of outward thrust of medieval Christendom had been in Iberia, in the Levant and round the Baltic. In the sixteenth century the most powerful and determined of the marcher states tempered by crusading expansion was Spain. Spain and the similarly conditioned but more maritime state of Portugal agreed to share the continuation of the *reconquista* by expansion overseas; and both derived considerable power, wealth and experience from their colonial achievement. The Habsburgs used these traditional marcher resources, including the 'wealth of the Indies' and the unequalled Spanish infantry, in their bid for hegemony in Europe. But the prolonged hegemonial effort, together with the continuing development of the overseas empires, proved too much for the Iberian states. The Habsburg dominions on the upper Danube were also a border state. The names Ostmark, Steiermark, Krain (eastern march, Styrian march, border) indicate the frontier character of those provinces. With Hungary they formed the barrier of Europe against the powerful and warlike Ottoman Turkish Empire, itself a marcher state of an expanding Islam that had driven the Latins from the Levant and was now pursuing them up the Danube into the heart of Europe. Spanish and Austrian ways seemed harsh to the more civilized Italians and Netherlanders over whom the Habsburgs ruled, and to the rest of Europe too.

Why then was the combination of these two marcher traditions, along with the other resources controlled by the Habsburgs, not sufficient to establish a durable hegemony over the emerging European society of states? We can discern three main reasons. First, during the

194

whole period of the Habsburg bid for hegemony, the Ottoman thrust up the Danube and in the Mediterranean was too strong to allow the Habsburgs a free hand in Europe. The marcher states that made themselves masters of the other civilizations did not have a power anything like as formidable as the Ottomans threatening them in the rear. Second, the colonization of the New World made greater demands on the manpower and other resources of Spain, and provided the state with less net strength, than was then supposed. Third, there was the great and enduring power of France, the geographical and cultural centre of western Europe.

France was able to re-establish itself in the seventeenth century as the most powerful state in the European system. Louis XIV's and Napoleon's bids to establish a French hegemonial order as the basis of the European society of states came not from the periphery but from the centre. They nearly succeeded. In fact Napoleon did succeed on the European continent, and his imperial order was only broken by the two most peripheral European powers, Britain and Russia. Though France with its access to the Atlantic was able to conduct significant operations overseas, its anti-hegemonial opponents derived a substantial net balance of strength from outside Europe. The same was true in the two twentieth-century wars against Germany. In those great military struggles the periphery proved stronger than the centre.

SOME CONSEQUENCES OF WESTPHALIA

The seventeenth century was decisive for the European society of states. The broad outlines of that society developed out of the efforts of Richelieu, and also the Dutch and the Swedes, to forge the disparate elements in Christian Europe opposed to the Habsburgs into a co-ordinated anti-hegemonial camp. The continuous diplomatic and strategic dialogue which co-ordinated the wartime coalition included the Ottomans; but it became much more intimate between the Christian princes and cities, who shared a cultural outlook and faced similar problems. All the Christian members of the coalition, great and small, down to minor princes of the empire, treated each other on a basis of *de facto* equality because they had to be persuaded rather than obliged to co-operate. In the same way new forms of international jurisprudence developed in the anti-hegemonial camp. These wartime practices were established by the Westphalian settlement as the rules of the new commonwealth of Europe. The rules were then developed by *ad hoc* practice into the **constituent legitimacy of the European society of states**.

But hegemony was not long in abeyance. Because the Westphalian settlement was formulated by the anti-hegemonial camp, it established the legitimacy of the European society considerably further along the spectrum towards multiple independences than the distribution of power in Europe and the propensity to hegemony in the system warranted. A gap soon opened between the premises and the practice of the new commonwealth, between the 'is' and the 'ought'. Into that gap stepped the new Bourbon–Habsburg hegemony of Louis XIV. Thus **hegemony continued to be an integral and constituent feature of the practice** of the European states system, despite the anti-hegemonial legitimacy established by Westphalia. For, as so often before and since, the leader of the anti-hegemonial coalition became the new hegemonial power, and incorporated into its hegemonial structure much of the machinery and many of the states of the victorious coalition, alongside the hegemonial practices of its predecessor. The pendulum of European practice swung back from Westphalia, but only part of the way.

Among the significant features of the new society for the future was the independent sovereignty of the princes and cities of the empire. Many German and Italian rulers and cities had long since acquired varying degrees of freedom of action, and maintained relations and alliances with other European states. The Westphalian settlement legitimized and standardized the practice. More than a hundred small principalities, some no more than the personal estates of a noble family, were invited to the negotiating table and acquired a sacrosanct quality of sovereignty, while remaining nominally within the empire. The new order allowed each state to take the place in the wider international society of Europe that its strength and geographical position made possible. They all participated independently in the diplomatic dialogue: not merely within one of the two competing networks of alliance that had organized the long military struggle, but henceforth able to switch from one side to the other. Some of the smaller states based their relations with other states under the Westphalian charter on religious, dynastic or other issues of principle; some were anti-hegemonial, determined to conserve their sovereign freedom from imperial or other control; and some pursued a policy which their critics called 'harlotry', contracting with the highest bidder. The concept of independence for a smiliar multitude of small states in our present international society, formed from the fragmentation of empires, and their presence at the permanent congress of the United Nations, has evolved from the Westphalian settlement and bears an inherited resemblance to it.

NOTES

1 H. Bull, *The Anarchical Society*, London, Macmillan, and New York, Columbia University Press, 1977, p. 13.
2 Richelieu, *Political Testament*, Chapter VI.
3 Letter from King Gustavus Adolphus of Sweden to Oxenstierna of 1 April 1628. See also G. Parker, *Europe in Crisis*, London, Fontana, 1974, p. 14.
4 C. V. Wedgwood, *The Thirty Years War*, London, Methuen, 1981, p. 525.

18

THE AGE OF REASON AND OF BALANCE

The eighteenth century, from the Utrecht settlement to the French Revolution, was a period of order and progress in Europe. An international society of states, or princes, functioned well, with rules and institutions and underlying assumptions which its members accepted. Wars, in the sense of conflicts between states involving military operations, there certainly were. But they were not wars for great religious causes, or about how hegemonial the states system should be. They were minor wars of adjustment: the final means, after other pressures and inducements had not succeeded, of compelling those modifications of the balance between the states of the system which the logic of changing power dictated. In this chapter we will look at the main formative elements of eighteenth-century European international society, and the premises on which it rested. The next chapter will deal with the activities of the Europeans outside Europe, and the impact of those activities on the evolution of the European society of states.

The Utrecht settlement of 1714 took a stage further the anti-hegemonial assumptions of Westphalia. The experience of seeing France assume the hegemonial aspirations of Spain and Austria convinced the leaders of the coalition against Louis XIV, especially English and Dutch statesmen, that it was necessary to go beyond the negative anti-hegemonial principle to the more positive concept of a **continuous mobile equilibrium**, in which every state in the system had its part to play. The way Louis XIV stepped into the shoes of the Habsburgs, says Butterfield, 'added a new chapter to the history of man's modern experience; and if the appropriate conclusions were soon drawn from it, we might say that whenever they have been forgotten since that date, the world has been the loser'.[1] The Venetians, who as much as any community in Europe lived by international trade and wanted to preserve their freedom of action from hegemonial control, had advocated the extension of the Medici concept of the balance of power to the whole system, so that the affairs of all Europe would hang in a complex balance. The Venetian formula had also long been favoured in England, and the Utrecht settlement was quickly nicknamed 'la paix anglaise'. The concept of equilibrium was paramount in the redistributions of territory and other provisions of the settlement, and was most clearly formulated in the treaty between England and Spain, which accepted Louis's grandson as king of Spain but prohibited a union of the crowns of Spain and France. The operative part of the preamble reads:

> Whereas the war, which is so happily ended by this peace, was at the beginning undertaken, and was carried on for so many years with the utmost force, at immense charge, and with almost infinite slaughter, because of the great danger which threatened the liberty and safety of all Europe, from the too close conjunction of the kingdoms of Spain and France; and whereas, to take away all uneasiness and suspicion concerning such conjunction out of the minds of people, and to settle and establish the peace and tranquillity of Christendom by an equal balance of power (which is the best and most solid foundation of a mutual friendship, and of a concord which will be lasting on all sides); as well the Catholic King [of Spain] as the Most Christian King [of France] have consented, that care should be taken by sufficient precautions, that the kingdoms of Spain and of France should never come and be united under the same dominion, and that one and the same person should never become king of both kingdoms.

This passage is also notable for the strength of language, in a treaty, against the disasters of a major war. The sentiment helped to ensure the moderation of eighteenth-century conflicts, as the same sentiment after the Napoleonic Wars helped to ensure moderation in the nineteenth.

The **balance of power** became a feasible practice for eighteenth-century statesmen, in spite of the increased complexity resulting from the fusion of the northern and western systems into one, because Louis XIV's bid for hegemony was broken by a coalition of states in which no one was dominant. There was no successor to Louis's claims, and no state felt strong enough to challenge the prevailing assumptions against hegemony and in favour of balance. During the long ineffectual reign of Louis XV the great potential strength of France was only partially mobilized. France and Austria were now both reasonably satisfied powers. Both recognized an interest in the functioning of the system itself, and were occasionally willing to co-operate with each other to prevent disruption of it, for instance by the rise of Prussia. Russia, westernized and modernized by Peter the Great, became an accepted great power in the system. Its tsars intermarried with European dynasties and became leading members of the sovereigns' club.

The system became much less bipolar. The multilateral balance of power turned on five major states or great powers: France, Austria, Britain–Hanover, Prussia and Russia. All five accepted the system as such, although the two newcomers, Prussia and Russia, considered that the distribution of territory inadequately reflected their increased relative power. Ottoman Turkey continued to be very much a part of the system while remaining largely outside the rules and institutions evolved by the Europeans for themselves. The complex balance between the great powers was steadied and reinforced by a number of powers of the second rank. These included Spain, the Netherlands and Sweden, which had been exhausted by war and reduced in power, and other states such as Denmark, Bavaria, Saxony and Poland. French policy makers felt and sometimes publicly argued that the idea of the balance of power, though formulated in different ways by different foreigners, was fundamentally anti-French. This was only another way of saying that France remained, actually or potentially, the strongest power in Europe. British statesmen were aware of this, and threw their weight fairly consistently against France throughout the period.

The eighteenth century was the age of reason and of mathematics. Reason in public affairs meant the calculation of self-interest. Externally a state had many interests, any one of which if pressed too far would cause disadvantage elsewhere; and it was considered possible to work out the optimum course mathematically after taking every aspect into account. The light of reason was cold, a matter for the mind and the brain rather than the emotions: it was what distinguished men from animals. Eighteenth-century statesmen distrusted the passions, especially powerful herd emotions like race, religion and loyalty to a dynasty. Men and groups of men, they held, were not profoundly different but essentially the same, and so were governments. Territories could be transferred and rulers changed. A balance of power between states in a system corresponded to the parallel ideas of a multilateral balance of trade and to the multiple checks and balances which constitutionalists thought should operate within a state, and indeed to the laws of physics.

European statesmen recognized that affairs of state, both domestic and external, involved power. Power was in principle measurable, and the states system could be portrayed mathematically as a diagram of forces, analogous to the solar system revealed by Newton's discoveries. States great and small exercised attraction and pressure on each other, in proportion to their mass and the distance they kept from one another. If one power in the system grew stronger or weaker, other states moved – or according to others should move – away from it or closer to it. If the mobile balance was continually adjusted, all the states in the system would be checked and held in restraint.

Adjustment – keeping the balance just – was not merely the business of the strongest states. The complex mobile was also affected, like Newton's solar system, by the movements of smaller states. It ensured their autonomy and gave them real and positive roles in the system. The lesson of the previous century was that once any state accumulated the power to lay down the law, it would exercise that power. It then became at best a very painful business, involving protracted and damaging warfare, to reduce that state again to manageable size; and because warfare was unpredictable it might not be possible at all. Dominant power in the system was therefore unacceptable, no matter how legitimately it might occur. The answer in the minds of eighteenth-century statesmen was to prevent the accumulation of such power, and so preserve both the independence of the member states of the system, great and small, and also something close to peace. Therefore neither dynastic connections, nor formal alliances, nor commercial ties, nor religion, nor admiration for the civilization and culture of the potentially hegemonial power must stand in the way of mobility between the member states if a 'just balance' was to be preserved and adjustment was to be continuous. The concept of a just balance, publicly proclaimed, consciously maintained and overriding other considerations, was a significant advance on the anti-hegemonial policies of the previous century or of the ancient world.

Reason and enlightenment were also the order of the day in the domestic affairs of states. In Britain and the Netherlands political theory moved away from the need for a strong state to provide security against domestic and foreign violence, towards more Calvinist ideas, that the social contract involved the continuous consent of the governed and that governments were consciously instituted among men for specific purposes. These ideas gradually spread in France and to a limited extent elsewhere. But most European states were governed by absolute executive authority, with the concentration of power first achieved by the techniques of the *stato*, and often with a remarkable amount of enlightenment and progress dispensed from above. The state was now distinguished from the ruler, who was no longer accorded Louis XIV's personal apotheosis. Louis's heir, the Duke of Burgundy, declared that a king is made for his subjects, not they for the king; and the most thoughtful of the enlightened despots, Frederick the Great of Prussia, described himself not as the incarnation of the state but as its first servant. The distinction between interests of state and the will of the prince helped the system to function more responsibly, though few European rulers admitted an obligation to further the system as a whole.

Within the overarching framework of the balance of power, which restrained the wilful exercise of sovereign independence, the commonwealth of European states managed their international society by four constituent institutions. These were: first, international law, the rules of the game and the codes of conduct derived from a common culture; second, the concept of legitimacy, usually dynastic but modified by treaties; third, a continuous diplomatic dialogue conducted through permanent resident embassies; and fourth, limited war as an ultimate means of adjustment. All four institutions have been bequeathed by the European system to the present global one, and form important elements of it.

International law

The independent sovereigns who made up the European society of states found the untrammelled wilfulness of the Italian Renaissance too disorderly and too unpredictable. Their subjects too, especially the bourgeois and trading classes, became increasingly appalled by the carnage and destruction of religious and acquisitive wars, which reached their climax in the horrors of the Thirty Years War in Germany. If life was not to be so nasty, brutish and short, in Hobbes's famous phrase, then authority, order and law were necessary within a leviathan-state, and so was some equivalent between the sovereign states of the European commonwealth. The appeal and justification of a hegemonial system was that it would provide such an order, and that the hegemonial power would lay down the law. If there was not to be a Habsburg or Bourbon hegemonial order, which its opponents were determined there should not be, then other means of maintaining order were required. Anti-hegemonial princes came to realize that though the conscious maintenance of a balance of power was essential, it was not enough, and that in addition rules were necessary. If they were not to be laid down by a hegemonial power, they must be established by contract: in other words, the sovereign members of the commonwealth of states must bind themselves by rules which they would negotiate together and which would codify and standardize their actual practices. These practices had been partly shaped by medieval rules regulating war and commerce between different realms, and the revival of classical learning stimulated interest in the Roman *jus gentium* and other codes handed down from antiquity; but chiefly they were empirical responses to changing circumstances. For instance, if coastal guns could hit an intruding ship up to a range of three miles, they commanded that area of sea; and since a ship's captain from elsewhere could not know just where the coastal guns might be, it became the practice to keep three miles from all the shore. This practice was codified into the three-mile limit of sovereignty, beyond which lay the open sea free for all to navigate.

The work of the seventeenth-century lawyer-diplomats was continued in the eighteenth century by Vattel, a Prussian subject from Switzerland who became a prominent statesman in Saxony. Vattel tried to introduce a Swiss clarity into the unresolved conflict between the regulatory and the ethical aspects of what he called *le droit des gens* or 'law of nations', by which he meant states. He insisted on the equality of all states with respect to the law: 'A dwarf is as much a man as a giant is: a small republic is no less a state than the most powerful kingdom.'[2] But he recognized that this juridical equality of sovereigns would not mean much unless it was protected by a balance of power.,

The eighteenth-century European commonwealth was a sovereigns' club, and **international law** was the rule book of the club's independent and juridically equal member states. The substitution of human reason for divine fiat involved the secularization of international law. Statesmen agreed, privately if not publicly, that human societies were not natural or God-given, but as Polybius had said emerged as a response to chaos. They were held to be social contracts to protect the individual interests of the consenting members. The rules of the European commonwealth were therefore not immutable ethical commandments; they could be modified by negotiation to keep pace with changing practice. Their function was to make international life more orderly and more predictable, safer and more civilized, and also to induce greater conformity in the practices of states and persuade them to modify their behaviour. The actual rules were reinforced by custom and by codes of conduct.

The fact that European international law was mainly a codification of customary practice, and shaded off into custom not formulated in the form of law, reflected the common culture and what Heeren called the manners and religion of the member states. But not all international law merely codified the particular conventions of European sovereigns. The *jus gentium*, and much of the regulatory pattern in general, had universal assumptions, supposed to be applicable to all governments and peoples whatever their culture or religion. Europeans in Asia were forced to ask themselves what rules could be applied and what conduct expected between states in the multicultural world outside Europe. The beginnings of their search for an answer are discussed in the next chapter.

International law was thus very different from domestic law, which was decreed or enacted by the sovereign for the subjects and enforced by a judiciary backed by the machinery of internal authority. The sovereigns' club constituted a jury of sorts, and an offender could be disciplined by the pressure of his peers; but that was all. The distinction was obvious to eighteenth-century statesmen; the confusion caused by treating the rules of a sovereigns' club as analogous to law within a leviathan-state came later. What did strike eighteenth-century statesmen was the conflict between the law and the balance. Law though mutable took time to alter, and it set up certain norms. It was therefore more rigid than the mobile balance, to which most practising statesmen gave priority, especially as the complex equilibrium of power was what ensured respect for the rules. Men like Vattel saw both sides of the argument, which lasted until it was resolved by the Vienna settlement.

Legitimacy

The society of European states was also based on a complex concept of **legitimacy**. Sovereignty and non-interference, which had evolved as expedients in the two previous centuries, now acquired the status of principles. Some ruler or body was the legitimate sovereign of each state, with the right to speak and act for that state, and it was this person or body with whom other sovereigns dealt and to whom they accredited their envoys. Most states had a hereditary ruler who inherited by primogeniture, and one ruler might inherit more than one state. But the hereditary principle was not absolute. The balance of power might require it to be set aside, as in the Spanish succession. A ruler might prove unsatisfactory to his subjects, as James II of England did, or wish to abdicate; in which case another member of the royal family would succeed. Some states elected their rulers, and others had no crowned head. Moreover, states were constantly acquiring and ceding territories as part of the process of adjustment, regardless of tradition or the views of the inhabitants; so that legitimacy derived also from formally ratified treaties and agreements. Hereditary right and the endorsement of the constituent local authorities were no longer sufficient by themselves to secure sovereignty over a territory. After Utrecht legitimation by the international society of sovereigns was now also required. The legitimacy of possession was conditioned by the fortunes of war and the expediency of the balance.

The accepted members of the sovereigns' club recognized each other's rights, and the need for subjects to accept authority legitimated by inheritance or due process of election, or by cession. Consequently there was a general decline of subversion and stasis. The legitimacy bestowed by heredity and by treaties was a formula of convenience rather than of absolute right. It made for order and predictability and was also flexible enough to allow for the changes which were deemed necessary.

Diplomatic dialogue

The third organizing institution of the eighteenth-century commonwealth of Europe was a continuous multilateral **diplomatic dialogue**.
The Italian innovation of conducting business between princes through
a network of resident agents was developed by the Spanish and French
courts, reaching a climax in the complex diplomacy of Louis XIV.
Richelieu had emphasized that the dialogue should be continuous.
After Utrecht sovereigns took continuity for granted, and diplomacy
became a permanent dialogue. The main lines of communication were
the bilateral confidential exchanges between sovereigns through resident ambassadors and ministers. The representatives of monarchs continued to carry out the negotiating and reporting functions of the
Renaissance agents; but they were now aristocrats in an aristocratic
age, able to play an active part in the life of the court to which
they were accredited. At the same time diplomacy was also becoming
professionalized. Young noblemen learnt diplomacy as subordinates
before receiving posts of responsibility, in the same way as in eighteenth-century armies. Moreover, some of these professionals served
spells at home, to deal with the flow of reports, submit them to their
sovereign and his or her ministers and compose appropriate replies.
In this way foreign offices and ministries of external affairs came into
being. The diplomats in each court or capital recognized each other
as colleagues, though they represented different interests, and learnt
to exchange information and judgements as well as to co-ordinate their
actions where it was to their sovereign's advantage to do so. The *corps
diplomatique*, as the body of diplomats at a court was called, was thus
collectively aware of what a sovereign could be expected or persuaded
to do. They acted as brokers; and the aims of the various sovereigns
were mediated by the brokerage of the diplomatic corps throughout
the system.

The dialogue between sovereigns took a more overtly multilateral
form when congresses were convened, at which statesmen and professional diplomats met together to settle collectively a number of
issues which required widespread consent. The Utrecht settlement was
the most far-reaching of the eighteenth-century congresses, most of
which were convened to establish an accepted position after a resort
to war, as Utrecht was. The diplomatic dialogue, continuously bilateral
and intermittently collective, made possible the operation of a mobile
of rapidly shifting relations between member states and the preservation of a balance of power, as well as the continuous revision of
international law and other features of the society of states.

The use of force

The diplomatic dialogue was principally concerned with power. The persuasion, inducements and threats which it used were designed not to preserve the status quo but to mediate the subtle adjustments which changes in the relative power of member states made it possible to effect by force if persuasion failed, combined with the shift in the mobile needed to preserve a just balance. Ideally the sovereigns' club could make a concession to the increased power of one of its members here, or contain it there, without the need to resort to force. But in practice the mobile did not always function quickly or smoothly enough, and sovereigns were not always willing to adjust to the logic of changes in their power. The ultimate sanction, when other inducements and deterrents failed, was to **resort to force**. The eighteenth-century balance of power preserved the liberty of the member sovereigns of the European system, and especially of the smaller ones, but it did not always keep the peace.

However, war in eighteenth-century Europe was a moderate affair. War was now once more a matter for professional paid armies in uniform, carefully drilled and provided for at considerable cost to the state, and in which casualties were to be kept to a minimum. The trouble with war, said Frederick the Great's father, is that it damages your army so. It was better and cheaper for a state to use its armed strength as a demonstration of its power, without having to prove it by fighting. The Maréchal de Saxe, a distinguished French general, thought that it should be possible to wage a successful campaign without actually having to fight a battle at all. This ideal was not achieved, but the element of violence gradually faded away. 'Armies', says Professor Michael Howard, 'declined from wolf packs to gun dogs, and often to performing poodles.'[3] From Utrecht to the French Revolution, war in Europe was disagreeable and destructive, but it did not set back the rapid progress of European civilization, and far from disturbing the smooth operation of the international system on balance it assisted it. Minor wars adjust, it was said, whereas major wars destroy.

Three eighteenth-century descriptions of the new international society give us a useful picture of how its contemporaries saw it. The first is by Voltaire, writing about 1750. His memorable phrases outline the accepted eighteenth-century European picture of the system, as a backdrop for his account of the age of Louis XIV:

> For some time now it has been possible to consider Christian Europe, give or take Russia, as 'une espèce de grande république' – a sort of great commonwealth – partitioned into several states,

some monarchic, the others mixed, some aristocratic, others popular, but all dealing with one another; all having the same basic religion, though divided into various sects; all having the same principles of public and political law unknown in the other parts of the world. Because of these principles the European nations [i.e. states] never enslave their prisoners, they respect the ambassadors of their enemies, they jointly acknowledge the pre-eminence and various rights of certain princes like the emperor, the kings and the other lesser rulers, and above all they agree on the wise policy of maintaining an equal balance of power between themselves so far as they can, conducting continuous negotiations even in times of war, and exchanging resident ambassadors or less honourable spies, who can warn all the courts of Europe of the designs of any one, give the alarm at the same time and protect the weaker from the invasions which the strongest is always ready to undertake.[4]

The second is by Vattel, setting out the background to his 'Law of Nations' at about the same time as Voltaire:

Europe forms a political system in which the Nations inhabiting this part of the world are bound together by their relations and various interests into a single body. It is no longer, as in former times, a confused heap of detached parts, each of which had but little concern for the lot of the others, and rarely troubled itself over what did not immediately affect it. The constant attention of sovereigns to all that goes on, the custom of resident ministers, the continual negotiations that take place, make of modern Europe a sort of 'république' [commonwealth], whose members – each independent, but all bound together by a common interest – unite for the maintenance of order and the preservation of liberty. This is what has given rise to the well-known principle of the balance of power, by which is meant an arrangement of affairs so that no State shall be in a position to have absolute mastery and dominate over the others.

The surest means of preserving this balance of power would be to bring it about that no State should be much superior to the others, that all the States, or at least the larger part, should be about equal in strength. This idea has been attributed to Henry IV, but it is one that could not be realized without injustice and violence. And moreover, once this equality were established, how could it be regularly maintained by lawful means? Commerce, right of inheritance, even in favour of women and their descendants, which has been so absurdly established for succession to the throne, but which after all has been established, would over-turn your arrangement.

It is simpler, easier, and more just to have recourse to the method indicated above, of forming alliances in order to make a stand against a very powerful sovereign and prevent him from dominating. This is the plan followed by the sovereigns of Europe at the present day. They look upon the two principal powers, who for that very reason are naturally rivals, as destined to act as a mutual check upon each other, and they unite with the weaker of the two, thereby acting as so much weight thrown into the lighter scale in order to make the balance even. The House of Austria has for a long time been the predominant power; now it is the turn of France. England, whose wealth and powerful navy have given her a very great influence, without, however, causing any State to fear for its liberty, since that power appears to be cured of the spirit of conquest – England, I say, has the honour to hold in her hands the political scales. She is careful to maintain them in equilibrium. It is a policy of great wisdom and justice, and one which will be always commendable, so long as she makes use only of alliances, confederations, and other equally lawful means.[5]

The third description is by Heeren, a Hanoverian subject of George III and the great historian of the states system who wrote during the Napoleonic occupation when it was in suspense:

[From the preface:]

Among the remarkable phenomena which the general history of mankind presents to our notice, that of the European states-system or confederation of states, during the last three centuries, is the greatest, and at the same time, with reference to ourselves, the most important. The states-systems which were formed in ancient Greece, and in Italy during the Middle Ages, are far inferior, as regards both their power and their extent; and though the Macedonian system which arose out of the division of Alexander's universal monarchy may perhaps be compared with it in this respect as well as in some others, it still altogether failed to attain to such an exalted degree of maturity and refinement.

Whoever undertakes to write the history of any particular states-system (by which we mean **the union of several contiguous states resembling each other in their manners, religion and degree of social improvement, and cemented together by a reciprocity of interests**) [my emphasis] ought above all things to possess a right conception of its general character. In the system of

208

European states, it is obvious this character must be sought for in its internal freedom, or in other words the mutual indepen- dence of its members, however disproportionate they may other- wise be in regard to physical power. It is this feature which distinguishes such a system from one of an opposite class, that is, where an acknowledged preponderance of one of the member states exists.

[From the introduction:]

The European states-system displays all the variety of which it is susceptible. It is undoubtedly to this practical variety that Europe is chiefly indebted for her enlightened and enlarged views in general politics: to which must be attributed not only her superior policy, but in a great measure her rapid advancement in civilization.

The European states-system also acquired firmer stability from the fortunate circumstance of having its centre composed of a state, the form of which, imperfect as it was in itself, was never- theless of the greatest advantage to the whole system. This was the German Empire. Without such a central state, important to all but dangerous to none, this system could scarcely have grown up as it has. Enlightened policy soon perceived that on the pres- ervation of this Empire the welfare of the existing order of things mainly depended.

The principles which held this system together, and guaranteed the security and independence of the weak against the strong, were of various kinds. . . . [Heeren here discusses the law of nations and the sanctity of recognized legitimate possession.]

Another important support of this system was the adoption and maintenance of the principle of a balance of power: that is, the attention paid by the different states to the preservation of their mutual independence, by preventing any particular one from rising to such a degree of power as should seem inconsistent with the general liberty. . . . The maintenance of this principle led to the following consequences:

(a) It led to a vigilant attention of the states to the affairs of each other: and to a multitude of new and various relations between them, by means of alliances and counter-alliances, especially among the more distant ones.
(b) It gave a greater importance in the political system to states of the second and third order.
(c) It promoted a general feeling of respect for independence.

The European political system found a third support in the

establishment of maritime states, which more than all others have contributed to maintain the balance of power. The rise of maritime states, and the peculiar nature of their influence in the political balance of Europe, prevented land forces from alone deciding everything.[6]

These three passages formulate the assumptions of eighteenth-century practice. All three writers saw the balance of power as the determining characteristic of the states system. They describe a deliberate balance, which is far from automatic, and which is to be directed not against this or that dominant power but against hegemony from any quarter, and which protects the independence of the weak against the strong. Its purpose is to keep a system far towards the multiple independences end of the spectrum. The balance of power is the particular concern of maritime states which derive their strength largely from outside Europe: Venice, then the Netherlands, then Britain.

The eighteenth century also thought of the European society of states as a commonwealth much more closely knit than some later historians of individual states have realized. Burke referred to Europe as a federative society, in the sense of one united by treaties, and as a diplomatic republic, like Voltaire and Vattel. Heeren significantly took it for granted that such a commonwealth or union required common values and a shared background of tradition and custom, in other words a unity of culture, as well as a roughly level stage of material development. Eighteenth-century Europe, excluding the Ottoman Empire, met Heeren's requirements in a way which the diverse states of the modern world clearly do not.

Heeren regarded the German or Holy Roman Empire (which he still called a state) as important to all but dangerous to none, because it acted like a sponge, absorbing and balancing the pressures of the great powers that maintained an influence there either through territory or through client allies, and was composed of so many pieces that small shifts of power could easily modify the balance. His comment raises the question whether a balanced system of independent states requires a sponge area of this kind. Heeren also saw the Macedonian system as the one most resembling his own. Men of his age were always on the look-out for classical models, of course, but there are some striking analogies. The Macedonian system had a common Hellenistic culture; it was dominated by powerful and absolute monarchies with interrelated royal families; it was in an approximate though not a consciously formulated balance; Greece itself within the system was important to all and dangerous to none, fragmented and acting as a sponge; largely mercenary armies fought and manoeuvred for advantage rather than for causes; the Rhodians, in some ways the Dutch of that time, were evolving a code of maritime law; and there are many other resemblances.

As a way of managing diverse communities, admittedly within the same culture, the eighteenth-century European system worked well – certainly better and less dangerously than Europe had known at any time since the high Middle Ages, and conspicuously better than the devastating wars and stasis of the age of religious conviction or the struggle for and against hegemony. Europeans held – and still hold – that their dynamic civilization was enriched by the variety of its many individual manifestations. As in ancient China, a man who did not like one society or its ruler, for reasons of religion or political conviction or opportunity, could move without much difficulty to another. Personal security, population, wealth, standards of living, the sciences and especially the application of reason to human affairs advanced prodigiously. So much so that the eighteenth century was an age of enlightenment and of optimism, and of a widespread and heady belief in progress.

However, the eighteenth-century society of sovereigns had unsatisfactory features. It was a gain that war had become professionalized, and a demonstration of power rather than an orgy of destruction. But the competitive nature of the states system led sovereigns and statesmen to devote to the power struggle what seemed to many an undue amount of attention and of resources. Moreover, the commitment to preserving a balance of power led to the transfer of territories from one sovereign to another regardless of tradition, the wishes of the inhabitants or other considerations. This was particularly true of the fragmented territories of Germany and Italy. The process reached its climax in the partitions of Poland at the end of the century, when it seemed more important to preserve a general equilibrium in the east of Europe by assigning large areas of that ancient kingdom to Prussia and the Habsburgs, rather than to allow the whole weakened and ethnically mixed state to fall under Russian control. The partitions were the outcome of the struggle over the Polish succession, and a logical extrapolation of the methods used to resolve similar struggles over the Spanish and Austrian successions. Eighteenth-century sovereigns considered the equilibrium of Europe more important than the consent of the governed.

Thus the eighteenth-century European system assured the independence of its member states, by and large, though not their territorial integrity. But though the destructiveness and horrors of warfare were greatly reduced, it continued. Statesmen and others who applied reason to politics questioned whether a wilful sovereign might not get out of hand, and whether the existing checks and balances, internal and external, were adequate to restrain such a ruler. While such men devoted much thought and argument to constitutional means of controlling the executive power within the state, they gave much less consideration to the more difficult question of constitutional restraints by the system on the external conduct of the states comprising it.

The philosopher Immanuel Kant, watching the operations of the eighteenth-century system from the Baltic, where provinces frequently passed from one sovereignty to another, considered that it did not matter much which sovereign a piece of territory and its inhabitants came under, provided the state was adequately enlightened and just. In most of Europe enlightenment, where it existed, was rational and came from above. Emotional nationalism, and especially linguistic nationalism, was not yet an active force. Kant thought the next necessary task for the diplomatic republic of Europe was to prevent war, with its attendant waste, damage and chanciness; and thereby to reduce considerably the degree of preparedness and the competitive participation in the balance of power, which cost states so much money and effort even if they were not engaged in military operations. His proposal for *Perpetual Peace*, couched in the form of a draft treaty, recognized that it was not desirable or possible to abolish separate sovereignties in favour of a single imperial government. He also saw the value of the balance, and held that states keep each other straight like pine trees in a forest. The way to ensure peace was for the most powerful states, and especially those with constitutions which restrained the will of the ruler, to join together in a perpetual league and covenant. Kant's league was not committed to the status quo. Its purpose was to maintain the peace, and to effect necessary corrections of the balance by negotiation and where necessary the reassignment of territory. He proposed that the moderate sovereigns (who he hoped had a preponderance of force as well as reason on their side) should agree to impose the adjustments required by the balance instead of leaving the task to the ultimate argument of kings, the resort to war. *Perpetual Peace* is one of the first examples in European international society of a proposal put forward not by a statesman as a generalization from practical experience, but by a thinker on the basis of theoretical reasoning, and which nevertheless came to be substantially adopted, though in a modified form and after the devastations of the Napoleonic Wars. Kant's formulation reflects the eighteenth century, but the basic ideas are strikingly contemporary.[7]

The eighteenth-century European *grande république* stands out among states systems and phases of systems as exceptionally successful. It was well managed by the conscious co-operation, or at least restraint, of its member sovereigns, who valued their independence within a non-hegemonial framework of balanced order. The circumstances in which the eighteenth-century system functioned were also exceptional. Most notably, no power was in a position to make an effective bid for hegemony; and there was a prevalence of reason, an absence of passionate causes like religion or nationalism. The sovereigns' club could make and observe the rules. These circumstances were partly a fortunate accident, an interlude like the century of the Renaissance in Italy. It was a situation that statesmen could maintain but hardly bring about by design. Its rules and practices cannot be applied as they stand to other systems which are dominated by a hegemonial power, rent by popular passions or too diverse in culture and degree of development to form a *grande république* at all. Nevertheless the level of creative statecraft of the European eighteenth century is so outstanding that many of its concepts and much of its machinery continue transmuted in the present very different global system, and much of the wisdom which was then acquired remains relevant to other international societies including our own.

NOTES

1 H. Butterfield, 'The historic states-systems', paper for the British Committee on the Theory of International Politics, 1965.
2 Vattel, *Le Droit des Gens*.
3 M. Howard, *War in European History*, Oxford, Oxford University Press, 1976, p. 73.
4 Voltaire, *L'Histoire du Règne de Louis XIV*, Chapter 2.
5 Vattel, op. cit., Book III, Chapter 3, sections 47–8.
6 H. A. L. Heeren (1834) *History of the Political System of Europe and its Colonies*, trans. from the German, Oxford, Talboys, 1834, preface and introduction.
7 See, in this context, F. H. Hinsley, *Power and the Pursuit of Peace*, Cambridge, Cambridge University Press, 1963, pp. 62–80.

19

EUROPEAN EXPANSION
Overseas and overland

The expansion of Europe into the rest of the world, by conquest and settlement, by trade and administrative empire and by the diffusion of its civilization and its unique technology, was a major event in the history of mankind. It was a slow and complex process that took place over many centuries and took many different forms. This chapter is concerned with European expansion before the radical change of the nineteenth century. In that century the Europeans created the first international system to span the whole globe, and established everywhere a universalized version of the rules and institutions and the basic assumptions of the European society of states. Our present international society is directly descended from that universalized European system.

The fitful and diverse expansion of some European states over the rest of the world took place in parallel with the gradual process of organizing the vertical states of Europe into a *grande république* or anti-hegemonial international society. The expansion inevitably altered the nature and the balance of the European system. Its member states did not have a set of established rules and institutions which they attempted to impose ready-made on the rest of the world. On the contrary, they continually modified the rules and institutions of their evolving international society to take account of its wider range.

The west Europeans found that the world into which they expanded consisted of two different types of community. On the one hand were the high civilizations of Asia, which were as developed as the European civilization, and in many ways more so. On the other hand were the more primitive peoples whose existence was largely unknown to the civilized world. The most striking feature of the highly civilized area to the east of Latin Christendom was the continuing and successful spread of Islam, with its special adaptation of the earlier near eastern and Hellenistic civilizations. The Arab–Persian world from Morocco to Afghanistan was solidly Muslim. Beyond that Muslim conquerors were extending their dominion over vast territories and immense numbers of subject peoples in three directions. Muslims of Afghan and Turkic origin were establishing a fluctuating rule or suzerainity over the whole Hindu world from Persia to the Pacific. The Ottomans were similarly conquering eastern Europe: they took Constantinople in 1453 and within three-quarters of a century were besieging Vienna. In the north the semi-nomadic Tartar rulers of the steppes were also converted to Islam, though by 1500 their dominion over Russia was beginning to ebb. To the east of Islam was the Chinese imperial system, at that time under Mongol domination, and the similar civilization of Japan.

Professor Hedley Bull and I have summarized as follows the main features of the developed Asian systems, which distinguish them from the emerging European system:

> These regional international systems were, of course, very different from one another: the Arab–Islamic and Indian systems, for example, were in practice composed of a number of independent political entities, whereas the Mongol–Tartar and Chinese systems were more effectively centralized. But they had one feature in common: they were all, at least in the theory that underlay them, hegemonial or imperial. At the centre of each was a suzerain Supreme Ruler – the Khalifa or Commander of the Faithful, the Emperor in Delhi, the Mongol Great Khan, the Chinese Son of Heaven – who exercised direct authority over the heartland; and around this empire extended a periphery of locally autonomous realms that acknowledged the suzerain's overlordship and paid him tribute. Many peripheral states were able to maintain a complete independence in spite of the nominal claims of the Supreme Ruler. Beyond each fluctuating periphery there lay kingdoms and principalities which were recognized, even by the Supreme Ruler, as independent, although not as his equals – for example, the reduced state of Byzantium before its final collapse in 1453, the kingdoms of the Deccan and Java, some Russian principalities, and Japan.
>
> Within each of the suzerain-state systems, different as they were, relations among political authorities were regulated by specific treaties as well as by traditional codes of conduct, governing such matters as the movement of envoys who came and went, the payment of tribute, commercial exchanges, and the waging of war. States of the periphery maintained relations with each other as well as with the Supreme Ruler. But they did not combine to overthrow the central authority. They might disobey it or rebel against it, and sometimes a powerful king might aspire

to take it over; but they all assumed that some hegemonial focus would continue to exist, to lay down the rules and determine the nature of relations among the members of the system. There was no attempt, within these major, extra-European international systems, to question the underlying hegemonial concept.

Contacts among these regional international systems (and with the different world of medieval Latin Christendom) were much more limited than contacts within them. There was trade, especially by sea across the Mediterranean and the Indian Ocean. There was some diplomatic communication and military conflict, in some cases severe, as between Latin Christendom and the Arab–Islamic system. The Arab–Islamic system, to a limited extent, provided brokers and middle-men between the other systems; Islamic geographers, for example, had a much more accurate concept of the Old World than either the medieval Europeans or the Chinese, Marco Polo notwithstanding. But not even the three Islamic systems (Arab–Islamic, Mongol–Tartar, and Indian) may be said to have formed among themselves a single international system or international society, in the sense in which we use these terms; much less did any such system embrace the world as a whole.[1]

The **Ottomans** played a major part in the European states system from its sixteenth-century beginnings down to its merger into the present global system. The trade with the Levant was a vital component of the economic life of Europe. Strategically the Ottomans occupied about a quarter of the continent until the end of the seventeenth century, and were as formidable a military and naval power as any in Europe. The Habsburg bid to establish a hegemonial system in Christian Europe was defeated, and the decisive Westphalian formulation of the anti-hegemonial nature of the European international society was made possible, by Ottoman pressure on the Habsburgs, co-ordinated by the Franco-Turkish alliance which brought the other anti-hegemonial powers into friendly relations with the Ottomans. Even in the centuries of the empire's decline Ottoman policy remained a prominent factor in the calculations of the European powers.

In spite of this close involvement, for most of the period the Turks were not members of what Voltaire called the *grande république* and Burke the federative society or diplomatic republic of Europe. Commanders of the Faithful disdained membership of the European society of Christian states, and were (perhaps therefore) not considered eligible by the Europeans. The Turks were not Christians. They did not accept the European principles of international law, which for instance forbade enslaving prisoners of war and guaranteed immunity for diplomats. The Ottomans were absent from the settlements of Westphalia, Utrecht and Vienna. They were not formally accepted into the European international society until 1856, after the Crimean War, and in practice hardly even then. Nevertheless, from the beginning they and the European powers together formed an international society of a looser kind: in Bull's terms they conceived themselves to be bound by a common set of rules in their relations and shared in the working of common institutions.

The most characteristic of these institutions were the 'capitulations' governing trade and residence for Europeans in the empire. These were, as their name indicates, *capitula* or chapters of detailed rules, mainly concerned with the regulation of trade and extraterritorial jurisdiction. In origin they were unilateral Muslim formulations of rules to govern relations with citizens of infidel states. Harun al Rashid granted them to the Franks; and his successors drew up similar sets of rules in the eleventh and twelfth centuries to regulate the activities in Muslim territory of Italian merchants. The Byzantines made similar arrangements. Both in the *dar al Islam* and in medieval Christendom the sovereignty of a ruler covered only those who owed allegiance to him. It did not extend to aliens. But aliens whose presence and activities were profitable, such as traders, must be subject to some laws; and those laws must be sufficiently acceptable to the traders to ensure that they came. Muslim rulers found that the most expedient solution was to make each alien community subject to its own laws, which its members knew, and which could be administered by a local representative of their prince or government. This solution was in fact an extension of the arrangements for managing subject nationalities under Muslim rule.

The Ottoman sultans continued the established Muslim practice. Capitulations were established in 1536 for subjects of the king of France, in 1583 for subjects of the king of England and in 1613 for Netherlanders. The Europeans in the Ottoman Empire were under the jurisdiction of consuls, who could call on the aid of the Ottoman authorities to enforce both the capitulatory rules and the laws of their own state. The Ottomans regarded capitulations as unilateral and only valid for the lifetime of the sultan who proclaimed them, so that they had to be renewed after each accession. The Europeans regarded them as contractual treaties between sovereign states; and indeed they did contain reciprocal provisions that regulated the situation of Ottoman subjects in the European state concerned. As the Europeans grew more powerful and the Ottomans relatively weaker, the capitulations were modified for the benefit of the Europeans, especially in matters concerning investment of capital and immunity from Ottoman law. What began as a Muslim contribution to the rules regulating intercourse between separate states systems was in the period of Ottoman strength still largely formulated by the Muslims; but by the nineteenth century the rules were rewritten and prescribed by the Europeans, as one would expect.

The Ottomans also used the machinery of European diplomacy, and in some respects helped to shape it. The sultans at an early stage accepted resident European ambassadors at Istanbul, though they did not bother to send envoys in return. The European concept of consulates grew out of relations with the Ottomans, and for instance the first English consulate was established at Aleppo. The French–Ottoman agreement contained secret and oral strategic provisions directed against the Habsburgs, and the Ottomans supported the German Protestants for the same reason. In the period of Ottoman strength their support for the anti-hegemonial forces in Europe was not in itself anti-hegemonial, but designed to weaken the main barrier to the expansion of Ottoman hegemony up the Danube. Louis XIV's grand design and relative Turkish weakness made Ottoman support for France more ambivalent. The diplomatic envoys of Britain and the Netherlands were able to mediate peace between the Holy Roman and the Ottoman empires at the Congress of Karlowitz in 1698–9 in order to free the hand of the Habsburgs for the anti-hegemonial struggle against Louis. There was a similar evolution of the codes of conduct that regulated warfare between the Ottomans and their European allies and enemies.

In sum, the Europeans and the Ottomans, like the states of today's multicultural world, formed an international society in the sense that they co-operated in the working of agreed procedures of international law, diplomacy and general international organization, and certain customs and conventions of war. But the institutions and conventions that regulated the involvement of the two civilizations were much more restricted and more explicit than those of the European *grande république*.

The first expansion of western Europe over the Atlantic was eminently orderly and imperial. A proclamation by the pope and a negotiated agreement, the **Treaty of Tordesillas** in 1493, established hemispheres of exclusive jurisdiction for Spain in the west and Portugal in the east that avoided conflict between the two Iberian powers and excluded the rest of Christendom.

From the beginning the **New World of the Americas** was treated very differently from the ancient and highly developed civilizations of Asia. The Spaniards, and the Portuguese who owing to geographical ignorance were accidentally awarded the eastern part of South America that is now Brazil, treated American territory as an extension of the Reconquista, to be colonized and settled in the same way as the southern parts of their European kingdoms. The Spaniards gave their great new domains names like New Granada and New Spain, and introduced Spanish law and other institutions with the Spanish settlers. The Iberians found that most of the New World was inhabited by what they called wild men, and therefore belonged to no civilized authority. The Spaniards found two wealthy and developed but (by European standards) oppressive Stone Age empires in Mexico and Peru; and these also they destroyed in the same way as they had just liquidated the emirate of Granada in southern Spain. There was thus a sharp discontinuity between the Amerindian societies and the new European dependent states which came into being, and which were governed even more directly than European Spain and Portugal by the bureaucratic authority of the crown. A great deal of Spanish and considerable Portuguese effort was directed towards the establishment of these states, which remain today an enormous and lasting achievement. From the beginning the colonial states of the New World were an extension of Christian Europe, European in form and run by Europeans.

Naturally the Iberian kings, and especially the Habsburgs during their bid for hegemony in Europe, expected their new provinces to contribute as much as possible to the strength of their *stato*. But the contributions of the New World were somewhat illusory. Precious metals, especially silver, were shipped back to Europe in large quantities, and some tropical agricultural produce was also exported, especially after the first turbulent century of colonization. The colonists exploited the local population in spite of opposition by the church, and achieved a higher standard of living than they had enjoyed at home. A few merchants and others in Europe also made fortunes. Moreover, the possession of a great empire in the New World impressed other Europeans and added to the weight of Habsburg power. But the New World imported much from Europe; and when the heavy costs in defence, administrative talent and immigration are taken into account, it is today a matter of controversy how much net benefit, if any, European Spain derived from the American 'Indies'.

The most commercially developed area of Europe was the Netherlands. There the Protestant Dutch were fighting to make good their secession from the Habsburg Empire and were the animators of the anti-hegemonial coalition. They deemed the hegemonial partition of the outside world into hemispheres of monopoly by the pope and the Habsburgs to be devoid of legitimacy. The Dutch prudently left alone the Spanish colonial states in the Americas, and concentrated on taking over the positions of their commercial rivals the Portuguese. A prolonged attempt to establish themselves in Brazil finally failed, and other Dutch ventures in the Americas were minor.

Two other peoples on the Atlantic seaboard of Europe, the French and the English, followed in the wake of the Dutch, disregarding the hemispheres of monopoly and joining the competitive free-for-all. In North America and the Caribbean both powers founded new dependent settler states. The English and French colonies were less directly administered than the Spanish ones, and much authority was delegated in practice to the emigrants and chartered companies who pushed out the frontiers of European settlement. The English colonists especially considered themselves, and in fact were, increasingly autonomous. But all the European settler colonies in the Americas were tied to their European homelands in many ways. The ties included: shared culture and civilization, continuously reinforced by immigration; trade, because the colonies produced for the European market, selling to the 'mother country' and buying from it; and above all defence, for the European powers and their colonials fought each other incessantly in the wealth-producing Caribbean islands and on the mainland, and the settlers needed the resources of a powerful and vigilant European state to protect them. During the period of Louis XIV's bid for hegemony in Europe the French conceived an imaginative imperial plan for North America under royal direction, based on the St Lawrence and the Mississippi. The English colonies were particularist, many of them founded by different sects of religious dissenters who applied an American version of the *cujus regio ejus religio* formula; and their anti-hegemonial attitude to their French rivals was stiffened by Huguenots opposed to the French crown who came to America after Louis revoked the Edict of Nantes in 1685. The French bid for hegemony was muted after the Utrecht settlement, and their hold on North America was broken in the middle of the eighteenth century by Washington's capture of Fort Duquesne (renamed Pittsburgh) and Wolfe's capture of Quebec.

It is instructive to compare the west European colonization of the Americas with the Greek colonies round the Mediterranean and the Black Sea in the period of the city states. There were the same cultural links, not merely with Hellas or Europe as a whole but with a particular mother state, and similar commercial ties. The competition and warfare between the new Greek city states were as intense as between the European colonies. But a new Greek polis was independent from its foundation, and its defence links with the parent city were tenuous at best. In contrast the states of western Europe retained what they called sovereignty over the dependent states which they had created, along with the responsibility for their defence and a trade monopoly to pay for it. Yet underneath the superstructure of imperial authority the European settler states from Canada to Chile were moving in practice steadily towards the independences end of our scale. The

New World colonies attracted the self-reliant and those who wished to escape from authority. Consequently within the external framework of dependency the European settlers developed an increasing capacity to manage their own affairs, and acquired the experience of government required for independent statehood and membership of the European international society when the time came.

The maritime European experience in **Asia** was quite different. Mediterranean trading cities like Venice, Genoa and Barcelona had grown rich on the trade with the Levant, importing luxury goods from the highly developed civilizations of Asia through Muslim intermediaries into Europe, in return for what Europe could produce or pay for. The Portuguese purpose in undertaking the long and hazardous voyages round Africa into the Indian Ocean was to cut out the Mediterranean middlemen and to trade with India and the Spice Islands direct. The Portuguese enterprise was maritime and commercial, and they wanted only minimal bases, little more than fortified warehouses and dockyards, at the other end of the voyage. Sometimes they bought or otherwise acquired small areas of land round their bases, but with no thought of establishing settler colonies like those in the New World. They remembered the injunction of Almeida, the first viceroy or representative of the Portuguese state in the Indies: 'The greater the number of fortresses you hold, the weaker will be your power. Let all your forces be on the sea.'

While the Europeans dominated the New World, in the east they were the clients of Asian authorities. The Portuguese traders in the Indian Ocean were in the same position as the Arabs who sailed between India and the Levant, and the Chinese who plied between the Indian Ocean and the Pacific. They fitted into the usual pattern of trade between different civilizations, which in addition to actual buying and selling involves dealings with the local authorities and perhaps relations of some kind with the ruler of the area. The Portuguese commanders were representatives of their king, and they dealt with the non-Muslim authorities which they found in Asia formally as other European rulers, and in practice much as the Italians and French dealt with the Ottomans. At the end of long lines of communication, they were willing to accept a client relationship in return for trading privileges. In addition to selling European goods and bullion at cheaper prices than Arab middlemen, the Portuguese had a technological advantage to offer local rulers: they commanded the sea by means of naval guns that far outclassed anything else in the east. They were therefore effective allies and enemies in local conflicts. In the sixteenth century the conceptually hegemonic Indian system was in one of its periods of disintegration into a great variety of Muslim and Hindu principalities, comparable with the situation described in the *Arthashastra*. The Portuguese hostility to Muslims, derived from the reconquest of their own country from the Moors and then their involvement on the Habsburg side against the Ottoman Turks, made them especially welcome to Hindu princes. But local rulers, while accepting the commercial and strategic advantages of the Portuguese presence, did not modify their concepts or their practices to suit European ones.

Portuguese commercial enterprise in the Indian Ocean was very profitable, and soon attracted the attention of merchants and bankers in the Netherlands. In their struggle against the Habsburgs the Dutch relied on their commercial classes to provide the financial sinews of the war. When in 1580 the crown of Portugal was inherited by the Habsburgs, the Dutch could no longer obtain the wares of the east from Portugal, and they began trading directly with the east on their own account. Dutch operations were not conducted under orderly state direction, like the Portuguese, but by private merchant companies. The Dutch attacked the Portuguese where they could, and were glad to co-operate with Muslim rulers because Ottoman attacks on the Habsburgs greatly helped the Dutch struggle for independence. They were soon providing armed protection to Muslim rulers in Java and the Spice Islands in return for a trade monopoly. Dutch political involvements in the Indian Ocean grew out of local circumstances rather than from any imperial design in the Netherlands.

European ventures into the Pacific were even more tenuous. The Spaniards colonized the Philippines as a westward extension of Mexico. The Portuguese and Dutch came from the Indian Ocean. The Portuguese established a trading post in China, for which they paid 'tribute', in 1516, and one in Japan in the 1540s. The first Dutch expedition arrived in China in 1542. The Europeans introduced some technical innovations such as firearms and clocks, and carried silks, tea and similar luxuries back to Europe. But their contacts with China and Japan were sporadic.

The Portuguese and Dutch ventures mark the beginning of the economic and strategic involvement of the European system with the high civilizations of Asia east of the Ottoman Empire. The Europeans transported the goods and supplied some naval technology; but, few in numbers and far from home, they had to conform to the ways and learn the languages of their Asian trading partners. Consequently the degree and the shape of the relationship were determined in Asia by the Asian rulers concerned. The general nature of the relationship was similar to that of the Europeans to the Ottomans; and the arrangements in the Indian Ocean and with China and Japan were in fact different varieties of 'capitulation'.

Though the Dutch failed in Brazil, in the more lucrative east they got the better of the struggle. Their success broke up the orderly Iberian approach based on hemispheres of monopoly that excluded other Europeans, and substituted a commercial and military free-for-all of conflict and competition. European expansion beyond the Atlantic was transformed from trade and occasional conflict with non-Europeans into a long and complex struggle of European states and traders against each other. Overseas as in Europe the Dutch aim was to push the system towards the multiple independences end of the spectrum. Their anti-hegemonial assumptions and the principle of freedom of the seas for trade legitimized in their eyes their activities in the east, and strengthened their determination to incorporate those principles in the rules for the emerging European society of states. The extra strength which their overseas activities brought them contributed materially to their hard-won victories in Europe, and so enabled them to play a major part in shaping the rules of the emerging European society.

In addition to their practical experience with the Ottomans, the Europeans brought to their dealings with other peoples and governments their ideas of natural law. The concept of general or natural rules governing the relations between human beings everywhere, and evident by the light of God's reason, had for centuries formed part of their thinking. Natural laws were held to be formulated in practice by the Roman *jus gentium*, which regulated relations of peoples and states with each other in matters such as war and peace and the rights and obligations of resident foreigners. Because the laws of nature were universal and reciprocal, it followed that all *gentes* were to be regarded in the light of reason as moral equals, however different their beliefs and customs might be. There was some doubt about whether these reciprocal rules could reasonably be applied to wild men or savages. But the Europeans applied them as a matter of course to the highly civilized peoples of Asia, and were not surprised to find that the Asian authorities (except perhaps the Chinese) seemed to share their ideas. The Europeans supplemented the general principles of the *jus gentium* with the formalities and practices of European diplomatic intercourse. Envoys and sometimes merchant captains carried letters of credence authorizing them to act in the name of their sovereign. The European forms were tactfully modified to conform with Indian and far eastern usage, at first by Asian intermediaries and then by the Europeans themselves as they learnt Asian languages and customs, and saw the need for elasticity. What a European envoy might report back to his sovereign as an exchange of gifts between equals could be treated by an Asian ruler as an offering of tribute and a grant of aid to the European petitioner (cf. Chapter 12).

The rival British and French maritime trading companies shared Dutch ideas about a commercial free-for-all, though they were also aware of the advantages of local monopoly. They concentrated their attention on India, where they largely supplanted the Portuguese. They fortified their depots and ports of call more against each other than against local rulers, who usually found their presence advantageous. During the seventeenth century the brilliant Mogul Empire, Muslim but necessarily pluralist in face of the Hindu majority, reasserted the suzerainty over India which the former sultans of Delhi had exercised, and by the end of the century had made it effective in the south where the main European trading centres were established. The European companies acted like the local Indian rulers: they accepted subordinate positions in the new hegemoninal pattern, and gradually extended the areas of their administration within the constitutional framework of the Mogul Empire, as agents of the emperor or a vassal prince. The relationship of the Europeans to the imperial and local Indian authorities was facilitated by the formula that both the English and the French in India were members of private merchant companies rather than representatives of their kings. In China and Japan, Europeans operated more as individuals and in more subordinate positions, except for Dutch control of the island of Formosa.

In the eighteenth century the grip of the Mogul Empire weakened, and power in India again became more diffused. Competition between the British and French trading companies now took the form of an armed struggle, reflecting the conflict between the two powers in Europe. While the two European companies held each other in check, many Indian rulers and pretenders, freed from the restraints of hegemony, resorted to war to extend their domains, and granted one European company or the other the exclusive trading privileges which it wanted in return for a military alliance. Eighteenth-century Euro-Indian alliances were modelled on the treaties in force between European sovereigns. The British especially talked in anti-hegemonial terms of maintaining or restoring a balance of power in the subcontinent as though it was another European system. They did not yet think of establishing their own hegemony, let alone dominion, over India as a whole.

An important stage in the expansion of Europe was reached in the eighteenth century when two states that had been created or greatly influenced by Europeans – Russia and the United States – became members of the European society. Although those two states had a European heritage they were historically and geographically peripheral to Latin Christendom and on a vaster scale. They became the two superpowers of the global system.

The consequences for the European system of the independence of the United States and the other American states that followed suit are discussed in Chapter 22.

At the same time as the Atlantic Europeans were enlarging the westward scope of their states system by Europeanizing the New World and forming it into a number of dependent settler states, a similar enlargement of Europe was taking place to the east as a result of the Europeanization of **Russia** and the acceptance of its tsars as members of the *grande république*. In the late Middle Ages the Slav peoples were divided into a western group, members of Latin Christendom and in the Polish case its chief champions against the east, and a number of Russian and other principalities with a Byzantine culture. The east Russian princedoms acquired increasing autonomy under the military Tartar suzerainty of the Golden Horde (*hurdu* = army). The princes of Muscovy co-operated with the Tartars, from whom they learnt some military and administrative techniques and an imperial vision extending across northern Eurasia. In the fifteenth and early sixteenth centuries Muscovy established a hegemony in the east of Russia under Ivan the Great and Ivan the Terrible who made Muscovy into an effective but non-western *stato*. When Muscovy relapsed into the chaos known as the 'time of the troubles', the western half of Russia came under Polish dominion, and the rest under Polish influence through client tsars installed in Moscow with Polish help. The independent Romanov dynasty from 1613 systematically set about westernizing and expanding Muscovy.

For the first century or so the western model for the Muscovite court and administration was Poland. But Peter the Great (1689 to 1725) preferred to learn military techniques from Russia's principal enemy, Sweden, and the other mechanical and technical aspects of westernization from the most advanced states of his day, Holland and England. Peter was in love with the west, and he did not westernize the Russian Empire, as he now called his state, in order to defeat the west but in order to join it. He abandoned Moscow for his new western city of St Petersburg, built to be the capital of modernized Russia and also a great port on the Baltic, a new Amsterdam. The Romanov dynasty, and particularly Peter, created that characteristic phenomenon of the spread of European ways to other societies, a westernized elite. With the help of that elite Peter erected a European *stato* on the backs of the uncomprehending and often resentful Russian people. 'Russia in effect adopted the aesthetic and philosophic culture of Poland while rejecting its Catholic faith, and the administrative and technical culture of Sweden and Holland.'[2] Peter in particular, by concentrating power in his own hands, did for Russia what Louis XI, the Catholic kings and the Tudors had achieved in western Europe

225

two centuries earlier. Like them, he recruited his new elite from people of all classes, and so provided an unusual degree of upward mobility for those willing and able to take advantage of it. Such upward mobility is often a characteristic of marcher societies: it was also a feature of the European settler societies in the Americas.

The combination of new talent, western technology and the determined westernizing drive of the Romanovs brought Russia into the European system and established it as one of the five great powers in the society of European sovereigns. But the new empire was on a larger scale than the old European states. It stretched what was to Europeans the almost unimaginable distance overland to the Pacific, as far as any of the maritime powers by sea. Much of the energies of Russia, both state and private, during all the three centuries of the Romanov dynasty was spent on landward territorial expansion: to 'reunite' the Russian lands, to fill the void in north and central Asia left by the disintegration of the Golden Horde and to reach the sea. In contrast to the long conflict between the west Europeans for the control of North America, the Russians expanded eastward virtually unchallenged until they encountered China, with which they signed a spheres of influence treaty in 1689. Permanent Muscovite positions were established on the Caspian and the Pacific more than a century before Peter reopened Russia's window on the Baltic and gained his foothold on the Black Sea. While the Americas inherited the European pattern of a *grande république* divided into several states, the Russians were heirs of the limitless, monocentric authority of Byzantium and the Tartars.

During the two centuries of the Petersburg era (*circa* 1717 to 1917) westernized Russia was a European power. The mass of the people and the forms of domestic government remained very different from Latin Christendom. But the tsars were now partly western by blood (the two ruling empresses Catherine I and Catherine II wholly so); and their ministers who conducted Russia's relations with other European states were westerners or westernized Russians. By the middle of the eighteenth century the Romanov dynasty was accepted into the sovereigns' club, and conformed to its rules. From then on Russia has played a major part in shaping the destinies of Europe and of the world. At the beginning of the nineteenth century only three major European powers remained in the arena of the Napoleonic Wars: France, Britain and Russia.

By the end of the eighteenth century Europeans controlled the Americas, which they formed into dependent states or provinces of their European society of states, the sovereigns' club. Europeans were also reaching out into Asia by sea and by land. The operations of the west

European maritime states and merchant companies overseas, from the Ottoman Empire to Japan, were still in the main subordinate to local authorities; but the Europeans were beginning to introduce rules and concepts derived from their own experience. The European states operated separately, in competition and conflict with each other. They did not yet dominate the other systems of states in the world, and had not yet created a single global system. That was to be the achievement of the nineteenth century.

NOTES

1 H. Bull and A. Watson (eds), *The Expansion of International Society*, Oxford, Oxford University Press, 1984, pp. 3, 4.
2 Billington, *The Icon and the Axe*, New York, Knopf, 1966, p. 114.

20

THE NAPOLEONIC EMPIRE

The previous chapters have shown that since geographically sovereign states replaced the horizonal structure of medieval Christendom, a propensity to hegemony, that is a tendency to move back from the more absolute forms of multiple independences, was inherent in the European system. The desire of the strongest state to lay down the law for the whole system, at least in the external relations between its members, was made more acceptable by the advantages that a measure of authority in the system brought to others too. It was not that the kingship must reside somewhere. The pre-eminence claimed by the Holy Roman Emperor and the king of France, and the rights and obligations that were held to go with this claim, did not amount to hegemony. The legitimacies established by the settlements of Westphalia and Utrecht were anti-hegemonial, Utrecht explicitly so. But even anti-hegemonial statesmen were aware that hegemony brought certain benefits; and they intended the conscious observance of the balance of power and of international law to provide some of these benefits in other ways. Such was the propensity to hegemony that even the anti-hegemonial alliances which such statesmen formed to resist a specific bid for hegemony installed, by their very success, the strongest power in the coalitions – first the Spanish and Austrian Habsburgs and then the Bourbon–Habsburg king of France – in a hegemonial position. The formal commitment of the eighteenth-century sovereigns' club to a multilateral balance of power at Utrecht lasted for three-quarters of a century. During that time power was effectively balanced. No state was conspicuously stronger than the others; and France, potentially the strongest state in the system, did not at that time achieve its potential.

The French Revolution stimulated new energies and aspirations in France, and in most of Europe, that Napoleon was able to harness and exploit. Napoleon's imperial order was the furthest point of the pendulum's swing away from the orthodoxy and legitimacy of multiple independences in Europe. It carried the European system well past hegemony, and brought much of Europe under his dominion. It made radical changes both in the relations between the communities in the European system, and in the internal government and social structure of those communities. Though Napoleon's order lasted only briefly, the changes which it induced were lasting. After his downfall the pendulum swung only part of the way back towards the multiple independences end of the spectrum.

By the end of the eighteenth century the middle and lower middle classes of Europe were more educated and prosperous than ever before. Two important and successful western states, Britain and the Netherlands, (as well as some smaller polities), had ceased to be *ancien régime* societies, governed by an absolute prince. They owed their power and success largely to the contribution of the trading and professional classes, and to the benefits of participation in public affairs by a much wider segment of the population than elsewhere, including many of its shrewdest and most innovative elements. English and Dutch ideas and practices, which reflected this new type of society, acted as a leaven elsewhere. They were particularly influential among the highly developed French middle class. The ideas of the French *philosophes* derived from England and Holland, and gradually spread over the rest of Europe. In France a few bold spirits wanted 'the people' to take the government entirely into their own hands.

In most European states the middle classes threatened from below the rule of the sovereign princes and their international society. The hereditary absolutism of kings and princes and the dominance of the hereditary nobility seemed to have increased since the heady days of the Renaissance when, first in Italy and then elsewhere, so many 'new men' rose to positions of power and influence. Most rulers, and especially the enlightened ones, gladly recruited administrators from the bourgeois or middle class, because they were more competent and more obedient than noblemen who were willing to serve. But those who served the ruler surrendered their independence. The great majority of the middle classes, who were not subordinate members of the executive, were effectively excluded from government. The educated and wealthy professional and trading classes of the towns were less willing than Kant to leave power in the hands of sovereigns, even when enlightened: they aspired to some say in the direction of public affairs, both domestic and foreign. They knew how much their administrative and financial ability could contribute to what seemed to them incompetent government, and considered that they were denied their rightful place in the direction of public affairs and in society by the *anciens régimes*. With the demand for more efficient and representative government went a wider reaction, by no means limited to France, against the artificiality of eighteenth-century court life and art, court politics and warfare, and less consciously against cold autocratic reason in favour of warm popular passion.

The French Revolution was the most dramatic act of self-assertion of the middle class in European history. The *tiers état*, as those who demanded change called themselves, swept away the old regime with an explosive force that profoundly changed the relations between the various European communities which since Westphalia had been organized in a society of similar states in some sort of balance. The great increase in power that the revolution released in the most important state in the system was reinforced by the ideas, couched in universal terms, that it developed and spread, and which appealed to the restless equivalents of the *tiers état* in other continental states. The revolution produced, and its leaders actively encouraged, a general stasis in Europe to the east of France.

The self-assertion of the middle class in Europe took two forms: the demand for participation in government, and nationalism. To the *tiers état* and their equivalents at that time, it did not seem possible to have the one without the other. They no longer accepted that a state should be composed of any chance collection of territories inherited or acquired by a prince, or assigned to him to preserve a balance of power. The sovereignty of the people implied that the only legitimate state was one based on and expressing the will of a particular kind of collective entity called a nation. Wherever the German tongue is spoken, sang Arndt, there is the German fatherland. In central and eastern Europe this was a revolutionary idea indeed, and had a disruptive effect on all the *anciens régimes* there, great and small, as it also did in the settler colonies of the Americas. It was a solvent of empires as well as of petty princedoms, but not of the idea of sovereignty painfully established by princes. It raised an issue which, in different forms, has played a major role in European affairs ever since: how to decide what territories a given state should legitimately comprise.

The revolution, by sweeping away the artificialities and inefficiencies of the old regime, legitimized the positions which the French middle classes and the peasantry had acquired *de facto*, and provided new opportunities in every walk of life. '1789 would not have been possible', says Jean Blondel,

> and its effects would not have been so easily accepted, had French society not already become in part, and even in large part, a rural democracy. In many areas peasants had already acquired the land in all but name, and the end of many estates, and particularly the end of Church property, merely enabled peasants to acquire a little more, and in a wholly secure fashion, of what they had already come to have.[1]

The revolution also let loose a tidal wave of national and doctrinal enthusiasm. The effect was to liberate and revivify the tremendous creative energies of France. The period of the Terror abandoned the restraints and decencies of eighteenth-century civilization and instituted a dictatorship that was blood-soaked, arbitrary and at times absurd. All real revolutions (as opposed to secessions like the American 'revolution'), says Bertrand de Jouvenel, aim at increasing liberty; but there is always less liberty after than before.[2] Even so, the revolution mobilized the patriotism of the French, who responded to the call of *allons enfants de la patrie*. The revolutionary armies were recruited by general mobilization: men said and believed that to die serving one's *patrie* was too noble an act to be left to mercenaries like those who served kings for pay. This new kind of army, with its huge numbers, living off the land and fighting for a cause, was more than a match for the aristocratic officers and uninspired rank and file fielded by the kings and princes who tried to restore the Bourbon monarchy. If the energies and enthusiasm which the revolution released could be organized and harnessed, France would stand unchallengeably powerful in continental Europe.

The great and often decisive importance of the individual in history, sometimes overlooked by social historians who concentrate on vast impersonal forces, is graphically illustrated by Napoleon, the astonishing and many-sided genius who achieved single-handed control of revolutionary France and then of much of Europe. Born into the impecunious petty nobility of Corsica, an Italian island possession of France, he embraced the revolution and rose to impose on its turbulence the controls and organization of the Renaissance Italian *stato*. A professional general, he transformed every aspect of warfare, from the mobilization of the nation's resources to campaign strategy and the tactical command of a battle; and he paid particular attention to maintaining the revolutionary enthusiasm of his men and to choosing his officers on the basis of ability rather than class. In one sense he was the *condottiere* of the revolution; and like other *condottieri* he wanted, and secured for himself, absolute and untrammelled power. He brooked no argument against his judgement and no check or balance to his will. The French people acclaimed him because of his military victories, and also because he seemed able to assure them most of the advantages of the revolution without its drawbacks. But he was more than the last and greatest *condottiere*: he was also the last and greatest eighteenth-century enlightened despot. His organizing ability showed itself in every aspect of statecraft. His autocratic and successful hand directed the government of his empire, from the redrafting of a uniform code of law to details of local administration, with a lucidity that was characteristically French, a disregard for tradition that derived from the revolution, a reason that derived from the Enlightenment and a practical genius that was his own.

This Renaissance *condottiere* and self-made prince used methods not very different from those recommended by Machiavelli to bring the greater part of Europe into an imperial super-*stato*. The creation and maintenance of his empire depended on military success. War was not a last resort, but a means to getting his way, and his victories were regular and decisive demonstrations to France and to Europe of his invincibility. In negotiations he was tactically elastic, using diplomacy to bribe, threaten and cajole the eighteenth-century states arrayed against him, with no regard for the validity of his promises. He also exploited the revolutionary appeal which good government and a society open to talent had for the middle classes. His empire was a colossal adjustment to the new realities of power and the strength of the rejuvenated French state.

Napoleon had a broad vision which stretched beyond France to the whole of Europe. His imperial system was organized in the concentric circles familiar to us. At the centre was the area of direct administration, which he continually expanded beyond the previous boundaries of France until at the height of his power it stretched from the Baltic to Rome. The kingdoms of Holland and Italy, at first satellite states in his circle of dominion, were soon incorporated in the area of French administration. This expansion of direct rule was due to the exigencies of war, rather than to a desire to extend French rule as such. But once annexed, those Dutchmen and Italians who had welcomed the Napoleonic reforms were left with nothing round which their nationalism could crystallize, and found themselves divided into departments of France.

In the area of his dominion Napoleon set up satellite kingdoms and principalities. They were precarious entities, dependent only on his will, with their rulers and boundaries constantly changed. They were ruled on his behalf by members of his family, his military marshals or local kings and princes. His attitude towards these subordinate states is illustrated by his description of his family as 'a family of kings, or rather of viceroys'. The key to the control of the European system was the Holy Roman Empire. After the collapse of Louis XIV's attempt to focus the allegiance of the German principalities on himself, the mosaic of smaller states had reverted to its function of a sponge absorbing the pressures of the system, 'important to all but dangerous to none' as Heeren said. Austria and Prussia were great powers; but Napoleon succeeded in bringing all the rest of the empire, which the French called 'la troisième Allemagne', under his suzerainty. He focused the allegiance of its rulers not on Paris, but on himself as protector, wherever he happened to be. The Kingdom of Westphalia and the princes who made up the Confederation of the Rhine retained separate identities. So outside Germany did two other former Habsburg fiefs, Spain and Naples, and some other small states. Most of this area had come under French influence before the revolution. Now Napoleonic ideas of law, commerce, education, the metric system, local government and much else were steadily introduced: the pace varied, but the direction was the same.

Beyond the area of dominion or indirect rule lay an area of hegemony, comprised of independent states like Austria and Prussia that had hitherto been reckoned as great powers, and Scandinavia. They were gradually reduced from Napoleon's independent enemies to his quasi-allies, reluctant yet also afraid of Russia; but they retained control of their own internal affairs.

Napoleon polarized the European system, and integrated it round one dominant power, more than at any time before or since (except for the brief Nazi occupation of the continent, 1940–4). The pendulum had swung with one of its great lurches, comparable to that under Alexander. Such a large swing was too far for stability. Napoleon's power was too new and too innovative to be legitimate. Like the Italian Renaissance princes who founded *statos*, he tried to legitimize his power, both domestically and abroad. In a society which had overthrown traditional authority, and where government depended to some extent on popular support, good government provided a degree of legitimacy; and Napoleon provided good though autocratic government. The symbols and slogans of the revolution evoked new loyalties, especially in France but also to some degree outside it; and in order to preserve revolutionary legitimation Napoleon was careful to retain the tricolour, the rhetoric and other revolutionary trappings while in effect establishing a hereditary monarchy. In this he may be compared to Augustus; and the comparison was present in his own mind, for he consciously followed Roman models, symbolically in his titles of consul and emperor and the eagles for his legions, and more fundamentally in Roman law, Roman conquest and Roman imperial administration. For an age highly conscious of classical examples this was also a form of legitimation. Nor did he neglect the legitimation which the Catholic Church could confer after its persecution by the revolution. Internationally there were conscious echos of Charlemagne in his bringing the pope to Paris to crown him emperor and in proclaiming his son King of Rome. But his most striking bid for international recognition was his marriage to a Habsburg princess, which legitimized him as the heir of the hegemonial tradition, and along with other Bonaparte royal marriages made the new dynasty acceptable to the intermarried royalty of Europe.

Napoleon's imperial order did not have the chance to settle down, to realize the benefits of empire and to be made acceptable by the passage of time. Those European states which retained any freedom of action became increasingly concerned that the empire was too strong for a balance of power, and seemed bent on further conquests. After his fall Napoleon claimed that he wanted peace in the later years of the empire; but his policies at the time give little indication that he was willing to stabilize Europe on any basis acceptable to the independent states. In the century since Utrecht the European international society had become committed to the principle of an anti-hegemonial balance. The states allied against Napoleon in 1813 – Britain and Russia, joined by Austria, Prussia and others – declared that they were ideologically opposed to the doctrines of the French Revolution which Napoleon claimed to champion, and particularly upheld the legitimacy of the deposed sovereigns. They declared that they were not fighting against France, but against the preponderance which Napoleon exercised. The allied statesmen regarded legitimate French power as one of the corner-stones of the European system, and they were willing to allow Napoleon a territory greater than France had previously possessed. But they insisted on ending Napoleon's dominion over Germany and Italy, and on a peace settlement based on a Utrechtian just balance and distribution of power, which would protect the peoples of Europe from the misery of war that they had experienced for twenty years.[3]

At the height of Napoleon's dominance the only genuinely independent states left in Europe were Russia, at times an enemy and at others an ally, Britain, which was more or less continually at war with him, and the Ottomans, who were outside the European society of states. All three powers were on the margins of Europe, beyond the effective reach of Napoleonic conquest and largely immune to the revolutionary appeal of his empire. The sources of British strength were the Industrial Revolution, which produced more and cheaper goods, and the power of money which subsidized the continental armies against Napoleon. British gold sovereigns, known as 'the cavalry of St George' from their design of George and the dragon, played the same role as the Persian king's gold archers in city-state Greece and Richelieu's subsidies. Moreover, Britain was an island state able to defeat Napoleon at sea, and thus to maintain its independence in a way that Holland was not. Napoleon could exclude Russia from the *grande république*, but it was too remote and too geographically immense for him to conquer with an army of foot soldiers. The revolutionary appeal of Napoleon's empire had little effect in Russia: the country had not yet developed an independent and excluded middle class, and the peasantry, then as in previous invasions, rallied to the defence of Holy Russia against the alien invader. The Ottoman Turks and their subjects were also effectively beyond the appeal of the revolution and Napoleon's military capacity. His early invasion of Ottoman Egypt was frustrated largely by British sea power. The Ottomans were aware of Napoleon's subsequent designs against them; but intermittent Russian operations against the Ottomans drove them to look to their traditional French ally until Napoleon's invasion of Russia in 1812 persuaded the sultan to make an anti-hegemonial peace with the Russians.

An imperial system that went beyond hegemony to effective dominion over much of Europe could not have been expected to appeal to those who believed in a balance of power. Its appeal was directed towards client rulers, but especially towards their subjects, to whom it offered better government. That appeal had made Sforza fear that the Venetians would make themselves *signori di tutta Italia*. How far was the Napoleonic system acceptable to those outside France who came under its sway? Many of the middle classes in Germany and Italy shared Kant's view that it did not much matter which state one found oneself in, if there was a reasonable constitution or if the despotic ruler was enlightened and just. Napoleon's rule, and that of his satellite kings, was impressively enlightened and provided enticing opportunities to the middle class. In Germany men like Goethe and Beethoven began by welcoming the extension of Napoleon's power; and even at the end many in the satellite states of Westphalia and the Confederation of the Rhine remained loyal to the new order. In Italy the attachment to the regimes which he set up was still more marked: French imperial rule was more congenial than Austrian, though its grip was firmer. French rule was much less popular in established west European nation states like Holland and especially Spain, where genuine national sentiment existed, though many members of the Spanish middle class supported the Napoleonic regime.

The main problem for Napoleon within his imperial system was not the attachment of the people to their former regimes, but the new force of nationalism, which ironically French teaching and example did much to foster. The people attracted to his government wanted to be treated as equals, and felt loyalty not to a small sovereign state but to their nation, their *patrie*. Frenchmen could be proud of an empire that dominated Europe and gave them the important positions; but other Europeans who welcomed Napoleon's reforms resented their subordinate position in his imperial design. For instance, Napoleon wanted the Spanish 'rebellion' against his puppet government to be ruthlessly crushed so that Spain, under an efficient, progressive government, could better serve both her people and the empire; and he spoke of 'the chance which fortune gave me to regenerate Spain.'

But the Spanish guerrillas who resisted Napoleon were fighting against a foreign occupation.

Neither popular national resentment against foreign conquest and domination, nor the anti-hegemonial commitment of statesmen to a Europe of independent states, nor the British blockade and the Russian 'wind from the hungry steppe' could alone bring down Napoleon. His imperial system was the most ambitious and the most successfully implemented bid to shift Europe decisively towards the imperial end of our system; and all three opposing forces needed to work together to overturn it. When after twenty years of struggle they finally succeeded, the victors were not able, or willing, to restore the eighteenth-century pattern. A large part of what the revolution and Napoleon had swept away was gone for good. Many of the advantages of a hegemonial structure for the states system had to be incorporated in new forms. Socially the middle classes were stronger and more assertive; and popular national sentiment, with all its force for good and ill, become rampant in Europe until at least our own day.

Napoleon's bid to impose an imperial unity of government on Europe came close enough to success, and was sufficiently like what the Habsburgs and Louis XIV's France attempted before him and the Germans later, that it is useful to our enquiry to ask what would have happened if his system had succeeded and become stabilized? Professor Owen Connelly puts the question well: 'Overall would Europeans generally have had more liberty, equality and prosperity (not to speak of unity and power), if they had sacrificed temporarily to allow Napoleon to achieve his vaunted "general peace"?'[4] The advantages of the imperial end of the spectrum are real, and were not unwelcome to many Europeans in spite of the tradition and the rhetoric of multiple independences. That an imperial Europe would have had more unity and more power is clear. It would doubtless have been more prosperous. The lower classes in central Europe would have enjoyed more personal liberty than in fact they achieved for some time after Napoleon's fall – though politically his system was a benevolent autocracy not a democracy. There would also have been more equality in the sense of greater upward mobility for individuals. But the empire involved domination by Frenchmen and French methods, and other Europeans were and would have continued to be faced by the choice between second-class citizenship and assimilation. There would certainly have been internal peace, for this is the great boon that imperial systems have to offer; but externally the European empire would doubtless have found itself at war with Russia and other powers. Though Napoleon's system was too brief to acquire general acceptance, after it was overthrown its advantages were impressive enough to make liberated Europeans want to see which of its merits could be negotiated by co-operation between the great powers and implemented by their concerted action, rather than imposed by unilateral force.

NOTES

1 Jean Blondel, *Contemporary France*, London, Methuen, 1974, p. 5.
2 Bertrand de Jouvenel, *De la Souveraineté*, Paris, Médicis, 1945.
3 See in particular Henry Kissinger, *A World Restored*, New York, Universal Library, 1964, p. 103.
4 Las Cases, *Mémorial de Ste. Hélène*, Paris, 1823, vol. iv, p. 287.
5 Owen Connelly, *Napoleon's Satellite Kingdoms*, New York, Macmillan, 1965, p. 336.

21

COLLECTIVE HEGEMONY
The nineteenth-century Concert of Europe

Napoleon's imperial authority took the European system of states further towards the empire end of our spectrum than ever before. It was successfully opposed both by other states and by anti-French nationalism outside and inside the area of his hegemony. These external and internal constraints worked to push the whole system back towards the independences end of the scale; but they were not able to bring it all the way back to the eighteenth-century pattern. Napoleon's empire changed the social structures of west and much of central Europe, and permanently altered men's ideas about what was desirable and attainable. The system which emerged from the Vienna settlement of 1814–15, at the end of a quarter of a century of upheaval and warfare, stands about halfway between the Napoleonic and the eighteenth-century systems on our spectrum. In some ways it was a synthesis between two opposing ways of organizing Europe.

Napoleon's defeat in Russia restored Austria, which had become a client state of the French Empire, to independence as the mobile element in what was again a complex balance. Metternich, the architect of Austrian policy, like Lorenzo dei Medici saw the threat from more than one quarter. Whole-hearted co-operation with Russia to destroy Napoleon would put Russia in too strong a position, and he therefore worked for a compromise. Fortunately for Metternich, Britain emerged from the war industrially and financially strengthened; and its increased power and wealth could be enlisted to oppose the domination of Europe by any single power. The difference between the view from Vienna and from London was that, since Austria had no possessions across the ocean, Metternich thought of the balance only in European and Ottoman terms, whereas the British with their global commitments saw 'the continent' as one element in a wider economic and strategic system that included the Americas and the Indian Ocean. Britain was now the dominant power in the overseas extensions of Europe; and in order to exploit that dominance it needed equilibrium and peace in Europe itself. These objectives also suited Russia, which

238

was equally interested in expansion outside the area of what had been Latin Christendom. To direct Russian energies into the Ottoman Empire and further east seemed to Tsar Alexander more feasible than to aim at a demanding and perhaps unattainable hegemony in Europe. He therefore also opted for stability to his west. The two powers thus agreed that their policies within the *grande république* required limitations that did not apply outside it.

So it was that Castlereagh and Wellington, acting for Britain, and the tsar, acting for Russia, found themselves with similar objectives after the collapse of their common enemy Napoleon. It suited both states to re-establish Austria and Prussia as independent great powers nominally equal to themselves, and also more strikingly to accord the same position to a restored Bourbon France. They and Metternich recognized that the system would be unstable if so dynamic an element as the French were fundamentally opposed to the settlement, and that therefore a strong and satisfied France was essential to a stable and balanced Europe. The restored kingdom should not be punished or deprived of territory in Europe that had been French before the revolution; and moreover, though still potentially dangerous, it should be welcomed as an equal partner by the four major allies.[1] This prudent and imaginative statesmanship stands in striking contrast to the treatment of Germany after the First World War.

Superficially the anti-hegemonial allies reverted to the eighteenth-century pattern of five major powers that checked and balanced each other. But the statesmen who congregated at Vienna had learnt hard lessons from the revolution and Napoleon. They understood, more clearly than they are sometimes given credit for, the advantages of order and tranquillity which Napoleon's empire had brought to the great areas of Europe which he controlled, and were well aware that it was undesirable as well as impracticable to revert to the eighteenth-century system. The tsar and Metternich in particular, but also the other statesmen, considered that international peace and order and the domestic tranquillity of their states were threatened both by an imbalance of power, which allowed one state to bid for dominion as Napoleonic France had done, and also by what they regarded as the disruptive effects of revolutionary principles. A cardinal and prudent principle of the eighteenth-century sovereigns' club was that its members should not interfere in each other's domestic affairs. But the French had used revolutionary doctrines and slogans to sanction crusading interventions in the internal affairs of other states, and these doctrines were now too widespread to permit a return to eighteenth-century codes of restraint. The counter-doctrine of dynastic legitimacy and the practical desire to manage the system seemed to the statesmen at Vienna to justify equally ideological interventions to repress revolutionary bids for power in any state. Such interventions, for the purpose of preserving international peace and security, put the practice of the early nineteenth century in Europe somewhat nearer the imperial end of our spectrum than hegemony as we have defined it.

Europe was not to be divided into separate spheres of influence: the five powers agreed that collective machinery was needed to maintain and modify the settlement. A collective institution or league to manage the system had been proposed by Kant's draft treaty for perpetual peace and other projects, but it was something new in post-medieval European practice. It took the form of a compact of the five most powerful sovereigns. The tsar originally established what he grandiloquently called a 'holy league of Christian princes', but the informal machinery agreed at Aachen was more modestly described as a 'concert of the great powers'.[2] The five powers did not trust each other to intervene unilaterally in order to deal with threats to peace and security; but where they agreed to act together, or at least acquiesced in action after consultation, they could collectively exercise a diffused hegemony which none would agree to another exercising alone. They could together lay down the law: and since future adjustments were presumed to be necessary, they could also amend it. Harmony between them would orchestrate a **Concert of Europe**.

It soon became clear that the five powers would not maintain for long the close similarity of purposes that marked the immediate postwar years. First, their interests diverged. The territorial and other arrangements of the Vienna settlement were negotiated compromises reached after much bargaining, and were not regarded as immutable: the maintenance of the mobile balance would inevitably make modifications necessary as time went on. But the five powers recognized that their interests were broadly compatible, and that each had certain areas (in the cases of Britain and Russia very large ones outside the *grande république*) in which their interests would be allowed to prevail. In additon they all shared an interest in the successful operation of the new concert. *Raison de système* does not exclude conflicts of interest; it is the recognition that the advantage of all the parties is to resolve such conflicts within the framework of the system and, as the architects of the Vienna settlement saw it, according to the rules and codes of conduct of their revised international society.

Second, those in a position to shape the policies of the major powers had principles as well as interests; and their principles also conflicted. In London the control of policy quickly passed from Castlereagh and Wellington to men like Canning, who was more in tune with the increasingly important middle classes and who reflected the British commitment to liberalism and constitutionality. French policy inclined in the same direction, in spite of the jibe that the restored Bourbons had learnt nothing in exile. The three east European monarchies supported absolute authority; in Petersburg under Alexander I and Nicholas I this support amounted to a conviction that went deeper than Metternich's expediency. Principles are less easy to bargain about than interests. But even the clash of principles could be mitigated by the Concert of Europe. Acquiescence and acceptance were felicitous concepts of the diplomatic dialogue that enabled a great power, by judicious abstention from certain decisions and their enforcement, to maintain intact both its principles and its partnership in the concert, while permitting developments to occur that it could not in practice prevent. The history of the European states system in the nineteenth century is largely concerned with the efforts of these five powers to mediate their relations with their yoke fellows and with the forces of nationalism and democracy in such a way that divergences of interest and principle did not damage the advantages which all five derived from maintaining an orderly international society.

The other member states of the system resented their exclusion from the diffused hegemony of the five great powers. The anti-hegemonial principle had been an implicit premiss of European international society since Westphalia and an explicit one since Utrecht, and it was the proclaimed purpose of the allied struggle against Napoleon. The new hegemony also damaged the interests of the smaller sovereigns in practice. These criticisms have been echoed since. Surely if states were to be regarded as juridically equal, a status confirmed by the diplomatic protocol of the Treaty of Vienna, the smaller sovereignties of Europe should have been represented in the informal but decisive international institution of the new society? The balance of power system of the eighteenth century enabled each state to exercise influence in proportion to its power; and twentieth-century formal international machinery has been theoretically omnilateral (though practice has fallen short of the nominal aim). But in the decades following the Vienna settlement the European system shifted only part of the way back from Napoleon's imperial authority towards the independences end of the spectrum. Moreover, the hegemonial authority was too diffused, and too inclusive of all the main centres of power, for an anti-hegemonial coalition to be practicable.

How far are these charges justified? Certainly the five powers deliberately set up a hegemony. Systems of independent states have a propensity to move back along the spectrum towards greater integration; and Napoleon's imperial system had shown unmistakable benefits as well as unacceptable disadvantages. The statesmen of the five great powers gathered at Vienna and at subsequent congresses and conferences thought that the diffusion and balance built into the concert system would provide what they considered the essential advantages of hegemonial authority while strictly limiting its disadvantages. They also had two further considerations in mind. First, the five powers made up some three-quarters of the population of the European society of states (and the same was true of the four powers if Russia was left out of the equation); and they held more than three-quarters of the effective power, especially when the resources of Britain and Russia outside Europe were taken into account. A policy agreed between them would prevail whatever the rules and legitimacies of the society. Second, the medium and small powers took part in the diplomatic dialogue, and where their direct interests were affected their desires and interests were known to the great powers, one or more of which could be relied on to urge that they should be taken into account. The concert system of the early nineteenth century reflected realities; but the great powers arrogated the duties and privileges of operating the concert to themselves, and the smaller European states did not give their consent, though they acquiesced.[3]

The operation of the system in Europe itself can be divided for our purposes into three periods. The first three decades, from 1815 to 1848, were a period of peace between the great powers, and repression of social and political revolution. The second period, from 1848 to 1871, was marked by revolutionary nationalism and wars of adjustment. The third period, from 1871 to the end of the century, was again a period of peace in Europe, with the concert largely dominated by Bismarck. The more momentous changes in the field of our enquiry that took place outside Europe are discussed in the next chapter. We must now look briefly at each phase in turn; remembering that the developments we are examining were a continuum, that the division into periods is for our analytical convenience and that events inside and outside Europe intimately affected each other.

THE FIRST THIRTY YEARS

During the thirty years from the Declaration of Aachen in 1818 to the year of revolution in 1848, the five great powers came close to functioning as a directorate. The first phase of the Concert of Europe was rather more than a diffused hegemony. By claiming and exercising the right to collective intervention, the great powers were able to maintain something like a dominion over the fragmented quarter of European society outside their administration. The disagreements between the five concerned the management of the system, rather than bilateral conflicts of direct interest. The aristocratic statesmen who managed the affairs of Europe during those three decades felt a solidarity of purpose: they feared the dangers that threatened their world, but not each other. The Rhinelander Metternich was the most important single statesman of the period. The central position of Austria, his continuity in office and his acute sense of *raison de système*, summed up in his phrase 'my country is the whole of Europe', enabled him to exercise a leadership in the concert greater than the military and economic strength of the Austrian Empire justified. His opposition to popular nationalism and democracy and his insistence on maintaining the Austrian position in Italy have led liberal writers to dub the 'Age of Metternich' a period of reaction, which in the main it was, and forcible preservation of the status quo, which it was not. In fact many adjustments took place, some of them major. In western Europe the former Austrian Netherlands obtained their independence from Holland as the Kingdom of Belgium, and the western great powers intervened to install more liberal governments in Spain and Portugal.

The two powers that had been beyond Napoleon's reach, Britain and Russia, both derived much of their strength and resources from outside Europe. At the Vienna settlement and during the following decades Britain and Russia acted in Europe like a pair of book-ends, pushing against each other and holding the whole system in place, while outside Europe they extended their influence and their empires in parallel across Asia from the Ottoman Empire to the Pacific. By checking and balancing one another, in a mild form of cold war, and yet at the same time recognizing their responsibilities to the European society of states and to each other, they provided the essential framework in which the Concert of Europe could function and manoeuvre. Britain and Russia were the superpowers of that time.

The five great powers were not opposed to the use of armed force or committed to the status quo. In the first thirty years they used armed force by agreement or acquiescence. In the middle period of the century their interests and principles diverged so far that the concert was sometimes in abeyance. Popular nationalism strengthened to the point where the great powers were prepared to use armed force to a limited extent against one another, in order to bring about adjustments for which there was no general acquiescence and which therefore could not be negotiated without a demonstration of superior force. In the last thirty years European states also used armed force, but not against each other. Throughout the century the brief and comparatively minor wars in Europe, and the colonial operations outside it, were usually little more than military expeditions. Even the most important – the Crimean and Franco-Prussian wars – did not seriously interrupt the progress of European civilization and the advance of material wealth and the arts and sciences in the states involved, much less in Europe as a whole. To many they seemed glorious and exciting episodes. There was nothing like the loss of life and the material, social and genetic damage caused by the American Civil War. The European minor wars of the second period, while admittedly expensive, cruel and destructive, did not therefore seem unacceptable means of settling differences and bringing about adjustments.

THE MIDDLE PERIOD: REVOLUTION AND ADJUSTMENT

The second period, from 1848 to 1871, was one of an upsurge of popular nationalism, of revolution against the established political order and of wars of adjustment between the great powers. In the year 1848 middle-class discontent with the 'Metternich system' and with dynastic legitimacy boiled over into genuine revolution in many European communities, notably France and the German and Italian lands. A new legitimacy was now in a position to challenge the old: the right of 'peoples' to determine for themselves what state they should belong to and how that state should be governed. Peace seemed less important than other values.

Three related trends, towards nationalism, democracy and popular interest in external affairs, exercised an increasing influence on the functioning of the European states system. Nationality is not the sole fundamental political category into which people naturally and always group themselves. Other groups of men at other times have been held together by equally strong allegiances to a religion, a dynasty, a class or order of society, or a political creed. In the nineteenth century in Europe it was the 'nation' that came to be accepted as the basic political unit, and other forms of organization and loyalty had to accommodate themselves to it.

What did nineteenth-century Europeans mean by a nation? The ideas of nationalism and democracy were related. Both challenged the legitimacy of the European states, and of their society, the sovereigns' club. Democracy meant that the *demos* – the people, the *Volk* – should rule, or at least elect its rulers; and that the legitimacy of governments derived not from the mere consent of the governed, but from the periodic exercise by the *demos* of free choice. But what did a *demos* consist of? Which individual wills should make up what Rousseau called the general will? To this question there were a variety of answers. In the west an arc of state nations stretched from Iberia through France and Britain to Scandinavia, each welded together within the hide of a leviathan-state by shared hopes and fears and homogenized by the spread of education. West Europeans now felt themselves to be, in the main, citizens rather than subjects; and they came to see their monarchical states as the constitutional and political expression of their nations, rather than as merely the institutionalized *statos* of a princely family. In the centre of Europe, by contrast, religious passions had for centuries helped to focus loyalties on local states and dynasties rather than on nations; but in the nineteenth century the haphazard mosaic of large and small states ruled by sovereigns who allowed little popular participation in government failed to evoke the loyalty of the *demos*. Nationality was a linguistic and cultural matter, with no adequately representative state to give the nation form. The newly independent settler communities across the Atlantic developed a third version: they saw membership of a national *demos* as an act of individual choice. But all the democratic answers assumed that a nation ought to be sovereign and entitled to act as it wished, and that the most natural form of state was one composed of a single people with a single 'national character'. In other words **each *demos*, each nation, should have its own independent state**.

The major restructuring of Europe, and particularly central Europe, on that basis seemed to liberals and nationalists inevitable as well as just. They accepted that force would be necessary, certainly in the form of revolutions and probably also in the form of armed intervention by foreign supporters of nationalist movements. However, once the new nation states came into being, central European nationalists and their western supporters were inclined to assume that the boundaries between national homelands, and thus between the new nation states, could be acceptably drawn. Unlike greedy princes, democratic nation states, once constituted, should be able to live in peace. The states system and international society would be changed but not impaired: what had been a sovereigns' club would become a family of independent nations. Nineteenth-century nationalists also disliked suggestions that their nation state should be trammelled by an international system or concert. They looked forward to a more total independence, freedom from external restraints and sovereign exercise of the popular general will. Nationalism and democracy pushed the European states system further towards the independences end of the spectrum.

Conservatives were alarmed that, among other things, the complex and interlocking equilibrium of the states system, which had been established and modified over a long period and often at considerable cost in blood and money and considerable sacrifice of dynastic legitimacy, would be irredeemably upset if central and eastern Europe were reorganized according to an exclusive legitimacy of nation states without regard for other needs or criteria. The editors of *The Cambridge Modern History* wrote as the nineteenth century ended: 'the passion for nationality was to prove the revolutionary force most fatal to the established order'.[4]

The most dangerous immediate threat to the European balance was pan-Germanism. The people who considered themselves to be Ger-

245

mans and whose mother tongue was German had become the most numerous people in Europe, and in the second half of the century they entered a phase of development which led others to feel misgivings about their competence; and moreover, they occupied a central position in the continent, stretching from Holland to Russia and from Italy to Denmark. A nation state comprising all the Germans would be more powerful than any other in Europe and in a permanently hegemonial position, manageable only by a permanent anti-hegemonial coalition of the other great powers, instead of a more elastic concert of great powers of comparable strength. Beyond pan-Germanism loomed the remoter but even less manageable threat of pan-Slavism. If Russia and the other Slav peoples were to establish a nationalist union or state in Europe, reaching west to Bohemia and south to the Mediterranean, what could redress the balance in Europe? In the nineteenth century the great state most threatened by nationalist fervour, especially pan-Italianism, pan-Germanism and pan-Slavism, and which therefore represented the bulwark of the existing system, was the multinational and absolutist Austrian Habsburg Empire. To weaken Austria, and eventually dissolve it into national states, was the prime immediate goal of nationalists and liberals.

The aims of nationhood and popular sovereignty were rooted in the ideas of the French Revolution. Their champion in Europe was Napoleon's nephew, who was brought to power in France by the revolution of 1848 and in 1853 took the title of Napoleon III. The new emperor considered that to justify himself as his uncle's heir he needed to upset the Vienna settlement, to make France again the foremost power in Europe, to liberate Italy from Austrian control and generally to pose as a champion of national aspirations. But he did not have an alternative design for the ordering of the *grande république*, as his uncle and Louis XIV and Richelieu had. Democracy was also another matter, dangerous to his authority. It was necessary, and seemed to him and many Frenchmen also desirable, to carry out his policy by means of military force. During the twenty years of his reign, therefore, Napoleon III involved France in a series of minor wars and expeditions ranging from the Crimea to Mexico and China.

French military intervention against Austria to unify Italy into a national state would enhance the prestige of France. But Austria, the foremost German power, was the only effective obstacle to the unification of Germany under Prussian leadership, which would gravely damage French interests. Napoleon III was almost as inept as his uncle had been able. He blithely embarked on the destruction of Austrian power in Italy. His later efforts to prevent or at least to obtain territorial compensation for German unification embroiled him in a war which cost him his throne. Napoleon III ignored maxims of *raison d'état* that

246

had guided far-sighted European statesmen since the Renaissance: do not gravely weaken a power which you will need at a later stage; and do not encourage passions in one area which will damage you if they spread to another.

Prussian policy during those twenty years was as calculating as Napoleon III's was impulsive. Prussia had always been a state but not a nation. It was also conspicuously the weakest of the five great powers. Its policy was guided by Bismarck, who also preferred to act independently of the concert unless he could control it. He distrusted the popular German nationalism that aimed to disrupt the Prussian and Austrian monarchies, and to create a new superstate which he knew would not be acceptable to the other great powers. German nationalism was too general and too deeply felt to suppress; but minor wars between the other four great powers allowed Prussia to gain some control over the movement and limit its achievements to partial unification excluding Austria. A short military campaign to remove the Austrian veto caused the minimum of damage and resentment, and Austria soon became the ally of the new Germany. Bismarck was not so successful with France, where national humiliation in the war to prevent the unification of Germany caused lasting bitterness.

Though the revolutions of 1848 against princely absolutism seemed to fail, over the next quarter-century the middle class substantially achieved their aspirations in Europe, and especially in the centre. Most of Italy was united in a nation state under the leadership of Savoy, and most of Germany under the leadership of Prussia; while inside the defeated Habsburg Empire the German and Hungarian elements worked out their own bargain at the expense of other aspiring nationalisms. Social compromises made Italy and the new German *Reich* significantly more democratic, and brought the middle classes into active partnership. The new states adopted many west European features, especially constitutional monarchy in which the crown symbolized the sovereign nation and shared political power with its citizen-subjects. In the past much warfare had been waged in Europe by kings and aristocrats. The resorts to force in the middle years of the nineteenth century were nationalist and democratic, inspired by the middle class and directed by rulers who wanted to harness and control middle-class emotions.

The effect of these changes was to loosen the system, and to make its member states less conscious of *raison de système*. Moreover, there simply was not room in Europe for the national aspirations of all its peoples. But even in these difficult circumstances the concert continued to function. Most statesmen remained aware of the dangers of irresponsible wilfulness. A series of congresses and conferences, sometimes after a trial of force, achieved compromises acceptable to the five great states and others directly concerned. These acts of balanced management ranged from the general settlement elaborated at the Congress of Paris after the Crimean War down to more specific issues like the international status of Luxemburg or Crete.

The attenuated functioning of the concert was facilitated by the attitudes of the two 'book-end' powers on the edges of Europe. Though Britain and Russia came to blows over their policies towards the Ottoman Empire, they continued to favour equilibrium in Europe's affairs. British governments avoided military involvement in central Europe. Liberal Englishmen supported democracy and applauded national liberation, especially in Italy, and opposed the reactionary influence of Russia. But when territorial claims overlapped, and nationalism pitted European liberals against each other, isolationists in Britain considered that this was not their business.

> What a notion a man must have of the duties of the people living in these islands if he thinks . . . that the sacred treasure of the bravery, resolution and unfaltering courage of the people of England is to be squandered in a contest . . . for the preservation of the independence of Germany, and of the integrity, civilization and something else of all Europe . . .

declared John Bright.[5] The tsars and their advisers, more aware of the advantages of the Vienna settlement, intervened in central Europe to rescue the Austrian monarchy from Hungarian and German national revolutionaries, and encouraged Prussian attempts to curb German nationalism. While Russian foreign policy remained under the control of the tsar, nationalist and pan-Slav sentiments also spread in Russia: Russians declared that they were Slavs, and would soon declare that other Slavs were under Russian protection. However, the two 'book-end' powers dominated the system less than they had in 1815. The Petersburg empire especially, after making great strides forward in the eighteenth century, now began to fall behind England and France and especially Germany in economic, political and technical development.

BISMARCK'S EUROPEAN ORDER

The third period, from 1871 to the end of the century, was again one of peace. The peace was uneasy. The central European sponge of smaller German states, which Heeren had called important to all but dangerous to none, and which had been an indispensable element in the Westphalian and subsequent settlements, was gone. In its place stood the new German *Reich*, the strongest power on the European continent. The balance which had maintained and adjusted itself since Vienna, first in peace and then in minor wars, became unstable. For some years Bismarck's considerable restraint and skilful diplomatic juggling maintained the European order. Remembering the fate of Napoleon, he was determined to avoid a quarrel with either Russia or Britain. The renewed alliance between the three east European powers, the *Dreikaiserbund*, reinforced by his secret 'reinsurance treaty' with Russia and his refusal to become involved in the problems of the Ottoman Empire ('The eastern question', he declared 'is not worth the bones of one Pomeranian grenadier'), removed the threat to Germany from the east. Throughout the system he made his enlarged Prussia behave as a sated and co-operative power.

Meanwhile the Industrial Revolution and popular nationalism generated increasing pressure in Europe. The last three decades of the century were therefore a period of accelerating economic and territorial expansion outward, away from the pressure at the centre, by the great powers and some lesser ones. One of the most successful achievements of the concert, described in the next chapter, was to manage this competitive expansion by agreement. But the new state at the centre became more potentially hegemonial. The economic and then political integration of most of Germany, and the social reforms that accompanied it, released new sources of energy similar to those released in France by the revolution. That was an ominous precedent for the peace and stability of Europe. By the time of Bismarck's fall from power in 1890 the new Germany had overtaken Britain to become Europe's greatest industrial power, and the Germans stood at least equal to the British and French in scientific, medical and other achievements. The German army had demonstrated its superiority in generalship, equipment and martial determination, like the French army in Napoleonic times. German governments after Bismarck behaved in a more nationalist and assertive manner, and neglected his careful cultivation of relations with Russia and Britain. Russia, the bulwark of conservatism, contracted an anti-hegemonial alliance of expediency with dissatisfied republican France.

The nineteenth century was a period of growing success and prosperity in Europe. There were dramatic advances in material living standards, health and education, and also in the sciences and the arts. It was an age of industrial and technical revolution, and of great strides in man's mastery of the environment. The middle class acquired an increasing say in most of the communities of Europe, with a new industrial working class crowding on its heels. The whole world seemed to become Europeanized. It became difficult not to believe in progress. To echo Gibbon's description of second-century Rome, if a man were asked when Europeans felt most proud of their achievements and most confident of the future, he would say the period from Waterloo to Sarajevo.

The society of states which provided the framework for these remarkable advances was based on the concert of its five largest states: none in a position to dominate the others, but unchallengeable if they acquiesced in each other's actions. The concert combined the advantages of hegemony and the balance of power. It was a considerable creative improvement on the eighteenth-century sovereigns' club, in less manageable circumstances. As in the eighteenth century, the monarchs and statesmen who directed the external policies of the five states shared an aristocratic outlook, and most of them thought in terms of Europe as a whole, of *raison de système*. Many were anxious, sometimes over-anxious, to restrain and bridle the passions and prejudices which threatened their concert. However, by the end of the century, growing industrial capacity combined with nationalist rivalries, and a faded memory of the damage which a major war could do, to make the European society of states increasingly fragile. The elasticity needed for the concert to operate gave way to rigidity.

Impressive as the nineteenth-century concert was, the conditions which made it possible and the long evolution which generated it were exceptional, not only in Europe but in any states system. A concert of great powers today or in future would have to operate in very different circumstances.

NOTES

1 The partnership of the five great powers was formalized in 1818 by the Declaration of Aachen (Aix-la-Chapelle) in which they stated their intention to maintain an intimate union of regular consultation for the preservation of peace on the basis of respect for treaties, and agreed to invite other states to their meetings where the affairs of such states were concerned. A protocol confirming the joint responsibility of the four allies to guard Europe against a French threat remained unpublished but was communicated to the French government.

2 Professor Enno Kraehe, an authority on Metternich, defines the concert as co-operative action among the powers with the aim of preserving international tranquillity, whether, at one extreme, Castlereagh's idea of *ad hoc* consultation strictly limited to territorial issues, or, at the other extreme, Tsar Alexander's concept of a great power oligarchy empowered to intervene in the internal affairs of other states. E. Kraehe, 'The concert in the age of Metternich', paper read to the Southern Historical Association, 11 November 1983, Charleston, South Carolina.

3 For discussion of a range of conflicting views about the concert by a Danish scholar, see C. Holbraad, *The Concert of Europe*, London, Longman, 1970.

4 S. Leathes (ed.), *The Cambridge Modern History*, Vol. I, Cambridge, Cambridge University Press, 1902, p. 2.

5 John Bright quoted in A. J. P. Taylor, *The Troublemakers*, p. 62.

SUMMARY

We are now in a position to see what conclusions can be drawn about the European society of states. The themes listed in the preface to this section as particularly significant were: the principles and organizational practices of the European society – the *grande république* – including the significance of hegemony, of legitimacy and of the swing of the pendulum; and on another plane, the continuity with previous systems and with our contemporary global society, and the relevance of cultural unity, especially in relation to the European system's worldwide expansion. Though we may distinguish these themes for the purpose of analysis, in practice they were so closely interwoven, and each so affected the others, that they need to be considered together.

We can also try to see where the European society stands in comparison with others discussed in the first section of the book. In doing so we must bear in mind that the *grande république* formed the core of a wider network of strategic, political and economic interests and pressures. The wider network or system closely involved the Ottoman empire and gradually covered the whole planet. Neither was static; both the European society itself and its relations with the outside world continually changed and expanded through the four centuries of its history.

PRINCIPLES AND PRACTICES: INDEPENDENCE AND HEGEMONY

Let us begin with the distinctive principles and practices of the European society. Perhaps the most distinguishing feature of that society was the unusual determination of its member states to exercise untrammelled freedom of action, both internal and external. The Italian Renaissance princes, the princes and cities of the Holy Roman Empire, the victors who made the Westphalian settlement, the eighteenth-century theoreticians, the settler colonies in the Americas and as much as any the nineteenth-century nation states, all wanted to push the practice of the society, and many of them also its legitimacy, far towards the multiple independences end of our spectrum. To a substantial degree they succeeded.

The question of **order** between the member states of the European society became more acute in proportion as the demand for independence was realized, and the power of the states increased. First, the more closely that independent states are held together by an impersonal net of interests and pressures, the more they are driven to make alliances and other agreements that bring a form of order into what would be an inchoate system. Second, order is further promoted by voluntary general agreements and rules that restrain and to some degree benefit members of a system and make it into a society. Indeed, it is possible to regard all societies of states, with their laws and institutions and codes of conduct, as attempts to ensure order.

However, as we saw with the ancient systems, the freedom of action of independent states is limited not only by the pressures of interdependence and by voluntary choice. Usually it is also limited, more effectively, by a third factor, **hegemony**. The experience of the European society illustrates the pull of the **pendulum** – the propensity, in systems towards the independences end of the scale, for the strongest state or states not merely to assert their own advantage but to establish a degree of hegemonial order, and for many other states to acquiesce in it. Martin Wight indicated an integral feature of the European society of states when he called it 'a succession of hegemonies'.[1] The hegemonies, and the corresponding anti-hegemonial activities – the coalitions, the wars, the concept of the balance of power and the other rules which were designed to check hegemony – are the leitmotiv of the European society.

The operational practice of the European society thus reinforces the definition in Chapter 12 of a society in the independences half of our spectrum as an international system of political control, with a powerful state (or group of states) as its focus. Such systems are in fact **societies of multiple independences moderated and managed by hegemony** – corresponding to Larsen's supernational systems of political control in the tighter half of the spectrum, which are imperial structures moderated and made more manageable by autonomy.

These generalizations throw light on the **historical development** of the European society of states. Medieval Christendom saw itself as, and substantially was, a single horizontally organized society, held together by a common cultural tradition (with local variations) and a common religion, which among other things laid down rules governing the external conduct of its princes. The medieval unity of Christendom was slowly eroded, especially in the west, by the growing effective power of local rulers and their administrations. It was further fragmented in Italy in the Renaissance by a new desire to see political realities as they were, outside the Christian context. Expediency as the test of conduct emancipated rulers from medieval obligations in their relations with each other, and the remarkable development of the *stato* concentrated as much power in the hands of a ruler as he could manage to wield. The wilful Italian princes whom Machiavelli appreciated fiouted the rules, but did not put forward a theoretical right to independence.

Those who governed the new European states wanted to liberate themselves from the old rules and also from new constraints imposed by the pressures of greater state power, and especially from a hierarchical or hegemonial ruler capable of regulating their conduct. So arose the conscious concept of the **balance of power**, that characteristically European contribution to anti-hegemonial practice, and more significantly to the precepts of a society of states. The purpose of the balance of power was, in Heeren's words, 'to protect the weak against the strong' (that is, weak states or princes against stronger ones, not subjects against princes – unless they rebelled and set themselves up as autonomous states).[2] But the concept was much more than a mere succession of anti-hegemonial coalitions. It put a high premium on elasticity, on the maxim that the enemy of yesterday is the ally of today and that therefore the ally of today may be the enemy of tomorrow. In order to achieve the imperative aim of untrammelled freedom of external and internal action, it elevated the practice of the Renaissance Italian *stato* to a principle: the ruler must be prepared to sacrifice other commitments such as treaties, family ties and religious loyalties – his word and his bond – to the preservation of a wary, non-hegemonial independence.

If for convenience we take the European society of states as beginning at the start of the sixteenth century, the characteristic features of the society took about a century to emerge, and its rules and institutions were not formally promulgated until the landmark Westphalia settlement a half-century later. During that first century and a half the Habsburgs groped for ways to preserve what they thought of as the unity of Christendom. They operated strictly according to the legitimacies of the time, and their hegemonial authority was based on the accepted laws of princely inheritance. The Habsburgs were able to exercise a **de facto hegemony** in the emerging European society of states, but they were too weak to establish their hegemony on a regular and accepted basis. They recognized that Europe was not a single realm but in a sense a *res publica* of realms and princes. The maintenance of order within and defence without would therefore have to be achieved, not by a formal suzerain but by the hegemonial authority of a leader or family. In a similar way Augustus did not establish himself as king or *dominus* but, constitutionally at least, exercised his *auctoritas* as *primus inter pares*.

In the long struggle against the Habsburgs the anti-hegemonial camp of forces opposed to integration came to accept a goal of full freedom of action for every member of the coalition, though many princes and cities of the empire and other participants were not legally sovereign. The members of the coalition also developed the practice of treating each other as *de facto* equals. The European members – for the Ottomans had their own policies – did not want anarchy. They saw the need for order between the princes and states of Europe. But they were not prepared to accept an order imposed hegemonially by the Habsburgs: they wanted a **non-hegemonial order** such as operated between themselves under the pressures of war, to be formulated after victory by international agreements and operated by means of new 'international' rules and institutions (which in their developed form are briefly described in Chapter 18). This seminal idea continued to inspire the legitimacy of the European system throughout its existence; and has been taken over, sometimes with exaggerated legalism, by our contemporary international society. But the formula of genuinely anti-hegemonial society imposed on Europe by the victors at Westphalia had little chance to operate. As the Habsburg plans were too hegemonial for the realities of Europe, so the Westphalian concept was too far along the spectrum towards multiple independences. It was soon replaced by the hegemony of Louis XIV. His hegemonial methods were elastic, and could be made quasi-legitimate by observing the forms of the new Westphalian society.

Exceptionally, the seventy-five years after Utrecht were non-hegemonial. In that particularly interesting phase the *grande république* functioned on the basis of a multiple balance of power maintained by minor wars of adjustment. The achievement was regulated by the laws of the European society. Its operation was made possible partly by the restraint and sense of collegiate self-interest of the members of the princes' club in the age of reason, but largely by the chance that the hegemonial potential of the strongest power was temporarily in abeyance, that is France was too weak to assert the primacy which it exercised earlier and later.

Napoleon, heir to the revolution and the energies which it released in France, had much more imperial aims: to dominate the *grande république* and perhaps the Ottoman Empire, and also to remodel the internal government of the member states, to 'regenerate' them according to his own ideas. He was able for a time to exercise more than hegemonial authority in the European society, and to convert it into an imperial structure recognizably akin to those of the ancient world, with a large core of direct administration, a penumbra of dominion and an area of hegemony, beyond which only Britain and Russia were genuinely independent European powers.

The nineteenth-century **Concert of Europe**, which the five strongest powers agreed to operate together, was a collective hegemony tempered by the balance of power, and thus a synthesis of the two opposed traditions of the European society's quest for order. It was, so to speak, close to the low point of the pendulum. How well did it work in practice? In the first period the informal pentarchy functioned adequately to preserve order and peace, while managing a degree of change and acquiring a certain legitimacy. In the second period it functioned less well: collective authority was loosened by the forces of change and the nationalist desire for unfettered independence, and minor wars occurred between the five members of the concert. The mantle of legitimacy which the collective hegemony acquired survived the weakening of its practical effectiveness. In the last three decades of the century the concert functioned more consciously and responsibly again, notably over areas outside Europe; but it operated largely under the personal orchestration of Bismarck, and revealed its inelasticity in an age of nationalist self-assertion when 'the pilot' was dropped.

A powerful state or states may have defensive as well as offensive reasons to institute a hegemonial order. In the European system the Habsburg bid for hegemony was essentially defensive rather than acquisitive in concept, given the Habsburg concept of what belonged legitimately to the family. The framers of the Westphalian settlement organized a similar order anti-hegemonially. Louis XIV had a more manifest desire to assert his power in the system and to expand territorially; but his basic design resembled that of his Spanish and Austrian cousins. Even the policy of conquering Napoleon acquired some defensive aspects, difficult though it is to reconcile the march to Moscow with them.[3] The collective hegemony of the Concert of Europe was more defensive, especially at first, and later it regulated the expansionary aims of its five directing powers. The conservative role of hegemony in the ordering of today's international system is discussed in the next section of the book.

How did the struggle between hegemonial and anti-hegemonial concepts of order affect the **legitimacy** of the system? Neither those who favoured hegemony nor those who opposed it were strong enough to impose their aims definitively on the European society of states. A degree of hegemony was an integral part of the **practice** of the *grande république*. The Austro-Spanish Habsburgs and the Franco-Habsburg Louis were able to operate a *de facto* hegemony, and Napoleon moved the society far towards dominion. But they were not able to establish the **principle** of hegemony; and each of the hegemonies was ultimately overthrown by an anti-hegemonial coalition. The anti-hegemonial powers were able to legitimize their concept of a society of independent and juridically equal states, and to enshrine it in the succession of great peace settlements. But they were not strong enough to ensure obedience to the legitimacy except in the eighteenth century after Utrecht.

The juridical equality of states, in the sense that every member of the club of princes (and by analogy republics) was master in his own house and free to decide how to conduct his external relations, became a reality in the seventeenth century. That did not preclude the exercise of hegemonial authority by the strongest power. However, the principle of juridical equality was then magnified into the idea or legal claim that nothing should be permitted to any state that was not permitted to all, and that any claim to primacy, or even to special rights and responsibilities as a great power, ran counter to the fundamental rule of the society. The gap between that claim and the realities of the system had a damaging effect on the orderly functioning of the European society.

COMMON CULTURE: THE SOCIETY AND THE SYSTEM

We saw that in the sixteenth century the Italian concept of the *stato* combined with the traditional practices and assumptions of late medieval Christendom, and with concepts inherited from classical Greece and Rome, to form a new society of vertically integrated states within a common cultural framework. What general and comparative conclusions about the nature of states systems can we draw from the **worldwide expansion** of the European international society? It was a complex process, with many important strands. The Europeans were the primary actors throughout, but played different roles. They determined the relations with the new states which they created in the Americas, and later in sub-Saharan Africa and Oceania. In Asia, from the Ottoman Empire to the Pacific, the European expansion was a process of mutual adjustment and synthesis.

The expansion of the European overseas empires was not a collective enterprise. It was carried out by individual states, and often by companies of private entrepreneurs within the states; and it involved armed struggles between rival imperial powers, deriving partly from local competition and partly from conflict in Europe. But neither was it a free-for-all. The expansion of the European society of states was largely regulated by collective agreements, and occasionally by joint intervention, within the developing framework of the society's institutions and codes of conduct, in which military operations found their place. The members of the European society regulated their expansion between themselves, from the first orderly partition of the transatlantic world between Spain and Portugal down to the nineteenth-century arrangements for Africa, Oceania and Asia which avoided the colonial wars between Europeans that had previously marked their expansion. In the process the rules and institutions, and even more so the practice, of the European society adapted themselves to the realities of overseas expansion, and thus incidentally became somewhat more acceptable to non-Europeans when they were admitted.

Let us take first the **European settler states** overseas. The Europeans regarded their colonies in the New World as dependent realms of European settlers, and later as overseas extensions of the European *grande république*. When the settler states shook off their dependence that is how they continued to see themselves, both culturally in general and in relation to that particular product of European culture, the society of states, though they avoided some of the entanglements of their fellow states in Europe. Like European rulers they wanted to be independent members of the society, not independent from it. They added to the European legitimacy and rhetoric of independence the rhetoric of decolonization. The European settlements in southern Africa, and in the nineteenth century in Australasia and some smaller islands, were also increasingly self-governing and potentially independent members of the European society of states. In all these areas the cultural divide was taken for granted. The non-European elements of the population were subordinate, though in some cases a majority. Nor did either colonial authorities or settlers regard local peoples outside their direct administration as constituted into proper states, though they made treaties and agreements of a kind with them. The closest parallel in the ancient world is perhaps the Greek settler colonies in the west described in Chapter 5. They saw themselves as extensions of Hellas in the same way, with the difference that they were politically independent from their foundation; and their relations with local peoples were similar. Educated Europeans both in Europe and in the Americas had the parallel in mind, and it coloured their thinking about their own colonies.

In **Asia**, on the other hand, the Europeans were faced with highly civilized and powerful states. Their formidable neighbour, the Ottoman Empire, for most of the period controlled up to a quarter of geographical Europe, and always bulked large in the economic and strategic calculations of the Europeans. Why, if the Ottomans were so much part of the system, did they not become members of the society? The evidence is that each side regarded the other as too alien. The Ottomans especially disdained the rules and institutions of the European society, though as they grew relatively weaker they increasingly

257

accepted some of them. But both they and the Europeans of course saw the need to regulate their close involvement. They worked out rules called capitulations, which were largely based on Ottoman practice at first but subsequently modified in favour of the Europeans. Those bicultural rules, and the experience gained in operating them, governed the dealings of the Europeans with the Ottoman Empire, and were adapted to cover relations with the Asians beyond the Ottomans, at the end of the long sea route round the Cape of Good Hope. The principal interest of the Europeans who came into actual contact with the remoter Asian states was trade; however, in order to develop and protect their trade, the Europeans found themselves increasingly involved in administrative and military functions within the framework of the Asian systems. Until late in the eighteenth century Asian governments were usually able to determine the terms of their trade and other relations with the Europeans, who had to adapt themselves to Asian practices. After that, as the Industrial Revolution increased the power of the Europeans (including the United States) and the desirability of the goods they had to offer, the hybrid arrangements under which the Europeans operated in Asia tilted increasingly in favour of the Europeans, without losing their essential hybrid character. Structuralist and Marxist analysis offers the valuable insight that in any given system the underlying economic and strategic realities produce a superstructure of rules and ethical norms which reflect those realities; this is a useful way to look at the changing position of the Europeans in Asia. Thus the relations of Europeans with the Ottomans and other Asian states derived elements from more than one cultural tradition. The arrangements varied in different places and at different times, but were everywhere in practice a compromise or hybrid, and were understood to be so by both parties.

However, in the second half of the nineteenth century and the first half of the twentieth, the rules and institutions of the European society gradually displaced the hybrid arrangements, and membership of the society became open not merely to European settler communities but to any state that was willing and able to comply with the rules. Nevertheless it was the Europeans, including Russia and the United States, that decided who should be admitted to their club. When Europeans took it for granted that all other independent states should be admitted to their international society on the same terms as themselves, the European society can be said to have given way to a global one. The element of continuity is illustrated by the impressive way (discussed in the next section of the book) in which most of the rules and institutions of the European society, and to a lesser extent its values, continue in force in modified form today.

The evidence therefore indicates that the formal rules and institutions of a society of states, and especially its assumptions and codes of conduct, are formed within the matrix of a single culture. When states belonging to different cultures are involved in the pressures of the same system, regulatory machinery will be devised and adjusted to manage their relations. If a society of states becomes dominant within a wider system, as was the case with the European society in the nineteenth century, other states in the system can become members of the society or be associated with it, provided they conform with its rules and assumptions, perhaps with marginal modifications.

There is room for debate about why the European society pervaded the whole system as it did, displacing the earlier bicultural arrangements. But it is not disputed that European dominance in the highly civilized societies of Asia (as well as in Africa and Oceania) was made possible by the enormous advances in technology which were achieved in Europe and North America in the nineteenth century. It was a spectacular example of the process which Professor McNeill and others see as the spread of superior technology.[4] Part of the reason for the striking spread of the rules and institutions of the *grande république* is that technology includes, alongside manufactures and innovations in the military, medical and other fields, techniques of government and of managing relations between governments. The spread of European techniques was accelerated in the nineteenth century by westernized elites of non-western cultures, whose aim was usually to westernize their countries as fast as possible. They resented the inferior status imposed on them by westerners, and many of them wanted to master the technical and administrative know-how of the west in order to stand on a more equal footing with it; but they did not doubt the superior value of what they were learning. The great majority of those concerned with relations between states wanted, not to establish a new international society, but to make their state an independent member of the European society on an equal footing. In this they were like the European settlers.

It is difficult to imagine a scenario in which the European states, by sustained self-denial or indifference, refrained for centuries from all protection and support of their traders and settlers, and allowed European contacts with the rest of the world to be regulated entirely by other governments where these existed. But it seems certain that, had European military and administrative imperialism not occurred, the goods and services offered by the European economy and the other advances of technology would have spread in any case. Their diffusion would have taken place more slowly and with more disorder no doubt, but inexorably, because of the superior power which they generated and the attraction which they exercised for the non-European world. It is pertinent to observe that, if so, the rules and institutions of

259

contemporary international society would have remained more obviously multicultural, more purely regulatory and less committed to specifically western values. It may be that, following the collapse of European dominance, discussed in the next chapter, the rules and codes of conduct of our international society are now moving in that direction.

COMPARISON WITH OTHER SYSTEMS

The European states system operated during the four centuries of its history very largely in the independences half of our spectrum; and the rules, institutions and legitimacies of the *grande république* were firmly anchored to the concept of multiple (though not equal) independences. The one significant exception, Napoleon's imperial structure, was indeed a dramatic tightening of the system; but it lasted only a dozen years and despite its wide acceptance in practice did not have time to become wholly legitimate. However, the rhetoric of independence was more extreme than the practice: and as the evidence of the earlier systems led us to expect, one feature of the independences half of the spectrum which emerges very clearly in the European case is the propensity to hegemony. The formation of anti-hegemonial coalitions is itself part of the evidence. But the successive European hegemonies, real as they were, and tacitly recognized as each one was by most member states of the society including those that opposed it, never acquired legitimacy. The nearest the *grande république* came to legitimized hegemonial authority was the nienteenth-century Concert of Europe.

The *de facto* nature of the European hegemonies puts the European society alongside the polis society of classical Hellas and the elaborate society described in the *Arthashastra*, well towards the multiple independences end of our spectrum. In those societies there was no principle of suzerainty, no assumption that the kingship must reside somewhere. Even so, hegemony played an important role in maintaining order in the *grande république* as in other comparable societies of states. A hegemony is not a series of dictatorial commands. The hegemonies which we have looked at in Europe and elsewhere, whether formally established or not, whether exercised by an individual power or by a small group, involved continual negotiation between the hegemonial authority and other states, and a sense on both sides of the balance of expediency. In the European society the hegemonial powers had to rely more than in some others on negotiation and inducement, because they did not have legitimacy and the acceptance of suzerainty to support their authority, and because of the strength of the actual or potential forces arrayed against them, which eventually brought each one of them down.

Martin Wight, after describing the European system as hegemonial, went on to ask whether there is always a hierarchy in any system based on independent states, always the equivalent of great powers with special rights and responsibilities. The evidence we have examined suggests that this is so. In classical Hellas, for instance, the legitimacy, or rhetoric, of the independence of every polis was conspicuously different from the practice, which included the exercise of dominion by the stronger states (the Athenians, the Spartans, the Thebans, the Persian Empire) over certain others, and the hegemony of one or two of the most powerful over much of the society. The Chinese society of the warring states, the Macedonian system and others illustrate the same point. The ubiquity of hegemony, and of a special status for the largest powers, in other systems predicated on multiple independences, shows these aspects of the European society to less anomalous than they seem if measured only against its legitimacy, and especially against the egalitarian extrapolations of that legitimacy. It is also interesting to note that the systems in the tighter half of the spectrum – the area of dominion and imperial authority – had a corresponding gap: the written and sculptural rhetoric of empire of the Assyrians, the Persians and even the divine emperors of silver-age Rome contrasted with the expediency and the economy of force with which they exercised their authority in practice.[5]

The **expansion of the European society** beyond Latin Christendom offers instructive analogies with the diffusion in the ancient world of techniques used by the Assyrians, the Hellenized Macedonians and the Romans for managing relations between a number of different communities in an imperial framework (along with military, engineering and other skills). We noted the parallel with the competitive colonization by Greek city states in less developed areas to the west and north; and the Phoenician cities expanded to Carthage and beyond in the same way. The earlier diffusion of Sumerian trade, culture and technology, and the later extension of the fringes of the Byzantine *oikoumene*, followed similar patterns. The Romans in particular offer an instructive parallel. They behaved in the areas to the west of Italy in a similar way to the Europeans in the Americas, whereas in the more civilized east, in Egypt and Athens for example, they were readier to make use of local institutions. It has been claimed that the mercantile quest for gain through trade played a larger part in the eastern expansion of the European system, especially in Asia, than in most earlier empires. This may be so. But the support of traders for imperial order, and the economic advantages brought by trade, also provided significant motivation and resources for the expansion of other empires: it did so in the case of the Assyrians and their Phoenician associates as well as more obvious examples like the Athenians. More generally, looking at the ancient imperial structures from our millennial distance, we can appreciate the real benefits which they brought in the form of peace, order, personal security and technical advance, as well as the brutalities and exploitation involved, particularly in the initial stages. In our own age of decolonization we keenly realize the very real injustices and suffering inflicted by European imperial expansion, and its racial and cultural arrogance; but it is important not to allow this awareness to obscure the benefits which, like all imperial structures, it also brought to the areas it dominated.

Moreover, since both the letter and the spirit of the European society of states were essentially non-imperial, and fluctuated within the independences/hegemony half of the spectrum, the nineteenth-century European dominance over the rest of the world proved to be less durable than it once seemed. It carried within itself the seeds of its own dissolution – in the rhetoric, and the less absolute but still real practices, of multiple independences. As the European settler states shook off their dependence and became members of the *grande république*, and as the capitulatory relations with Asian powers gave way to the diffusion of the institutions and legitimacies of the European society of states, the global system experienced a great loosening. The European relationship with the 'outside world', which in the nineteenth century had seemed so firmly imperial and colonial, dissolved into a worldwide society nominally committed to the principles and practices hammered out in Europe. The next and final section of this book examines that transformation.

NOTES

1 M. Wight, *Systems of States*, Leicester, Leicester University Press, 1977, introduction.
2 H. A. L. Heeren, *History of the Political System of Europe and its Colonies*, trans. from the German, Oxford, Talboys, 1834, preface and introduction.
3 See J. Tulard, *Le Grand Empire*, Paris, Michel, 1982.
4 William McNeill, *The Shape of European History*, Oxford, Oxford University Press, 1974.
5 See Chapter 12, and also the discussions in M. T. Larsen (ed.), *Power and Propaganda: A Symposium on Ancient Empires*, Copenhagen, Copenhagen University Press, 1979.

THE GLOBAL
INTERNATIONAL
SOCIETY

22

THE EUROPEAN SYSTEM
BECOMES WORLDWIDE

During the nineteenth century the Europeans brought the whole world for the first time into a single net of economic and strategic relations. They achieved this worldwide unification, which laid the foundation for our present global system, by expanding the European system, and they continued to make the rules.

European expansion, which had continued since the medieval crusades, had already brought about massive changes in the relations between the communities of the world by the time of the Vienna settlement. The west Europeans, in their sailing ships which seem to us so inadequate for their global task, and equipped with what were at the time new forms of military technology, had explored and settled large parts of the New World and incorporated the Americas into their system. With the same means they pushed into Asia, eastward across the Indian Ocean and westwards across the Pacific. In Asia they achieved less. Their efforts before the Napoleonic Wars to bring China and Japan into their economic system had failed. But British merchants had with their government's help established themselves as one of the major powers in India, where the Mogul imperial system had broken down into multiple warring independences, and Dutch merchants had achieved a form of dominion in the East Indies. Similarly Petersburg Russia had continued the Muscovite landward expansion 'with the icon and the axe' across northern Asia in the wake of disintegrating Tartar suzerainty. The Russo-Chinese state treaty of Nerchinsk in 1689, written in several languages including Latin, can be regarded as a landmark in the slow process of incorporating China into a world society of states; and by the Vienna settlement the Russians were finding their way along the Pacific coast of America as far as San Francisco, overlapping with British and American expeditions. The Europeans were encountering some resistance in Asia, but no Asian imperial power was at that time capable of expansion beyond the confines of its own civilization.

The European expansion into the rest of the world had by no means reached its climax when its second stage, **decolonization**, began in the second half of the eighteenth century, with the assertion of independence by European settler states in the Americas. Some statesmen like Burke in Europe, and many more in the Americas, thought of settler colonies in classical Greek terms, and expected them to drop off the parent tree when they were ripe for independence. But most European statesmen valued colonies in the New World and elsewhere as extensions of state power and territory, the loss of which would weaken the state in Europe. European statesmen calculating the balance of power between the states of their *grande république* included European possessions and activities in the rest of the world. Nevertheless the legitimacy of multiple independences, which had animated the European international society since the Westphalian settlement, inspired an increasing number of European settlers in the Americas. They wanted to extract themselves from dependence on one European power and involvement in the European balance, and look after their own interests as independent members of European society.

The United States had obtained its independence by armed secession from Britain in the eighteenth century, with the help of Britain's enemy France. The importance of the United States in the international system needs no emphasis. The new state was dominated and largely settled by peoples of British and other European stock, and based on principles and traditions that were profoundly European. Made powerful by expansion from the eastern seaboard into a rich and almost untapped continent, it ranked by 1900 as one of the great powers of the worldwide international system, equipped like other great powers with colonial territories and bases where 'the flag outran the constitution'.

As France supported the independence of the United States from Britain, so during and after the Napoleonic Wars Britain actively supported the independence of Latin America: both for economic reasons, in order to open the doors of that continent to what was then the world's most expansive economy, and for strategic reasons, in order to establish new and supposedly more democratic states there to balance what were considered in London the reactionary tendencies of the Holy Alliance. Nearly a score of Latin American settler states became independent and were accepted as associate members of the European international society. The most important of them, Brazil, did so with an emperor from the Portuguese royal family who was married to a Habsburg princess and therefore enjoyed Metternich's support.

European acceptance of new Latin American states fitted in with the aim of the United States to keep the western hemisphere insulated from European colonialism and power politics. The British navy and the American Monroe Doctrine effectively froze the post-liberation status quo and excluded the European powers from further colonial activity in the Americas. Consequently the powerful thrust of European imperial expansion in the nineteenth century was directed eastwards. Consequently also some American statesmen (though not the public) began to see a joint responsibility with Britain for ensuring the special position of the Americas. This shared commitment foreshadowed one of the main developments of the twentieth century, when a stronger America became obliged as a result of irremediable British weakness to assume other British responsibilities in the system.

A third and different kind of nation began to form in the Americas from the end of the eighteenth century. When the dependent states constituted in the New World by the English and the Iberians acquired their independence, the settlers who became their citizens were Europeans, or the descendants of Europeans, who had come there by individual decision. The dependent American states, though under the same sovereign as their mother country, offered a different way of life, and in some English colonies a different religious establishment. After independence the citizens of the states in the temperate zones of North and South America recognized that many more immigrants were needed. They welcomed Europeans who were attracted by their new nation's way of life and wished to become members of it by an individual and voluntary act of choice. This phenomenon was not wholly new. In Europe itself there had been considerable migration: notably the three-pronged expansion of the crusades, the mobility of priests and merchants and the extensive migration for religious reasons in the period of sectarian passion. Nevertheless the idea of a state with a thinly populated territory inviting like-minded immigrants from different European nations to come and be citizens seemed new and exciting. A largely empty state in search of a nation to be formed by voluntary individual adherence is different from a pre-existing and homogeneous ethnic group becoming a nation within the hide of a dynastic leviathan, and still more so from an ethnic nation in search of a state.

The independent European settler states of the Americas regarded themselves, and were regarded in Europe, as members of the family, though country cousins. They exchanged diplomatic envoys, subscribed to treaties and towards the end of the century became members of international organizations like the Hague Court of Permanent Arbitration, which became the Hague Court of International Justice. Above all they traded actively with Europe; and the United States also operated in the Pacific. But they all, except sometimes Brazil, kept themselves aloof from involvement in the interests and pressures which formed the nub of the European system, and played no part in European politics. Similarly, except for Napoleon III's intervention in

Mexico, the Europeans left them strategically to themselves. What really and decisively made the settler states of the Americas consider themselves, and be considered, members of the European family was that they were all states on the European model, inhabited or dominated by people of European culture and descent (in the marginal case of Haiti, Euro-African descent). None of them was a restoration of a pre-Columbian community. The end of dependence of the European states in the Americas was a significant move towards the multiple independences end of the spectrum. But because they were Europeans and remained in the system and joined the society, and also because they were insulated from the strategic pressures of the European net, the disintegrative effect was not as great as it would have been if a non-European system had reasserted itself in the Americas. The world-wide expansion of the European international system was not set back by the secession of American states from European empires, which took place within the compass of that system.

While most of the European dependent states in the Americas were decolonizing themselves in this way, the Europeans in the course of the nineteenth century brought the whole non-European world to the east and south of Europe, the high civilizations of Asia and the Mediterranean and the more primitive communities of Africa and Oceania, under the collective hegemony of the European concert. Individual European powers incorporated large areas of those continents into their separate 'empires', while other areas like the Ottoman Empire and China remained a collective responsibility.

This momentous expansion of the European system to cover the whole world was one result of the sudden and kinetic advances in technology, sometimes called the Industrial Revolution, which greatly increased the economic and strategic power of Europeans relative to non-European communities. In Europe the power of the states grew as the Industrial Revolution spread, and the pressures within the system increased. The power required for expansion in Europe yielded increasingly greater benefits if directed outwards along lines of less resistance. The Europeans could now sell all but the finest goods better and cheaper to Asians than the Asians could produce for themselves. The Europeans regarded the technical and scientific advances which their society indisputably produced as aspects of a general progress and superior civilization that included other fields as well, particularly the ordering of society itself. They wanted to use their superiority to Europeanize and modernize the non-European world, to bring 'progress' to it. Non-Europeans were deeply impressed by the spectacular increases in European technology. Whether they welcomed or disliked the Europeans, they found it difficult to resist what the Europeans

268

had to offer. European states were in a position, individually and collectively, to lay down the law and to lay down the terms of trade.

The nearest field of European expansion eastwards, and the most divisive for the concert, was the **Ottoman Empire**. Although the weakened Turks still ruled a large part of geographical Europe, they took no part in the Vienna settlement, which was negotiated only by the European society of states.[1] During the nineteenth and early twentieth centuries the Ottoman regime appeared ever less able to achieve the technical progress that was gathering momentum in Europe, or to maintain the inward authority and outward power that had made it so formidable in the past. The Ottoman Empire was not a power vacuum, but was certainly an area of lower power pressure than Europe. The Europeans had no thought of disengagement from it. Its weakening posed what European statesmen and publicists called the eastern question. 'We have on our hands a very sick man. It would be a pity if he were to pass away without the necessary arrangements having been made,' the tsar was reported to have said.

The communities of south-east Europe which were or had been under Ottoman rule had long been conscious of their ethnic and linguistic identity, and were administered by the Ottoman authorities on this basis through their religious leaders, so that nationalism there was associated with religion. But the peoples of Ottoman Europe who in the nineteenth century developed active nationalist aspirations were not geographically divided into separate ethnic groups: in many areas the population was ethnically very mixed. Nationalism was infused, everywhere in Europe but especially in the Balkans, with romanticized history. Most of the peoples of Ottoman Europe, especially the Greeks, the Serbs and the Bulgars, had folk memories of imperial states that they had established at different times in the distant past and that encompassed much of what later became Ottoman Europe; and therefore their nineteenth-century nationalist successors maintained implausible and overlapping claims to the mixed areas.

While all the Europeans wanted to bring progress to the great Ottoman area, they did not agree about how to do so. In the eyes of nationalist liberals the Christian peoples of Balkan Europe were rightly struggling to be free of 'the unspeakable Turk'. The liberals wanted Ottoman Europe to be divided into independent and more or less ethnically homogeneous nation states with democratic institutions headed by imported European monarchs. To achieve this liberal end, the Ottomans must be driven out of Europe by force, and ethnic minorities could migrate on the *cujus regio ejus natio* principle. The champions of liberal nationalism were not concerned with the strategic consequences. The Ottoman Empire's two great neighbours, Russia and Austria, both had a centuries-old tradition of wars of liberation against the Turks, which formed part of the moral justification of the two marcher empires. In particular the tsars and the majority of Russians regarded themselves as the champions and ultimately the suzerains of their co-religionists the Orthodox Christians throughout the Ottoman Empire, in the same way as the Soviet government and many Russians in the years after the Second World War saw themselves as the protectors and suzerains of governments and parties that acknowledged their orthodox form of communism. Both Russia and Austria therefore saw the crumbling of Ottoman rule as an opportunity and an obligation to expand their imperial authority. The decline of Ottoman power sucked them forward. Britain and France were ambivalent. They intervened jointly with Russia to establish an independent Greek state. Later some statesmen continued to support liberal nationalist secession, while others like Palmerston and Disraeli in Britain and Napoleon III in France thought it more prudent to maintain and reform Ottoman authority. Prussia alone of the European great powers remained aloof from the eastern question in the nineteenth century.

The great powers recognized that it paid them to pursue their conflicting purposes outside Europe within the framework of the concert system. The consequence was a series of compromises on the eastern question. Only once did events spin out of control, when Britain and France fought the Crimean War to block the expansion of Russia into the Ottoman area. Diplomatic compromises did not aim at permanence or justice, as the ardent nationalists did, but were designed as adjustments that corresponded to the changing strength and determination of the states involved and gave to each what it wanted most at the time. The three major compromises negotiated by the concert on the eastern question were the treaties of Adrianople and London in 1829–30, mediated by Prussia, to set up part of Greece as an independent state; the Treaty of Paris in 1856, mediated by Austria following the Crimean War; and the Congress of Berlin in 1878, mediated by Prussia (Germany) following a further Russo-Turkish war. Ottoman suzerainty in Europe gradually gave way to a number of feuding independent states. The rest of the empire was partially Europeanized, reformed and induced to progress, and involved in the rules and institutions of Europe. It was formally recognized as a member of the European society of states in the Paris settlement. But in practice the Europeans did not treat the Ottoman Empire as a European state. Capitulations continued, modified by the Europeans to ensure that their nationals and their trade were subject to European rules and practices, and that Ottoman administration observed some European standards in dealing with the communities under its jurisdiction.

Further east the principal feature of European expansion was the parallel extensions of Russian and British imperial administration across Asia between the Ottoman Empire and the Pacific. Less importantly, the Dutch retained substantial possessions in south-east Asia, and the French and later the Germans and Americans acquired new ones there and in Oceania.

The Russians continued to push out their land frontiers. They consolidated their authority in Siberia and central Asia, brought in settlers and began the assimilation of the native populations. It was a solid expansion, and impregnable in the absence of any power capable of major military operations against Russia in that great area. The British reached out to Asia along the sea routes. The focus of their power was the spectacular British raj in India: a richer prize than the Russian acquisitions further north, and one that provided the resources and the manpower for a semi-autonomous imperial structure all round the Indian Ocean. But the British position was much more fragile than the Russian, for three main reasons. First, the maritime link was tenuous and depended on British control of the sea, as opposed to the uninterruptible massive Russian access by land. Second, settlement from Britain was only possible at the extremities of the Indian Ocean, in Australia and to a limited extent in South Africa, whereas most of the Russian Empire in Asia was suitable for immigration from European Russia. Third, the British made no attempt to assimilate their Asian and African subjects. Instead they trained and educated local Asian elites, who gradually took over all but the highest levels of separate though dependent Asian governments. The British dependencies, unlike the Russian, became progressively more autonomous.

A REGULATED SYSTEM

Economic and strategic pressures can and often do hold together states from different cultures or civilizations in a single system. The rules and institutions which states of different cultures work out in response to the challenge of those mechanistic pressures tend to be essentially expedient and **regulatory**, designed to give the system order and predictability, like the honouring of commercial contracts, the immunity of envoys and perhaps of traders and the synchronization of military operations. The arrangements which the European states and the Ottoman Empire worked out together are a classic example. Both sides were conscious of belonging to different cultures or civilizations, and the arrangements between them were determined by expediency. Those arrangements were designed to manage the close involvement of the two sides in the same system, and therefore needed to be much more detailed and elaborate than the general assumptions and practices that regulate intermittent contacts between different systems.

271

But they did not go far enough for us to call the Euro-Ottoman system a society, let alone what Heeren meant by a union.[2]

It is the regulatory arrangements that spread if a heterogeneous system of this kind is enlarged. The rules and institutions which the Europeans spread out to China, Persia and Morocco in the nineteenth century were those which they had evolved with the Ottomans, including capitulations and consulates with jurisdiction over their nationals, rather than those in use within Europe itself such as free movement and residence virtually without passports. In fact neither the Ottoman Empire, nor China, nor Persia, nor Morocco, nor other non-European independent states like Siam, ever really belonged to the *grande république*, whatever the formal and theoretical position may have been. Even Japan, accepted as an equal ally and a member of the world concert of great powers that asserted collective international authority in China, was not a member. The states that made and modified the rules and institutions of the worldwide European international society of the nineteenth century were the members of the *grande république*.

A remarkable achievement of the nineteenth-century concert was the avoidance of fighting between the European states outside Europe in the course of their competitive expansion, in striking contrast to the incessant acts of war against each other overseas in previous centuries. The rival colonial powers established their authority in the interior of Africa in the later years of the century according to partition agreements reached largely at the Congress of Berlin in 1884. The complex arrangements in the strategically situated sultanate of Morocco dated from 1880, and led to disputes but not conflict between the European states that exercised capitulatory privileges there. Even more impressive was the collaboration over China, where the collapsing Manchu dynasty was unable to maintain order and the Boxer rebellion endangered foreign traders and besieged the foreign legations in Peking. The collaboration of the concert in China reached its climax in 1900, when all the great powers of Europe, notwithstanding the tensions that divided them, joined with the United States and Japan in a combined military and policing enterprise, which went well beyond the immediate purpose of rescuing their diplomats besieged in Peking. So genuinely collective was the intervention that the various contingents exchanged parts of their uniforms and operated with a symbolic medley of clothing and equipment. Undoubted wrong was done to China, which according to European international law was theoretically an independent state, by this and other foreign interventions. The significant aspect for the system was the unanimous decision of the great powers that it was necessary to intervene in the internal affairs of China on behalf of the international community. It may be compared with similar interventions under United Nations sponsorship in the Congo and other chaotic areas in our own times. The concert ended the century in China as it began in Europe in the years after Vienna, with a diffused hegemony of the great powers acting together to achieve what they would not trust one another to do alone.

The principal aim of the imperial powers both in Africa and in China was to make those great and turbulent areas safer for trade, and for mines and plantations to supply the developed economies with raw materials and tropical produce. But a secondary and more ethical purpose induced the Europeans and Americans to go beyond the regulatory and expedient arrangements which they were now able to enforce. They began to insist on the observance of normative rules and institutions which they had developed within the matrix of their own culture. The most conspicuous example was the abolition of the slave trade, first proclaimed in the Vienna settlement, and then the insistence on abolishing slavery itself. The concert regulated the implementation of these aims, to avoid conflict between the imperial powers and to organize collective intervention where necessary.

As the European system spread over the world, many non-European rulers wanted to join the European society of states, in order to be treated as equals rather than as inferiors, and if possible to have some say about how the new global international society was run. When the Europeans, about the middle of the nineteenth century, began to stipulate that other states which wanted to join their international society should accept not merely its rules but also some of its values and ethical codes, the criterion they used was the 'standard of civilization'. Non-European states were admitted as members of the society (though not of the *grande république*) provided that they adopted its rules and were able to attain an acceptable level of civilization in their activities as members. Nor were European standards of civilization understood as broad generalizations only. European international law, for instance, had developed into an elaborate set of very precise rules. The great powers also insisted that all governments should observe certain European economic standards and commercial practices, particularly where they affected foreigners. Non-European candidates were judged not merely by how they conducted their external relations, but also by how they governed themselves. Communities that were culturally non-European had to learn these laws and practices and adjust to them, often at some cost to their own societies. The insistence on western values (recognizable as such though of course not observed everywhere by every westerner) can reasonably be considered a form of cultural imperialism. It played an important part in the integrating process which established the European-dominated global international society. Those who led the historic revolt against the west resented cultural imperialism as much as or more than strategic domination or economic exploitation.

By 1900 the reach of the system had expanded slowly and piecemeal across Asia, Africa and Oceania. It brought **the whole world**, not into a single empire but into a **single set of economic and strategic relationships**. Europe remained its strategic and economic focus, and what happened in Europe was still decisive for the system as a whole. However, by 1900 two great independent non-European powers, the United States and Japan, were making their weight felt in the system, especially in eastern Asia and the Pacific, thus breaking the monopoly of control from geographic Europe; and a score of smaller independent states in the Americas, Asia and Africa played marginal roles. The wealth and power of the imperial states, great and small, and therefore the network of interests and pressures that held the new global system together, were more directly affected by their dependent territories. The dependencies of the European powers, the United States and Japan covered about half the land surface of the earth. They were concentrated mainly in Asia and by the end of the century also Africa. The degree of imperial control ranged through the concentric circles in which empires tend to be organized, from some directly administered extensions of Russia and France to the self-governing British settler dominions. The dependencies also varied enormously in the degree of their economic development; and the relative weight of the extra-European dependent states in the system grew as they became more significant to the world economy – and in some cases strategically more important too.

During the nineteenth century the concert of great powers set up by the Vienna settlement became progressively looser, as described in Chapter 21, and the strategic pattern of the European system moved a certain distance along our spectrum towards greater independence. But it would be wrong to deduce from this loosening of the *grande république* that the system as a whole swung from a jointly managed order towards an international anarchy. Europe and indeed the whole world became more closely knit into a single global economy, and the economic independence of even the greatest member states progressively diminished; though the actions of their governments showed little awareness of the growing inroads into their economic sovereignty, and popular nationalist sentiment would have indignantly rejected the idea. The economic integration of the world was less visible because it was not imposed or managed by any single economic great power or group of such powers, but was brought about by the relatively free play of increasingly worldwide markets. Moreover, the eastern hemisphere outside Europe, which by 1900 bulked so large in the strategic and economic pressures of the system, did not appear to be something separate from Europe; most of it did not consist of politically independent states like the Americas.

Thus by 1900 the world was much more integrated than our hindsight and the rhetoric of multiple independences indicate, or than the European powers realized. It was bound together by a tightening economic network, and by the empires of its leading powers; and also united into an international society by the global acceptance, outwardly at least, of common rules and assumptions for the conduct of international relations. But even while the member states of the European international society elaborated its rules and institutions, and imposed them on the rest of the world, in another sense that society became less coherent, and its position shifted towards the independences end of the spectrum. The Concert of Europe, which started as a diffused and collective hegemony exercised by the cosmopolitan statesmen who directed the policies of the five great powers, was transformed in the course of the century into a society dominated by nation states whose increasingly sovereign peoples felt more in common with their fellow nationals perhaps, but less in common with other nations. Nationalism pushed the European nation states further apart from each other, and statesmen increasingly reflected this alienation.

Outside Europe the sense of obligation to the European *grande république* was even weaker. The United States and Japan were both remote from Europe, psychologically as well as geographically. The United States and the more important Latin American republics, though culturally European and largely populated by people of European stock, avoided entangling alliances and involvement in European affairs. Their feelings of detachment were reinforced by the stream of European immigrants who poured into the New World, turning their backs on the old continent and committed to new nationalities. Japan for all its new and successful outward conformity with European standards remained psychologically very different. The Japanese and other culturally non-European states admitted as members of international society made it more heterogeneous, especially in its underlying assumptions and values.

Consequently nineteenth-century international society was pulled by nationalism and democracy and the growing importance of its non-European members away from the tight hegemony instituted by the Vienna settlement towards a much looser attitude of mind that emphasized independence, at the same time as the advances in technology and other factors were integrating the worldwide system into an ever closer economic and strategic net of involvement and interaction. The European ideas of sovereignty, independence and juridical equality, which provided the formal legitimacy of the international society of states in 1900, put that society *de jure*, that is so far as law and theory were concerned, appreciably nearer to the independences end of the spectrum than the operational practices of the system justified. This dichotomy between practice and theory was to grow wider in the twentieth century.

NOTES

1 The absence of the Ottomans from Vienna followed the traditional pattern of their absence from Westphalia, Utrecht and other settlements, and their disdain for involvement in European institutions, as well as the technical point that they had not been at war with Napoleon.
2 H. A. L. Heeren, *History of the Political System of Europe and its Colonies,* trans. from the German, Oxford, Talboys, 1834, preface and introduction.

23

THE COLLAPSE OF EUROPEAN
DOMINATION

The twentieth century requires different treatment from the past systems we have been examining. This is our century. Much of it is familiar to us through direct experience and living memory, and the sequence of events is too well known to need recapitulation. But it is too recent, and its outcome and consequences too unpredictable, for us yet to be able to look at it in adequate perspective. We cannot see the wood for the trees. We are intellectually and emotionally children of our era, with commitments and loyalties which come from our involvement in the struggles of the time. Since we cannot view our own century with the same detachment as the Mauryan Empire or the European wars of religion, we need to make a special mental effort to apply to it the same analysis as we have to the past: retaining our convictions but recognizing that others, and especially future generations, will question them and be puzzled by the importance which we attach to them.

There is no abrupt gulf or revolutionary dividing line between the European states system and the present global one. The European system was never confined to Latin Christendom or to the European continent. From its sixteenth-century beginnings both the Americas and the Ottoman Empire figured inescapably in the economic and strategic calculations of its members; and so to a lesser extent did Russian states like Muscovy. Further east and south, the Europeans were from the start of their system in contact with highly civilized communities in Asia and primitive ones in Africa. They had just expanded their system to cover the whole globe when in the twentieth century they lost control of it.

Once the global system emancipated itself from control by the Europeans, it became visibly new and different. The economic and strategic pressures that hold the present system together are quite unlike those of the era of European dominance. But the legitimacy, as usual, lags behind the realities of change. The great majority of members of our worldwide international society are non-European; but the rules and institutions of our society are still largely inherited from Europe, and it was generally perceived until quite recently as merely the European society writ large.

The twentieth century opened with a worldwide international system. It was still dominated by European powers; but outside Europe and especially round the Pacific the Europeans already shared their dominance with the United States and Japan. Within fourteen years of the joint intervention to restore order in China, the Europeans plunged into a most devastating war – which after a twenty-year interval of disorderly peace was resumed in a different form from 1939 to 1945. By then it was abundantly clear that Europe no longer dominated the world's affairs, and that the interests and pressures of the system were truly global. This change would no doubt have occurred in any case in the course of the century; but the self-destruction of European power greatly speeded up the process.

The Europeans lost control of the worldwide system, and a new international society emerged, not all at once but gradually and steadily, over a period of half a century. We can distinguish four principal phases. The first was the destruction of the European society of states as a consequence of the First World War. The second was the twenty years of the Versailles settlement and the League of Nations, which disintegrated into the Second World War. These two phases are discussed in this chapter. Third came the reorganization of the global system and of the new international society following the Second World War. Finally, and interwoven with the others, was the major change brought about by decolonization. The last two phases are discussed in the following chapter.

The **destruction of the European society of states**, which had developed uniquely and successfully over four centuries, had many and complex causes. We are particularly concerned with the inability of that society to adjust without catastrophe to the pressures set up in the system by the growth of German power. At the beginning of the twentieth century the great powers of Europe moved from an elastic concert, which had allowed them to line up in different ways on different issues, into a rigid confrontation of two rival blocs. The triple alliance of Germany, Austria-Hungary and Italy bound together the former eastern half of Latin Christendom, where nation states were still a novelty. Opposed to it stood France and Russia, two dissatisfied great powers. But at a deeper level than these formal alliances, almost all the powers of Europe became increasingly disturbed by the rapid growth of the industrial and military capacity of

278

the new German *Reich*. The population of the new *Reich* was the largest in Europe outside Russia, and superior in education and skill.

In the European states system the growth of the relative power of an individual state led to adjustments in its favour. The strongest state was usually able to focus much of Europe hegemonially round itself. These adjustments were balanced by many other states moving politically away from it and closer to each other. While Britain and Russia were also major Asian powers and France and Austria-Hungary had areas of imperial expansion at hand, Germany was locked into the centre of Europe. Could the major displacements required for a balance between Germany and its neighbours be achieved by peaceful compromise? Or did the strength of Germany pose the same kind of problem to those who opposed hegemony as the France of Napoleon and Louis XIV, insoluble except by a major war? The Germans did not at that time claim additional territory in Europe, but they saw themselves as hemmed in, *ein Volk ohne Raum* – a people without room. Now that the scope of the system had become worldwide, many Germans argued, surely the other powers could make room to absorb the new *Reich*'s restless energies.

Other European states were not prepared to be so accommodating. After the fall of the cautious Bismarck the Germans acquired a dominant position in the dwindling Ottoman Empire that impinged on both Russian and British interests; their overseas colonialism competed with Britain and France; and they thought it necessary to protect their eminently legitimate worldwide trade drive with a powerful navy. Along with these specific challenges went what seemed, in the fears of Germany's neighbours, to be a hegemonial tone in Europe itself. In fact the German government in the years before the First World War was markedly less hegemonial, in its actions and in its intent, than the Habsburgs, Louis XIV or Napoleon; but the idea of hegemony in Europe was even less acceptable than formerly, and the power of Germany was growing. All these factors had the familiar effect on what was left of the European mobile: other states felt themselves pushed towards each other by the new challenge. The *entente* between France, Russia and Britain saw itself as a genuine anti-hegemonial coalition, with France as the animating power. Unfortunately the concert no longer worked effectively in Europe, and no mutually tolerable compromise could be negotiated. Nor were statesmen or their publics seriously disturbed by the alternative: the prospect of war had lost its terrors. So the stage was set for a resolution of the tensions in Europe by a major war between the great powers, such as had not occurred for a century.[1]

Much the same problem was posed in eastern Asia by Japan. The modernization and westernization of Japan released an expansionist dynamism comparable to that of Germany in Europe. The Japanese also saw themselves as a people without room; and imperialism was the fashion among the other members of the great power club which they took for their models. Fortified by an alliance with Britain they evicted Russia from Manchuria, and then proceeded to establish a special position for themselves there and in northern China, comparable to the European empires elsewhere in Asia. The authority of the Chinese government and the traditional British policy of the 'open door' for trade had collapsed; and the complex collective arrangements for protection of foreign nationals and their commerce in China seemed likely to be replaced by a division of that immense country into protectorates of individual imperial powers. However, Japanese expansion was opposed by the United States. The Americans, involved in the area by their own recent annexations, belatedly championed the open door and the integrity of China. Imperial possessions and spheres of influence acquired before 1900 were legitimate, the Americans and others seemed to the Japanese to be saying, but now the game must stop, leaving the 'have' powers with their gains and the 'have-not' powers without. The Japanese did not want to raise the global issue, as the Germans did; they counted on the Anglo-Japanese alliance to protect them from unmanageable opposition by the United States and Russia to their Chinese plans.

Thus the worldwide expansion of the European society of states did not provide adequate scope for two of the four most powerful and capable communities of our century, Germany and Japan.

The war of 1914–18, now usually called the First World War, was in fact a European war, fought for European reasons and fuelled by European passions. The extent of German strength, and therefore the genuinely anti-hegemonial nature of the war in Europe, was demonstrated by the fact that Germany was fully a match for the coalition marshalled against it, though its principal allies, Austria-Hungary and the Ottomans, were weak states on the verge of dissolution into their component national communities. Not until the overseas resources of the United States were also brought into the struggle was the hegemonial power of Germany temporarily broken.

The First World War remains, as Gibbon said of Constantine's establishment of Christianity, a subject which may be examined with impartiality, but cannot be viewed with indifference. A very great deal has been written about the many contributory causes and the appalling effects of that great and indecisive conflict, which we need not recapitulate here. Its cardinal importance for us is that it effectively destroyed the European states system beyond the possibility of repair. George Kennan graphically describes the damage as it appeared at the end of the war:

The equilibrium of Europe had been shattered. Austria-Hungary was gone. There was nothing effective to take its place. Germany, smarting from the sting of defeat and plunged into profound social unrest by the breakup of her traditional institutions, was left nevertheless the only great united state in central Europe. Russia was no longer there as a possible reliable ally, to help contain German power. From the Russian plain there leered a single hostile eye, skeptical of Europe's values, rejoicing at all Europe's misfortunes, ready to collaborate solely for the final destruction of her spirit and her pride. Between Russia and Germany were only the pathetic new states of eastern and central Europe, lacking in domestic stability and in the traditions of statesmanship – their peoples bewildered, uncertain, vacillating between brashness and timidity in the exercise of the unaccustomed responsibilities of independence. And to the other side of Germany were France and England, reeling, themselves, from the vicissitudes of war, wounded far more deeply than they themselves realized, the plume of their manhood gone.[2]

The First World War precipitated the Russian Revolution. That complex of events has been hailed by Marxists and sometimes by non-Marxists as the most important event of the twentieth century. Though few would make such extravagant claims today, the influence of the Russian Revolution was and remains very considerable. Its impact on the society of states was largely negative. The Germans negotiated the Treaty of Brest-Litovsk with the Bolsheviks; but the allied great powers, including America and Japan, were less in touch with Russian realities. They reciprocated Lenin's hostility, and tried a collective military intervention to restore an internationally acceptable order, as they had done successfully in China twenty years before; but in Russia their half-hearted efforts failed. Russia remained a major constituent of the states system; but it withdrew into itself. The Soviet government stood largely outside the international society of states, with which it maintained relations similar to those of the Ottomans with the European *grande république*. As Peter the Great's move from Moscow to Petersburg symbolized the opening of a window on the west and the entry of Russia into the *grande république* as a great power (Chapter 19), so Lenin's move back to Moscow symbolized the closing of that window.

The embittered peoples who had suffered the ordeal of the First World War emerged from it in a mood of feverish resentment, psychologically unwilling to restore the system to which they attributed the disaster.

A decisive break with the past and a fundamentally new international order had become essential.

The **Versailles settlement** (including the minor treaties and the establishment of the League of Nations) is often counted as the first constituent act of global self-regulation by a society that had become worldwide. But in retrospect it appears increasingly as a transitional arrangement. In the absence of Russia and Germany, the settlement was the work of the western great powers. They aimed at producing both a workable settlement for Europe and a blueprint of rules and institutions for a world society capable of maintaining order and preventing war. In contrast to its great predecessors, Westphalia, Utrecht and Vienna, the Versailles settlement was so defective, and so much less congruous with the realities of the situation, that it failed to achieve either aim. It is sometimes said that suffering makes men wise. That was not the case with the First World War.

The elements of continuity with the European past were still powerful, perhaps uppermost, in the minds of the assembled statesmen. The peace treaties themselves were legally binding documents in the European tradition, though the terms were more nakedly dictated by the victors. The victors redrew boundaries, abolished states (notably the Austro-Hungarian and Ottoman empires) and created new ones, and imposed financial indemnities, less wisely than their predecessors but visibly in the same manner. The design for the new global society, the **League of Nations**, perpetuated the practice of five great powers which, except in cases of open disagreement, were intended to constitute a sort of concert of the world by dominating the League Council. The design for the new global society also incorporated almost all the rules and practices which had developed in the European *grande république*, including its international law and diplomacy and its basic assumptions about the sovereignty and juridical equality of the states recognized as independent members of the society. Alongside these non-discriminatory European concepts, the new design left virtually intact the capitulations and other practices which the Europeans had collectively instituted in countries from Morocco to China, as well as the great imperial structures of dependent states controlled by the victors and certain neutrals.

Both the public in western democratic countries and the statesmen they elected were dismayed and horrified by the carnage and ruin of the war, and by what they came to realize was the destruction of the European system. They concluded that major wars were no longer tolerable, and that their most important task was to prevent another Armageddon by creating a system of security. In other words, they wanted to move away from the perils of uncontrolled multiple independences towards a tighter system, and especially to 'outlaw war'.

The American President, Woodrow Wilson, spoke for internationally minded Americans and for many Europeans who regarded the prewar international society as an anarchy of sovereign states. To rely only on the restraint of statesmen and the balance of power seemed to them a recipe for disaster. International order must be maintained by means of an overarching machinery of restraint. The machinery was not to be a world government but a league of states willing and able to prevent disturbances of the peace. In practice that meant that the great powers of the day must lay down the additional rules and institutions of a new, more tightly structured international society, and where necessary enforce compliance with them.

The Covenant of the League of Nations was drafted in accordance with anti-hegemonial legitimacy, as the keystone of a society of sovereign states who voluntarily agreed to provisions for collective security. In fact it was imposed by the principal western victor powers, and could only be expected to function effectively if those powers agreed to act as a collective hegemonial authority to regulate and when necessary enforce the new international society. The League was a permanent compact committed to keep the peace on Kantian lines, and also a holy alliance of victorious and virtuous powers determined to make the world safe for democracy. In this general sense it can be said to resemble the Vienna settlement: but it proved much less effective than the Concert of Europe which emerged from Vienna, for two major reasons.

First was a lack of elasticity. The western allies, instead of restoring mobility to the balance of power, renounced the whole concept of balance, which they held largely responsible for the catastrophe, in favour of the more rigid idea of collective security. In place of the Austro-Hungarian integration of the Danubian area and the Ottoman integration of Anatolia and the fertile crescent, they opted for the Balkanization of the whole area between Switzerland and Persia. In so doing they made a half-hearted attempt to apply the nationalist principle of 'self-determination'; and they declared that, once boundaries had been 'permanently' settled, either in this way or by the victors' fiat, a state that resorted to force to alter them or to establish control over areas not assigned to it was to be regarded as an aggressor. It would be the duty of the peace-loving members of the League to restrain it by counter-force. The problem of the League as a means of managing change and adjusting the system to shifts in the power of states was that it almost ruled out change. It represented the satisfied powers, those who wished – not necessarily in every detail but by and large – to maintain the territorial status quo.

Second, the League proclaimed a new legitimacy, but was too weak to enforce it. The governments of the four most powerful and assertive communities of the twentieth century, the Americans, the Russians, the Germans and the Japanese, were uncommitted to its provisions for the maintenance of international order. Germany and Japan remained unsatisfied powers, whose relative strength in the system was greater than their say in managing it. We saw that, after Napoleon's wars, Russia and Britain had acted like a pair of book-ends, opposing each other in many ways but together rescuing and restoring the European states system in a modified form. But now neither book-end was available: the United States and the Soviet Union were for different reasons dissociated from the League. But the United States in particular remained a full member of the wider international society, and took an active part in it. The decline of the power of Britain and France, discernible by 1919 and increasingly obvious since, was obscured by their still extensive colonial empires and their networks of client alliances. But they were not strong enough to maintain the settlement hegemonially by themselves, with such help as some lesser members of the League might give them. The result was a disturbing dichotomy between the elaborate and formal apparatus of a collectively guaranteed world society of states that existed only as an idea, and the reality of an unmanaged and disorderly power-political struggle concerned with the inescapable problems of change. It is important not to confuse the two. The powers committed to the League made up only part, and not the strongest part, of the international community. To see the two out of six great powers that supported the League and the status quo as trying to operate the rules of international society, and the other major states as seceding from that society or actively trying to subvert it, is to misunderstand the increasing pressures and the ineffective regulatory machinery of the worldwide states system between the two world wars.

Nevertheless the League, however flawed in practice, was the first attempt at a constitution for the new global society of states. It incorporated three principles of importance to smaller states and to those who aspired to a new world order. First was the presumption of universality. The League was open to all states recognized as independent. Half of its fluctuating membership of about sixty states were geographically outside Europe. Second, it provided a permanent forum, where smaller states could make their views known and play a part in deciding international issues, particularly in defining the new legitimacy. Third, the League represented the principle of collective security, the protection of the weak against the strong and the special responsibility of the great powers to provide the collective protection. A standard justification of the balance of power was its claim to protect the weak against the strong; the League was intended to do so more

284

effectively. All these three principles, in new guises, remain part of today's legitimacy.

If the mobility of the system had been restored, the terms of the Versailles settlement, which reflected the momentary superiority of the western victors, could perhaps have been adjusted later. This was the hope of the more detached peacemakers. General Smuts wrote in his statement on signing the treaty: 'There are territorial settlements which will need revision. . . . There are punishments foreshadowed, over most of which a calmer mood may yet prefer to pass the sponge of oblivion.' In the 1920s the process of adjustment in Europe was tentatively begun: strategically by Germany's Rapallo agreement with Russia and Locarno agreement with its western neighbours, and economically with the American-sponsored Dawes and Young plans. But the sponge of oblivion did not wipe the slate nearly clean enough; the adjustments which the western powers and their clients were prepared to make seemed quite inadequate to the Germans and the Japanese. It sometimes seemed that the sponge had passed over the memories of western statesmen, so that they forgot the lessons of experience, like the need to preserve legitimist and co-operative governments in major but dissatisfied states. The unwillingness of the French and their client allies to implement the promise of Locarno helped to cause the fall of the Weimar Republic and the rise of Nazism in Germany. American efforts to block Japanese aspirations in China continued; and Britain, under pressure from her independent 'dominions' and the United States, broke off the most stabilizing feature of the east Asian system, the Anglo-Japanese alliance. The consequent frustration in the two powerful 'have-not' communities contributed, along with other causes, to militant totalitarian regimes bent on achieving by force what could not be obtained by negotiation. At the same time an economic recession, which the economic integration of the system made worldwide, proved beyond the ability of statesmen to control. The process of adjustment became steadily more ragged and dangerous.

The weakness of the satisfied and peace-loving democracies of western Europe in face of this threat was most clearly perceived by the realistic French leader Laval, who put French material interests above principles. He almost succeeded in bringing communist Russia and fascist Italy into a traditional anti-hegemonial alliance with democratic France and Britain. Italy's conquest of an empire in Africa, though like those of the western democracies, so incensed public opinion in the west and in the League that an anti-hegemonial alliance became impossible. Laval therefore decided to accept German hegemony in Europe and to protect France's interests by becoming a client associate of Hitler, comparable to the relation of many German states with Napoleon. But the day for such cynical calculations of self-interest was past. The majority of opinion in the west was revolted by the excesses of totalitarian dictatorships, and opposed to ideologically unacceptable alliances: it preferred the law to the balance.

Soon no effective balance remained. Stalin, obliged to choose either a bargain with Hitler on the lines of Alexander I's deal with Napoleon or membership of an anti-hegemonial coalition against him, opted like Alexander for a deal with the hegemonial power which shifted the weight of Germany against the west. Hitler's wilful and quasi-Napoleonic bid to dominate Europe, and the Japanese strike against the United States, led to a massive resumption of warfare, in which the four most powerful communities of the system emerged as the protagonists. Three of these – Germany, Japan and Russia – had totalitarian regimes, and only America a democratic one. Each fought for its own interests and principles, linked by a loose alliance of convenience rather like that between the Ottomans and France in the European system.

Hitler's area of occupation in Europe and the Japanese 'co-prosperity sphere' in eastern Asia were ephemeral attempts at imperial control. They were both regional within the global system; they lasted only about four years each; and they were largely provisional, dominated by the exigencies of total war. Both showed signs of becoming organized like other imperial systems, in concentric circles of direct rule, dominion and hegemony. A Nazi European empire seemed to envisage Italy, France and some other states not as annexed provinces but remaining as client allies in a hegemonial relationship with the *Reich*. The Japanese did not think of formally annexing China. In spite of the oppression of totalitarian rule, and particularly the attendant horrors of racism and genocide which we in this century cannot forget, even those transient imperial experiments brought about, or indicated, some of the advantages associated with the imperial end of the spectrum. In Europe the vision of political union and economic co-ordination in a single market so appealed to many of those fighting Hitler that after his downfall they were unwilling to return to the feuds and barriers of the inter-war years, and worked for a diffused supranational authority in the form of a European union of independent or autonomous states. As Napoleon's imperial Europe led to the diffused hegemony of the concert, so Hitler's imperial co-ordination of Europe led to two much closer regional economic and political integrations. West European integration is being achieved by the voluntary decisions of the member states. In eastern Europe the Soviet Union imposed a dominion which effectively, but not permanently, integrated the area. The Japanese occupation made it impracticable to restore European colonial rule, or moral authority, in eastern Asia. The 'co-prosperity sphere' did not develop into an integrated system, though the ASEAN group of south-east Asian states is moving towards a closer union. The Japanese-occupied area was not and has not become a *grande république* comparable to Europe.

The states system in the first half of the present century (*circa* 1900–45) was worldwide, but still centred on Europe. Both before and after the First World War the system became increasingly constricted by the pressures of development and the growing power of its leading states, combined with inadequate arrangements to manage the pressures. In other words, the international society in both periods was so loose and so near the multiple independences end of the spectrum that it was in fact a recipe for disaster, as President Wilson and his supporters perceived. At the beginning of the century a diffused authority managed by the great powers successfully imposed its order in China. A barely adequate flexibility in the relations of the powers might have been preserved by the project for an Anglo-German alliance or reinsurance treaty, which would have prevented the division of the great powers into two rigid blocs; but the talks failed. In the twenty years between the two wars the sense of unmanageability increased. Though the League machinery for maintaining order was not negotiated among the great powers but devised by the western allies, it might have proved effective if the most powerful of them, the United States, had remained an active member, and if it had retained the full co-operation of the democratic government of Japan; but probably some working arrangement with both Germany and the Soviet Union would also have been necessary.

NOTES

1 George Kennan, on reading these chapters suggested that nationalist passions, and particularly irresponsible chauvinism in influential French and Russian circles, should be given greater weight than I have done.
2 G. F. Kennan, *American Diplomacy 1900–1950*, London, Secker & Warburg, 1952, pp. 68–9.

24

THE AGE OF THE SUPERPOWERS
AND DECOLONIZATION

The second phase of the emergence of the global international society, namely the two decades between the wars, discussed in the last chapter, had been a period of unusual disorder, which amounted in practice to an interregnum of authority in the system. The four decades that followed the Second World War (1945–85) were a period of much greater order and authority. The damage inflicted by that war on Europe and Japan destroyed the capacity of the Europeans to control the system, and left the United States and the Soviet Union (despite the grave damage inflicted by the war there also) to step into the shoes of the Europeans.

In that third phase of the emergence of the new global society, following the havoc of the Second World War, the victors were faced with two major questions of world order. The first was how to respond to the unfamiliar pressures of a reshaped system that held them in a tighter grip than before. The second was what rules and institutions should be given to the new and no longer Eurocentric international society.

THE TWO SUPERPOWERS

The great general wars of the European states system were followed by congresses of statesmen from the victorious and the defeated powers, who recognized that they were revising the rules and institutions of an international society. That society was essentially European, held together not only by common experience of what was expedient but also by common values and a common civilization. No such congress was possible after the global conflict of the Second World War. The power of the two great vanquished states, Germany and Japan, was briefly but utterly destroyed; their territories were occupied and administered by the victors, and in the case of Germany partitioned between them. The victors were two superpowers: a badly damaged Soviet Russia and the United States, which had taken

Britain's place in the system. Britain, unconquered but severely wounded, France and other states of western Europe, and Kuomintang China were restored much as the European states conquered by Napoleon were restored in 1814.

The United States, the Soviet Union and Britain had formed their temporary alliance only to counter the threat of German and Japanese power, and only after military operations had begun. Once this power was destroyed, the basic reason for the alliance disappeared with it. The wartime conferences of the three allied powers at Tehran, Yalta and Potsdam merely settled spheres of dominance *de facto* and in broad terms. Power in the global states system quickly rearranged itself round two opposing poles, the Soviet Union and a western alliance in which the United States was very much the strongest partner. The two superpowers were not 'book-ends' holding together a single closely involved society of states; they were centres round which largely separate societies developed, locked against each other strategically but insulated by geography and ideology.

THE FORMAL INTERNATIONAL STRUCTURE

Both of the new centres of world power belonged to the European cultural tradition, but both lay outside the original Europe. The European tradition of an organized international society was so strong that they and their allies agreed that the rules and practices of the previous period should remain provisionally in force with minor changes. The overarching international institution was not to be a world government but a permanent diplomatic congress to which each state would appoint a delegate, and which would eventually become omnilateral by the admission of all 'peace-loving' states. The framework for such an organization existed in the League of Nations; and such was the instinct and desire for continuity that, notwithstanding the League's conspicuous inadequacy, the three wartime allies decided to establish a reformed version of it. One reason for the failure of the League was rightly perceived to be the absence or indifference of the most powerful states in the system. This time the Soviet Union and the United States would be the leading members of the new organization, called the **United Nations**.

Whether the great powers would collaborate to make the new machinery work seemed dubious from the start. The Russians therefore proposed, and the other major states accepted, a formula based on the experience of the great powers in the Concert of Europe. There would again be five great powers, permanent members of the Security Council; and the active opposition of any one of these powers could block a mandatory decision of the council, so that the support or at least acquiescence of the five powers was necessary for the United Nations to take any significant collective action. The Soviet Union regarded the United Nations machinery as inappropriate for resolving conflicts between the great powers, which would have to be handled by direct negotiation if at all; I myself heard Molotov make this explicitly clear. But where the great powers agreed, the United Nations might prove a suitable means for establishing and implementing a joint plan of action. The 'veto' was and remains unattractive to idealists, and to states that cannot exercise it; but it was shrewd and traditional statesmanship, for which the Russians must be given the credit, and which all five 'veto powers' have used. It has acted like a safety valve, easing the strain on the institution.

In other respects the United Nations aimed at universality rather than effectiveness. Membership would be the symbol of independent statehood and of acceptance into the global international society. In a General Assembly like that of the League each state had a vote, with the tacit assumption that such votes would be 'advisory' and not make much difference. British Prime Minister Macmillan described the attitude of the founders: 'It was because they knew that one man one vote and rule by the Assembly was unworkable that the founders put all their faith in the Security Council.' The United Nations also established a number of specialized omnilateral organizations to diffuse and exchange between governments various aspects of technology, such as health and medicine or food and agriculture.

The United Nations as originally constituted did not in fact function as a concert of the larger powers, or effectively maintain order. It served the interests of lesser powers better, as we shall see.

A BIPOLAR SOCIETY

While the rules and institutions of the worldwide society emphasized continuity, the pressures of the system were now too altered for a restoration to be possible. The reality was not a diffused hegemony over the system; nor was it a tightly knit international society based on voluntary commitment according to the theoretical design of the League and the United Nations; nor an anarchy of multiple independences. Its characteristic was the dominance of the two superpowers, and the separation of the two systems which they proceeded to construct. The five great powers after Vienna acquiesced in each other's actions within a single concert: the two superpowers after the Second World War acquiesced in the establishment of two separate spheres of authority.

The United States, with about half the functioning industry of the world concentrated within its borders, and the sole possessor of the atom bomb, was unchallengeable. Americans did not want to dominate the world. There was still a strain of isolationism in their make-up. But powers that find themselves able to lay down the law in a system in practice do so. The USA was no exception: it wanted to make the rules, and to see that others abided by them. Americans considered the rules of the new world order which they favoured and which favoured them – democracy, the rule of law, decolonization and an open door for American business – to be just and universally valid, giving equal independence to every 'nation'. The extent to which the ailing Roosevelt expected Stalin to co-operate with him to achieve these American ends is well illustrated by his naïve statement to Bullitt, his ambassador to Moscow: 'If I give Stalin everything I possibly can and ask nothing from him in return, noblesse oblige, he won't try to annex anything and will work with me for a world of democracy and peace.'[1]

But of course this was not how Stalin saw it. He thought of politics largely in terms of raw power, and especially his personal power. Stalin had made himself *imperator* of the Soviet Union; and at the end of the Second World War he saw the opportunity to expand his empire and insulate it from external threats. He occupied a circle of subordinate states, with regimes which recognized him as their autocratic overlord. Beyond this zone of dominion Stalin hoped, through the influence of communist parties obedient to him (the Cominform) and through other forms of pressure, to establish a hegemony over western Europe and parts of Asia, or at least to block tendencies and policies there which he considered hostile to his interests.

The likelihood of a Soviet hegemony over all of Europe, if Stalin's designs were not opposed, is disputed by historians today. At the time the prospect alarmed Churchill and most other Europeans. He and many other European statesmen accepted the recurring lesson of European and classical history that the ally of yesterday can become the enemy of today, and the enemies of yesterday the allies of tomorrow. Now that German capacity to dominate the continent had been destroyed, they saw a restored western Germany as the allies in 1814 had seen France: a valuable component of the European concert and an indispensable partner in a new coalition to oppose Russian hegemony. Churchill launched an anti-hegemonial appeal to the American public, in language similar to that of the Corinthian envoys appealing to the Spartans (Chapter 5). He spoke about an iron curtain coming down across the middle of Europe.

The makers of American policy thought it necessary to contain Soviet power all round the world. In Asia, Truman refused Stalin a zone of occupation in Japan, and helped China and Iran to recover Russian-occupied territory. But soon after the war the communist party of China established effective control over that huge community, which was then estimated to contain between a fifth and a quarter of the population of the world. The assumption that all communist parties were under Soviet control gave the impression that the globe was divided ideologically and strategically into two great hemispheres of influence. The reality was more complex than that simple illusion.

THE COLD WAR

The cold war was a global but restrained struggle, marked on both sides by defensive strategy and by competition for the allegiance or sympathy of people all over the world. In some respects it resembled its even more muted predecessor, the nineteenth-century rivalry between Russia and Britain in Asia. The cold war remained cold partly from war-weariness, but principally because of the deterrent effect of nuclear weapons. The Soviet armed forces in Europe were designed and equipped for offensive war; but statesmen on both sides understood very clearly that war between great nuclear powers was no longer the last resort: it was altogether too destructive to achieve any political goal. They have in practice backed well away from the threshold of mass suicide (despite some assertions to the contrary). The whole developed world has become what some commentators call a zone of presumed peace. The resort to force, excluded at the centre, was driven outward and downward, away from nuclear annihilation towards what the jargon calls 'low-intensity conflict' and guerrilla operations. The forty years after the Second World War were marked by minor wars which, like those of the mid-nineteenth century in Europe, might damage the combatants but did not upset the general course of civilization in either of the great blocs. This is a major change from the two catastrophic world wars of the first half of the century.

In the cold war the Soviet Union operated essentially alone. It exercised dominion over the contiguous client states in which it had garrisons, notably in eastern Europe and Mongolia; and it later offered a measure of protection and support to small states that feared a powerful neighbour and adopted an approximately Soviet form of government, like Cuba, Vietnam, Angola and South Yemen. The impressive Soviet imperial structure was a remarkably Byzantine *oikoumene* (Chapter 10), derived from a millennium of inherited experience that was partly overlaid but not lost during the two westernized Petersburg centuries. As Byzantine authority was shaped and legitimized by Orthodox Christianity, so Soviet authority was shaped and legitimized, in the Soviet Union and outside it, by the doctrines of Marxism-Leninism, which were authoritarian, Moscocentric and universalist. But Marxist ideology was not enough by itself to make other states submit to Soviet control or even leadership. Yugoslavia and China,

with communist governments but no Soviet troops, detached themselves from the Soviet bloc and became leaders of the non-aligned
movement (see p. 297). There was the same sort of modified continuity
before and after the Russian Revolution as between the French *ancien*
régime and Napoleon. And it is worth remembering that for the last
three centuries Russian policy has usually shown a considerable prefer-
ence for stability in the European *grande république* and for expansion
elsewhere.

The much looser strategic hegemony of the United States permitted
other states greater freedom of action. It was expressed institutionally
in a chain of alliances, which extended from Britain and France, and
soon the restored Japanese and West German states, to smaller clients
in Europe and Asia. In all of them American power was preponderant.
Furthermore, the industrial and financial strength of the United States
had grown so much, and that of the rest of the developed world had
been so damaged, that an American economic hegemony was also
inevitable. American hegemony was negotiated as much as it was
imposed; like that of Louis XIV, it was maintained by a defence
capacity which the client states could not muster for themselves, by
financial subsidies and by a continuous and detailed diplomatic
dialogue.

American hegemony, though mild, stimulated the inevitable **anti-
hegemonial reaction** in its junior partners and clients, which were
insulated from Soviet pressure by the American shield. De Gaulle took
France out of NATO, the integrated American defence structure for
western Europe, while remaining in nominal alliance; he concentrated
on building a west European Economic Community of states under
French leadership, with political overtones and memories of the *grande*
république, and on relaxing the tensions between western Europe and
the Soviet system. The West Germans welcomed the economic community and the *détente* with Russia; but like the rest of western Europe
were unwilling to give up the American shield. Britain remained a
more willing junior partner of the United States. However, French,
German and British policies were still rooted in their experience in the
European system which had now disappeared; and they had to be
painfully adapted to the very different patterns of power which now
prevailed in the world.

The rift between the two super-systems was not as great as it is
sometimes portrayed. The world remained very much one system
strategically, and each superpower was the principal military concern
of the other. The world also remained formally one international
society, with a common structure of international law, diplomatic rep-
resentation and other rules and institutions inherited from the European society. What both the superpowers, and particularly the Soviet

Union, disregarded was the theoretical legitimacy of multiple absolute sovereignties. The European system was a succession of hegemonies, in which the practice was tighter than the theory: the practice of the global system in the decades following the Second World War was somewhat, but not much, more hegemonial than the European norm.

During the cold war the relations between the two superpowers were chilly but correct. But following the death of Stalin, Khrushchev and then particularly Nixon and Kissinger explored the possibilities of containing their antagonism, and conducting it in a less expensive and dangerous way, especially by means of a more realistic confidential dialogue and arms limitation agreements. These attempts to moderate the arms race seemed inadequate and ineffective at the time; but cumulatively they developed in the minds of the negotiators a familiarity with the idea of a wider understanding, which became more attractive as the relative power of the two superstates declined.

DECOLONIZATION

Meanwhile the spectacular but brief European dominance of the outside world continued to disintegrate. The fourth phase of the emergence of the new international society, the **decolonization** of the postwar years, was part of the more fundamental ebb tide of European power. We must look back briefly at the European commitments which led to it.

When the Concert of Europe regulated European activities in Africa at Berlin in 1884–5, it formulated the international obligation of colonial powers to act as **trustees** for the welfare and advancement of primitive and dependent peoples. This obligation was often treated in a cavalier fashion; but it created an important new legitimacy. The concepts of trusteeship and advancement implied that colonial tutelage would in due course come to an end. They later became the basis of the League of Nations mandates and the United Nations trusteeship system.

After the First World War, **self-determination** replaced imperialism as the fashionable doctrine of the age, and the acquisition of colonies no longer seemed legitimate. The victor powers did not annex the dependent territories of the German and Ottoman empires, but formed them into League of Nations mandates, each administered by a mandatory power.[2] The essence of the mandate system, formulated in article 22 of the League Covenant, was the international accountability of the mandatory powers, who had to submit annual reports on how they were discharging their 'sacred trust of civilization'. Britain brought Iraq to formal independence in seventeen years. After the Second World War the same system was continued by the United Nations Trusteeship Council for those mandated states which had not yet achieved independence.

The concept of general decolonization spread rapidly between the two world wars. A wide body of western opinion, and western-educated elites in the dependent states, applied the mandate concepts of sacred trust, accountability and self-determination to all colonies, and regarded imperialism as racist and as economic exploitation. The British government accepted independence for the white settler 'dominions' within a Commonwealth that retained close ties to the imperial 'mother country', and the process of giving India the same status was well advanced. It was assumed in Britain that the reins of government in less developed colonies would gradually be handed over too. The French and Portuguese programme was to assimilate the subjects in their outremer empires, to make them into French or Portuguese citizens in the same way as imperial Rome had done. The French parliaments came to have some eighty deputies from the overseas provinces.

At the end of the Second World War the European colonizing states were acutely aware of their weakness. At first, while accepting responsibility for the welfare of colonial peoples, they still assumed that their empires, which had increased their power and pride in the past, would help them to revive their economic strength and political influence. They did not yet see how transitory the overseas empires established in the previous century really were, especially the most recent colonization in tropical Africa. But within ten years it had become clear to political leaders and to the majority of informed opinion in the democratic countries of the west that colonialism had by then become as unacceptable as slavery a century before, and that the time had come for all the dependent states set up by the west Europeans to achieve political independence.

Both superpowers encouraged decolonization, and applied pressure to speed it up. The Soviet attitude was influenced by Lenin's questionable analysis of imperialism, and by the valid assumption that decolonization would make western containment of the Soviet bloc more difficult. US policy makers, brought up on anti-colonial rhetoric, had a clearer and earlier realization than west Europeans that retention of colonies was no longer practical (they did not count their own overseas possessions as colonies); but they made the unrealistic assumption that the European dependencies which acquired their independence would look towards the United States.

Though colonies were all bracketed together in one doctrinal condemnation, in practice there were great differences between them. In the ancient civilizations of Asia, western-educated elites had learnt European administration and technology, and usually understood better than Europeans how to adapt imported know-how to their own people. The imperial authorities had come to rely on westernized Asians in all but the top echelons of government. The dependent states established by the Europeans in Asia were thus obviously capable of independence. After the Second World War it was quickly achieved, though not without bloodshed, throughout that continent from the Mediterranean to the Pacific. The decisive step came two years after the war, when the British carried out their long-planned withdrawal from their Indian empire, which accounted for half of the colonized population of the world. The standards and values of the high civilizations of Asia were substantially modified by the period of western administration, law and education; so that Asian communities emerged from the European ebb tide with a blend of the two cultures and traditions, in the same way as the Hellenism of the Macedonian world was a blend or hybrid of Greek and near eastern traditions. After independence the east Asian states especially entered a period of impressive economic prosperity and cultural adjustment, consonant with their millennial achievements in the past.

By contrast the more primitive peoples of tropical Africa and Oceania seemed to the Europeans not yet ready to assume the duties of citizenship in a modern state. Whether or not that judgement was justified, the pressure of events was too great for gradual solutions. The west Europeans had lost both the capacity and also the popular will to continue colonization. More important, the economic argument, which had always been the main motive for colonization in areas that were unsuitable for European settlement, faded also. The European governments calculated the balance of advantage, and except for the Portuguese dictator reckoned that if the imperial power yielded to liberationist sentiment and departed by negotiated consent, economic, cultural and other links would probably survive; but that whatever happened after their departure, it would on balance pay the Europeans to go.

With such a general demand for decolonization and so little opposition to it, the United Nations General Assembly had little difficulty in passing Resolution 1514 (14 December 1960) that

> immediate steps shall be taken in Trust and non-self-governing Territories, or in all other Territories which have not yet attained independence, to transfer all powers to the people of those Territories without any conditions whatsoever. . . . The inadequacy of political, economic, social or educational preparedness should never serve as a pretext for delaying independence.

Within twenty years after the end of the war the larger dependent states created by west Europeans overseas had achieved political independence, followed soon after by almost all the rest. The concept of many small independences achieved its ultimate extension in the subsequent decolonization of the Soviet Union.

The states which emerged or re-emerged into independence from the ebb tide of European dominance did not turn in gratitude to either the United States or the Soviet Union. Like the states of the Americas when European colonialism ebbed from the New World, the newly independent countries with few exceptions wanted to be free of entangling relations, and in particular to avoid becoming client states of either imperial superpower. In Asia and Africa there was also a more general revolt against the west, born of deep resentment against the racial and cultural superiority presumed by 'white men'. Under the leadership of India and China the newly independent states proclaimed the goal of non-alignment, at a congress at Bandung and several subsequent congresses. They called themselves the third world, as distinct from the two hegemonial systems. The anti-imperial appeal of the third world concept was strong enough to bring the Latin American states into the non-aligned bloc.

Decolonization was a massive political decentralization, and a substantial swing of the pendulum towards the multiple independences end of the spectrum. The new and restored states now constituted the majority of the members of international society. They insisted on the European concept of the equality of all sovereign states. But most of them were without tradition or experience in international affairs, and many were mini-states too small to be economically viable. Many of them recognized that economic and administrative, as opposed to political, independence was impracticable. They therefore quickly came to consider what international arrangements would mitigate the poverty and loneliness of too absolute an independence.

Both the new superpowers were heirs to the European tradition of managing an international society. Perhaps the most significant feature of those forty years was the considerable stability of the system, able to absorb such great changes as decolonization. That stability was ensured by the hegemonial control and in some cases dominion exercised by the two superpowers within their own constellations, together with the nuclear balance of terror which kept the cold war cold. However, in the course of the period the dominance of the two superpowers gradually waned. The economies and the morale of the other highly developed states, particularly the Japanese and the Germans, recovered, and consequently also their weight in the world system. The developed world became more polycentric.

The fragmentation of the west European empires into a number of states entitled and able to achieve a circumscribed independence can be compared with the similar fragmentation of the Holy Roman Empire legitimized by the Westphalian settlement (Chapter 17) and the break-up of the Austro-Hungarian and Ottoman empires after the First World War. It is a mistake to see the polycentrism and decolonization as seriously increasing anarchy in the practice of the system. Certainly the formal international society shifted nearer to the multiple independences end of the spectrum during the period; but growing economic integration and the economic inadequacy of most of the newly independent communities held the member states of the non-communist world in an increasingly tighter net. Nevertheless many statesmen and political observers around the world wondered to what extent the proliferation of independent states without previous international experience, belonging to very different cultures and at very different stages of development, and the shrinking preponderance of the superpowers, would make it harder to manage the system and diminish the prospects for order. The following chapter looks at the responses of the contemporary society of states to these challenges.

NOTES

1 A. Eban, *The New Diplomacy: International Affairs in the Modern Age*, London, Weidenfeld & Nicolson, 1983, p. 6.
2 The Versailles settlement determined that the Arab peoples of the Middle East could be quickly brought to independence by Britain and France; that the tribal peoples of tropical Africa would require a longer period of European tutelage by Britain, France and Belgium; and that primitive and island peoples would best be eventually absorbed by five non-European mandatory powers: Japan, the United States, Australia, New Zealand and South Africa.

25

THE CONTEMPORARY
INTERNATIONAL SOCIETY
Heir to the past

It is notoriously difficult for a member of a society to describe it, because it is impossible to distance oneself far enough from it. However, in the light of the previous chapters we can perhaps note some significant aspects of our contemporary society of states.

The collapse of European domination did not dissolve the worldwide network of interests and pressures that involved the whole planet in a single system, organized by a single society. European control has ebbed, in a gradual and ragged fashion; but the global nature of the **system** has survived, with such a degree of continuity that it is difficult to say where, in time or function, the system ceased to be European. The explosive development of technology, especially the speed of communication and the range and deadliness of weapons, continues to make the world more integrated, so that every state becomes more constrained by its pressures than before. Within this shrinking world new patterns of pressure and interest have arisen.

When we turn from the pressures of the system to the rules and practices of the international **society** with which we attempt to order it, we see that the society also continues to encompass the whole of mankind in a single set of rules and institutions, and to a limited and often nominal extent common values. But it differs from the substantially imperial global society of the previous century, whose rules and values were imposed by the Europeans as an extrapolation of their own experience, and differs indeed from all previous societies that we have examined, by having in principle no dominant or determining cultural framework. There has been a huge swing of the pendulum, notably in Asia and Africa and less importantly in Oceania and the Caribbean, from the west European overseas empires, through a transitory hegemonial pattern of the British Commonwealth and the French Communauté, to a fragmented society of nominal multiple independences; and in eastern Europe and elsewhere the Moscocentric area of Soviet dominion has also disintegrated, and the republics of the Soviet Union have regained at least their formal independence. A large number of states now accept only the regulatory aspects of the present society, and do not feel bound by values and codes of conduct derived from Europe. The legitimacy of the society is exceptionally far towards the independences end of the spectrum.

However, there is more continuity in practice than the legitimacy suggests. The new and non-discriminatory global society was not brought into being by a radical break with the past, but as explained in the last chapter it has inherited its organization and most of its concepts from its European predecessor. There was a conscious effort after the Second World War to maintain a continuity with the existing rules and institutions, including even the League of Nations; and the League was itself an extension, with some modifications, of the principles and practices developed in the very different context of the European *grande république*.

THE POSITION OF THE LESS POWERFUL STATES

The most important feature of the present international society is the extension of political sovereignty throughout the system, even to small and impoverished islands that de Gaulle called the dust of empires. The 180 or so states into which it is divided are, at least nominally, independent and juridically equal. The system has been further loosened by the increasing **outlawry of the use of force**, which has largely, but not altogether, inhibited the strong from imposing their will on the weak. The degree of immunity from physical coercion that small states currently enjoy is historically exceptional; but the fate of Kuwait shows that it is far from absolute.

The non-aligned majority of the member states of the current international society value their external as well as internal independence. As the disintegration of the Holy Roman Empire enabled a number of minor European states to acquire domestic sovereignty and to have their external independence legitimized by the Westphalian settlement, so broadly speaking the disintegration of European power enabled large numbers of former colonial and other dependent states to become politically, but in most cases not economically, independent. Politically and strategically they are anxious to avoid entanglement in a hegemonial alliance; or, if that is not practicable, to mitigate the consequences of client membership. But they do not want to leave the global society of states. On the contrary, they attach great importance to being accepted as members on an equal footing with other states. Indeed, most of them depend to an unprecedented degree on the benefits which the current international society provides for small and poor states.

The attitudes of the westernized ruling elites of former dependent states reflect those of liberals in Europe. They also echo those of their predecessors, the European settlers in the Americas, who initiated the movement for decolonization of the overseas European empires and developed its rhetoric of independence and avoiding entangling alliances. This European inheritance is lamented by those members of other cultures, notably in Africa and the Arab world, who consider that the western model of statehood was imposed by the Europeans and is unsuitable for their societies.

The coveted status of reacquired or newly acquired independence and membership of the 'world community of nations' is symbolized by participation in the institutions of the society. The exchange of bilateral diplomatic representatives with other states and membership of the omnilateral United Nations are the visible evidence of recognition. **Membership of the United Nations** also provides every member state, however small, with a voice, and a chance to participate in reformulating the rules, institutions and proclaimed values of the worldwide international society, or in other words the society's ostensible legitimacy. The United Nations' specialized agencies concerned with fields like health and agriculture make the technical know-how of more developed states available to the weaker ones without political strings. The majority of member states of our international society have had virtually no experience of international affairs. The principal contribution of the United Nations to world order is that it offers them a highly precious moral position, a say in the management of the society, and some real material advantages. The potential advantages to the larger members are discussed below. The United Nations is not a legislature or a world government. Nor has it been the voice of the world community, though the end of the cold war may make it more effectively so. But it (particularly the General Assembly) is the voice of the newly independent majority of member states.

The more important states of the society now formally endorse the legitimate right of all small states to choose their own form of government free from outside interference. They also recognize the responsibility of the strong to protect the weak: a function which was enshrined in the Wilsonian League of Nations, and which Heeren claimed for the balance of power. However, the current formula for sovereignty does not preclude the most powerful states from determining the rules for the conduct of international relations (especially but not only in the economic field), which is how we have defined hegemony. Nor does it preclude major powers, individually or collectively, from withholding protection and assistance, which smaller states want and may have to purchase by acceptable behaviour. The operational practices of the system are considerably more integrated than its fragmented legitimacy suggests, and the gap between the practice and the theory of the system is unusually wide.

STRATEGIC FLUX

In Chapter 23 we identified the United States, Russia, Germany and Japan as the four major centres of power in the twentieth-century system. The destruction of German and Japanese power in the Second World War was temporary; but as a result the **strategic** configuration of the worldwide system was set for nearly half a century in a relatively stable bipolar pattern, focused round the two military superpowers, with a 'third world' that wished to keep as non-aligned as practicable.

Then in the 1980s the international system underwent a dramatic change. In the contemporary world, economic as well as strategic strength is necessary to hold together an imperial system. The failure of Marxism-Leninism has led to the disintegration of the Soviet Union, and has sent Russian power into temporary abeyance, despite its massive strategic capacity. Russian power has collapsed before, and then recovered; and the great nation that stretches from the Baltic to the Pacific will doubtless soon resume, and never wholly lose, its major influence on world affairs. The eclipse of Russian power has left the United States, once more and unexpectedly, in a position of sole leadership or hegemony. At the same time Europe, not merely the Community of Twelve but the whole continent up to the Russian border, seems to be coalescing piecemeal but steadily into an economic and then probably a political and strategic confederacy. Successful integration would certainly make Europe a stronger economic and political force. More generally and less dramatically, our pendulum, which in the age of decolonization swung so far towards multiple and fragmentary independences (and in the Soviet Union has not finished its anti-imperial swing), now appears to be moving back towards greater authority and order, both strategic and economic.

Meanwhile the strategic thinking and dispositions of every state in the system previously affected by Soviet power are being rapidly and rather confusedly modified. The other great structure of alliance and protection amounted to a pooling of defence capacity against the Soviets, and was organized round the strategic and economic strength of the United States, which in practice held a hegemonial position among its allies. As Soviet capacities and hostility to the United States and its allies decline, and as American economic capacity loses its relative predominance, American forces permanently garrisoned abroad are being reduced partly by agreement with the host states and partly unilaterally. It is not yet clear what new functions the alliance structures may have. There are other potential threats to the allies' interests and principles; and the alliances legitimize American bases and the US 'leadership role' as the protector of the independence and democracy of smaller states.

Until the mid-1980s the two superpowers seemed to be feeling their way towards joint responsibility for order, based on compromise between opposing views. That might have led to a diarchy. In Kimon's words, they were coming to think of each other as yokefellows.[1] But the new and temporarily much weakened Russia has also normalized its relations with the other powers from which it needs help: western Europe under German leadership, Japan and China. A concert of world powers, with its practice based on agreement and acquiescence, is beginning, jerkily, to take on the management of the international society, even in such difficult areas as the Middle East, Indochina, the Balkans and the reconstruction of the ex-Soviet economies. The concert will function hesitantly at first, with reluctant American leadership; and where practicable under the auspices of the UN Security Council. The state whose acquiescence is necessary for Security Council resolutions, and which therefore now sets effective limits to action by the concert through the UN, is China.

How will such concert policies be legitimized? The founders of the United Nations intended it, and particularly the Security Council, to be machinery for their management of the system, if they could agree on what they wanted to achieve. In contrast to the value of the institution to smaller states, its contribution to joint hegemonial management has hitherto fallen far short of its potential. But where the world's strongest powers, or more accurately the five permanent members of the Security Council, agree or acquiesce, the United Nations is able to play a useful peacemaking role. It has sponsored peacekeeping forces to keep apart actual or potential combatants, and has also prevented or helped to end a number of minor wars between its members, though not others. The United States is now considering with its major partners how they can use the weight of their authority to obtain consensus or endorsement by the UN of the arrangements they are able to work out between themselves. The permanent omnilateral congress would thus fulfil its ratifying and legitimizing function, and also provide machinery for the largest powers to implement their concerted decisions.

ECONOMIC INNOVATION

The most striking innovations in the organization of international society since the Second World War have been in the **economic** field. The tightening economic integration of the system makes new practices and institutions necessary. The economic order is now more integrated, and more managed by an institutionalized directorate of economic great powers, than anything previously attempted by a society of politically independent states. The novelty and immensity of this undertaking are still not fully realized.

One major change is in the attitude of industrial powers to their sources of supply. The Athenians in their heyday, and the British in the nineteenth century, established their imperial control over at least some of their sources of supply; and the Germans and the Japanese in the first half of this century tried to do the same. Modern industrial technology makes the possession or imperial control of large territories a much less important factor of economic power now than when land and raw materials were the principal source of wealth, so long as an orderly economic system ensures that **high concentrations of technological skill in a small area have access to supplies of food and raw materials on the one hand and markets on the other.** The question for world order is therefore: what institutions, what practices, can make the present international economic system orderly and predictable enough to assure supplies and markets to Japan, western Europe and other concentrations of skill?

The governments of the leading states agree that they have to guide and nurse orderly economic development throughout the world in proportion to their capacity: in other words, to accept the responsibilities of economic *raison de système*. (How well they discharge these responsibilities is open to debate.) Economics is the field in which leadership comes most easily to Americans. The institutions which they devised for managing a new economic order provide the foundation of the present machinery, and have developed into the economic counterpart of the United Nations. The principal instruments are the intergovernmental Bank for International Reconstruction and Development, known as the World Bank, the International Monetary Fund and other multilateral bodies established to promote and monitor economic growth. They are supplemented by bilateral aid and significant non-governmental sources of aid and credit. The United States still holds a preponderant position in these institutions.

Meanwhile some states in the long-civilized areas of Asia, particularly those of its Pacific rim, have reached the political and economic levels of the most developed societies, and so regained the relative positions which they held in their dealings with the west before the nineteenth-century European expansion. Japan may now have the most developed economy in the world. Elsewhere, by contrast, many newly independent states are sinking below their relative levels in colonial times, towards the positions which they held before the era of European dominance.

The most significant of the experimental arrangements for managing international finance and trade is the informal Group of Seven. It enables the leading economic powers to discuss and co-ordinate more or less continuously their efforts to direct the world's ever more integrated economy, which now includes the former Soviet empire. In ways reminiscent of the Concert of Europe, the group includes all the economic great powers of the day, which realistically arrogate to themselves, where they agree, the responsibility of determining the rules and day-to-day arrangements of the economy. It is a **diffused economic hegemony**, combining the laying down of the law with an internal balance within the group.

Two realistic features of the new machinery of economic co-ordination increase its effectiveness. First, the weight of each state in the multilateral economic bodies depends on its contribution, which relates the economic dialogue to the power of the states concerned. The international financial institutions are thus enabled, in Frederick the Great's phrase, to produce concerted music instead of a babel of discordant sound.[2] Second, western governments are uneasily aware that economic activity is like quicksilver, and that their efforts to conduct or even regulate it have unpredictable results. The intergovernmental machinery has moved towards stimulating and harnessing not grandiose state planning but domestic private enterprise.

Facing the diffused hegemony of the economic great powers is a kind of anti-hegemonial coalition, still loosely and inadequately known as the 'third world'. This coalition to some extent co-ordinates the policies of the weaker majority, and so contributes to the integration of the economic system. Its members are committed to political independence, but they realize keenly how much they need **collective economic security**, including aid, investment and markets for their exports (which are the industrial countries' sources of supply), so as to satisfy the rising expectations of their increasing populations.

The donor states offer the recipients increased economic security and a considerably faster rhythm of development, but at a price. The international financial institutions and the parallel consortia of 'donor powers' insist that, as a condition of continuing aid and investment, recipient states should observe not only external standards for debt servicing, currency and foreign trade, but also standards acceptable to the donors for the management of their domestic economies. These western standards correspond to the standards of civilization and security for foreign commerce which the Concert of Europe laid down and enforced in the nineteenth century (Chapter 21). It is entirely understandable that the recipients should vociferously demand that the western economic standards laid down hegemonially by the donors be modified in their favour. The 'Group of 77' recipient states, formed to press for a second 'new economic order' and a more just distribution

305

of wealth and technology (inevitably at the donors' expense), has grown to include some two-thirds of the member states of international society. The 'North–South dialogue', if we include in it the crucial negotiations of recipient states with the international economic organizations about debts and aid, is the first concern of most of its members. But the economic hegemony of the donor powers and their ability to make the rules have been modified remarkably little.

The power of money, that haunting phrase of Thucydides, was also important in ancient systems. Money did not always flow one way; imperial rulers often found it expedient to subsidize those whom they wished to keep quiet or loyal. The Persians (Chapter 4), the Ptolemies (Chapter 6), the Byzantines especially (Chapter 10) and the imperial Chinese (Chapter 12) expended large sums of money in this way. So did seventeenth-century France (Chapter 17) and eighteenth-century Britain. The major role of economic power in managing systems of states is not in itself new.

The economic machinery of our international society is innovative and experimental. It is well that it should remain elastic; that gives it a chance to adapt to new pressures and requirements such as the diffusion of economic strength, the closer incorporation of the ex-communist bloc into the world economy and the decline of American dominance. There are institutions; but the pressures of a changing system are transforming some, making others obsolete and inducing member states and confederations to try out new ones.

A MORE INTEGRATED SYSTEM?

In the last few years the temporary abeyance of Soviet (or perhaps one should say Russian?) power and the visible resurgence of Germany and Japan have thrown the pressures of the global system into a considerable flux. In such periods of rapid change and readjustment it is especially difficult to see what the next phase of the system will be like.

Two longer-term trends are likely to help shape the system, and to determine what modifications the rules of the society will need. The pressures of world economics – the global market – and the ease and speed of communication seem to be constraining us into a tighter, more integrated system. This is now the conventional wisdom. Though the legitimacies of our international society remain unusually far towards the multiple independences end of the spectrum, the pendulum seems to be moving back. But a firmer global net of interests and pressures may not prevent traditional cultural affinities and practices from reasserting themselves, if the revolt against western dominance pushes our society towards groupings of similar states. Regional

306

confederations, communities and similar groupings seem likely to reflect cultural affinity and geographical proximity as much as economic complementarity.

The awareness that states are being constrained into a tighter system, especially in the economic field, has led to increasing doubts about the continuing relevance, and even the reality, of independent sovereignty. The real sovereignty of the *stato*, established by Italian and German princes and maintained by the princes' club and the romantic nationalists, remains precious, especially to the governing elites of states recently emancipated from imperial rule. But the external and internal freedoms of action associated with independent states no longer seem to be bound together into a monolithic whole. In the rhetoric of statehood, the different elements in the bundle – from defence and immigration to currency and human rights – can be assigned to various confederal or society-wide bodies without destroying the identity and ultimate sovereignty of the state. Or to put it more prosaically, the modern successors of the European princes find themselves constrained by the pressures of a tightening system and by the institutions and practices of a more integrated society to act increasingly in ways that deprive them of independence de facto, externally and internally, so that their governments no longer control a *stato*; while leaving intact the symbolic legitimacy of the state and varying degrees of real autonomy.

The historical evidence, including that from Europe, shows that hitherto all international societies with shared values and assumptions have evolved within the matrix of a dominant culture. Does such a global framework exist in practice today? Two schools of thought consider that it does. One school maintains that the ethical standards put forward by western and non-western leaders still derive essentially from western values. The other school believes that technology and continuous contact have enabled a new modern global culture to develop, which determines the life-style and the values of virtually all the elite statesmen who take international decisions.[3] On the other hand, many believe that non-western values and standards, often in hybrid forms, are reasserting themselves regionally, and that the worldwide society established by the Europeans, which separated politically into some 180 nominal sovereignties, may perhaps reintegrate into a number of distinct *grandes républiques*. The regional societies would still be bound to each other by the interests and pressures of a global system, which they would manage by means of a developed version of the arrangements between Europe and the Ottomans: that is, with regulatory rules and operational practices, including legitimacies, but with few or no common values or codes of conduct.[4]

The most impressive evidence of the trend towards regional associations based on a common culture and traditions is the gradual tightening and geographical enlargement of the European Community. The European states, previously so determined to assert their anti-hegemonial independence, are moving towards a confederation which will cover most of what was Christendom (but not, for instance, the oil-rich Arab states of north Africa across the Mediterranean). Voltaire's *grande république* will remain divided into a number of states, which will retain their identity though they may give up their external and much of their domestic autonomy, as they would have if Louis XIV had succeeded. This voluntary pooling of sovereignty in a European confederacy is acceptable because it brings economic and other advantages, and because the area is now only a part of a much wider system. Many republics of the former Soviet empire may establish a similar confederation of nominally independent states. The cultures of the non-European world, now blended with European ones, may be on the same tack. Associations of states with geographic and cultural ties are beginning to take shape in Latin America, tropical Africa, south-east Asia and, cutting across others, the Islamic world from Morocco to Malaysia.

A world organized on those lines would gain significance from the fact that it would resemble what might have developed if the European expansion of the nineteenth century had not taken an imperial form. It could clearly function tolerably well. It would not exclude a great and growing volume of economic and other intercourse between the regional groupings. Indeed, the European capitulations with the Ottomans and other states were expressly designed to facilitate trade. Both economic integration and regional groupings would move the system away from multiple independences.

But it may be that **something new** is taking place, comparable to the innovations that we saw at the Westphalian settlement and after the death of Alexander. Almost all the members of our worldwide international society now insist or at least accept that, like its predecessor which was imposed by the Europeans, our society too should take account of principles as well as interests, and have some common values as well as regulatory rules. The states of the world, forced into unprecedentedly close interdependence and unwilling simply to accept 'western values', may be working out, as the Hellenistic civilization did, ethical standards and codes of conduct which span more than one cultural frame. Significantly the United States, now the only effective superpower, is multiethnic and gradually becoming more multicultural. But it is far from clear what such system-wide values and standards, if they did evolve, would be; alongside the western tradition, an especially significant contribution would be likely to come from the high civilizations of Asia.

When we compare the present international pattern with others discussed in this book, our society appears to be nominally fragmented into multiple independences, with a number of real but not wholly legitimate sources of hegemonial authority trying to manage a system closely integrated by technological and other pressures. Our society's formal institutions and legitimacy, inherited selectively from Europe and reinforced by the demands of the newly independent majority of member states and the anti-imperial spirit of the age, place it exceptionally far towards the independence end of the spectrum. But the strategic, economic and other operational practices of the society are significantly more adapted to realities, and therefore more integrated, than the legitimacy; and the society is drawn by the gravitational pull of the pendulum towards more hegemonial and more workable arrangements, which are tacitly accepted by the majority. As a result, the gap between the practice and the theory is unusually wide. A global multicultural society is still something new and still experimental, which has not yet found a form that adequately fits the realities of the system.

NOTES

1 See Chapter 5, p. 59.
2 See A. Watson, *Diplomacy: The Dialogue between States*, London, Methuen, 1983, pp. 53–4.
3 See H. Bull and A. Watson (eds), *The Expansion of International Society*, Oxford, Oxford University Press, 1984, chapters 26 and 27, and conclusion.
4 The honouring of contracts and the immunity of envoys are not common values in this sense, but matters of expediency, like saying that honesty is the best policy. Such rules are recognized between communities that maintain only sporadic contacts.

CONCLUSION

We have now looked at a number of cases where communities are sufficiently involved with one another to form what we have called a system. We can draw some conclusions from the evidence that takes us beyond the familiar platitudes and controversial claims.

SYSTEMS AND SOCIETIES

Our examination shows that the network of economic and strategic pressures that holds a system together constrains its members to act and to refrain from acting in certain ways. These pressures act mechanically, in the sense that they operate outside the will of the community concerned. Except in the most directly administered empires, the mechanical pressures leave a large area which governments and spokesmen for communities can influence by conscious choice. Communities can to some extent organize their system, making it into what we have called an international society.

A set of rules and institutions devised by statesmen for an international society is a superstructure, consciously put in place to modify the mechanical workings of the system. The rules are likely to be largely a codification or 'capitulation' of the practices which the rulers and statesmen have developed in response to the pressures of the system. Codification is a conscious act, and the operation of a code of rules involves the assent of a number of adherents. Institutions require a more specific commitment and participation. The rules and institutions of an imperial society are brought into force, as the significant phrase goes, by a single dominant power, such as the empires of the ancient world or Napoleon, and subsequently modified in the same way. Near the middle of the spectrum a hegemonial power, such as the Athenians in their heyday or the Habsburgs and Louis XIV, is able to 'lay down the law' governing relations between the members of a system of more independent states. As we move closer to multiple independences we find more diffused and uncertain forms of joint hegemony by a group of major powers, such as the 'king's peace' and the Concert of Europe after the Vienna settlement. Finally but rarely, a set of anti-hegemonial rules may be devised for a society consisting of independent and effectively equal communities. Even where states locked into international systems do not constitute what we have called a society, they evolve regulatory rules and institutions and formulate them in capitulatory agreements because they cannot manage without. No system has existed without rules and conventions of some kind, and it is hard to see how one could.

The lawless 'state of nature' postulated by Hobbes and others is an allegory. Nobody regards Rousseau's statement that man was born free but is now in irons[1] as an anthropological observation about solitary hominids coming together in a clearing, as Jouvenel mockingly says, in order to bind themselves and their descendants in a social contract.[2] But the relations between geographically separate communities are much looser and more voluntary. Communities have existed within sporadic striking distance of each other and without any jointly accepted rules to regulate their conduct, in what some Europeans called a state of nature. We may therefore more reasonably describe the conscious establishment and subsequent modifications of a society of communities, and also more limited regulatory machinery such as operated between the European *grande république* and the Ottoman Empire, as deliberate social contracts. Such contracts are binding not from generation to generation, but for so long as the members, or those able to lay down the law, find the rules and institutions advantageous. They have been and will be constantly revised.

In addition to a contractual area of explicit rules and institutions, the members of past international societies also observed certain unwritten codes of conduct, values and non-contractual assumptions. They derived these from a common civilization which was dominant in the society, and which communities belonging to other civilizations could not be expected to understand or practice. Such non-contractual links were taken for granted in eighteenth-century Europe (Chapter 18). The distinguishing characteristics of a consciously ordered society of states can be seen most clearly in the areas of non-contractual practice, and it is in these areas that an international society develops its individual style. They raise pertinent questions for the worldwide and multicultural society which we are trying to shape at the present time.

CHARACTERISTICS OF SOCIETIES

Our examination has thrown into relief a number of intertwined characteristics that play important parts in the ordering of societies made up of many communities. We can look at some conclusions about them conveniently under the separate headings of hegemony, legitimacy, sovereignty, culture and inheritance.

Hegemony

The most striking feature of ancient systems in the independences half of our spectrum is the **propensity to hegemony**. There the gravitational pull towards a more integrated pattern sometimes manifested itself as a movement towards hegemonial or imperial authority over the whole system, and at other times as two centres of bipolar hegemony. In the European society also hegemonial tendencies were always present. A degree of hegemony was an **integral feature of the practice** of that society. The issue was the extent of hegemonial authority over the *grande république*, not over the whole system, and the Ottoman Empire operated outside the society as an anti-hegemonial makeweight. In our still somewhat inchoate global system two centres of hegemonial authority, the United States and the Soviet Union, polarized the system for forty years after the Second World War; but the Russian pole is temporarily in abeyance.

The European experience emphasizes what is already clear from our examination of ancient systems, that the propensity to hegemony in a system of multiple independences cannot simply be equated with the urge to conquer and dominate. Certainly a state whose relative strength in the system has increased may want to assert its power and even to expand its territorial boundaries. This ambition can sometimes push the whole system along our spectrum: but not always, and not often to a determining extent. Defensive as well as offensive reasons may impel a single power (in the European society the Habsburgs, for instance) or the great powers in a society collectively (the Concert of Europe) to institute a hegemony – that is, to introduce a greater degree of order into the system, to lay down the law on the relations between the component states and even to intervene in the domestic government of some of them.

A commitment to an anti-hegemonial principle, the insistence that independent states must in the last resort be free to act as they see fit, acknowledges that hegemony may be legitimately resisted by force, and therefore accepts the risk of war. Even in today's international society, where war is formally condemned, the resort to force is not really illegitimate, and there are elaborate rules of war. The inability to avoid major wars was one of the destructive liabilities of the European system, as it was of other systems inclined to multiple independences such as the classical and Macedonian Greek systems or the Chinese period of the warring states. We need to ask ourselves how far their failure to avoid catastrophic war was due to their underlying

313

anti-hegemonial assumption. In particular, was the European society anchored too far to one end of the spectrum to adapt itself successfully to the pressures that developed in the system in our century? Might a society more tolerant of hegemony, nearer the middle of the spectrum, have shown itself more elastic?

The Sumerian society of city states was too different from the Europe of a century ago for detailed comparison. But the general idea, that an overarching authority ought to reside somewhere and that the advantages of a degree of hegemony outweigh the loss of freedom of action of princes and states, was present in the European society, though it did not become generally accepted as legitimate. The Habsburg bid for hegemony in its Spanish–Austrian form was perhaps too rigid, too unable to incorporate and harness the new forces that were transforming Europe; but its French version under Louis XIV showed a more Persian mildness and adaptability. Napoleon's imperial system seemed ephemeral and artificial at the time, and more so in retrospect; but had it settled down it might have provided a framework, and more important a habit of thinking about the relations between European communities, that would more easily have accommodated the explosive growth of wealth and power in central Europe. The diffused hegemony of the Concert of Europe after Vienna did not prevent resorts to war; but it kept the practice of the society a long way from the mere clash of multiple independences, and restrained the use of force to acceptable levels and limited objectives, so long as it remained flexible. The ossification of alliances after 1900 made a concerted harmony impossible.

The gravitational pull towards hegemony, and the ubiquity of some hegemonial authority in societies of independent or quasi-independent states, stands out so clearly from the evidence that the question arises why studies of states systems and political theory underestimate or even ignore it. One main reason, I think, is that we are not used to thinking of systems of communities as ranging from independences to empires. Our vision is constricted by the assumption that the independent sovereign state is the basic or even the sole unit of a states system. Any attempt by a state to exercise hegemonial control over the society, let alone the degree of dominion exercised by Napoleon, is regarded as a misuse of power and as a throwback to a less law-abiding past. This is especially true of American and British writings on the subject, many of which lose interest in a system at the point where its active members are not independent. French historiography has had a wider horizon, partly because of the hegemonial position of France in most of the European story. This disapproval of hegemony makes it difficult to understand the relation of multiple independences to other ways of managing a system of communities.

Legitimacy

In Chapter 12 we identified **legitimacy**, and in particular the degree of independence and imperial authority which the communities involved thought right – the position along the spectrum – as one of the factors determining the stability of a system at a given time. The mythology of Chinese history helped to pull the Chinese system away from the independences half of the spectrum towards the imperial. But the opposite was true of classical city-state Greece, where the mythology of the independent polis as the natural way to organize a community helped to hold the system close to the independences end of the spectrum. The Hellenic assumption was revived in the Italian Renaissance. The seminal Westphalian settlement established a definitive anti-hegemonial legitimacy for the European society of states. Reinforced by practice, by the interests of princes and by some of the most effective political theory ever written, the classical Greek legitimacy of independence has continued to exercise a powerful effect on the European system and on the contemporary world, little though a modern 'nation state' is like a Greek polis, and though in fact the nominal multiple independence of the Greek cities was tempered in practice by leagues, hegemonial alliances and a succession of hegemonies and bids for domination of the whole society (Chapter 5). The same was true of the European *grande république*. In such cases the practice is more hegemonial than the legitimacy.

Legitimacy in the ancient world was the oil that lubricated the operative machinery of a society. The more its rules and institutions were considered legitimate, the more easily it could change its practices. The experience of the European society confirmed the lubricating role of legitimacy; but it also showed how the anti-hegemonial legitimacy established by the Westphalian settlement and explicitly confirmed by Utrecht could operate as a check on the swing of the pendulum, as it was designed to do. Even so, where the pressures for change were great, practice disregarded legitimacy, or found a way round it; and over a period the legitimacy adjusted to take account of the practice. In the contemporary world the rules and institutions (notably the United Nations) and the nominal values of our international society give a stamp of legitimacy to a very high degree of multiple independence. Even the strongest powers profess to respect the independence of all members; and this reassurance makes the hegemonial reality more acceptable.

Sovereignty

Legitimacy leads on to the European concept of sovereignty. Many statesmen and scholars have held that the most distinctive feature of the European system, and of our own, is the **sovereign state**. It has been portrayed as the essential characteristic that sets the ancient Greek and European civilizations apart from the suzerain systems that have prevailed elsewhere. It is constantly hailed as the goal to which dependent and colonized communities should and do aspire, and equated with liberty itself. It has also been condemned as the root cause of international anarchy and of war, the evil idol which must be overturned if mankind is to achieve a more civilized future. Others claim that it is now disintegrating.

The European concept of sovereignty had its roots in the practices of the Renaissance *stato*, and in the influence of Hellenic and Hebrew traditions. As its name implies, it was an aim of rulers and princes, who wanted to be masters over all their subjects but to acknowledge no master over themselves. The concept of sovereignty protects the weak prince against the strong. The sovereignty to which Westphalia committed the European society of states was essentially domestic. What a sovereign did in the territories recognized as legitimately under its government was not the business of other sovereigns. In principle sovereign princes and states were also free to act as they saw fit in their external relations. Indeed, the ability to conduct an independent foreign policy was widely regarded as the test of genuine sovereignty. But the relations of a sovereign state with the other members of the sovereigns' club were constrained by the pressures of the system and by the rules of the club, and also most of the time by a degree of hegemonial control.

The distinction between hegemony over the functioning of an international society and interference in the internal affairs of its members was and is clearer in theory than in practice. Stasis, the attempt to overthrow an established government by force, was a common phenomenon in the European system, as in ancient times and since. The intervention of other governments, which as Thucydides said brought calamity, was not mere wilfulness or ideological emotion. Strategic and other compulsions often made it dangerous or impossible for other states to avoid involvement – particularly in periods of war.

The ban on intervention imposed by the European sovereigns' club worked well enough in Europe from Westphalia to the French Revolution. It collapsed in face of the commitment of the revolutionaries to the export of revolutionary ideas and that of other sovereigns to restore their French colleague. Napoleon systematically reshaped the domestic policies of the states under his dominion. The nineteenth-century concert accepted the practice of hegemonial intervention. In the twentieth century interference again became as widespread and as passionate as in the wars of religion. After the First World War a wave of ideological stasis spread through Europe. Communist and fascist parties received open support from other governments. Elsewhere decolonizing revolts led other states and non-governmental organizations to arm and encourage liberation movements. The United Nations intervened collectively in the chaos of the Belgian Congo, an action similar to the collective intervention in China half a century before. Intervention today takes other forms, often connected with human rights. In addition, great powers like the United States and France maintain an old-fashioned periphery or backyard of dominion where they determine, to a greater or lesser extent, the domestic policies of client governments. The effective European ban on intervention was exceptional and short lived.

Even so, the concept that intervention in the domestic affairs of sovereign states is illegitimate is one of the important legacies of the European system to our own. Decolonization is the achievement of sovereignty by dependent states. What Westphalia legitimized for the princes and cities of the Holy Roman Empire, admission to the United Nations legitimizes today for newly independent states, many of them tiny, and their rulers, many of them tyrannical. The theoretical legitimacy of our present global society expressly forbids intervention in the internal affairs of a member state, by another member or by the collective institution of the United Nations. But in practice the distinction is as smudged as it ever was.

Culture

The assumptions and operational practices of Europe also illustrate the **cultural limitations** of a society of states. One of the most striking features of the European system was that, in spite of the major role played by the Ottoman Empire in that system's strategic and economic network of forces, the society of European states, the *grande république*, did not cover the whole system but developed only within the matrix of Latin Christendom; and that a separate set of capitulatory rules and institutions was evolved for managing the relations between the Europeans and the Ottomans. In the nineteenth century the cultural criterion included the settler states of the Americas and Australasia in the European society of states, while excluding in practice non-European states ranging from the ancient highly developed civilizations of Asia to primitive communities. Similarly the ancient Greek cultural distinction between Hellas and the diverse outside world excluded the Persian Empire from the Greek society of city states in spite of its major role in the system.

317

We may conclude that regulatory arrangements always come into being between civilized polities when the volume of contacts becomes worth regulating. Anything more intimate, a society that goes beyond rules and institutions to shared values and assumptions, has hitherto always developed within a cultural framework, even if some of the values and assumptions are later adopted by communities outside the culture. The pertinent and unresolved question for our multicultural society is: to what extent must an effective international society develop its codes of conduct, its values and its non-contractual assumptions within a common dominant culture?

Legacy of the past

The evidence of past systems also makes it clear that the pattern of an international society, its social contract so to speak, is not drawn up afresh for each society. It is to a large extent **inherited** from previous societies; though its practices, and thus with a certain delay its legitimacies, continually alter. The Persian Empire inherited much from Assyrian and Babylonian systems. The Macedonian kingdoms and to a lesser extent the Mauryas were successors of the Persians. The Romans, whose empire after Augustus became increasingly Hellenistic, were the heirs of the Macedonians. The Byzantine *oikoumene* and the Arab caliphate were the heirs of the Romans. The European society, which began with the spread of the ideas of the Italian Renaissance over Latin Christendom, was in many ways a continuation of the Middle Ages, and also looked consciously back to the classical models of Rome and Greece. The pressures and interests of our heterogeneous contemporary global society are very different from those of its European predecessor, but our society too carries a large and prominent hereditary element, which current practice is gradually adapting to new pressures and problems. Whether we regard this element of continuity as a transcultural legacy, or regard cultures and civilizations themselves as descended so to speak from previous ones, whether we want to understand our present international society or to change it, we need to recognize how much both the conscious rules and institutions, and also the practices and assumptions, which any international society adopts are inherited from the past.

NOTES

1 J. J. Rousseau, *The Social Contract*, opening sentence. 'Man is born free' is a mistranslation.
2 B. de Jouvenel, *De la Souveraineté*, Paris, Médicis, 1945, p. 42.

EPILOGUE
Some indications for the future

WHAT CHOICES ARE AVAILABLE?

We can decide which advantages we wish our present worldwide society to ensure and which ends we wish it to promote. An understanding of the workings of international societies in the past helps us to translate our wishes realistically into practice, by showing us what modifications of our present international society are practicable, what advantages they might bring and at what price. A realistic understanding is very difficult to obtain if we remain imprisoned in the conventional legitimacies and half-conscious assumptions of our own time. We need a broader base of comparison. As the natural sciences and medicine look for many examples of a phenomenon in order to understand it well enough to modify it, so history can enable us to distinguish the area of necessity from the area of choice.

Let us start with the recognition that some systems of communities are more imperially organized than others, and that different positions along the spectrum have corresponding advantages and disadvantages. Then in order to see what our options are, the first question we should ask ourselves is: how far along the spectrum from the theoretical absolute of anarchic independences must a society of states be, how much does the freedom of action of its member states have to be controlled, in order to establish some authority that can enforce the rules? The authority may be a single power, e.g. the United States; or a group of great powers, e.g. the five permanent members of the Security Council or the Group of Seven; or it may be a collective authority somehow representing the majority of communities involved.

Many people may not want to go very far towards establishing such an authority: the legitimacies and to a large extent the preferences of our present society of states are well towards the independences end of the spectrum. Those imperial systems we have examined were established by force of conquest; and though some of them soon

319

became bland enough to win acquiescence and the active approval of certain communities and classes, and an imperial system does not necessarily imply less liberty for the **individual** than a system of more independent communities (rulers can tyrannize their subjects as much in small communities as large ones), yet an imperial system does by definition involve less freedom of action for the **communities** involved in it, and especially for their rulers and leaders. It has long been recognized that effective power in a society of states must be able to override the freedom of the member communities, what the Europeans called the sovereignty of princes. This is not the only disadvantage. The outstandingly creative periods in other civilizations were usually those, like city-state Hellas and the warring states of China and the European *grande république*, which were far towards the multiple independences end of the scale. The price at which the peace and order of an imperial system have to be bought is high.

Nevertheless peace and order are great boons; and in times of anarchy men become especially anxious to find means of ensuring them. How can this be done? In our century the ideal of **world government** for 'spaceship Earth' is widespread. When it is not a utopian yearning for the calm of paradise where the lion lies down with the lamb, the ideal boils down to tightening and ordering a too anarchic international society by a global quasi-legislative authority which reflects in some way the diverse opinions of mankind, and whose decisions are enforced by an executive capable of doing the job. Advocates of world government in western democracies postulate that the means of enforcement would be, not a hegemonial state or concert, but 'peace-keeping forces' so powerful that no state or coalition could breach the peace. Otherwise warfare would remain a possibility. Such concepts of world government are a semi-instinctive hankering for the advantages of order, security and peace that the imperial half of the spectrum can provide, without paying the price. More recently human rights, egalitarian economic justice and protection of the environment have been added to peace and strategic security. A world government would have a considerable agenda, and would need to deploy considerable force. World government is not a likely option in the medium term.

Fortunately for practical statesmen, and for the prospects of all of us, the evidence of other systems is that most of the benefits of the imperial half of the scale can be obtained, not absolutely but to a considerable extent, with less integration than a single system-wide government. The Sumerian kingship, with which our analysis began, addressed itself to the problem, and evolved a solution that was no more than halfway along the spectrum. 'The kingship must reside somewhere' can be rephrased as 'someone must maintain a degree of order'. The European concert after Vienna was a loose collective hegemony which laid down the law for the society of states, while leaving the great powers independent of each other and smaller states a large degree of independence also.

Like order, independence has a high price. Classical Hellas, the warring states of China, Renaissance Italy, for all their other glories, were periods of danger, disorder and war. All but the largest powers found client membership of a hegemonial alliance preferable to lonely independence in the maelstrom. But even so, most of us do not want to move further from multiple independences than is necessary to achieve our other objectives. Thus we should also ask ourselves a second and opposite question. How far from the multiple independences end of the spectrum can a society move in its quest for peace and order, and yet ensure that its member communities continue to enjoy the advantages of independence, meaning substantial freedom of action in their domestic affairs and in their relations with other communities or states?

TOWARDS A HEGEMONIAL CONCERT?

Our system is becoming more integrated, strategically and economically, and its member states more functionally interdependent. As the impersonal pressures increase, so does the need for conscious regulation. Hobbes stated, and few have argued to the contrary, that what makes men give up their independence of action is not reason but fear. The city corporations of classical Hellas did not look on armed conflict with horror; but as technology becomes more dangerous and the damage done by major warfare more irreparable, the fear of war makes us more willing to sacrifice a degree of independence in order to place effective limitations (but not a total ban) on a resort to force. The fear is justified. Though the most developed nuclear powers are aware that they are capable of mutual and assured destruction, and so cannot go to war with each other, below the nuclear level the use of force continues to be the ultimate argument of several states, large and small (not to mention civil wars within states). In addition, most of the less developed majority of states fear economic insecurity more than invasion, and are reluctantly prepared to sacrifice a degree of internal independence to obtain the help of economically stronger powers.

To think that we can achieve a more peaceful, orderly and prosperous society without any sacrifice of independence is to ignore what Clio might call the great lesson of international history. If we are willing to pay some price, what arrangements are we likely to get?

Until the mid-1980s the most likely move towards an effective strategic authority seemed to be for the two superpowers to assume more consciously the role of 'book-ends' which Russia and Britain played in Europe in the nineteenth century. But detailed prediction of the course of international events is dangerous. As a result of the dramatic changes described in Chapter 25, the exercise of joint responsibility by the major states of our society now seems to be developing under American leadership into something like a concert, a diffused hegemony. A concert of this kind could go some way towards imposing peace and order without seriously limiting the freedom of action of other states in fields other than a resort to force. But in practice it is unlikely to restrict itself to that one issue.

The evidence indicates that to function successfully a concert of great powers needs a number of conditions. First, none of the states that operate the concert can be stronger than the others combined. However, they need not be equal in strength; nor need all, or indeed any, be 'satisfied' powers, committed to the status quo, as is sometimes argued, though in practice one or more of them usually will be. Second, the concerting powers need not agree all the time; but they must all recognize the advantage of managing the pressures of the system and making the society work: they must have a sense of *raison de système*. They must be willing to implement 'the principles of prudence and moral obligation that have held together the society of states'.[1] Third, the tension and watchfulness between them must be combined with a degree of mobility in their relations, so that if one of them seeks an undue advantage, the others are prepared to collaborate on that issue to preserve the balance. It is possible, but not certain, that present international practice can evolve to meet these conditions.

JOINT HEGEMONY AND LEGITIMACY

A hegemonial concert would be resented by many other states. This raises the question of its **legitimacy**. Some people argue that a naked joint hegemony would in fact destabilize world order; but that the great powers are not 'acting hegemonially' when they exercise the weight of their power and authority through a reactivated Security Council of the United Nations (as has happened in the Kuwait crisis), because that involves them in consultation with other states and respect for the rules of the global society. Some go further, and want the more powerful states to take action to promote peace and order only when they can obtain a consensus in favour of such action by all or at least a majority of the member states of the UN. These arguments are partly based on using the word 'hegemony' in a pejorative sense (which we have not), implying that it is arbitrary and excludes consultation with other states and respect for the rules. This as we have seen is not how hegemonies actually operate. Louis XIV, for instance, was in more continuous and detailed consultation with other states than any other member of the *grande république*, and was at pains to operate his hegemony through the Westphalian rules which his government had played a major role in formulating. A concert of great powers that acts with the endorsement or acquiescence of the Security Council may be acting 'legally'; but it is still a hegemonial concert, and the procedures of the council were devised by the three greatest powers of that time in order to make such a hegemony legitimate. The consensus of all the members of the United Nations, or even a majority, would be another matter, and beyond the bounds of practicability.

A tighter political, strategic and economic order will have to cover the whole world. It may not develop into a single international society, for the reasons given in the last chapter. But if it does, it will doubtless be based on a good deal of bargaining between the great powers, resulting in partnership in some fields and acquiescence in others, as the European concert was. A tighter **strategic** order seems likely to accept American leadership or tacit hegemony for a while;[2] to achieve its results by intense diplomatic dialogue; and to express itself through the agreement or acquiescence of the five permanent members of the Security Council.[3] The **economic** hegemony of the Group of Seven, which fortunately includes Japan and Germany, may well become more tripartite in practice (North America, Europe and east Asia) for a time before associating Russia. It is able to legitimate its insistence on certain codes of conduct by operating through established collective machinery like the World Bank and the International Monetary Fund, and through client associations like the Lomé conventions which provide a degree of collective economic security. In general a concert of the major powers will operate more effectively to the extent that its members conduct an active diplomatic dialogue with other states and respond to their needs; and to the extent that they cloak hegemonial decisions in the legitimist rhetoric of independence for every member of the international society. For legitimacy is the lubricating oil of international societies, and especially of arrangements for international order.

It may thus be possible to strengthen international order, and to move the evolving practice of our society quite a distance along the spectrum towards hegemony, while leaving the legitimacies in place. Legitimacy usually lags behind practice. But a conspicuous and growing gap between legitimacy and practice causes tension and the impression of disorder. For this reason a number of statesmen and jurists are asking themselves two complementary questions. First, how far should expedient practice be limited to conform with cherished though perhaps outdated legitimacies? Second, how far should the legitimacies themselves be recodified, as they have been in the past, to legitimize expedient practices? In the sensitive field of domestic sovereignty, for instance, almost nobody still maintains that, however repugnant or dangerous to others the domestic behaviour of a member state may be, there should never be either individual or collective intervention from outside.

Fortunately legitimacy, like all the schemes of mice and men, is subject to change with the passage of time. According to Professor Rosalyn Higgins:

> the task of the international lawyer over the next few years is surely not to go on repeating the rhetoric of dead events which no longer accord with reality, but to try to assist the political leaders to identify what is the new consensus about acceptable and unacceptable levels of intrusion.[4]

It is also possible to recast the legitimacies of our society in less absolute form. The concept of *dike*, as practised by the Greek cities and Persia, is relevant today (see Chapter 5). Less rigid than international law and the concept of blind justice, it also took account of the situation on the ground and relied on the good offices of third parties. But *dike* was more than mere expediency: its resolutions of international issues might not be permanent in a world of change, but they had to seem right and reasonable to the principal contenders at the time.

We concluded in Chapter 12 that the optimum mix of three factors largely determines the most stable and generally acceptable point along the spectrum for a system at a given time. The three factors are: the balance of material advantage, for both the rulers and the ruled; the point of greatest legitimacy; and the gravitational pull of the pendulum away from empire and anarchical independences towards the middle of the spectrum. That optimum mix was approached in the European system, so far as such theoretical concepts can be realized in practice, by the concert system of the century following the Vienna settlement. We cannot see ourselves as others will see us. The experience of the past can nevertheless help us to make a guess as to what is today, what may be tomorrow, the optimum mix for us.

The weight of events themselves is helping to pull the present system towards a stronger authority. A concert or multiple hegemony of the strongest powers, operating to their own advantage but also with an adequate balance of advantage for other states, would soon find itself near the mid-point of the spectrum: able to control the external relations between states, and also to intervene to a limited degree in their internal affairs. The significant question is not whether there will continue to be some degree of hegemonial direction in the management of the global international society (there will certainly be some), but how much hegemony there will be in practice.

In this Epilogue we have been trying to set the parameters of the probable. Where along the spectrum we would personally like to see the rules of our society established and its practices operate is a question that each of us must determine for ourselves. Some of us are inclined towards multiple independences, in which communities can work out their diverse destinies and achievements with greater immunity from outside interference and a greater risk of armed conflict, while others may prefer the more mundane blessings of peace and prosperity at the expense of independence. The experience of the past is only one guide to the options for the future, but I believe it is an indispensable one. Whatever arrangements our system of communities may develop, it will remain substantially the heir of its own past.

NOTES

1 H. Butterfield and M. Wight (eds), *Diplomatic Investigations*, London: Allen & Unwin, 1966, p. 13.
2 But see the final chapter of P. Kennedy, *The Rise and Fall of the Great Powers*, New York, Random House, 1987.
3 The composition of the Security Council is anachronistic. There is pressure to increase the number of permanent members, perhaps without veto rights. Any additional vetoes will make the use of UN machinery more difficult.
4 Rosalyn Higgins, *Intervention in World Politics*, Oxford, Oxford University Press, 1984, p. 42.

BIBLIOGRAPHY

This Bibliography lists books which I have found especially useful and relevant for the study of states systems. I have omitted familiar standard texts such as the Bible, Thucydides, Voltaire, Gibbon and Kant. The list does not pretend to be exhaustive; many of the books in it contain a fuller bibliography of their subject. I have added some comments which may help the reader to make his or her own choice.

THE ANCIENT STATES SYSTEMS

Arnold, Sir T. (1965) *The Caliphate*, London, Routledge. A standard text on the organization of the Islamic system in theory and practice.

Badian, E. (1968) *Roman Imperialism*, Oxford, Blackwell.

Boardman, J. (1980) *The Greeks Overseas*, London, Thames & Hudson. Useful on the expansion of the classical Hellenic system.

Burn, R. (1972) *Persia and the Greeks*, London, Arnold.

Cahen, C. (1970) *L'Islam des Origines au Début de l'Empire Ottoman*, Paris, Borden.

The Cambridge Encyclopedia of Archaeology (1980), Cambridge, Cambridge University Press.

Cambridge History of Islam (1970), P. M. Holt and A. K. S. Lambton (eds), 2 vols, Cambridge, Cambridge University Press.

Cook, J. M. (1983) *The Persian Empire*, London, Dent. Informative, but anti-imperial and somewhat hostile to the Persians.

Diehl, C. (1943) *Les Grands Problèmes de l'Histoire Byzantine*, Paris, Colin. The chapter on exterior policy gives a useful survey of the range of the Byzantine system.

Doyle, Michael (1986) *Empires*, Ithaca, Cornell University Press. Useful theoretical discussion of the nature of empires, and a good account of the differences between Athenian empire and Spartan hegemony. See my Introduction.

The Encyclopedia of Islam (1971), Lewis *et al.* (eds), Leiden.

Franke, O. (1967) *Geschichte des Chinesischen Reiches*. See Vol. I on the period discussed in Chapter 8 of this book.

Garnsey, P. D. O. and Whittaker, C. R. (eds) (1976) *Imperialism in the Ancient World*, Cambridge, Cambridge University Press.

Hirth, F. (1923) *The Ancient History of China*, New York, Columbia University Press.

Kangle, R. P. (trans.) (1960–5) *The Kautilya Arthashastra*, 3 vols.

Karlovsky, Sabloff and Lemberg (eds) (1976) *Ancient Civilization and Trade*, University of New Mexico Press.

Kramer, S. N. (1959) *History Begins at Sumer*, New York, Doubleday. Useful texts and inscriptions on the working of the Sumerian system.

Larsen, M. T. (ed.) (1979) *Power and Propagada: A Symposium on Ancient Empires*, Copenhagen, Copenhagen University Press. Several valuable essays, especially by the editor. See my Introduction.

Luttwak, E. N. (1976) *The Grand Strategy of the Roman Empire*, Baltimore, Johns Hopkins University Press. Useful on the external and defensive aspects of the Roman imperial system.

Mahdi, M. (1957) *Ibn Khaldun's Philosophy of History*, London.

Mann, Michael (1986) *The Sources of Social Power*, Cambridge, Cambridge University Press. An exceptionally thoughtful sociological study of the ancient systems. See my Introduction. The section on Europe is less relevant.

Meiggs, R. (1972) *The Athenian Empire*, Oxford, Oxford University Press. A valuable account.

Millar, Fergus (1977) *The Emperor in the Roman World*, London, Duckworth. Among the most valuable books on the Roman imperial system.

Nozick, R. (1974) *Anarchy, State and Utopia*, New York, Basic Books. The first two sections describe a state of nature with protective associations (alliances) and domination.

Obolensky, Dimitri (1971) *The Byzantine Commonwealth*, New York, Praeger. The most useful work for our purposes.

Oppenheim, A. L. (1977) *Ancient Mesopotamia*, Chicago, University of Chicago Press.

Ostrogorsky, G. (1969) *History of the Byzantine State* (trans. of *Geschichte des byzantinischen Staates*), Princeton, Princeton University Press. A substantial standard text.

Rubin, V. A. (1976) *Individual and State in Ancient China*, New York, Columbia University Press. A translation of a valuable work by a Soviet scholar on Chinese political theories in the period of the warring states.

Schmandt, Besserat (ed.) (1976) *The Legacy of Sumer*, Malibu.

Schmidt, Nathaniel (1930) *Ibn Khaldun: Historian, Sociologist and Philosopher*, New York, Columbia University Press. Still the best introduction to ibn Khaldun.

Thapar, Romila (1966) *The Penguin History of India*, Vol. 1, Harmondsworth, Penguin. A recognized authority, Ms Thapar emphasizes the Indian cultural roots of the Maurya Empire.

Urbanski, A. B. (1968) *Byzantium and the Danube Frontier*, New York.

Watson, A. (1964) *The War of the Goldsmith's Daughter*, London, Chatto & Windus. A study of the states system and Islamic–Hindu relations in medieval southern India.

Weber, Max (1968) *Economy and Society* (trans. of *Wirtschaft und Gesellschaft*), Berkeley, University of California Press is a standard text on authority and legitimacy.

Wessen, R. G. (1967) *The Imperial Order*, Berkeley, University of California Press.

THE EUROPEAN INTERNATIONAL SOCIETY

Historical works

Albrecht-Carrié, R. (1968) *The Concert of Europe*, New York, Walker. Contains most of the relevant documents up to 1914.

Braudel, F. (1972) *The Mediterranean and the Mediterranean World in the Time of Philip II* (English trans.), London, Collins. A detailed sociological survey which gives the background of the Habsburg hegemony in the European society of states and the involvement with the different Ottoman system.

Butterfield, H. (1956) *Napoleon*, New York, Macmillan. This and H. A. L. Fisher's book remain the two best short books on the significance of Napoleon.

The Cambridge Medieval History (1911), H. M. G. Watkin and J. P. Whitney (eds), 9 vols, Cambridge, Cambridge University Press. Perhaps the most useful standard reference work.

Cipolla, C. (1965) *Guns and Sails*, London, Collins. For the vital role of technical progress in the expansion of Europe.

Clark, I. (1989) *The Hierarchy of States. Reform and Resistance in the International Order*, Cambridge, Cambridge University Press.

Connelly, O. (1965) *Napoleon's Satellite Kingdoms*, New York, Macmillan. The most useful account of the areas of Napoleonic dominion, beyond the French empire proper.

Dehio, Ludwig (1965) *The Precarious Balance: Four Centuries* (trans. of *Gleichgewicht oder Hegemonie*), New York, Vintage. A useful analysis of the interplay between hegemony and multiple independences in the European society of states.

The Encyclopedia of Islam (1971), Leiden. For aspects of Ottoman policy, especially Vol. 3, *Imtiyazat* (= 'Capitulations'), the best summary I have found.

Gulick, E. (19) *Europe's Classical Balance of Power*, Ithaca, Cornell University Press.

Howard, M. (1976) *War in European History*, Oxford, Oxford University Press. A short readable work of remarkable clarity.

Kissinger, H. (1964) *A World Restored*, New York, Universal Library. Outstanding, with many perceptive insights, some inevitably controversial. My Chapter 21 is indebted to this work.

Koenigsberger, H. G. (1971) *The Habsburgs and Europe*, Ithaca, Cornell University Press (first two chapters reprinted from *The New Cambridge Modern History*).

Leathes, S. (ed.) (1902) *The Cambridge Modern History*, Cambridge, Cambridge University Press. The original edition of 1902 has been superseded for many purposes by the *New CMH*, but the original often provides more detailed evidence of the relations between the European states.

McNeill, W. H. (1982) *The Pursuit of Power*, Oxford, Blackwell.

Meinecke, F. (1957) *Machiavellism* (trans. of *Die Idee der Staatsraeson*), New Haven, Yale University Press. A classic study of *raison d'état* which deserves its considerable influence (the English title is misleading).

Mowat, R. B. (1930) *The Concert of Europe*, London, Macmillan. A standard and still relevant work.

Rosecrance *et al.* (1971) *Power, the Balance of Power and Status in Nineteenth Century International Relations*, California, Sage.

Schenk, H. (1967) *The Aftermath of the Napoleonic Wars*, New York, Fertig. A useful analysis: but regards the concert as ending in 1825.

Sieburg, F. (1979) *Napoleon und Europa*.

Tilly, C. (ed.) (1975) *Formation of National States in Western Europe*, Princeton, Princeton University Press.

Tulard, J. (1982) *Le Grand Empire*, Paris, Michel. Examines in detail the relevance to France of the empire and its satellites.

Theoretical studies

Work arising out of the British Committee on the Theory of International Politics

Papers written for the British Committee (1959–), unpublished, available in the library of the Royal Institute for International Affairs, London. These papers form the basis, or at least the point of departure, for many ideas in this book. Some have been reproduced in the following six publications. Of the unpublished ones, I am especially indebted to Geoffrey Hudson's essay on the ancient Chinese system. See Introduction to this book.

Bull, H. (1977) *The Anarchical Society*, London, Macmillan, and New York, Columbia University Press. Now a basic text, quoted in this book. Concerned with multiple independences, and especially the contemporary society of states.

Bull, H. and Watson, A. (eds) (1984) *The Expansion of International Society*, Oxford, Oxford University Press. A coherent account and analysis, with chapters by several authorities, relevant to both the European and the contemporary societies.

Butterfield, H. (1951) *The Whig Interpretation of History*, London, Bell.

Butterfield, H. (1973) 'The balance of power', in *The Dictionary of the History of Ideas*, New York, Scribners. Much the best piece on this subject.

Butterfield, H. and Wight, M. (eds) (1966) *Diplomatic Investigations*, London, Allen & Unwin. Makes several early papers of the BCTIP available in book form, especially two seminal essays: Wight on 'Why is there no international theory?' and Butterfield on the balance of power.

Wight, M. (with introduction by H. Bull) (1977) *Systems of States*, Leicester, Leicester University Press. Essays on the Graeco-Persian and European systems, and the invaluable 'De systematibus civitatum' – see Introduction to this book.

Other works

Cobban, A. (1945) *National Self-Determination*, Oxford, Oxford University Press. A valuable study of a major issue of the last two centuries.

Craig, G. L. and George, A. L. (1983) *Force and Statecraft*, New York, Oxford University Press. Part I, 'The International System from the Seventeenth Century to the Present', covers usefully and concisely several aspects of the European society of states, with bibliographical comments.

Dehio, L. (1959) *Germany and World Politics in the 20th Century*, London, Chatto & Windus. Written from the centre of the network of European pressures (in contrast to much British and US observation from the periphery of Europe).

Donelan, M. (ed.) (1978) *The Reason of States*, London, Allen & Unwin. Useful essays on international political theory and the European states system by leading British academics.

Hinsley, F. H. (1963) *Power and the Pursuit of Peace*, Cambridge, Cambridge University Press. A standard and indispensable work: puts the theory before the practice. See Introduction to this book.

Kennedy, P. (1987) *The Rise and Fall of the Great Powers: Economic Change and Military Conflict from 1500 to 2000*, New York, Random House. See Introduction to this book.

Mommsen, W. (1980) *Theories of Imperialism* (trans. of *Imperialismustheorien*), London, Weidenfeld & Nicolson. Concise summary of contending theories, including Marxist.

Morse, E. (1976) *Modernization and Transformation of International Relations*, New York, Free Press. Useful but sometimes unreliable survey. See especially Chapter 2 on the Westphalia settlement.

THE GLOBAL INTERNATIONAL SOCIETY

Historical studies

Eban, A. (1983) *The New Diplomacy: International Affairs in the Modern Age*, London, Weidenfeld & Nicolson. Many shrewd insights, especially on American–Soviet relations and the myth and reality of the United Nations.

Kennan, G. F. (1952) *American Diplomacy*, London, Secker & Warburg. An effective realist commentary on the distortion caused by (US) ideology and dogma to the operation of international society.

Theoretical studies

Aron, R. (1973) *Peace and War: A Theory of International Relations* (trans. of *La Paix et la Guerre*), New York, Anchor Press.

Claude, I. (1962) *Power and International Relations*, New York, Random House. Valuable critical analysis of the balance of power, collective security and the concept of world government.

Donelan, Michael (1990) *Elements of International Political Theory*, Oxford, Oxford University Press. Useful and readable guide to international theories, more concerned with individual states than the system. Dedication to the British Committee.

Gilpin, R. (1981) *War and Change in World Politics*, Cambridge, Cambridge University Press. A sociological study emphasizing history as well as change. The introduction and the chapters on hegemony and continuity are the most relevant. See Introduction to this book.

Morgenthau, H. (1978) *Politics among Nations*, revised edn, New York, Knopf. A classic study of power politics and national interests, especially during the cold war. See Introduction to this book.

Porter, B. (ed.) (1972) *The Aberystwth Papers*, Oxford, Oxford University Press. Part II contains useful essays by several authorities, notably Howard, Claude and Butterfield.

Watson, A. (1983) *Diplomacy: The Dialogue between States*, London, Methuen. Contains a fuller account of the evolution of the ancient and European diplomatic dialogues into contemporary practice.

See also several works cited in the European list.

INDEX

IMPORTANT TERMS AND CONCEPTS

IMPORTANT NAMES AND PLACES